# www.wadsworth.com

*wadsworth.com* is the World Wide Web site for Wadsworth and is your direct source to dozens of online resources.

At *wadsworth.com* you can find out about supplements, demonstration software, and student resources. You can also send e-mail to many of our authors and preview new publications and exciting new technologies.

**wadsworth.com**
Changing the way the world learns®

# Ethics

## An Introduction to
## Philosophy and Practice

**STEPHEN J. FREEMAN**
Texas Woman's University

Australia • Canada • Mexico • Singapore • Spain • United Kingdom • United States

Counseling Editor: Eileen Murphy
Editorial Assistant: Annie Berterretche
Marketing Manager: Caroline Concilla
Project Editor: Pam Suwinsky
Print Buyer: Mary Noel
Permissions Editor: Joohee Lee
Production Service: Matrix Productions

Copy Editor: Victoria Nelson
Cover Designer: Ross Carron Design
Cover Image: PhotoDisc
Signing Representative: James Smith
Compositor: R&S Book Composition
Printer/Binder: Webcom Limited

Printed in Canada

2   3   4   5   6   03   02   01

For permission to use material from this
text, contact us by
    web: www.thomsonrights.com
    fax: 1-800-730-2215
    phone: 1-800-730-2214

Library of Congress
Cataloging-in-Publication Data
Freeman, Stephen J.
    Ethics: an introduction to philosophy and
practice/Stephen J. Freeman.
        p.   cm.
    Includes bibliographical references and index.
    ISBN 0-534-36638-4
    1. Counselors—Professional ethics.
    2. Psychotherapists—Professional ethics.   I. Title.
    BF637.C6.F683   1999
    174'.915—dc21                              99-41890

Wadsworth/Thomson Learning
10 Davis Drive
Belmont, CA 94002-3098
USA
www.wadsworth.com

International Headquarters
Thomson Learning
290 Harbor Drive, 2nd Floor
Stamford, CT 06902-7477
USA

UK/Europe/Middle East
Thomson Learning
Berkshire House
168-173 High Holborn
London WC1V 7AA
United Kingdom

Asia
Thomson Learning
60 Albert Street #15-01
Albert Complex
Singapore 189969

Canada
Nelson/Thomson Learning
1120 Birchmount Road
Scarborough, Ontario M1K 5G4
Canada

 *This book is printed on acid-free recycled paper.*

To Mary Lee, my partner, the one with whom I have grown—
the sine qua non of all my perspectives.
To Stephanie and Anna who are the light of our love.
To the memory of my parents Anne and Coy—we miss you.

# Contents

# III ETHICAL AND LEGAL ISSUES

＊

# Preface

I t is possible that many students in the field of counseling and psychotherapy are obtaining degrees without acquiring a proper introduction to professional ethics. No matter how well prepared otherwise, the professional not well enough acquainted with relevant ethical issues to understand their impact is missing something. As we enter the 21st century, questions about values and contemporary morality loom before us, and the demand for an educational response has been heard loud and clear. What is not so clear is what should be taught under the label of ethics. Even the definition of ethics is a matter of controversy. *Webster's* defines ethics as "the study of standards of conduct and moral judgment; moral philosophy." Does this mean that ethics requires an absolute set of global standards that apply to everyone everywhere? Or are all standards of what is right or wrong and what constitutes a good life or a good society merely relative to the individual or a particular group (Lavine, 1984)? Is there room for legitimate disagreement about what is ethical; about basic ethical principles? What are the basic principles? Are we really searching for a correct way of acting or should we consider the correctness of thoughts and feelings? Is it actions or the results of our actions that are of concern? Or must we concern ourselves with what we intend and the motives that cause our actions? Professional preparation is incomplete until the counselor or therapist understands the impact of moral conduct upon himself/herself, the client, the profession, and society.

The practice of counseling and related helping professions is regulated both by law and by professional standards of practice or codes of ethics. However, the laws and professional codes that govern practice provide only general guidelines, with few specifics regarding the actual circumstances of everyday practice. Codes of ethics are designed to guide practitioners, protect the welfare of clients, safeguard the autonomy of professional workers, and enhance the status of the profession (Mappes, Robb, & Engels, 1985). There are, however, times when these ethical guidelines and the law conflict, or occasions where no law or guideline is sufficient to cover the situation in question. The Code of Ethics of the American Psychological Association (APA, 1992) directs psychologists, in cases where conflicts exist between ethics and the law, to seek resolution in a way that complies with the law, and at the same time most nearly conforms with the APA code of ethics. In situations where neither the law nor professional codes provide guidance, one must consider the individual, the community, and the profession in consultation with one's own informed ethical conscience. The law as a guide reflects only the minimal standards of behavior that society will tolerate; ethical codes represent a higher standard but lack the specificity necessary to address many ethical dilemmas. The formation of an informed ethical conscience will provide the same guidance for the practitioner that a good theoretical foundation provides for practice.

In developing an informed ethical conscience one must first explore and develop a theoretical understanding of the subject—in this case, ethics. In this process one concomitantly explores theoretical approaches to ethics and begins the formation of an ethical conscience by asking questions such as, "What moral/ethical values do I hold and why do I hold them?" This approach is consistent with Tennyson and Strom's (1986) view that acting responsibly is an inner quality, not something imposed by an external authority. Values, while seen as enduring and stable over time, may vary in importance at any given time depending on the context (Schwartz, 1992; Feather, 1994; Braithwaite, 1991, 1994). This prioritization suggests that values are dynamic rather than static and change in level of importance according to contextual scrutiny. This observation is critical in understanding the dynamic difference between mandatory and aspirational ethics. Mandatory ethics may be viewed as the minimum, characterized by compliance with the law and with professional codes of ethics. Professionals who practice at this level meet the minimum requirements and are generally safe from legal action or professional censure. At the higher level are aspirational ethics. Here, practitioners' actions are guided not only by the minimal requirements, but also by an awareness of the effects that their actions will have on their clients, their community, and their profession. Movement between the two levels in part reflects the variation of importance of personal values at any given time relative to the circumstances. Knowledge of our own variability is a necessary requirement in the formation of an informed ethical conscience.

Helping professionals regularly make moral/ethical judgments about the appropriateness or inappropriateness of particular actions. They may judge it is morally/ethically appropriate to warn a third party about a threat posed by a client even if the client demands confidentiality. They may judge it morally/ethically appropriate to withhold client information obtained in counseling from third parties who legally request it. They may judge it morally/ethically appropriate to allow a client to commit suicide. The fact that those in the helping professions face such moral/ethical judgments should come as no surprise. What is the basis for such judgments? How can these judgments be justified? How can one's decision or judgment be defended against those who would make different decisions or judgments? Questions such as these require the decision makers to explore the epistemological basis of morality and ethics. Epistemology, the study of knowledge, provides the basis for knowing that various decisions/judgments are true or false.

There is no doubt that principles, standards, and codes of ethics are useful in the formulation of moral/ethical judgments. However, there are good reasons for believing that professionals must not adopt these as their foundations for ethical thinking. Review of the various principles, standards, and codes of ethics reveals conflicts, unclear implications, and a lack of real-life applications, including exceptions. What is *most* notably absent, however, is the overall integration into everyday functioning that comes with a larger theoretical framework. A moral/ethical theory is needed to provide the foundations of justification in moral/ethical decision making.

The principles of individual autonomy and justice are highly prized in the helping professions. But how do professionals determine if the principle of autonomy applies to adolescents as well as to adults? Is the magnitude the same? What about others, such as the elderly, the mentally ill (depressed), the mentally challenged, the newly born, and the not-yet born? Does the principle of justice mean treating everyone equally or fairly? How can we achieve justice when doing what is just for one creates hardship or injustice for another? Who should be considered and how? What are the implications for the individual, group, profession, and society?

The preceding paragraphs illustrate just two examples of the often felt but not often articulated challenges to the process of ethical decision making. A firm foundation on which to base moral/ethical decision making is required. An overreaching understanding of moral/ethical theory, one that allocates a proper place for the ethical principles espoused by the helping professions in the lives of individuals, is needed.

The goal of this book is to acquaint students with relevant ethical theory and to provide exposure to real-life ethical issues that are often messy, complex, multifaceted dilemmas defying simple solutions. In this process students are encouraged to explore their own moral/ethical value systems as well as the paradigms they work from, and to begin the formation of an informed ethical conscience for making sound moral/ethical judgments.

# PART I

# Ethical Issues
# and Ethical Codes

The enumeration of ethical standards enables a group to clarify to its current and prospective members and those served by its members the nature of ethical responsibilities held in common by its members.

# 1

✳

# Problems of Ethics in the Helping Professions

This book was written to provide a framework through which helping professionals can begin to develop a process for understanding the basic values that support and determine their appropriate actions. Helping professionals need to study and internalize a sound theoretical foundation and process for ethical thinking and decision making because they are often confronted with dilemmas that have no apparent correct or good solutions. In the helping professions, almost anything an individual does has potential ethical ramifications. We do not just behave according to instincts or impulse, nor do we live in a vacuum. We acquire values and ideals, form goals, and generally conform to patterns of acceptable social behavior. We usually obey the law. However, on occasion we disagree with some particular aspect of it on the basis of some higher principle. No matter how personal and individual we consider our values to be, we demonstrate agreement with society in our acceptance of certain general assumptions such as the right to live and be happy and the importance of doing the right thing—even though we cannot always agree on what exactly that is. People disagree in particular cases or in general philosophy because each of us believes we are objectively right. But ethics, unlike food, is not just a matter of taste or preference. Assuming that the study of ethics, theories, and concerns is a smorgasbord from which each person can pick and choose is grossly erroneous. Our moral judgments and subsequent actions may be challenged and we are expected to have a sound rationale for them.

The study of ethics should help us think about our actions in real-life situations and help us organize our opinions, beliefs, ideals, and values about what

**3**

is right and wrong. It should make us aware of the ripple effect our actions create, setting a precedent for future behavior, both our own and that of others. Like the domino effect, where one falling domino sets in motion a series of falling dominos, our actions may provide the impetus or validation for another's action though circumstances may or may not justify the action. This awareness adds a new dimension to our thinking and to our potential for action. Kant (trans. 1963) summarized this well in saying that ethics without reference to particular actions are empty, but actions devoid of ethics are blind.

The study of ethics involves not only our humanness but the appreciation of worthy beliefs, goals, ideals, and values. From the time of the earliest philosophers there has been agreement that there is a correct theory or approach to ethics—one that forms a consistent, coherent, and comprehensive system. Philosophers have, however, disagreed on which approach is the most consistent, coherent, and correct, with each attempting to improve or surpass the others. Many of their theories will be described in this book for the reader's own evaluation.

The following summaries of ethical dilemmas as well as those at the end of various chapters are true stories taken from my experience in clinical practice and university teaching. Significant changes have been made to protect the identity of all characters. Inclusion of real cases, instead of fictitious examples, demonstrates the complexity and untidiness that occurs in real life. These cases demonstrate the need for a well-grounded practical approach to clinical ethical judgments. My comments on the various ethical dilemmas and their resolution are post hoc.

As you read the following summaries of ethical dilemmas, record your actions and the rationale for them in detail for later reference. Refer as necessary to the various codes of ethics in the appendices. (The codes of ethics of related helping professions have been included because we do not work in isolation and increasingly must be able to interface and work as part of a multidisciplinary team. Effective multidisciplinary functioning and related problem solving requires one to have a working understanding of the ethical standards of the other team members.) After responding to these questions, read the rest of the book, including the codes in the appendices. In reviewing the codes of ethics of the various professional organizations be acutely aware of the similarities and differences that exist. When you have finished reading, you may wish to return to the summaries; you may wish to revise and/or add to your original answers. The stimulus questions posed at the end of the dilemmas are to stimulate more in-depth thought for your second round of responses as well as your rationale(s) for them. The goal of this process is to increase self-awareness and insight into the underlying reasons for your actions, leading to the formation of an informed ethical conscience and an increasingly sound ethical basis for decision making.

## ETHICAL DILEMMA 1

You are a counselor working independently in a private practice setting. After a lapse of some years, Mrs. M. calls for an appointment. You had originally worked with Mrs. M. when she sought counseling for bereavement after the death of her spouse from cancer some years ago. Your records reflect that she appeared to have made successful resolution of her bereavement. During this second intake appointment, you discover that Mrs. M. has remarried (approximately 2 years ago) and she reports a very happy life until three months ago when she was diagnosed with bone cancer. After numerous consultations, her case was labeled terminal and she was referred to hospice. She has come to see you again because she remembers how much you helped her after the death of her first husband. She states she knows you will be able to help her now. Following her diagnosis and dim prognosis, she had come across the book *Final Exit*. After reading it she decided that rather than suffering the ravages of bone cancer she would take her life ("self deliver" as she expresses it). Knowing you would understand, she requests that you see both her and her new husband to help him understand and cope with her decision, which he neither understands nor approves. You are not altogether sure Mrs. M. is not seeking counseling in order to bolster her resolve in this area of her own commitment.

### The Problem

As a supposedly unbiased counselor, should you agree to support Mrs. M. in her decision to commit suicide given her terminal diagnosis? What about her current husband and Mrs. M's request that you help him understand and cope with her decision?

### The Dilemma

The dilemma faced here is multifaceted and requires the counselor to address and consider the principles of autonomy, nonmaleficence, beneficence, compassion, fidelity, and justice.

1. Does an individual have the right to control his or her own body and his or her own life, including ending it?
2. Is morality defined by the wishes of the client? Is morality defined by the humane and compassionate values of those involved?

To assist you in the decision-making process answer the following questions:

1. What are the counselor's responsibilities to Mrs. M.?
2. What are the counselor's responsibilities to Mr. M.?
3. What impact do the wishes of Mrs. M. have on your recommendations?
4. What are the counselor's responsibilities to society (in the welfare of this individual and others and the issue of life and death)?
5. What are your possible alternative courses of action and why would you choose them?
6. What are the possible and probable consequences of the actions you take?
7. How do the ethical codes in the appendices apply to this case? How does this affect your decision?

8. In the final analysis, what are the implications for this particular case? For cases involving ethical questions of life and death?

9. As the counselor, what would you do and why?

# ETHICAL DILEMMA 2

You are on the graduate faculty of a small university in the counseling department. You teach various counseling related classes and serve as an advisor to many students. You also maintain an active private counseling practice away from the university. You are licensed and have appropriate academic credentials. One of your current graduate students approaches you with a request for personal counseling. You are not this student's advisor, though you have had her in class before. She is not currently enrolled in any of your classes, though it is possible she would be in the future. However, there are enough other faculty members teaching similar courses that she could switch to one of their courses.

## The Problem

Should a professor see a student in personal counseling?

## The Dilemma

The dilemma here has to do with dual relationships. Several points concerning dual relationships are seen here.

1. Is it ethical to draw clients from the ranks of your students (or other faculty's students)?

2. Does the role of professor bias the role of counselor, or the role of student dilute or bias the role of client? Does the role of client dilute or bias the role of student?

   To assist you in the decision-making process, answer the following questions:

1. What is your responsibility as a professor to this student?

2. What is your responsibility as a professor to your other students?
   a. To the other faculty?
   b. To your profession?
   c. To yourself?

3. What are your possible alternative courses of action and why would you choose them?

4. What are the possible and probable consequences of the actions taken?

5. Review the codes of ethics in the appendices. Are there any statements that would apply here? How do they affect your decision?

6. As the professor, what would you do and why?

## ETHICAL DILEMMA 3

As a counselor working independently in a private practice setting, you had previously seen Mr. and Mrs. S. in marital counseling. During the course of counseling, it became clear that Mr. S. desired to leave the relationship. He discontinued conjoint counseling, and divorce followed his move from the home. Mrs. S. continued to see you for individual counseling until after the divorce, and terminated based on mutual agreement between you. Approximately two years following the initial conjoint counseling, you receive a letter in the mail from a court-appointed ombudsman. The letter explains that the couple is engaged in a custody battle and your records will be used to aid the ombudsman in making a recommendation to the court on the issue of custody. You have serious questions regarding the applicability of your records of marital counseling to the question of custody. On further investigation, you determine the ombudsman is a volunteer with "appropriate training." This person appears to have no related academic training in the field, and no certifications or licenses.

### The Problem

You have signed releases from both Mr. and Mrs. S., but should you release the information?

### The Dilemma

The dilemma involves the clients' rights to information about themselves but also how and by whom this information will be used. There is a serious question as to whether or not your records contain information appropriate for drawing inferences about parental suitability for custody. In addition, there is the ethical question of disclosure of records to an individual unqualified to interpret them.

To help you in the decision-making process answer the following stimulus questions:

1. Exactly who is the client?
2. What are the counselor's responsibilities to Mr. and Mrs. S.?
   a. To Mr. and Mrs. S.'s children?
   b. To the court?
   c. To society?
3. What impact do the wishes of the couple have on the counselor's actions?
4. What are your possible alternative courses of action and why would you choose them?
5. What are the possible and probable consequences of actions taken?
6. What do the ethical codes offer as assistance in resolution of this dilemma?
7. As the counselor, what would you do and why?

# ETHICAL DILEMMA 4

You are a school counselor in an expanding middle school. Your responsibilities have increased in proportion to the school's expansion, which is significant. Despite the school's expansion there are no funds currently available to increase the counseling staff. You had previously been able to provide various counseling services to the students, including several groups. Now you face the undesirable possibility of having to discontinue these groups due to increasing administrative duties. Another counselor with whom you are acquainted and who is familiar with your situation approaches you with a possible solution. She says she has been approached by a private psychiatric hospital and asked if she would be willing to provide community counseling services for which they would reimburse her. She further explains she would be willing to do the groups that you have been doing as a community service paid for by the hospital. The school would in effect be gaining a free part-time counselor. You would then be free to attend to your other administrative duties and the students would not lose the experience of group, which you think is very beneficial to them. Your situation is growing more unmanageable and you know that very soon you will have to do something—but what?

## The Problem

As a competent school counselor you are concerned about direct services to your students. You are also aware that your job has necessary administrative duties, which take you out of direct contact with students. Are there any problems with the offer made by the other counselor?

## The Dilemma

Does the hospital not have the right to engage in community service? Who is the employer of the new counselor in this situation? Does this present any potential problems? Do the benefits outweigh the risks?

To assist you in the decision-making process answer the following questions:

1. What are the school counselor's responsibilities?
   a. To the school?
   b. To her students?
2. What are the other counselor's responsibilities to the students?
   a. To the hospital paying her?
   b. To the school?
3. What are the counselors' responsibilities to their profession?
4. What are the counselors' responsibilities to society (the welfare of the students and others)?
5. What are your possible courses of action and why would you choose them?

6.  What are the possible and probable consequences of the action you take?
7.  How do the ethical codes in the appendix apply to this situation? How does this affect your decision?

## ETHICAL DILEMMA 5

As a counselor working in an agency setting, you have seen Mr. and Mrs. D. in marital counseling for several weeks. Mr. D. requests some individual counseling with you in addition to the conjoint sessions. In the individual session Mr. D. discloses the fact that he had an affair some time ago, and he is experiencing significant guilt feelings. His desire to discuss this with you is several-fold. First, he feels significant guilt over the brief affair, especially because the marital relationship has improved so much since counseling. Second, he is concerned that if Mrs. D. should find out about the affair she would leave him. He points to her statement of such some time ago and to the fact that she is a somewhat fragile individual emotionally, something you as a counselor have also noticed. In stating his dilemma to you, Mr. D. expresses a strong desire to make his relationship work but is caught in a bind of guilt on one side and fear (possibly justified) on the other. He turns to you for assistance.

### The Problem

Mr. D. wishes to deal with his guilt feelings by confessing to his wife, but he is afraid she will leave him if he does.

### The Dilemma

The counselor is placed in a precarious position by Mr. D.'s disclosure. Should the counselor inform Mrs. D. or have Mr. D. inform her about the affair? What about confidentiality? What about the relationship? What about Mrs. D.'s emotional well being? What about Mr. D.'s increasing feelings of guilt?

Answer the following stimulus questions to help you decide what to do:

1.  Who is (are) the client(s)?
2.  What are the counselor's responsibilities to Mr. D?
    a.  To Mrs. D?
    b.  To the agency?
3.  Review the ethical codes. Are there any guidelines that may apply?
4.  What are your possible courses of action and why would you choose them?
5.  What are the possible and probable consequences of each action listed in Question 4?
6.  As the counselor, what would you do and why?

# ETHICAL DILEMMA 6

You are a female counselor employed in an agency setting. You have been on staff for approximately four years. You have appropriate academic credentials and are also licensed. While working at the agency you were once aware of feeling a significant attraction toward a client you were counseling. Your solid academic background made you conscious of your professional responsibility and you did not allow this to interfere with the therapeutic relationship. Your client successfully completed counseling and you had not seen him since. Now, some years later, you meet this individual several times in a social setting. You again become aware of feeling a significant attraction toward him, and begin to think he may also be attracted to you. When he realizes that you both are single, he asks you out on a date. He does this by saying he was attracted to you during your counseling together and now finds himself feeling the same attraction again.

## The Problem

Should you accept the offer of a date from a person who was once a client long ago?

## The Dilemma

As a counselor, should you engage in relationships with former clients? When does the professional relationship end? Or does it?

To assist in the decision-making process answer the following questions:

1. What is the effect of the therapeutic relationship on the counselor and the client?
2. When does the counselor's "influence" on the client end, if ever? When does the client cease to be a client?
3. What are the counselor's responsibilities to the client?
   a. To herself?
   b. To the agency?
   c. To the profession?
   d. To society?
4. What are your possible alternative courses of action and why would you choose them?
5. What are the possible and probable consequences of these actions?
6. What would you do and why?

# ETHICAL DILEMMA 7

You are a school counselor working in a high school setting. During the first few weeks of school, a student approaches you and requests individual counseling for some adjustment problems. The student is new, having transferred from another city to your school. Several teachers have approached you noting the student's request to be allowed to leave class to see you. They voice concerns that the student's behavior is a little odd in class and ask if you know what is wrong. During one of the early sessions with the student, she revealed that the reason her family moved was that her father had committed suicide approximately six months ago. Her mother had moved the family here to be close to her family of origin. At her old school, the response from the teachers and peers to her father's suicide had been negative. Fearing this reaction again, she asked you not to disclose this to anyone. The student's grief over her father's death is also affecting her schoolwork in that she finds it difficult to concentrate or attend to tasks while in class. The family has not sought counseling and now are attempting, according to the student, to put their lives together as if nothing had ever happened. She feels she can trust you but does not want anyone else to know. At about this same time the principal approaches you stating that several teachers have voiced concerns about this student and they want to know what she (the student) has told you in counseling.

## The Problem

One of the most difficult areas for school counselors concerns the disclosure of information obtained in a counseling session. The problem here is whether or not a counselor should disclose to a teacher or administrator what was disclosed in a counseling session if the material may have impact on school performance. The counselor is in a precarious position given the student's and the principal's requests. Should the counselor inform the principal of the student's problem?

## The Dilemma

When does the student's need for confidentiality outweigh the right of school officials to know? What if the principal and school policy mandate disclosure?

To assist you in the decision-making process answer the following stimulus questions:

1. What are the counselor's responsibilities to the student?
   a. To the principal?
   b. To the school district?
   c. To the profession?
   d. To society?
2. What guidance is offered by the ethical codes?
3. What are your possible courses of action and why would you choose them?
4. What are the possible and probable consequences of each action?
5. What would you do and why?

## ETHICAL DILEMMA 8

You are a school counselor in a junior high school working primarily with eighth-grade students. Last semester you had seen J. M., who is now a freshman, in individual vocational counseling sessions. During the course of one of the sessions, J. M. confessed that for several years he has been cheating on tests in order to receive good grades because he thinks this is his only way to ensure entry into a good college. J. M. further confided that increasing parental pressure to receive good grades and attend a good college is making him a "wreck." He related a recent incident in which he became so nervous before an exam he became physically ill. J. M. said he had tried to talk to his parents but they just wouldn't listen and continue to pressure him. He is afraid that if he does not achieve at the level his parents expect that they will forever be disappointed in him. Following this disclosure, J. M. became very concerned that what he had told you might not be held in confidence. He said that if his parents ever found out about his cheating he would kill himself. This semester, J. M. has been caught cheating on a midterm exam. J. M. pleads with the teacher, stating that he has never cheated before and panicked because he was unprepared for the exam. The teacher seeks consultation from the freshman counselor, who is a personal friend of J. M.'s parents and believes J. M. is sincere but is unsure of what action to take. The counselor, being unfamiliar professionally with J. M., sends you a note requesting a consultation regarding this incident. In the note are the following questions: Are you familiar with J. M.? Have you seen him for counseling? Are you aware of any reasons for this behavior or previous incidents? You are also asked for a recommendation on whether or not J. M. should be allowed to retake the exam.

### The Problem

The information you have has potential implications, both academic and personal. The problem is whether or not you should share the information you have about J. M. in a professional consultation.

### The Dilemma

When is academic counseling academic and when does it cross the line and become personal counseling and subject to different professional guidelines? When is it necessary and/or appropriate to consult with another professional without a student's/client's consent?

To assist you in the decision-making process answer the following stimulus questions:

1. What are the counselor's responsibilities to the student?
    a. To the school?
    b. To the profession?
    c. To society?
2. What guidance is offered by the ethical codes?

3. What are your possible courses of action and why would you choose them?
4. What are the possible and probable consequences of each action?
5. What would you do and why?

## ETHICAL DILEMMA 9

You are a counselor in a middle-class junior high school. You are seeing a 13-year-old female student for both academic and personal counseling. Her parents have recently divorced and she is having difficulty coping, as evidenced by a significant drop in grades and changes in social behaviors. Soon after her parents' divorce she had changed her peer group from other local junior high students to a mixed group of high school students and some recent dropouts. During one session she relates to you that she is sexually active with her new boyfriend, who is much older and a high school student. She tells you that they do not use any form of birth control as they see it as unnatural. She confidently tells you that she knows your concerns, but she won't be one who gets pregnant. Later in the session she acknowledges her desire to become pregnant and have a baby. She sees this as a remedy for her current family dilemma. She states that her new boyfriend is unaware of her desire to have a baby and that she has no intention of telling him until she is sure she is pregnant.

### The Problem

This situation presents several ethical as well as potential legal problems. The obvious is that your client is a minor and engaging in sexual activity which, given the age of the boyfriend, may be a crime. Another is her unwillingness to disclose to her partner her desire to have a child out of this relationship.

### The Dilemma

If a client, in this case a minor, is involved in potentially dangerous behavior, what should the counselor's response be? Also, if a client's behavior is placing another person at risk, what should the counselor do?

To assist you in the decision-making process answer the following questions:

1. What is the counselor's responsibility to the client?
   a. To the boyfriend?
   b. To the school?
   c. To the student's parents?
   d. To society?
2. What guidance is offered by the ethical codes (the law)?
3. What are your possible actions and why would you choose them?
4. What are the possible and probable consequences of each action taken?
5. What would you do and why?

## ETHICAL DILEMMA 10

You are one of six counselors in a fairly large high school with approximately 4,000 students. You are a new counselor who just completed your master's degree and counselor certification. Your school has a mentor program and you are assigned a mentor who has her doctorate and has been a school counselor for over ten years. You find the mentoring relationship rewarding and your mentor a very good role model. During an informal conversation with your mentor, you find out that she is in private practice. She acknowledges to you that her practice is doing well and inquires if you are interested in some part-time private counseling work. She says she has observed you and acknowledges that you have good counseling skills and would be a complement to her in her practice. She further states that both of you working at the school would be beneficial, as the majority of her referrals come directly or indirectly from the school. Because you are new to the field, you ask whether or not this is acceptable practice. Your mentor responds that as long as you do not engage in personal counseling with any students that you are seeing privately during school time there is no problem. You have a great deal of respect for your mentor, and, having just completed graduate school, you have a student loan on which you must begin to make payments. The offer sounds good but there is a nagging question in the back of your mind that prevents you from making a decision.

### The Problem

Should you dismiss your concern and take your mentor up on her offer? Should you, as a novice counselor, not accept the guidance of a much more experienced counselor, especially one you admire?

### The Dilemma

Do school counselors have a right to pursue private practice? What, if any, restrictions or concerns exist in a situation like this with respect to dual relationships?

To assist you in the decision-making process answer the following questions:

1. What are the counselor's responsibilities to the students?
   a. To the school?
   b. To her mentor?
   c. To herself?
2. What impact do her mentor's concerns or lack of concerns have on the decision?
3. What are your possible alternative courses of action and why would you choose them?
4. What are the possible and probable consequences of the actions taken?
5. How do the ethical codes in the appendices apply to this situation? How does this affect your decision?

# ETHICAL DILEMMA 11

You have just graduated with your master's in counseling and are interviewing for a job as a school counselor. The principal with whom you are interviewing appears interested in offering you the position. She hands you the job description and asks if you have any questions. You notice the job description includes responsibilities for testing and assessment. You query the principal, who explains that there is no diagnostician in the district currently and that the counselors have taken over that role. She goes on to say that the counselors are doing such a fine job that the district is in no hurry to find a diagnostician. Your master's program included only one course in testing and assessment and that was a survey course. You acknowledge to the principal that though you feel qualified in all the other duty areas listed, you question your qualifications and competency in the area of testing and assessment. Her response is that the district has the tests and the test manuals so it's not hard to give a test and figure out what it means. The other counselors are doing fine. She goes on to say she knows that with your background and teaching experience you will do fine also. After further discussion the principal says she thinks you are the best applicant and that the job is yours if you want it.

## The Problem

Should you accept a position when the duties include responsibilities you feel you are not competent to perform? What about taking a position in a school where you feel you cannot support the policies of the institution?

## The Dilemma

Does an individual have the right to employment even though they may not agree with the policies of the institution in which they are seeking employment? What about the fact that other counselors are performing the duties you are concerned about without apparent problems?

To assist you in the decision-making process answer the following questions:

1.  What are the counselor's responsibilities to herself?
    a.  To the school?
    b.  To the students?
    c.  To the profession?
2.  What impact does the fact that others are apparently doing well with the testing responsibilities have on your decision?
3.  What are your possible alternative courses of action and why would you choose them?
4.  What are the possible and probable consequences of the actions taken?
5.  How do the ethical codes in the appendices apply to this situation? How does this affect your decision?

# ETHICAL DILEMMA 12

You are the lead counselor in a middle school. The principal calls you in to inform you of an "experiential" learning exercise she and a teacher have planned for the students. She relates that on Thursday afternoon an announcement will be made that the president has been assassinated. This is planned to coincide with the history classes' study of the presidents and the assassination of President Kennedy. She hopes that the students will experience firsthand the importance of the office of the president in a democratic system and how disruptive the loss of the president can be. She knows that some students may have a strong reaction to the announcement and wants you and the other counselors to be prepared. She asks you to tell the other counselors to treat the announcement as real. The students will be told at the end of the day, before leaving school, that this has been an experiential learning experience and that the president is alive and well. Your first response is disbelief, but after a few moments, you realize that your principal is serious. You voice concerns but they are ignored. The plan is not going to change and your assistance is required.

## The Problem

As a counselor, you see the potential for emotional harm to the students. The principal and the history teacher disagree with you and plan to proceed with the exercise. Should you agree to participate because your superior and another teacher think it is all right and you are expected to cooperate?

## The Dilemma

Is it ethical to use human subjects in an experiment or to expose them to an experiential form of learning without consent? In a given situation, is it ethical to perform an action you believe is wrong because a superior told you to?

To assist you in the decision-making process answer the following questions:

1. What is the counselor's responsibility to the students?
    a. To the school?
    b. To the profession?
    c. To society?
2. What impact does your principal's "order" have on you and your decision?
3. What are your possible alternative courses of action and why would you choose them?
4. What are the possible and probable consequences of the actions you take?
5. How do the ethical codes in the appendices apply to this situation? How does this affect your decision?

# 2

# Codes of Ethics

"There is nothing more dangerous than ignorance being practiced" (Goethe). These words of wisdom urge the establishment of professional codes of ethics.

A profession can be defined as a vocation or occupation requiring advanced training in some liberal art or science. A professional, then, is one engaged in or worthy of the highest standard of a profession. Codes of ethics are developed to help guide the professional conduct of those in a given profession. They can be described as moral guides to self-regulation, reflecting the normative values of the profession. Levy (1974) provided a description of the nature and function of codes of ethics.

> Codes of ethics are at once the highest and lowest standard of practice expected of the practitioner, the awesome statement of rigid requirements, and the promotional material issued primarily for public relations purposes. They embody the gradually evolved essence of moral expectations, as well as the arbitrarily prepared shortcut to professional prestige and status. At the same time, they are handy guides to the legal enforcement of ethical conduct and to punishment for unethical conduct. They are also the unrealistic, unimpressive, and widely unknown or ignored guides to wishful thinking. The motivation to create a code of ethics may be a zeal for respectability. However, occupational groups are most often moved by genuine need for guides to action in situations of agonizing conflict and by a sincere aspiration to deal justly with clients, colleagues, and society. (p. 207)

The need for a moral perspective through which professionals can deal with practical problems results in the establishment of codes of ethics. Reflecting both the standards of the community and of the profession, codes attempt to define what the acts are that all decent people or members of a profession would agree are wrong. This represents a lofty expectation, possibly too lofty, which tries to be all things to all people. Mabe and Rollins (1986) express a fear that too many professionals may see a code of ethics as the sole basis for defining responsibility for its members. Various professional organizations have established codes of ethics for their members. Yet within similar professions, the codes of ethics and allowable conduct can vary greatly. The reader is urged to look critically at the various codes and note similarities as well as possible contradictions between them. Familiarity with the various codes becomes of critical importance where a practitioner possesses multiple certifications, licenses, or professional affiliations. This is compounded by the fact that multidisciplinary function is now the rule rather than the exception. Working collaboratively to solve ethical dilemmas involving other professionals in other disciplines requires practitioners to have a working understanding of the various ethical codes.

Becoming familiar with the ethical code of your profession and those of related disciplines will quickly expose the fact that ethical codes are not intended as a replacement for the use of judgment and conscious ethical reasoning. Ethical codes by their very nature represent self-imposed (general) regulations and some, but certainly not total, agreement among members of a profession as to what behavior is right and wrong. Codes of ethics cannot dictate or prescribe the behavior of members in all situations. Codes of ethics are written to reflect a rapidly changing profession and society; as such they echo the theme of ethical behavior and exemplary conduct rather than describe the specifics required of it. Codes of ethics do not provide an explanation as to why a given behavior is right or wrong in a particular situation. Smith, McGuire, Abbott, and Blau (1991) advise that codes of ethics are a combination of both rules and utilitarian principles, rather than precise dictates. They suggest that practitioners have the formidable task of clarifying and interpreting codes of ethics and then making personal judgments about how to apply these codes in various situations.

It is clear that codes of ethics do not represent a panacea dictating ethical responsibility; they cannot be applied in a rote manner. While serving a worthy purpose, much has been written about their limitations (Pope & Vasquez, 1991; Ibrahim & Arredondo, 1990; Pederson, 1989; Mappes et al., 1985; Tymchuk, 1981). These authors have noted that some issues cannot be resolved solely by relying on codes of ethics. There may be conflicts within the various codes of ethics of similar organizations as well as value conflicts of members with the codes. Codes of ethics can also conflict with institutional policies and procedures. Codes of ethics were never intended to remove the need for practical judgment and informed conscious reasoning.

Codes of ethics are in part designed to protect practitioners against charges of malpractice, for practitioners who practice within these accepted guidelines can use them as some creditable measure of defense in cases of accused malpractice. Generally in legal cases, a practitioner's behavior is judged by comparing it to the behavior expected of other practitioners in the same profession and in similar situations in accordance with accepted standards of practice. This reflects the community standard, which is what practitioners actually do, as opposed to the ethical standard of what they should do. Compliance with the code of ethics establishing ethical (not merely actual) standards of practice has some measure of validity in legal proceedings. When faced with an ethical conflict it benefits practitioners to think in terms of formal codes of ethics as providing the first (but not the last) line of assistance in the decision-making process.

## THE DEVELOPMENT OF CODES OF ETHICS

Organized groups within the helping professions have long struggled with the problem of right and wrong professional actions. Ethical standards are self-imposed regulations that provide rough guidelines for professional behavior and attempt to specify the nature of the ethical responsibilities of members, at least minimally. Ethical standards written by professional associations represent a consensus of members' beliefs and concerns about ethical behavior. They cannot tell counselors specifically what to do in all situations, and more importantly, they cannot address the question of why a certain action should be taken. Being self-imposed, they (the regulations) imply responsibility. Tennyson and Strom (1986) argue that, given the extraordinary ethical complexity of practical problems encountered in counseling, reliance on professional standards in making decisions is not enough. They advocate the development of professional responsibleness.

Kitchener (1984), addressing the issues of ethical principles in counseling, noted that when our ordinary moral judgment fails us, as professionals we must move to a more systematic and evaluative level in our ethical thinking. Tennyson and Strom (1986) suggest two conditions are necessary in the moral reasoning of counselors who exercise responsibleness. One is a commitment to rational thinking and the other an orientation to moral principles. They suggest professional ethical standards can be viewed as an attempt at the formation of ethical sense (responsibleness).

The codes of ethics of professional organizations are not static; rather, they are living documents that reflect movement and growth within the profession. The American Psychological Association (APA) established an ethics committee in 1938; however, it was 1953 before it adopted a formal code of ethics. Uniquely, this code reflected actual solicited input from the existing membership. Since that time the code has undergone several minor as well as major revisions (i.e., 1959, 1981, 1989, 1992). The American Counseling Association (ACA) code of ethics was adopted in 1961 and has also undergone several minor as well as major revisions (i.e., 1974, 1981, 1988, 1995). Most codes of ethics of professional organizations undergo revisions as the profession grows.

# ENFORCEMENT OF ETHICAL CODES

There are various mechanisms, both within the community and the profession, that have been established to oversee the conduct of practicing professionals. Hess (1980) outlines five sources, as follows:

1. Control and monitoring is established through general criminal and civil law that is applicable to all citizens including practicing professionals.
2. Control and monitoring is exerted on practicing professionals by their peers, with ethics committees emerging as the most relevant peer control mechanism.
3. Control and monitoring emerges from the legal power of professional (state) licensing boards and the accompanying establishment of entry-level standards (to the profession via licensure), definitions of practice, outlining or delineation of offenses, and sanctions.
4. Additional control and monitoring is achieved through civil litigation of malpractice complaints resulting from both the definition of practice that accompanies the development of licensure and the accompanying higher visibility of the profession.
5. Federal law and associated regulations provide another source of control and  monitoring. This is accomplished through the Code of Federal Regulations (CFR) as well as documents such as the Federal Regulations regarding the use of human or animal subjects in research. (p. 1)

The practicing professional will most likely be involved in some type of peer monitoring—formally, either as an individual or a member of a peer review or ethics committee; or informally, as an active responsible member of the profession. Most professional organizations have a formal ethics committee that oversees the conduct of their members. The main purposes of the committee are to educate the organization's members about ethical principles and practices and to protect the membership and the public from unethical practices. Bennett, Bryant, VandenBos, and Greenwood (1990) summarize the objectives of the committee as: formulating ethical principles for adoption by the organization; receiving and investigating complaints of unethical conduct by its members; processing and resolving complaints of professional misconduct and recommending a specific course of action in a given situation; and reporting on the types of complaints that are received by the committee to the organization membership.

The ethics or peer review committee investigating a complaint against a member has various avenues open to it in resolving the complaint. The committee may dismiss the complaint on the grounds that there is insufficient basis for the complaint; levy sanctions against the member; impose resignation or termination of membership; and/or require a specific course of remediation such as mandatory supervision or personal counseling or therapy. If membership in the organization is terminated, the termination is made public to all members. If the investigation involves the ethics committee of a state licensure board, the practitioner may also face the loss of his or her certification and/or license and the right to practice the profession.

Informal peer monitoring is a responsibility practitioners have to the profession and to the community. Most practitioners will be actively involved in the process as informal peer monitors. Keith-Spiegel and Koocher (1985) offer some hints for engaging in informal peer monitoring and confrontation.

1. Locate the relevant code of ethics and the section that applies to the suspected violation. Use this at the onset as a framework for evaluating the situation.

2. Evaluate the strength of the evidence that a violation has been committed. Determine if the evidence is hearsay or if the source of information is credible and there are verifiable facts.

3. Be aware of your own motivations to engage or avoid a confrontation with a peer. Seek consultation with a colleague to determine if some action is mandatory.

4. Schedule a face-to-face meeting in advance with the peer in question in a nonthreatening manner. A business meeting is usually more appropriate than a home or restaurant. Handling such matters over the phone is generally not recommended except where geographical conditions preclude a direct meeting. Do your homework in advance, clarify the nature of the violation, and have any necessary supporting material at hand.

5. When confronting the issue remain calm, and realize that the recipient may display considerable emotion. Expect it but do not become involved in it. Avoid moralizing; most people find this obnoxious and unhelpful.

6. Set the tone to be constructive and educational. Your role is not that of an accuser, judge, or jury; instead, your role is one of informing and educating as a team player in problem solving.

7. State your concerns directly and describe your ethical obligations. Reference the relevant section of the code of ethics that encourages your intervention and don't play detective. If confidences require protection (e.g., another person provided you this information, but insisted on remaining anonymous), explain this to your peer, but expect an uncomfortable reaction because no one appreciates not knowing their accuser.

8. Allow your peer time to explain and defend in as much detail as necessary. The experience can be flustering; be patient.

9. If the reaction is abusive or threatening, attempt to redirect the response. Some people need a chance to vent feelings and will calm down if they are not subjected to the same tone and response. If the negative reaction continues, acknowledge the upsetting nature of the situation and your inability to continue the interchange at present. Ask the individual to consider what information you have presented and ask them to contact you after a few days or a week. If no further communication is forthcoming, then other action must be taken. This might be involving another person,

informing the person of your next step (whatever that might be), or filing formal charges. (pp. 16–18)

When facing a dilemma of whether or not to confront a peer or colleague, one might be tempted to talk (gossip) to others about the situation. It is important to be ever mindful of the difference between gossip and consultation.

## ETHICAL DECISION-MAKING PROCESS

Before engaging in problem-solving activities, it is often helpful to determine what went wrong. Conditions that contribute to the formation of ethical problems often share some things in common. Knowing how things happen can be important in deciding how to resolve them, or even better yet, how to avoid them. "Forewarned is forearmed" (Cervantes). Sieber (1982) outlined six common conditions that result in ethical problems:

(a) an ethical problem may simply be unforeseen; (b) an ethical problem may be inadequately anticipated; the magnitude of the problem may be underestimated; (c) an ethical problem may be foreseen but there is no way to avoid it; (d) in a variation of the anticipated ethical problem, what to do may be unclear because of ambiguities of the consequences involved; (e) an ethical problem may arise when guidelines are inadequate or nonexistent relative to the situation; and (f) an ethical problem may arise when institutional policy or even ethical principles conflict with the welfare of clients. (pp. 12–13)

Responding to Sieber's conditions that result in ethical problems, and acknowledging that they may share similarities, several writers have developed models for ethical problem solving and decision making. Tymchuk (1981) developed procedural guidelines that can be used as an ethical decision-making model. The model begins with a thorough description of the situation and involves obtaining information from all relevant sources including the parties involved, sources in the literature, and collegial consultation. From the information that has been obtained the critical issues involved are ferreted out and defined. The codes of ethics or other professional guidelines may be helpful in seeking a possible resolution. These guidelines may include state or federal guidelines or laws, licensing statutes, and other educational and resource material such as published case studies that are similar to this situation. This process may not provide the right answer and might expose contradictory information; however, failure to find and acknowledge appropriate policies may have consequences later. With this additional information, evaluation of the rights, responsibilities, and welfare of all affected parties (including the community and the profession) may be assessed. When the issues have been defined and the affected parties identified, alternative decisions regarding each issue may proceed. This should proceed without regard to feasibility; the decision not to make a decision should also be included at this time. This process is analogous to a brainstorming session where ideas are generated and judgment is reserved for a later stage. This allows for the development of an array of options, possibly including the best-fitting one of all. Allowing for the possibility of each decision is followed by critical evaluation of the consequences of each proposed action and the time and resources necessary to effect each decision. The consequences should also be viewed from the standpoint of both short-term and long-term effects and their relevance to all parties identified. Finally, the probability of the actual occurrence of any of the identified consequences should be carefully weighed. Following the above process to completion results in as full a disclosure as is possible pertaining to the facts and circumstances relevant to the situation. Based on this, a decision is rendered. Ideally, this information (decision) should be shared with all parties involved to the extent possible.

Kitchener (1984) illustrates a critical evaluation model of ethical decision making that illustrates the role of virtues in decision making. Virtue ethics have been said to focus on the character of the practitioner (Jordan & Maera, 1990). Juxtaposed with principle ethics (which ask, "Is this situation ethical?"), virtue ethics ask, "Is what I'm doing the best thing for my client?" Jordan and Maera note that in the case of virtue ethics there is a consciousness (an informed ethical conscience) regarding ethical behavior, even in the absence of an ethical conflict or dilemma. Kitchener's model is based on four basic moral principles—autonomy, beneficence, nonmaleficence, and justice or fairness—that when superimposed on a situation provide moral/ethical guidance. As was noted earlier, principlists approach ethics by positing the existence of objective universal principles that ought to govern moral behavior. To the small cluster of fundamental values (autonomy, beneficence, nonmaleficence, and justice), one might add compassion and fidelity. Although these virtuous principles are meant to provide guidance, they must first be fully and adequately defined and elucidated before they can serve this purpose.

Autonomy has traditionally referred to the promotion of self-determination or freedom of the individual to choose his or her own direction. In addressing virtuous principles this definition is too brief and requires further elaboration. Autonomy is a virtue from which principles governing behavior arise. It endows rational beings with the capability of forming a conception of practical laws, which are principles we would act on if reason had full power over desire. To be autonomous, an individual must regard him/herself as a source of moral principles. Following the principle of autonomy, a human being is moral only to the extent that he/she is able to free him/herself from blindly following his/her own desires. The concept of free will is analogous to that of autonomy, in that to be the source of moral principles, one's choice must be free of the force of desire (Kant, 1956). Viewed in a narrow somewhat traditional way one might ask, "What are the implications of the principle of autonomy when it is applied to individuals who do not place a high priority on the value of being autonomous?" To answer this one must view autonomy in a much fuller way and in doing so expose an oxymoron. It might seem self-contradictory applying the principle of autonomy to individuals who do not place a high priority on it; however, to be truly autonomous individuals must be free of the desire to be autonomous.

Beneficence by definition is the act of doing good; active kindness. The focus here is on promoting good for others, which is seen as a professional duty. Issues involving the principle of beneficence can prove to be a slippery slope when the question to be answered is "In whose best interest?" Good for others is often viewed by practitioners as the client's good in a given situation, but again this view is too narrow. Value conflicts can arise when one is faced with respecting the autonomy of an individual and beneficence toward another person or group. To compound this problem one need only refer to Burt's (1979) brilliant and equally disturbing psychoanalytic interpretation of a burn patient's adamant refusal to be treated and request to die. Burt acknowledged the validity of the principle of autonomy as well as the sincerity of the patient's request to die. He enlarged the understanding of the case by attempting to place the patient's response in an emotional context. Burt suggests that perhaps the patient's refusal was less an unambiguous thrust of freedom than a plea for recognition, acceptance, and love from those around him. Instead of being a statement, perhaps it was a question in disguise. Clearly, the relevance of the principles of autonomy and beneficence for this case depends on whether one views the refusal as a statement or a question. Whether one agrees or disagrees with Burt's possible interpretations, the implications are clear that the search for moral justifications through the application of principles is far more complicated than it might first appear.

Nonmaleficence means doing no evil, mischief or harm; causing no harm. This refers to both acts of commission as well as omission. Certain behaviors will be appropriate for certain situations yet not for others. The principle of nonmaleficence is a caution to be ever vigilant and develop awareness and sensitivity to individuals and situations, ferreting out the unique requirements of each encounter. Rather than serving as a template to provide answers, this principle warns of the dangers of not viewing each encounter as unique and in need of unique answers.

Justice can be viewed as impartiality; fair representation of facts; consistency; actions judged similarly unless there are morally relevant dissimilarities between them; comparative treatment of persons or groups. Rawls (1971) proposed and defended two basic principles of justice. The first principle, the equality principle, stated that each person engaged in an institution or affected by it has a right to the most extensive liberty compatible with a like liberty for all. The second principle, the difference principle, states that inequalities as defined by the institutional structure or fostered by it are arbitrary unless it is reasonable to expect that they will work out to everyone's advantage. There is, as one can see, a balance between the rights of an individual and the needs of society.

The last two principles, fidelity and compassion, have to do with how we define a profession. Fidelity has to do with faithfulness; careful and exact observance of duty, or performance of obligations or vows; being trustworthy.

Compassion is defined as one's capacity to suffer with another; sympathy with a desire to help.

These last two principles form the cornerstones of the professions. A profession, according to Kass (1992), refers to an activity or occupation to which its practitioner publicly professes his/her devotion. Kass sees being a professional as more than being a technician. It is something that is rooted in our moral nature, being more than a matter of mind and hand but heart, not only of intellect and skill but of character. As a professional one is willing and able to devote one's self to others and to some higher good and in this way make a public profession of his or her way of life.

Thompson (1994) describes a limited but consistent number of universal values on whose account much of society's beliefs and attitudes rest. In working environments, the main values relate to the following four principles:

> (a) the principle of beneficence or the duty to care; (b) the principle of justice or the duty of universal fairness; (c) the principle of respect for persons or the duty to respect and protect; and (d) the principle of the rights of individual people. (p. 21)

Day (1996) described most codes of conduct as complex and multidimensional. She suggests that most ethics statements and codes can be classified according to three headings: professionalism, moral conscience, and political values. These principles represent a central feature or reference for the practitioner in determining what "ought to be" and they also help in determining one's perception of what is real and what is ideal.

Tennyson and Strom (1986) state that development of professional responsibility is a matter of personal interest, and that failure to understand the ethical moral nature of the practitioner's educative role has human as well as social consequences. They see the development of capabilities for moral reasoning as affected by cognitive and motivational factors. They believe that specific skills related to the structure of thinking involved in ethical moral reasoning are also important and can be learned. Some of the reasoning skills and dispositions practitioners can develop, according to Tennyson and Strom, include: critical consciousness of themselves as moral agents; identification and clarification of value questions and the worth of personal values; exploration and use of multiple perspectives; resolution of value conflicts and suspension of judgment while remaining open to new information.

According to cognitive developmentalists (Kohlberg, 1976; Piaget, 1932, 1965; Rest, 1979), the reasoning skills and dispositions related to moral responsibility can be acquired in environments where opportunity exists for critical reflection and dialogue about problems. Schon (1983) defined critical reflection as thinking about what one is doing. Howe (1966), addressing critical thinking through dialogue, described the process as a serious address and discussion between two or more persons in which the authenticity and truth of each is confronted by the authenticity and truth of the other. It must be a mature process on both sides.

## SUMMARY

Codes of ethics can be seen as both the highest and the lowest standards of practice expected of a practitioner, reflecting both the standards of the community and the profession. Codes, rather than being precise dictates, are actually combinations of rules and utilitarian principles that do not provide a rationale as to why a particular behavior is right or wrong in a particular situation or circumstance. Therefore, many issues cannot be resolved solely by relying on codes of ethics. Practical judgment and informed conscious reasoning are necessary in the proper application of codes of ethics. Various professional organizations have established codes of ethics for their members; however, in similar professions, the codes of ethics and acceptable behavior can vary greatly. When faced with an ethical dilemma, a practitioner would do well to think first of the formal code of ethics of his/her profession and then through a formal ethical decision-making process to expedite a sound solution.

## QUESTIONS FOR ADDITIONAL REFLECTION AND THOUGHT

1. Do facts alone decide the ethics of a situation? Does an ethical statement include more than facts?

2. Personally, as well as professionally, do you live by general rules or do you allow individual situations to influence your judgment of the most appropriate action to pursue?

3. What does it mean to say that something is right or wrong?

4. In what sense can a statement of ethics be said to be either true or false?

5. Is any profession's code of ethics as good as any other? If not, by what criteria can one decide which is better?

6. What are the reasons, in general, that punishment may be imposed as a consequence for ethical violations? State the bases or justifications for your answers.

7. Do professionals have an absolute duty to obey ethical codes of conduct? Are there occasions when it would be ethically right to violate established codes?

# PART II

\*

# Theoretical Orientations to Ethics

There is nothing so practical as good theory
KURT LEWIN

# 3

✳

# Introduction to Ethics

The unexamined life is not worth living (Socrates). What is right? What is wrong? Hamlet wonders, "To be or not to be," but according to Levine (1986), that is not the question. The question is, "How to be?"

In contemporary society there is an increasing opinion that there is no justification for moral judgments. A prevailing nihilism states that everything is relative and so there is no particular meaning (right or wrong) in the decisions you make today about how you act.

Are all standards of what is right and wrong, what constitutes a good personal life or a good society merely relative to the individual person or to a particular social group expressing nothing more than habit or prejudice and serving individual or group interests and needs? These are the questions of the branch of philosophy called ethics. Ethics asks if there is a highest good for human beings, an absolute good? What is the meaning of right and wrong in human action? What are our obligations? And why should we be moral? (Lavine, 1984, p. 3)

Ethics is a topic that holds some interest for everyone. Abortion, civil rights, civil war, ethnic cleansing, and politics are all issues that overtly or covertly provide us a steady stream of ethical questions. This short list suggests we are well aware of and have an interest in ethics.

## WHAT IS ETHICS?

The concept of ethics is not new. For centuries philosophers have wrestled with Lavine's question: What is the meaning of right and wrong in human action? Our founding fathers struggled with the concept of morality when in the Declaration of Independence they wrote, "All men are created equal . . ." So what happened? Blacks and women were excluded from the category of "all men" for generations; discrimination, gender bias, and other contradictions to these concepts linger today. Following W.W. II and Nazi Germany's crimes against humanity, the slogan was "Never again. The world must never forget." Unfortunately, since that time we have seen the killing fields of the Khmer Rouge in Cambodia, the "disappeared" in Argentina, and the ethnic cleansing in Bosnia.

## ETHICS AS PHILOSOPHY

To begin to understand or unravel this maze of apparent contradictions, we must first find the meaning of ethics. Webster defines ethics as "the study of standards of conduct and moral judgment; moral philosophy." Simply stated, ethics is the study of morality. What then is "moral"? According to Webster it is "the principles and practices in regard to right, wrong and duty; general conduct or behavior." A moralist, it could then be said, is concerned with behavior—sustaining worthwhile values, warning people of the dangers of their ways, and guiding them toward what is right. An ethicist is concerned with the examination of the underlying assumptions and principles of that which is considered right and wrong.

Ethics and morals are intricately connected but, as numerous writers note, have different denotations. Mowrer (1969) suggests that moral refers to the goodness or badness of a behavior while ethics is an objective inquiry about behavior. Van Hoose and Paradise (1979) suggest ethics is a theoretical examination of morals or morality. Peterfreund and Denise (1992) view moralists as those who tell us what they think is good, while ethicists question the underlying principles of what is good or right. The Roman poet Ovid acknowledged the relationship between ethics and morals when he wrote, "We know and approve the better course but follow the worse."

Returning to the question of what ethics is, we may say ethics is the branch of philosophy concerned with living a good life, being a good person, and doing the right thing. Ethics includes reasoning about general principles and using the process of reasoning to determine an appropriate action to take in a given situation. It attempts to identify explicit standards that are applicable to numerous situations. These standards identify for people the criteria necessary to judge an action or life moral. Ethics goes beyond formulating statements of general principles and attempts to find justification for the standards. It attempts to show that some standards are better or more sound than others. The study of ethics requires that we develop some objective rationale for the standards we use to guide us. Recent episodes of genocide show us that the discipline of ethics is necessary if humankind is to survive in this pluralistic society.

Morality is both the product of our pluralistic society and one of its constitutive features. Our personal values are in large measure learned and shared by many others like ourselves. The choice of values is an important and often confusing topic in the discussion of ethics. Do we choose our values, and does everyone have their own totally subjective values? Most scholars agree that we choose between already established possibilities and already available reasons. The choices are not unlimited, but have been preselected by tradition and culture. One chooses between these preselected choices. Values by their very nature are shared and transcend (go beyond) those who embrace them. The values that we cherish most, our personal values, are typically not idiosyncratic, but are those we share with the greatest numbers of others like ourselves (e.g., respect for life; compassion for others; quest for justice). However, our current society does not have one uniform set of moral standards. There are many different standards or customs and some of these contradict each other. Customs tell people how to live, what to do, and how to evaluate other people and what they do. If a person learns the customs of his or her society, do ethical or moral problems arise? Of course they do. People have many different reasons for not wanting to adopt some of the customs of their society. As standards of behavior, morals always place restrictions on individual behavior and gratification of desires. It is not uncommon, then, for people to question why they should follow the standards and customs of the group or society. Some people believe that they should be responsible for themselves and actively decide on their own standards, morals, and ethics. To them, what they receive from society is not really theirs until it has been explicitly chosen by them. To these individuals, making standards their own requires that they think about them and have a rationale for their actions and the lives they live. This is what Socrates meant when he stated, "the unexamined life is a life not worth living."

Ethics as a discipline refers to both the study of our values and their justification, and to the actual values and standards of conduct by which we live. A word of caution here—it would be a mistake to assume that ethical positions are just different personal opinions and that any opinion or position is as good as any other. Most people think there is an objective good; there are ways of behaving and treating others that are objectively good and others that are objectively bad. Morality is seen not just as a matter of personal opinion or customs. If we, at least in part, believe in objective goodness, then it behooves us to be sure that the standards we choose to live by are the truest according to our knowledge. It is not good enough to just do what we are told or what custom dictates; it is just as important to know the reason behind the action and to be able to say no when the action is wrong. Moral rules and the rationale for them form the preconditions necessary for the very functioning of society. The moral rule that it is wrong to lie seems to be a precondition to believing what others say, and even to communication itself. It is important not only to know the rule but to know why the rule is important. Watzlawick (1967) provides us an interesting example of the confusion that might exist if this were not so in the following case: A Cretin sage was brought before the King and said "All Cretins are liars. . . ." The ensuing problem is immediately apparent. Though this is an example of a principle in communication theory, it also points out that moral rules are the necessary framework that enables society to function. Without such rules we, like the king, would be left wondering, "If the Cretin Sage is lying when he says all Cretins are liars, what is one to believe?" It is necessary to study ethics in order to determine if our standards are true, and if not, to determine what standards are true. Ethics is more than a collection of do's and don'ts; it is a system of values and standards tied together in a coherent and reasonable way serving to show us the path toward the good life.

## RELATIVISM

In addressing relativism, the distinction between ethical relativism and cultural relativism is of paramount importance. Ethical relativism is a highly controversial philosophical theory, while cultural relativism is an accepted sociological description of some important differences between cultures (Westermark, 1932; Ladd, 1963). Ethical relativism concerns itself with the question, "What actions are morally right?" Cultural relativism concerns itself with the question, "What actions do different cultures believe to be morally right?" Because differing cultures have diverse moral beliefs, there is no way to decide whether an action is morally right or morally wrong other than by asking the people of that particular culture to judge. Ethical relativism may be seen as the view that if the members of a certain culture believe that a certain action is morally right, then it is morally right to perform that act in that culture. Likewise, if the members of a different culture view the same act as morally wrong, then in that culture to perform that act would be morally wrong (Westermark, 1932; Wellman, 1963; Brandt, 1959). With that basic difference noted, the larger questions involving relativism can be addressed.

Who are you to judge someone else's behavior? What gives you the right to impose your values on others? Some people doubt that the moral judgments of others can be valid. They reject the idea that there are valid universal moral principals applicable to everyone. Ethical relativism questions whether what is right for one person or culture or society is any indication that it is right for another. Relativism states that morality is relative to something else. It denies that there are any absolute moral standards and states that different moral standards exist for different cultures and societies. Relativism is one of the largest areas of controversy in the study of ethics. Holmes (1993, p. 20) distinguishes three theses relevant to relativism.

1.  Moral beliefs and practices vary from culture to culture.
2.  Morality depends on: (a) human nature (e.g., reason, motivation, emotions, and capacity for pleasure and pain); (b) the human condition (the natural order places constraints on human life such as death); (c) specific

social and cultural circumstances, or some combination of all three of the above.

3. What is right and wrong may vary from person to person and culture to culture.

Holmes (1993) states that thesis 1 simply affirms cultural diversity. Variations in moral beliefs and practices, some of which might be pronounced, are possible but not required in different cultures.

Thesis 2, the dependency thesis, states that morality is dependent on or conditioned by human nature and/or the world people live in. This view states that morality's function is to guide human conduct, and that it has evolved over time in response to human needs.

Thesis 3 is ethical relativism. It contains both theses 1 and 2 and goes beyond them. It is, according to Holmes, a statement about what is right and wrong and not just what is thought to be (pp. 20–21).

Ethical relativists believe in right and wrong; however, they contend that what is right for one person or culture has the possibility of being wrong for another. Relativism allows for the possibility of differing moral judgments about the same behavior being (relatively) correct at the same time.

## ABSOLUTISM

Throughout history there have been those who believe, in contrast to relativism, that there are absolute moral standards. Absolute moral standards are both universal and objective. They are universal in that they apply to everyone at all times and also apply to all situations equally. Consistency without contradiction is a key factor in this universal application. Absolute moral standards are objective in that they do not depend on a person's or culture's beliefs, thoughts, feelings, or customs. Objective moral standards have an existence that is independent of one's belief in them. Universal moral standards cannot be discovered by studying empirical data such as human desires or inclinations because by their very nature these vary from person to person. They are referred to as a priori, or existing prior to the creation of any particular situation or moral judgment. As such, they are not derived from experience but they are universally applicable to experience; and, they are the necessary preconditions of empirical knowledge. It is precisely this independence, this objectivity, that creates the categories of right and wrong relative to experience and one's belief about morality. Philosophers have always questioned whether truly absolute immutable moral standards (truths) are knowable by human beings. The agreed-upon answer has been no. Therefore, in an attempt to approximate this absolute moral standard the measure becomes the consistency with which the moral standard can be applied without contradiction.

The issue between absolutism and relativism is not about identifying the correct moral judgments. The issue between them concerns itself with the relationship among the correct moral judgments, whatever those judgments are;

specifically, whether those judgments are consistent with one another. Relativism allows for different judgments concerning similar actions to both be viewed as being true at the same time, thus holding that correct or valid moral judgments are not all consistent with one another. Universalists hold a contrasting view that the true moral standards or principles (knowable to us) are the same for all people and all situations.

## MOTIVATION IN MORALS

What motivates human beings to choose one action over another? Do we always act for the sake of our own self-interests, or do we sometimes act for the sake of others, or out of a sense of duty? The dichotomy between acting out of one's self-interest and acting for the benefit of others has been labeled egoism and altruism. Egoism is acting out of a sense of self-interest based in part on the belief that one ought to always act to maximize one's own personal good as an end. The term egoism or egoist should not be confused with the term egotistical or selfish. Egoists are no more conceited than anyone else, nor do they disregard the well-being of others, promoting their own welfare at the expense of others. Altruism is acting for the benefit of others based at least in part on the belief that one ought to act for the benefit of others as an end. This belief does not exclude the fact that the doer may also benefit from the action or act. Altruism may be based on some sense of compassion or possibly solely on principle. Egoism has as its basis for action the benefiting of self. Altruism has as its basis for action the benefiting of others. Motivation for acting is the primary meaning attached to both these terms.

Both egoism and altruism are subdivided into two distinct positions, ethical and psychological. Ethical egoism is the view that one ought to act in such a manner as to maximize one's own interests. Psychological egoism is the view that one is egotistically motivated and that everything that one does is for one's own interests and well being, self-love. Ethical altruism is the view that one ought to act for the benefit of others rather than self. Psychological altruism is the view that one is intrinsically motivated to act for the benefit of others.

Many ethical dilemmas arise as a result of the dichotomous demands between self-interest (egoism) and the interests of others (altruism). The problem is one of motivation—why should we be moral? This question has serious implications. In a society based on individual freedom, which cherishes virtues such as self-reliance and living up to your potential, self-interest (egoism) becomes more than a theory of moral motivation, it becomes a paradox. The paradox of self-interest grows out of egoism's implications for judgments about the conduct of others who are in their quest for their self-interest. In certain circumstances what is good for and in the interest of one person will conflict with what is good for and in the interest of another. A confirmed egoist would realize that both individuals should pursue what would maximize their own good. This means that each individual is obligated to follow his or her own course of action even though they (the actions) are incompatible. The question remaining unanswered is if moral actions are not based (at least partially) on self-interest, what rationale exists for the moral principle that people should act against their own self-interests and in the interests of others? The answer requires reasoning, reflection, and the need to justify one's actions. To act for reasons means that the question of justification or the "why" is relevant and important.

## SUMMARY

Moral rules are considered a basic prerequisite for the existence of society. Most people would agree some actions are right and others are wrong. The implication is that some actions are moral, what one ought to do, and others are not. To suggest some action "ought" to be taken implies that the action has meaning or purpose. Aristotle, in his theory of final cause (reason or purpose or intention of an event in existence), stated: To account for something, describe it in terms of that reason it has for being or the end (goal or purpose) toward which it is intending. The implied cause is that which is indicated to be intended, or desired. A teleological approach to the question of "what one ought to do" indicates the quest for one or more other causes in addition to the final cause (moral/ethical reasons for actions).

Moral relativism takes the position that there are no absolute standards, and indeed, in our introduction to ethics, we have found several variations in what different people, different customs, and different cultures believe is right and wrong. Absolutists insist that absolute moral standards exist and are both objective and universal. They are objective in that they transcend the customs and beliefs of a given culture or society. They are universal in that they apply to all people at all times. The actions dictated or allowed by societal norms are judged truly moral only if they agree with the absolute standards. Relativists argue against the existence of absolute moral standards, pointing out that different groups have had and continue to have different moral standards.

Which viewpoint is correct? What is the truth? Does true knowledge have its source in observation or human reason? Is truth fixed, absolute, or relative? What are the motivating factors in human beings' quest to live morally? Do we always act out of our own self-interest? Egoism is the term used to describe action taken out of self-interest. Altruism is the term used to describe action taken to benefit others. The primary meaning of egoism and altruism is in terms of motivation for moral action. One can, despite bad intentions, benefit others, but such action could hardly be called altruistic. One can also fail in an effort to help another and end up personally benefiting, but such action is not solely self-interest. The question has been asked, if one does not at least in part act out of self-interest, then why act morally? The relevant question is one of justification. In subsequent chapters we will survey some of the many ways philosophers have attempted to justify actions.

Values and beliefs are critical in determining behavior, but are they the same? Some might argue that they are, or at least that they are closely related. To look closely is to ascribe a somewhat different meaning to each term. Beliefs are convictions, aspirations, or ideals regarding how things ought to be. Values more closely align themselves with behavior. It is what we truly value that we choose. Values are hierarchically related to a greater or lesser degree of desirability. Values have to do with choice. The reason we select or choose an action, and the value we place on it are most important in determining the priority of the moral obligations. We must look behind the words (beliefs) to discover the reality (values) behind the facade. The congruence or lack of congruence between these two personal concepts has implications for ethics.

In closing our introduction to ethics, a note of caution seems in order. Dietrich Bonhoeffer, a Protestant clergyman imprisoned by the Nazis in World War II, reflected that action comes directly not from thought but from a readiness for responsibility. Carl Menninger, in his 1973 book *What Ever Became of Sin?*, identified this as a growing problem and joined Bonhoeffer in noting that there was a need for a return to common assent to the concept of personal responsibility and answerability both for ourselves and for others.

## QUESTIONS FOR ADDITIONAL REFLECTION AND THOUGHT

1. Pause for a moment to reflect upon conscious choices that you have made that have shaped your life. Every choice reflected the values and commitments that you held at the time you made those choices. Which do you now regret and which remain central to defining your identity?

2. What do you mean when you use the term ethics? How does it differ from morality?

3. What is meant by moral relativism? How does it differ from cultural relativism?

4. You are on a moral quest in search of maturity and integrity. Genuine choice is a matter of ethics. The moral quest is to set goals and to act decisively with conviction. How acutely aware are you of your moral/ethical values and choices and how they have shaped your life thus far? More importantly how can you heighten your moral/ethical awareness and use it to shape your life in the future?

5. How would you define the concept of virtues? Are you better having them or not having them? What role do virtues play in your choice of moral/ethical actions?

6. How influential are a culture's or society's customs, values, and practices in determining an individual's ethics/morals?

7. In your opinion, how do males and females differ in the way each approaches moral/ethical dilemmas?

8. In your opinion, should moral/ethical action be dictated by rules and principles or by the uniqueness of the situation?

9. Think about people who are determined to live their lives with integrity. Do they have the most comfortable, trouble-free lives?

10. What price are you willing to pay for integrity?

# 4

# Ethical Relativism: Knowledge or Opinion

**W**hat is right? What is wrong? What does life require of me? Clear thinking about the underlying assumptions and principles related to these ethical questions is no small task. John Ruskin (1905) in part addressed the problem when he said, "Modern education for the most part signifies giving people the faculty of thinking wrong on every conceivable subject of importance to them." He fortunately had a partial solution to the identified dilemma. Ruskin, in reference to reading Milton, said

> "Thus Milton thought," not "Thus I thought, in misreading Milton." And by this process you will gradually come to attach less weight to your own "Thus I thought" at other times. You will begin to perceive that what you thought was a matter of no serious importance—that your thoughts on any subject are not perhaps the clearest and wisest that could be arrived at thereupon—in fact that unless you are a very singular person, you cannot be said to have a 'thought' at all, that you have no material for them, in any serious matter—no right to 'think' but only to try and learn more of the facts. (p. 30)

This process of inquiry espoused by Ruskin is essential to the development of a set of principles for use in ethical reasoning. Epistemology, the branch of philosophy that asks the question "What is mere opinion and what is truth?", is intimately involved in searching for the underpinnings of ethics.

Ethics seeks reasons or rationale that support one position over another. People generally have views on a variety of topics and use these views as their basis for action. Consequently, people generally have a strong attachment (intellectually and emotionally) to their views. However, having a strongly held view about an ethical issue does not make that view right or lend justification for one's position. People have long held strong feelings or views that later proved to be grossly mistaken. The study of ethics requires, as Ruskin (1905) states, that we try to learn more of the facts. Our goal is not just to act but to act for reasons, intentionally, and with purpose. Ethics is ultimately about what should be; but the justification for what should be is found in the facts, not opinions.

## THE SOCRATIC METHOD

The Socratic Method or the Method of Dialectic is one way of seeking knowledge through question and answer. The question is usually a general one, such as "What is . . . ?" The answer offered by the respondent takes the form of a definition. Socrates would then refute each definition by offering a counter-example designed to show that the definition offered was too narrow, or in some way flawed. The final definition must state what all the examples, cases, instances, and particulars have in common. Sometimes the final definition completely reverses the original, or at times no definition is reached even though many are rejected in the process.

"There is nothing more dangerous than ignorance being practiced" (Goethe). This quote from *Faust* serves as a warning to those who believe they know more than they actually do. Socrates wrote that the only wisdom consists in knowing you know nothing. In his *Apology* he wrote "No one does evil voluntarily. Knowing the good, no man would voluntarily choose evil." To Socrates, having knowledge of what is true or right will bring about the correct action. But to gain knowledge of the truth we must first distinguish between knowledge and opinion. Socrates said that to know the good is to do the good and to know the good requires that certain conditions be met. They include sufficient reflection and full consent of the will. Sufficient reflection means that one is fully aware of the gravity of his/her proposed action. Full consent of the will means that the action is taken freely and not under the influence of limiting factors such as force, fear, or blinding passion.

Having knowledge of the good, no one would voluntarily choose evil. But we often say: "I acted against my better judgment" or "I really knew better." According to Socrates, this is absurd—if you had really understood the right thing to do you would have done it. If you really had possessed better judgment than you used, you would have acted on, not against, it. Socrates insists that when one does an evil act, it is always with the thought that it will bring one some good, some benefit. This is the misguided goal of striving to achieve happiness in life but never finding it, a life Socrates called unexamined and not worth living.

Plato expanded on Socrates' doctrine that to know the good is to do the good, developing a theory of the tripartite character of the human soul. Under Plato's guidance, human beings are seen as constituted by three distinct elements forming a hierarchical structure: the lowest the bodily appetites; next, the spirited elements; and then, the highest, reason. Plato proposed that though we may know the good, this knowledge may run into conflict with bodily desires. He additionally thought that reason, the desire to reach the truth or the ideal, comes into conflict with the bodily appetites that desire immediate gratification. The intermediate element, the high spirited self (emotions), serves as a mediator of such conflict and is capable of acting on behalf of either reason or appetite. An often-used example of a chariot and two horses illustrates the problem that reason has in managing both the appetites and the spirited element. One horse, the spirited element, needs not the whip but is guided by the charioteer's voice. The other horse, the bodily appetites, is more difficult to control and requires the use of the whip. The charioteer, reason, is pulling at both horses (Annas, 1981; Lavine, 1984). That potential for either success or disaster emanates from the conflict is clear in this example. While Plato provides us with an excellent example of the dynamics involved in the search for what is true knowledge, the question remains: What constitutes knowledge and what constitutes opinion?

Knowledge is a clear and certain perception of something. It is learning all that has been perceived or grasped mentally; it is understanding. Opinion, then, is a belief not based on absolute certainty or positive knowledge, but on what seems true; whatever one thinks. The struggle between believing that something appears true and therefore is true and understanding the truth, is illustrated by Plato in his famous Allegory of the Cave.

## THE ALLEGORY OF THE CAVE

Lavine (1984) provides the following description of the allegory:

> Socrates introduced the allegory by imagining humankind as prisoners living in an underground cave. Deep inside the cave, the prisoners face the inside walls, their necks and legs chained so that they cannot move. They have never seen the light of day or the sun outside the cave. A fire burns behind the prisoners; between the fire and the prisoners is a raised way upon which a low wall has been built, functioning much like a screen used in puppet shows to conceal the people working the puppets. Along the way, objects carried by people are seen by the prisoners only as their projected shadows on the cave wall. The prisoners, facing the inside wall, cannot see one another or the wall behind them. These prisoners live their entire lives seeing only shadows of reality, and the voices they hear are really only echoes from the wall. But the prisoners cling to the familiar shadows and to their passions and prejudices; were they freed and able to turn around to see there realities producing the shadows, they would be

blinded by the firelight. They would then become angry with anyone who tried to tell them how pitiful their position was preferring their familiar shadow-world. But if one were freed and permitted to see by the firelight the cave, his/her fellow prisoners, and if he/she were then removed from the cave into the light of the sun, he/she would see things of the world as they truly are indeed, he/she would see the sun itself. What would this now freed person now think of life in the cave and what the people there know of reality and morality? And if he/she were to descend once again into the cave, would he/she not then have great difficulty accustoming him/herself to the darkness, so that he/she could not compete with those who had never left the cave? Would he/she not be subject to their ridicule, scorn, even physical attack for describing a different reality from the one they knew? (pp. 27–28)

How does the Allegory of the Cave apply to the quest for knowledge and to our time? This question is most applicable. Many contemporary interpretations of the allegory are noteworthy; the reader is invited to supply current information regarding what is similar to the events described and contribute new interpretations.

Like Plato, we struggle to find the truth (knowledge), groping in the shadows and the darkness for standards of right and wrong that bring about the correct action. How does one ascend into the light and gain knowledge of what is right?

## METHODS OF KNOWING

A major problem that has always existed concerns the nature of knowing and the sources of information or knowledge. Peirce (1940) proposed three methods of knowing that are applicable here. The first method of knowing, the method of tenacity, states that people hold firm to truths they "know" are true. In establishing these truths there may be a tendency to omit evidence that does not support our beliefs and to find and include that which does. This represents the well-known problem of objectivity. Frequent repetition or reindoctrination of these assumptions or truths enhances their validity. This, simply stated, means one finds what one looks for. An eloquent example is provided to us by Viktor Frankl (cited in Fabry, 1987) in the following:

> Two men approach their rabbi with a dispute they could not solve. The first man says, "Rabbi, this man's cat ate my butter." The second man replies, "Rabbi, this is not true. My cat does not like butter." The Rabbi asked the first man how much butter the cat had eaten and he replied two pounds. The Rabbi then ordered scales be brought in and put the cat on one side. On the other he placed weights until the scales balanced, exactly two pounds. He then turned to the two men and replied, "Now we have found the butter, but where is the cat?" (p. 66)

When tenaciously held assumptions or truths are valid, they are a dependable source of knowledge. However, when they are based upon false beliefs they are a source of faulty knowledge.

The second method of knowing is the method of authority or established belief. This method has the weight of tradition and public sanction behind it. Many of the things we think we know have been handed down by tradition. People have also traditionally sought knowledge from those in positions of authority. History is replete with examples of kings and clerics who have dictated truth to the masses. Even now, this source is still used. The amount of information one is faced with is often overwhelming, and the method of authority allows it to be accepted at face value, without validation. When authority and traditions are valid, they are dependable sources of knowledge. However, when authority or expert opinion is based on sophisticated guessing, or tradition on mistaken beliefs and practices, then faulty knowledge results.

The third method of knowing is the method of a priori. This method responds to the question: "If facts are known, what is it that is known?" Lewis (1956) stated a priori represents the epistemic hypothesis for our classifying complex events into their factual categories. Katsoff (1947) answers that the fact is a proposition whereby supportive perception is the interpretation of sense data in the context of an existential hypothesis. Facts are different from sense data. Sense data is our perception of objects, our experience of what has occurred, but not as it necessarily occurs. It is our categories of understanding, a priori, not derived from experience, that are the bases of knowledge. Katsoff offers the following conclusions regarding a priori:

1. Sense data are not facts.
2. Facts result only as the interpretation of sense data.
3. Every scientific observation presupposes a set of categories (the requirement of the a priori).
4. A differentiation is to be made between the sense data events and the facts. Factual propositions are expressive of interpretative perception, never of the sense data. (pp. 688–689)

This method involves knowledge based on intuition and is self-evident; it represents evaluation based on an internal source, a higher authority. An example may be the section of the United States Constitution stating "all men are created equal." What makes this statement true? This statement is true because its validity is based on a higher authority; a moral law that was self-evident to our founding fathers and that existed prior to the writing of the U.S. Constitution.

Lewis (1929) stated that empirical knowledge without the a priori schemata of our definitive concepts would be impossible. Hayek (1952), on a priorism, stated that perception is impossible without prior categories or classificatory assemblies for the processing of input. Katsoff, (1947) however, cautioned that a fact in a foreign frame of reference is not false, it is simply meaningless.

Royce (1947) similarly postulated another three approaches to knowing. The first, the metaphorical, is possibly, according to Royce, the oldest. It involves knowledge based on intuitive or symbolic thought. It represents evaluation against an internal standard. An example might be knowing that a particular literary work is profound or that a work of art is beautiful. The second approach to knowing is rational, which is also an internal source of knowledge but based on the principles of logic and reason. An example might be reasoning by deductive thinking (all books have pages, this a book; therefore, this book has pages) or inductive thinking (a given solution worked in the past, therefore, it should work in the future). The third and final approach to knowing is empirical; that is, by objective observation. Of consequence is the sometimes erroneous assumption that our perceptions are correct (e.g., the professor with the slow watch who is always late and never knows the correct time though she gathers empirical data by looking at her watch frequently).

## ETHICAL GROUPTHINK

In My Lai, Vietnam, 16 March 1968, Lt. William Calley, U.S. Army, slaughtered helpless civilians. In 1971, he was convicted of what was described as the My Lai Massacre. Yet a great cry went up from sectors of the general public (as well as from the military) disputing the possibility that what Lt. Calley had done was a crime. He had obeyed orders, and had done as others before him (and since). Was his action morally right or morally wrong? What are the facts (truths) and what are the opinions?

Was Lt. Calley right in his actions at My Lai? After all, were we not at war? Few dispute the facts of what happened; however, some saw this as a crime while others did not—why? Carl Menninger (1973) labeled sin as the failure to recognize in conduct and character the moral ideal, at least as fully as possible under existing circumstances; failure to do what one ought toward one's fellow man. Identifying or defining the moral ideal here is the problem. What, under these circumstances, is the moral ideal? Some would say killing is never good, while others would say killing is allowable but only in war. If the latter is pursued, then what are the categories of acceptable killing? There are those who believe it is acceptable to kill enemy soldiers but not civilians or noncombatants. Some of those who would agree would add that civilians are often unfortunate casualties of war.

On such emotionally charged issues as this, we often encounter groups or factions who think alike. Irving Janis of Yale University coined the term "groupthink" in 1971 to refer to a kind of self-deception that groups of people working together fall into as a result of self-absorption. He noted that despite the advantages of group decisions there are also great problems; that groupthink can produce cataclysmic blunders that any single individual member might have avoided. Janis used as an example a statement supposedly uttered by

President Kennedy about the Bay of Pigs invasion: "How could we have been so stupid?" Janis listed several symptoms of groupthink applicable to the quest for knowledge.

1. Participants of groupthink ignore warnings and construct rationalizations in order to discount them.
2. Participants of groupthink have an unquestioning belief in the inherent morality of their group action.
3. Participants of groupthink hold stereotyped views of others who hold differing views.
4. Participants of groupthink apply direct pressure on any individual who momentarily expresses doubt about any of the group's shared goals or questions the validity of the arguments.
5. Unanimity becomes an idol. Participants of groupthink avoid deviating from what appears to be the group consensus; any misgivings are quickly silenced and the importance of their doubts is minimized even to themselves. (pp. 44–76)

Janis also lists some of the symptoms of the resulting inadequacy of problem solving. Among these are the limitation of discussion or focus, the failure to re-examine some previously acceptable alternatives or views that are now rejected, and the failure to seek information from other expert sources. Was Lt. Calley a victim of groupthink? What about those who supported him?

John Ruskin (1905) argued that

> to make our minds good ground for growth of the seeds which those kings of thought have to sow we must clear them of all weeds of prejudice, and uproot and utterly destroy whatever evil may have begun to grow therein. (p. 6)

## RELATIVISM

Is it all relative? Moral relativism is no new idea. O'Brien (1972) credits Protagoras, a Greek Sophist, as putting forth one of the most succinct statements regarding relativism. Protogoras stated that man is the measure of all things. This is based on a particular epistemology that reality is not the same for everyone. Certain or even reliable knowledge about the universe is regarded as impossible because our knowledge is based on idiosyncratic sensory impressions. It follows then that there can be no universal truth; and therefore, no universal good to which all lives should conform. Another Sophist carried relativism in the other direction. The Sophist responded to the question, "What is Justice?" with the reply, "Justice is nothing else than the interest of the stronger." As long as moral standards are interpreted to be nothing more than individual opinions, it is necessary to find some way of resolving the conflicts presented by them, so the strong must impose their morality on the weak.

Moral rules are the basic rules outlining the conditions necessary for society's existence. Morals are a prerequisite to the existence of a society; however, changing social and or economic conditions can bring about a change in a society's morals. Moral relativism is the position that moral standards are always relative to something else. Relativists deny that there are any moral standards that are absolute. They claim that different moral standards exist for different people, different societies, and different times, historically. They further state that there are no moral standards independent of societal moral codes; therefore, societal moral codes are the only objective standards possible. (Relativists, however, are not to be confused with nihilists. Nihilists are those who deny the existence of any basis for knowledge, truth, or ethical right and wrong. Relativists believe in right and wrong; but they believe that what is right for one person or in one culture may not be right for another.) Therefore, a relativist might say that a given act is, at the same time, both right and wrong—right for one culture, wrong for another. Relativism does not tell us which acts are right or wrong (absolutely); rather, it views the characteristics relative to cultural diversity and then describes them (relative to the culture) as being right or wrong.

There are several different types of relativism defined by how radically right and wrong are thought to vary. They all reject absolute moral standards but do so on differing grounds. The cultural relativist defines right and wrong acts as similar for people of the same culture but varying from culture to culture. Moral subjectivism or extreme relativism defines right and wrong as varying from person to person within the same culture. This position maintains that moral standards are always a matter of personal opinion based on the thoughts, feelings, or attitudes of the individual doing the judging.

The cultural relativist claims that people should live according to the moral code of their own culture or society, and they should also respect the moral codes of other societies. Additionally, the moral codes of a given culture should not be violated even if the individual finds him/herself in a different culture where the moral code is more relaxed and a prohibited act is allowed. However, in the case of extreme tolerance for moral codes, if your moral code dictates certain actions toward others that in another society would interfere or conflict with their moral code, then you should not follow the dictate of your moral code. Additionally, if the moral code of a given society is in direct opposition with your society's moral code, you should not interfere with or punish an action based on that moral code by a member of that society. This case of extreme tolerance paradoxically creates an absolute standard. Tolerance of others' moral codes now appears to be a universal requirement regardless of one's own societal moral code.

There appear to be some noteworthy problems with this logic. The most obvious is whether or not moral relativism can be logically obeyed. For example, the moral code of one's society dictates tolerance and respect for others' moral codes and at the same time requires adherence to principles of human rights that may require enlightening those others who currently do not subscribe to these principles. Would it not then be logically impossible to adhere to one's own moral code and at the same time respect others' moral code? Additionally, if relativism is true, then we cannot logically attempt to change one another's beliefs regarding human rights by producing moral reasons for our respective positions. As relativists we both know and agree that human rights are right for one society and wrong for another and we know why. Following this logic, relativism does not exclude the possibility of one individual judging the actions of another. However, from a moral standpoint the issue is moot because both may be right.

Tolerance now appears to be an absolute standard, but this is deceiving. Two people can disagree over an issue such as the morality of abortion and, according to moral subjectivism or extreme relativism, they can both be right in that subjectively it is right for the one and wrong for the other. Viewed from the standpoint of cultural relativism, however, both individuals cannot be right, at least not if they are both from the same culture or society. Within a given culture or society, though not between different societies, cultural relativism allows for an objective standard by which moral disputes are solved.

It is important to note in the above discussion that relativists are not necessarily subjectivists. Cultural relativists do acknowledge that there are objective standards of right and wrong that are external to the individual and personal judgment, but they contend that these standards vary from culture to culture and society to society. The reader is cautioned not to confuse ethical relativism and universalism with cultural relativism and moral subjectivism. Moral subjectivism states that objectively nothing is morally right or morally wrong. It views morality as a concept of human invention based on human needs and desires. Moral subjectivists see individuals as sharing certain human characteristics such as feelings for others (sympathy for the suffering). They also see groups of individuals with shared subjective needs and desires forming societies and exerting influence (socialization) on the subjective responses of all members of the society. This, however, does not exclude the possibility of different individuals having different subjective responses, needs, and desires. Anthropologist Ralph Linton (1976) argued that ethical relativism is false because it can be demonstrated that all societies have rules relating to certain universal categories of behavior (e.g., sexual behavior). Linton further asserts that morality is based on common human characteristics: needs, feelings, and cognitions. Unfortunately, the leap from this assertion of common human characteristics to an objective basis for morality falls well short of the mark.

Hume, having examined the case against reason as a source of morality, contends that sentiment is its source. Sentiments, according to Hume, are universally shared. Therefore, all people have some of the same (universal) subjective emotional reactions that can be the basis for shared moral views (Mackie, 1980). Nietzsche argued that there are no justifications for morality. He stated that traditional morality depends on belief in God, and according to Nietzsche, God is dead. To Nietzsche, it was the noble type of individual who regarded him/herself as a determiner of values; the individual is the creator of values. In general, Nietzsche's philosophy was that each person has to develop and express his or her own identity as well as values because God is dead. Therefore, we must bear the responsibility for what happens in our world and disregard our childish reliance on a superhuman power (Schutte, 1984).

Sartre similarly rejected attempts to justify morality, stating that justification only shifts the ultimate responsibility for what the individual does away from personal responsibility. Both the decision to act and the justification for it are nothing more than the individual making a choice and having to live with it. The individual is responsible for determining what is right and what is wrong. Living in good faith, according to Sartre, means being responsible for one's own free choices (Anderson, 1979).

## EMOTIVISM

Emotivism, or the concept of ethics as an emotive expression (Stevenson, 1944; Ayers, 1950), states that moral judgments cannot be based solely on facts and claims. They are rhetorical expressions of emotional reactions to events in the world and are attempts to influence others as to the rightness or wrongness of an act. Language is used to provoke emotion in others (through argument or expression of emotion) and to persuade them to make a similar judgment. Moral statements express the feelings of the speaker and are intended to influence the feelings of the listener. A statement has an emotive meaning if it is intended to produce a response in the person who hears it. Moral judgments then are reduced to and justified by expressions of emotion.

## SUMMARY

Absolute moral standards are those that are both universal and objective. They are universal in that they determine what is morally right for all people under all conditions. They are objective in that they exist independently of the beliefs, customs, and traditions of a culture or society. Moral relativism is the position that there are no absolute standards of morality. Morality is relative to something. Different standards exist for different cultures and societies. The most frequent tenet of relativism states that one should live in accordance with the moral codes of his/her society. Another states that one should live in accord with the moral codes of his/her society and also respect and tolerate the moral codes of other societies. An extreme view states that one should respect and tolerate the individual moral standards of all people.

Moral subjectivism expounds the view that moral standards are a matter of personal preference. Morality is a concept of human invention; therefore, there is no objective morality and no moral standard. Because morality is a subjective concept, it differs from person to person within a culture or society.

Emotivism argues that morality cannot be based on facts, but rather on emotional expressions of individual reactions to events in the world. To say that causing something to occur is morally wrong is not stating a fact according to emotivism. The statement is rather an evaluation followed by an emotional attitude toward what happened, and an invitation to others to join in making the same or similar judgment.

Is it all relative? The idea that what is right or wrong might vary from culture to culture and society to society can be an attractive as well as an untenable thesis. On the positive side, relativism encourages mutual respect and acceptance of differences, and may reduce tensions. Respect should not be confused with agreement. If one truly believes that the moral opinions of others are as valid as one's own, then one should have better tolerance for behaviors one disapproves. On the negative side, however, relativism can encourage avoidance and cowardice. "Well, let's agree to disagree and avoid the issue—after all, it's all relative."

Relativism, even if it is correct, faces formidable problems. This, however, does not mean that it has no applicability; rather, it means that relativists must find ways around these problems.

## QUESTIONS FOR ADDITIONAL REFLECTION AND THOUGHT

1. How should a person determine what is ethical and what is not? What method do you use?

2. Should one act on personal impulse, emotion, or intuition, or is there any objective guide that would assist one in determining a correct course of action?

3. The helping profession is not a valueless profession, but how does one determine what values to value?

4. What is the role of the group (e.g., profession, culture, or community) in determining what is right and what is wrong, what is ethical and what is not?

5. To what extent is any of us able to judge the choices made by others without experiencing directly the pressures and restrictions on their freedom?

6. How would you describe the difference between cultural relativism and ethical relativism? What are the implications?

7. What does a moral/ethical statement express?

8. Are there any objective criteria by which one can assess moral/ethical statements?

9. In what sense can a moral/ethical statement be true or false?

10. How does relativism speak to the need for a foundation for ethical decision making?

# 5

# Consequentialism
# or Justice

The most frequently asked question, "What makes a certain action wrong?" evokes the usual response: "The consequences." Consequentialists believe that the good is determined by the consequence of the act; nonconsequentialists deny this is true. It is a fact that all acts have consequences, even the most trivial; so the question now becomes which consequences are morally important and which are not. Which are good and for whom?

Ethical egoism is the idea that morality is defined as acting in one's own interest and in such a way as to maximize the consequences of good over bad. To amend this slightly and say morality is defined as acting in such a way as to promote the greatest balance of good over bad for all people is utilitarianism. Utilitarianism is a teleological, goal-directed theory emphasizing happiness as the end result of human action. Holmes (1993) describes two types of teleological ethical theory that are noteworthy here: micro ethics and macro ethics. Micro ethics regards the happiness of the individual as the highest good and defines what is right as the action that maximizes that end. Micro ethics can also have as its concern the good or well-being of the group; however, the good of the group is defined as the good of the individuals who comprise the group. Macro ethics, on the other hand, has as its concern the happiness or well-being of the group itself (city, state, nation, or race) and defines what is right as the action that maximizes that end. Macro ethics defines the group as being of greater importance than any particular individual or subgroup within it, because its good exceeds the sum of any and all of its parts. It is therefore potentially possible that any individual or part may be sacrificed for what is seen as the greater good of the group. A modern example of macro ethics might be the Chinese government's response to the student protests in Beijing's Tiananmen Square.

## ETHICAL EGOISM

Ethical egoism, according to Solomon (1993), can be viewed as a hedonistic version of consequentialism. According to this view, one should act in ways that maximize one's own personal good or happiness. This view is universal and seen as morally binding on everyone. It should be noted here that ethical egoists are not conceited or selfish, at least no more than anyone else. Their acts are dictated by the belief that they will bring about the maximum amount of happiness or good. Ethical egoists may very well be involved with and concerned about the plight of others. If they are, this action is based on the belief that this concern will bring about the greatest amount of happiness for themselves. Ethical egoists are not altruistic; however, without knowing something about the individual's beliefs you cannot necessarily tell an altruist from an egoist.

Ethical egoism has a universal mandate that says that each one of us has an ethical obligation to maximize our own happiness. The obvious question that arises is do morality and self-interest mix? In answering yes, one may consider goodness its own reward. In answering no, one may still consider goodness its own reward; however, this reward is outweighed by the gratification or reward of certain immoral actions, especially when the risk of discovery is nil. The most obvious problem with ethical egoism involves the conflict that occurs when what is good for one person directly conflicts with what is good for another person. The universal mandate becomes impossible because it obligates both parties to act in a manner that will maximize each one's own happiness. The collision is inevitable; in the worst case, one will prevail and the other will not. One's happiness may be maximized and the other's may not.

## UTILITARIANISM

Utilitarianism stresses that the greatest happiness of the greatest number should be the aim of all action, emphasizing that the value of anything is determined solely by its ability to bring about this end. Though what most naturally motivates one's actions may be one's own happiness, one should act not just for one's own happiness but for the greatest happiness for the greatest number. The focus is on the results achieved, which should be happiness for the greatest number possible.

Jeremy Bentham, an English philosopher and reformer, is considered the father of modern utilitarianism. Bentham held that pain and pleasure govern behavior and that any ethical system founded on anything other than maximizing the net balance of pleasure over pain is inherently in error. He is credited with borrowing the phrase "the greatest happiness of the greatest number" and extending it as the measure of value of all human action. Bentham, fearing that most people might not always choose correctly that which would bring the greatest happiness, went so far as to develop a "happiness calculus" to evaluate every action in the quest to achieve this end. Simply stated, the system was one of probability in which one would add up all the possible pleasure an action would bring and then subtract the amount of unhappiness the action would bring. Utilizing this formula provides one with a rational basis for making decisions regarding which action will (potentially) bring about the greatest amount of happiness. Obviously, there are large difficulties in making such calculations and the above description is a great oversimplification of the process.

John Stewart Mill, who at 15 years of age had become familiar with Bentham's ideas, went on to become the recognized champion of utilitarianism. Mill differed with Bentham in that he (Mill) concluded that pleasures must differ from one another in quality. Bentham believed that sensual or physical pleasure was the greatest good in life. Mill argued that if this were true and physical pleasure were the summum bonum, the highest possible good, then it would not matter whether the animal enjoying himself or herself were a human being or a pig. Mill (1897/1969) stated his view in the following:

> It is better to be a human being dissatisfied than a pig satisfied; better to
> be Socrates dissatisfied than a fool satisfied. And if the fool or the pig,
> is of a different opinion, it is because they only know their own side
> of the question. The other party to the comparison knows both sides.
> (p. 39)

Mill has shifted the focus from a quantitative measure of pleasure to a qualitative measure but there is still the problem of how to evaluate and measure these qualities.

Today, utilitarians are faced with yet another variation, made clear in the following two statements: (a) Always perform the act that will bring about the greatest good to the greatest number; (b) Always perform the act following the rule that will bring about the greatest good for the greatest number. The first statement is referred to as act utilitarianism and the second as rule utilitarianism.

## ACT UTILITARIANISM

Act utilitarianism states that an act is right if it produces at least as great a balance of happiness over unhappiness in its consequences for all people as any other act available. Any act is evaluated on the consequences that it produces and not on the general category of its desirability. An example is the act of lying; not telling the truth. Generally, lying is not considered to be desirable. If everyone were to lie, then chaos would exist, but are there not times when lying produces the greater good than telling the truth in a particular situation?

According to act utilitarianism, every time one acts one should consider the effects this act will have on this particular situation and the balance of good over bad. The following might serve as an example of both the process and problems encountered with the process. Utilitarian calculations are carried out for two given actions. One action includes telling a lie and cheating someone, and the other consists of telling the truth. Suppose the balance of the calculation were to come out even (the effect of either act being benign). If telling a lie would produce some personal benefit, then one might therefore increase the balance of happiness over unhappiness by telling a lie. The choice between lying and telling the truth is basically neutral. Critics of act utilitarianism object on the basis that clearly wrong acts might in a given situation be shown to maximize happiness and minimize unhappiness for everyone involved, thereby being acceptable. A variation in utilitarianism that addresses this concern is rule utilitarianism.

## RULE UTILITARIANISM

Rule utilitarianism is the view that an act is right if the rule dictating the act maximizes happiness or the greatest good for the greatest number. The rightness or wrongness of an act is not directly determined by the consequences of the act; but, rather indirectly by determining whether or not the act would be right according to established rules that maximize the happiness of the greatest number of people. Where act utilitarianism dictates that if all else is equal and what you desire to do would bring you more happiness, you should do it, rule utilitarianism dictates that you should follow the established rule(s) which maximize happiness for all people regardless of the individual situation.

Suppose that on a visit to the state of Hawaii you were to view the lava fields produced by the volcano Kilauea. You would like to take a piece of lava rock home with you as a souvenir. There is, however, a potential problem associated with this. There is a Hawaiian superstition that says the volcano god will be angered if anyone removes any of the lava from this place and bad luck will follow the person who defies this decree. Viewing this act from the perspective of act utilitarianism, the rightness or wrongness of the act would be dictated by the consequences of the act itself. The decision to take the lava rock would be determined by your belief in superstition and the consequences of taking the lava rock and of not taking it. Because the volcano is still active and you would take only one piece (and a little one at that) no one would notice. Therefore, the only person affected by your action would be you, and you would be happier if you took the rock. So according to act utilitarianism, you should take the lava rock. However, when this act is viewed from the perspective of rule utilitarianism the outcome is different. Rule utilitarianism states that one should compare the system of rules that allows one to take lava rocks from the lava fields with the system of rules that does not. Because Hawaii has so many visitors, millions and millions, if each one of them took some of the lava rocks as souvenirs this could have severe consequences for the lava fields. This effect on the lava fields would then have a negative effect on the future tourists who came to visit the lava fields. Therefore, under rule utilitarianism one should not take the lava rock. This is not to mention the possibility that one is wrong about the volcano god taking revenge.

Rule utilitarianism begins to move away from consequentialism in that it is no longer the consequence of the act itself that determines its rightness or wrongness. Instead, it is now the relationship of the act to the rule that dictates the rightness or wrongness of an act. An example might be the rule that one should not steal. In a given situation stealing may bring about better consequences than not stealing (e.g., hungry person stealing to feed one's family); however, one refrains from stealing because of the rule prohibiting it. Consequences obviously are appealed to in establishing the rule; however, action in a given situation is taken or not taken in reference to the rule.

There are some obvious problems associated with both act and rule utilitarianism. Moore (1956) pointed out that in considering the consequences of a given action in determining whether it is right, one is required to have knowledge of all of the possible consequences related to the act as well as all the possible consequences of every other action that is equally available at the moment. Compounding this is the fact that a comparison must then be made between all the rightness and wrongness of all the possible consequences. The final compounding effect to be considered is the ripple effect. Thought of as a rock dropped into a pond, the act is analogous to the point of entry of the rock; however, the ripples made by the rock extend far beyond the point of entry. Similarly, consequences of an act often extend far beyond the act itself. Knowledge of the foregoing spurs us on in our search beyond consequences toward the concepts of fairness and equality.

## JUSTICE

Protagoras, in Plato's dialogue, recounts the myth of creation in which various animals are equipped with the properties necessary to their preservation. Some have strength while others are swift. Only humans are left with no means of defense. Concerned for their survival, Zeus dispatches Hermes to confer on them a sense of justice to enable them to exist in community with one another. This endowment from Hermes has provided human beings with a most arguable task, the task of establishing social justice. Having a sense of justice or fairness has proven to be one thing; knowing the process and how to make it work have proven elusive. (Plato, trans. 1977, pp. 757–758)

Justice, it can be argued, is essential to political wisdom and to the process of government, which in turn is necessary if human beings are to exist in community with one another. Plato, in the above dialogue, acknowledges the importance of justice for social living. Today it continues to be one of the most pervasive issues permeating discussions of business, politics, and social well-being.

In orienting oneself to the concept of justice, three perspectives must be examined: the individual perspective concerned primarily with personal rights; the group perspective concerned primarily with furthering the good of all through furthering the interests of the group; and the institutional or societal perspective concerned primarily with the establishment and maintenance of principles and rules of law which in turn allow for its (the society's or institution's) very origin and continued existence.

Most discussions of justice center on legal justice, where the concern is to explain and justify the rules and procedures as they apply to the rights of individuals, groups, and institutions. Equally important is the concern with justice as understood in moral terms. The trial of Seaman Holmes (*United States v. Holmes,* 1842), a crew member of the American ship William Brown, serves as an example of both views of justice (legal and moral). The following is a brief summary of the accounts of the trial: The ship struck an iceberg and sank in the frigid waters of Newfoundland. Thirty-two passengers and nine crewmen crowded into a leaky lifeboat. Grossly overloaded and leaking, the lifeboat nevertheless held up throughout the night and into the next day, when it began to rain. The seas became progressively rougher and the rain heavier. Late that evening, it became apparent that something must be thrown overboard to lighten the load. Crewman Holmes ordered the other crew members to throw some of the passengers overboard, which they did. The next morning several more passengers were thrown overboard despite their protests. Early in the morning of the third day the weather cleared, the lifeboat was picked up by the ship Crescent, and all the passengers who had not been thrown overboard were saved.

At Mr. Holmes' trial, the prosecution argued that he (Mr. Holmes) had a duty to look after the well-being of the passengers, because as a crew member, he had agreed to serve and protect them. In his defense, Mr. Holmes argued that in a state of eminent peril, all men are reduced to a "state of nature," and that in such circumstances there is no distinction between the rights of a passenger and the rights of a sailor. Once adrift in the leaky lifeboat, the ocean had thrown them back into the state of nature where lawlessness is the norm and adhering to morality would probably cost one's life. The moral duties that make sense when people live in a well-governed social state become meaningless. In a state of nature where the agreements of an established orderly society no longer existed, he did not violate his moral duties to the passengers.

Mr. Holmes' unsuccessful defense was based in part on Hobbes' (1651) social contract theory. The theory acknowledges that there are morally significant differences between living in an orderly society and living in a state of nature and that these differences have implications for what must be done to preserve one's life. In an orderly society, people have agreed to adhere to moral norms in their relationships with each other, and the agreement to abide by these norms is enforced by society. Knowing that others will usually behave morally toward him or her, it is safe for him or her to act morally toward others. A state of nature is an uncivilized state because there are no agreements to keep people from harming or killing one another. Therefore, there is no morality in a state of nature and everyone legitimately can and will do whatever is necessary to preserve his or her own life. Once people move out of a state of nature and into a social state, a governing force has been created and the terms right and wrong all acquire a meaning based on the rules the society enforces. However, if the agreement ever breaks down (e.g., war, revolution, or absence of government) and people are once again fighting each other for their lives, they have returned to a state of nature and can no longer be expected to act morally. In other words, morality makes sense only so long as a social contract exists and there is force sufficient to compel everyone to keep his or her agreements.

## DISTRIBUTIVE JUSTICE

What is fair or just and how does one know? The concept of fairness implies openness; honesty; evenhandedness; hence equal or equitable. This concept of fairness can be used as a guide to determine what action is just. The task is to apply this concept to everyone equally. One method is the system of distributive justice. Distributive justice is concerned with how benefits and burdens are distributed equally in accordance with need and other mediating factors. The underlying principle of distributive justice is consistent equal treatment of all individuals or groups. This can be viewed as egalitarianism, the idea that everyone should be treated equally. Viewed from this perspective, it is unfair for anyone to have any more than anyone else. The distributive principle is to divide the total amount to be distributed by the number of individuals, thus assuring that everyone receives an equal amount. This approach is possible theoretically, but in practical application it runs into problems, especially when what is distributed is not quantifiable.

Another approach to distributive justice championed by Karl Marx in the mid-nineteenth century is from each according to his abilities; to each according to his needs. Such an approach was part of the former Soviet Union's Communist view of world order. This approach requires assessing what each individual should receive. Equal distribution then is viewed as being equal among equals but not among nonequals. The qualifying criteria for distribution becomes ability and need. How much one is given to bear depends on one's ability to bear the burden; how much one receives in benefits depends on one's needs. But many other criteria can be established for the distribution of burdens and benefits.

Yet another approach to distributive justice is the principle of equalitarianism. Equalitarianism is distinguishable from egalitarianism. Both require that everyone be treated equally; however, egalitarianism requires distribution to be made measurably equal, without regard to any criteria besides quantitative equality. Equalitarianism, however, requires that one assess the effects of distribution on the recipients to ensure the distribution constitutes equal treatment.

Then consideration is made as to whether or not some have an abundance while others do not have enough. Equal distribution, as defined by egalitarianism, may provide some recipients with too much and others too little. Equalitarianism, however, defines equal distribution as each recipient receiving or benefiting equally according to their ability, need, worth, and any other criteria that is applicable.

## SOCIAL JUSTICE

Given the underlying idea that distributive justice is consistency in the comparative treatment of all people, what is it to treat everyone equally? Rawls (1971) attempts this question, acknowledging that inequities exist in society and are inevitable; however, there are rational ways of justifying them. In his book, *A Theory of Justice,* Rawls sets forth his position on the principles of social justice. These two principles are the equality principle and the difference principle.

The equality principle states that each person in a society has an equal right to the maximum liberty compatible with the same amount of liberty for everyone else. This may be considered similar to the all men are created equal statement in the Constitution of the United States. This principle, according to Rawls, exists prior to the difference principle.

The difference principle states that inequality is permissible if it is reasonable to expect that it will work to everyone's advantage and that it arises under conditions of equal opportunity. If inequality does exist, it must in some way provide benefit for all, not just the one who has special advantage. An example might be the owners of a large corporation having greater wealth than the workers. The corporation, however, provides the goods and services, as well as the jobs, that result in a better quality of life for all.

Rawls goes on to say that if a conflict were to exist between the difference principle and the equality principle, the latter would take priority; the sole exception being a case of survival. This point makes it clear that Rawls is no utilitarian. His view is that "Each person possesses an inviolability founded on justice that even the welfare of society as a whole cannot override. . . . The rights secured by justice are not subject to political bargaining or to the calculus of social interests." (Rawls, 1971, p. 4)

Rawls' concept of justice, simply stated, is that people have the right to make agreements with one another and these agreements are binding on them. These agreements can be informal, as in making a promise; or formal, as in a contract in which you commit to perform a certain action. The agreement need not be a formally written contract, but in both cases a social contract exists which can be viewed as the key to the concept of justice.

The idea of the social contract is not new. Thomas Hobbes proposed a social contract theory, and acknowledged the Golden Rule (do unto others that which you would have done to you) as the rule by which individuals could agree and outline their mutual obligations and expectations. In his great work, *Leviathian* (1651), Hobbes states human beings have two main characteristics: First, they are generally equal in mind and body; second, they are all driven by a desire for gain, safety, and reputation. Because human beings are so equal in all areas and driven equally by desires, there is natural conflict but no mechanism to keep the peace and prevent constant war. War is every human being against every other human being. In the state of nature, just described, Hobbes believed human reason will come to certain conclusions about what must be done to preserve one's life. Hobbes called these conclusions natural laws. The conclusions (of which Hobbes had several) require agreement among individuals and a mechanism (government) by which to enforce the agreed-upon conclusions. Once a governing body has been created, terms such as "good," "bad," "right," and "wrong" can be defined. Morality then will be based on what the governing body enforces. Without these rules individuals leave themselves open to attack by others.

The social contract model suggests that everyone accepts or agrees to principles such as "I will not hurt or cheat you if you do not hurt or cheat me," and so forth. In doing so, everyone imposes the law (of agreement) on themselves rather than submitting under force to the dictates of others or society. The social contract model establishes the foundation of justice by mutual consent and agreement. Justice seen from this perspective is chosen rather than imposed. This approach requires rationality and the ability to see that one cannot pursue one's own self-interests without taking into consideration the interests of everyone else.

## THE ORIGINAL POSITION AND THE VEIL OF IGNORANCE

Differing from Hobbes, Rawls does not subscribe to the idea that individuals once lived in a state of nature necessitating agreement and enforcement of rules to ensure survival. Rather, he (Rawls) describes the social contract as an imaginary device that individuals use to discover our moral principles rather than to uncover them historically. Rawls begins by asking the question, "What principles would a group of rational, self-interested individuals agree to live by if they knew they would have to live together in a society governed by those principles but did not yet know what each of those principles would turn out to be like for them personally?" Rawls claims that a principle is morally justified if and only if it would be agreed to by a group of rational, self-interested individuals who did not know any particular characteristics (gender, race, social position, etc.) they would possess in this future society. This situation of an imaginary group of rational individuals is known as the "original position" and their ignorance of any particulars as the "veil of ignorance." In this situation the parties involved would logically and rationally agree first to accept the principle of equality; freedom for everyone. Secondly, they would protect themselves in case they turned out to be the least advantaged in the society. In doing so they would agree to the difference principle that allows for differences but also directs society to improve the circumstances of the less advantaged.

## RIGHTS AND JUSTICE

Rawls used the term "right," referring to one's right to the maximum liberty. Rights then are of significant importance when dealing with the concept of justice. By definition, a right is a just and fair claim to something—power, privilege, or the like—that belongs to an individual by law, nature, or tradition.

There are different kinds of rights. Some rights, such as those guaranteed by the U. S. Constitution or other laws (state or local), are considered legal rights. Clearly, these rights are relative to a particular group or society. The particular rights enjoyed by individuals in the United States are not merely rights by virtue of their inclusion in the Constitution. These rights are essential to our society's existence as we know it. In our society, these rights are known as civil rights and are based on the belief in equality of all people. Civil rights are usually written into law and therefore are legal rights as well as civil rights.

Civil rights are typically relative to the traditions of a given society; however, some of these rights appear more universally applicable as principles of morality. These rights are called human rights and are regarded as transcending social or cultural boundaries. They exist as a concomitant fact of humanness. Human rights need not be written formally or codified into laws; however, the Universal Declaration of Human Rights (1948), concretizes this abstract principle by enumerating 29 basic human rights. This document has been signed by representatives of almost all the countries of the world and supported by most, if not all, of the major religions. This document has served as a sound (although incomplete) basis for modern ethics.

## FORMAL CONSTRAINTS
## OF THE CONCEPT OF RIGHT

According to Rawls, the individuals in the original position had certain constraints placed on their knowledge of circumstances and consequently on the alternatives open to them. These restrictions are referred to as the formal constraints of the concept of right. Some constraints apply to all moral principles while others apply only to and depend on the reasonableness of the theory of which they are a part. These constraints are also applicable to one's right to maximum liberty as viewed from the perspective of social justice. Rawls identified the following five constraints: principles must be general in scope, universal in application, final, publicly held, and ordered.

Generality as a constraint of the concept of right means that principles must be general. According to Rawls (1971), "it must be possible to formulate them without the use of what would be intuitively recognized as proper names or rigged definite descriptions" (p. 131). The idea here is that moral principles should apply to classes or categories rather than to specific individuals or groups. Said another way, moral principles must be stated in general terms. Generality allows for a consensus by appealing to different principles. Paradoxically, this allows for agreement without dictating the [specific] principles of the agreement. This is the opposite of appealing to universal principles that provide an explicitly sound basis for particular judgments in regard to specific situations. Agreements, then, are not based on commitment to a particular group or agreed principle but to a shared perception of what is specifically at stake in particular kinds of human situations. Promotion of an individual's or particular group's interests above the interests of others is ruled out by this constraint.

Universality, the second formal constraint of the concept of right, says that principles must be universal in application, which is similar to generality. Katzner (1980) notes that Rawls makes two interpretations of universality, a weak and a strong. Rawls (1971) posits of universal principles (in the weak sense), "They must hold for everyone by virtue of their being moral persons" (p. 132). An example might be: If there is a right to life, it extends to all moral beings, not only to all men or all women or any other exclusive group or class. Rawls goes on to add a second and different interpretation of universality (in the strong sense), "Principles are to be chosen in view of the consequences of everyone's complying with them" (p. 132). Moral principles are to be assessed on the basis of the supposed consequence of everyone following them, as opposed to the realistic consequence of some people following them. Lying, for example, is wrong because the consequences of everyone doing it would be undesirable even if, as a matter of fact, so few people would actually lie that the consequences would not in reality be undesirable.

Katzner (1980) notes that Rawls is clear that the weak interpretation of universality applies to all moral principles; however, some do not conform to the strong interpretation. The weak interpretation, according to Katzner, carries generality to the conclusion that not only must moral principles be devoid of personal pronouns and other defined descriptions, they must hold for all beings. The strong interpretation of universality, which is based on hypothetical over actual consequences, can be viewed as being more reasonable in theory, but this cannot be viewed, according to Katzner, as a formal constraint on the concept of right.

The third formal constraint of the concept of right, finality, means that when moral obligations come into conflict with other kinds of considerations (e.g., self-interest, customs, or law) it is our moral obligations that prevail. This does not mean we should ignore the demands of self-interest, custom, or law, just that in cases of conflict, these are subordinate to the moral obligation that binds us. Basically, Rawls claims that all things considered, moral obligations are just that—obligations.

These constraints of the concept of right—generality, [weak] universality, and finality—are, according to Rawls, applicable when applied to the choice of any moral principles. Katzner (1980) notes this is true because of our conception of the nature of morality and not the reasonableness of the specific theory of which they are a part. He goes on to claim the function of these principles is to rule out of the moral domain any form of egoism. Katzner declares that the remaining three constraints of the right, (strong) universality (described above), publicity, and ordering, while placing constraints on the reasonableness of the specific theory of which they are a part, are not applicable to the choice of all moral principles.

Publicity is a constraint of the concept of right that insists on a public conception of morality. Not only must moral principles address the question, "What if everyone were to do that?" but one must also consider the effect of moral principles being publicly acknowledged as a fundamental rule of society. Publicity implies a public conception of moral principles as contractual and written as in a constitution and laws. This is opposed to one in which moral principles and human conduct are regulated by an intuitive and individual conception of morality. Here there is no public conception of law, but the rules are understood as universal. This can occur because each individual, in deciding what action to take, must be guided in assessing his or her own moral principles by asking the following: What would happen if everyone were to do that? Katzner (1980) asserts the reason that publicity cannot be a constraint for all moral principles should be clear—not all are contractual. That is, some individuals impose laws on themselves. Rather than agreeing to those publicly dictated by society, they choose the laws themselves.

Ordering is a constraint of the concept of right that tells us which one of the fundamental principles of morality, assuming there is more than one, takes precedence when there is a conflict. The idea behind ordering is that the purpose of moral principles is to guide one's action. Ordering provides an answer to the question, "What does one do when justice requires one thing and utility another?" Katzner (1980) clarifies why ordering cannot be a constraint for all moral principles. He notes first, not all moral orientations contain more than one principle (e.g., utilitarianism); and second, intuitionists rely on intuition to resolve conflicts between principles as opposed to ordering.

The concept of constraint has some very commonsense applications that are noteworthy. As Americans, we are accorded the right to free speech; however, this does not give us the right to stand up in a crowded movie theater and yell fire. As Americans, we are accorded the right to assemble; however, this does not give us the right to riot. The concept of rights is often and easily abused as witnessed by the proliferation of rights claims in our society. The ethic of radical individualism can be summed up in the principle, "I have a right to live my own life as long as I don't hurt anybody else." (Hurt means directly harming another's person or property.) Society, then, exists only as a means to protect one individual from another and to allow each to pursue his/her own private purposes. As Americans, we view our rights as precious;

however, rights are only one aspect of justice, and as such rights need to be balanced against the other components of justice that encompass society.

## SUMMARY

What makes a certain action right or wrong can be answered from several positions. Each position views the outcome or consequence from a different perspective. Theorists do not agree on the identity of the highest good, so there is little agreement on how to achieve it. Some theorists value the happiness of the individual while others value the well-being of the group. Acting to maximize one's own happiness or acting to achieve the greatest happiness for the greatest number are moral mandates for some, while acting fairly or justly is important to others.

The concept of rights plays a role in the defining of justice. Rights suggest a claim to power, privilege, and opportunities that belong to an individual and are deeply valued. Taken to the extreme, rights define society as merely a means to protect one individual from another while allowing each to pursue his/her own private purposes. Rawls identifies constraints that hold for the choice of all moral principles and that are also applicable to one's right to unbridled individualism.

## QUESTIONS FOR ADDITIONAL REFLECTION AND THOUGHT

1. How do you evaluate the result of an action? What is your criteria for a good result?

2. Is happiness evaluated by an individual's feelings, or is there some other more objective way of assessing it? Should one consider only the immediate happiness that an action produces, or should the long-term effect be factored in?

3. Whose happiness is more important, the individual's or the group's? How would a utilitarian determine an acceptable distribution of benefits and burdens?

4. Do you view human beings as basically barbarous and savage, restrained and subdued by society, but capable at times of reverting to their natural state? Or do you view human beings as naturally good and caring, shaped at times by society into antisocial animalistic beings, but, given the right environment, capable of maintaining their naturally good form?

5. Is there a place where social contracts (agreements) would allow for the personal development of each individual? Would personal development

not then enhance the relationships that make up the society? Is self-interest and human choice in this context an oxymoron?

6. How do you define rights? Are they specific or general? How do you determine when and why they are applicable?

7. If you were the founder of a totally new society how would you define justice and how do you see it working?

# USING THEORY FOR CONCRETE ETHICAL JUDGMENTS

## Ethical Dilemma

As a counselor in a private practice setting, you received a referral from a colleague (with whom you attended graduate school) of a couple (Mr. & Mrs. C.) for marital counseling. You saw the couple, minimal progress was made on the presenting problem, and termination of their relationship and discontinuation of counseling was decided on. Approximately six months later, Mrs. C. called requesting an individual appointment. During the initial interview, Mrs. C. detailed her prior individual counseling with the colleague who had referred her and her husband to you. Her presenting problem was vague and her focus was primarily on the differences she noticed between your methods and your colleague's. In the second session, she has direct questions regarding ethics, trust, and relationships. In this session, she discloses that she and her former counselor, your colleague, had engaged in sexually intimate behavior while she was his client. She states that during the time she was seeing him, their sexual relationship had not bothered her, but now she is finding it a source of great distress. After relating these facts to you, she voices extreme concern about what you will do with this information. She is confused and acknowledges strong mixed emotions about her former counselor and their relationship. She ends the session with the request that you not disclose this information to anyone.

Before this referral, you have been aware of several complaints and accusations of sexual improprieties against your colleague. Each time your colleague provided reasonable explanations and no action was taken by anyone. Recalling this, you also remember behaviors exhibited by your colleague that you considered mildly inappropriate but had passed off. Now, given this situation as well as previous accusations, you wonder if unethical sexual behavior could be currently occurring.

## The Problem

Should you honor the client's request and not disclose anything regarding the colleague's alleged behavior? Your dilemma is whether to keep confidential the information disclosed in the session or to take some type of action concerning the alleged ethical violations. The dilemma includes not only this client but perhaps other clients as well. Responsibility to the accused is also a question.

## The Case of Consequentialism

The basic theme of consequentialism is that actions and/or rules are right as long as they produce the most favorable consequences for those affected by the actions or rules. The ultimate goal dictated by the theory is doing on each occasion whatever will produce the best outcome possible. The right thing to do, then, is whatever will maximize the good. This provides an ultimate criterion of right and wrong. It does so by stating that whenever an act has a certain outcome, that of yielding the greatest possible good, then it has the moral property of being the right thing to do. Under this theory the procedure for making moral decisions should be deductive; that is, reasoning from the general to the specific or from a premise to a logical conclusion. Although this approach seems a very straightforward method of ethical decision making, it should be clear that consequentialist theories contain both an objective and a subjective component. The objective component is the criterion or basic goal that determines what is right, and the subjective component is the strategy for discovering what is right. We know, according to consequentialism, what the criterion of right and wrong is, but what is the recommended strategy for satisfying this criterion in specific cases?

## The Decision-Making Process

Knowing that the criterion is to maximize the good, you must now determine what action(s) will lead to the greatest good in this case and whether the criterion will apply more to the individual client or clients as a whole. Pragmatically, the first task is to determine whose welfare (the individual client's or clients' in general) is considered more important. Regardless of the choice, the decision should be based on the outcome of a cost-to-benefit comparison. This comparison must include your client's right to confidentiality and any harm that she might suffer (currently or in the future) as a result of disclosure. Additionally, the potential for current ongoing or future harm to other clients must also be considered. Competing strategies or alternative actions must be proposed and should be judged according to which best achieves the goal of promoting the greatest good. Realize in this process that there is no pretense of completeness in the possible discourse on available strategies, flawless exhaustive information, or infallible information processing. Also weighing in this decision-making process is the precommitment to following the ethical codes established by professional organizations. Ethical codes acknowledge that some antecedent goals have been judged to be optimal and are to be used as appropriate in developing strategies of action.

## Ethical Dilemma

You are a counselor working independently in private practice. Mr. K. has been in counseling with you for approximately three months, and you and Mr. K. both feel as though progress is being made. Mr. K. tells you during the session that his printing business is having difficulty and he has been forced to drop his insurance, which has been paying for his sessions. He is concerned over the prospect of discontinuing counseling but asks if you would be willing to consider a barter arrangement. You have just relocated your office and are in need of new business cards, stationery, and other business-related printing. Mr. K. proposes to provide you with letterhead stationery, brochures, and any other printing needs you may have in return for counseling. You would continue to bill for your services, for which Mr. K. would pay you in printing services you would otherwise have to purchase.

## The Problem

Should a counselor agree to barter with a client for services? Are there more problems here than meet the eye? The dilemma includes the question of dual relationship (boundaries) and role incompatibility.

## The Case of Justice

The basic theme of social justice is contractual in that actions and/or rules are permissible if they are compatible with the moral principles by which rational self-interested individuals in the right circumstances would agree to live their lives. Social contracts then, are devices through which individuals discover moral principles. The concept of right plays an important role in the defining of justice and the creation of social contracts. A right is a just and fair claim to something that belongs to an individual. The concept of rights establishes each person's equal claim to the most fundamental extensive liberty (autonomy) compatible with similar liberty (autonomy) for others. In the extreme, rights serve merely to protect one individual from another. However, constraints on the concept of right are applicable in providing guidance for making ethical decisions. Constraints on the right include generality, universality, finality, publicity, and ordering, though not all apply in our dilemma.

## The Decision-Making Process

You should apply the constraints on the right to determine if this action would be compatible with the way moral individuals would agree to live. The first constraint on the concept of right is the idea that moral principles should apply to classes or categories rather than specific individuals. The question itself—is it ethical to barter with our client?—is tantamount to applying moral principles to specific individuals, and therefore must be rejected. The second constraint on the concept of right is that moral principles must be universal in application. It states that principles must be chosen in view of the consequences that would result from everyone's following them. In agreeing to barter for services, both the client and the counselor become consumers and the professional boundaries are blurred. What consequence would result if all counselors and clients ignored professional boundaries? The third constraint on the concept of right, finality, means that whenever moral obligations conflict with other kinds of considerations our moral obligations hold sway. In this case, one is morally obligated to do no harm, which includes potentially biasing the relationship in any way. This takes precedence over the need for printing services. The fourth constraint on the concept of right, publicity, is not a constraint for all moral principles and is not applicable in this example. However, ordering, the last constraint on the concept of right is applicable. Ordering addresses the problem that occurs when justice comes into conflict with pragmatism. The thought here is that when two principles are viewed as different yet equal and conflict-ing, they must be ordered in accordance with their importance. Though not a constraint for all moral principles, ordering poses the confrontational question, "What does one do when justice requires one thing and utility another?"

# 6

# Kant and Deontology

I n a now-famous experiment, an experimental psychologist advertised for volunteers to serve as teachers in what he described as experiments in memory and learning. The protocol was simple. The volunteer teachers sat at the controls of an electric shock generator with a voltage range of 15 to 450 volts. The controls were labeled "slight shock," "moderate shock," "strong shock," "very strong shock," "intense shock," "danger: severe shock" and, on the last switch, "XXX." The volunteer teachers were then introduced to subjects whose task it was to memorize lists of words that were read to them by the teacher. As part of the experiment, each subject was strapped to a chair and fastened to electrodes. The teachers were instructed to administer shocks to the subject every time a wrong answer was given, increasing the voltage with each wrong response.

The experiment began and the subjects soon failed to provide correct responses. The teacher was instructed to administer the shock treatment. As the voltage increased with each error, the subjects began to emit mild responses of pain to the shocks, which increased proportionately with the level of shock administered. When the volunteer teachers first heard the subjects respond in pain they asked the experimenter if they should stop. Each time the response from the experimenter was no; that there was no danger and that he (the experimenter) took full responsibility. At 150 volts the subjects cried out and begged that the experiment be stopped. At 270 volts, the subjects were heard screaming in agony, followed shortly thereafter by silence. Under the psychologist's direction, 60% of the volunteer teachers continued to administer the shocks as directed until the subjects were silent, though they themselves became visibly shaken and agitated.

The suffering of the subjects had in reality only been acting. The experiment was actually designed to determine how volunteer teachers would respond when a trusted authority, the experimenter, ordered them to administer increasingly painful shocks to another person.

The experimenter described the results as creating extreme levels of nervousness. In some subjects (volunteer teachers) tension, profound sweating, trembling, and stuttering were typical expressions of the emotional disturbance. One subject, observed to be a mature and initially poised businessman, was within 20 minutes reduced to a twitching, stuttering wreck who was rapidly approaching the point of nervous collapse (Milgram, 1974).

The experiment received harsh criticism. The author, Milgram, defended his experiment by pointing out the social benefits derived from it. Several critics claimed that Milgram had merely used the subjects as a means to further his interests and research. They further stated that he had treated his volunteers in ways that no human being should treat another. This statement was made to be universal in that no one should treat another as the volunteers were treated regardless of the benefits. The final question asked was, "Would the experimenter be willing to be treated in the same way that he treated the research subjects?"

Milgram's critics, in arguing that it was wrong to use individuals as a means, were arguing a Kantian position. Kant stated two basic moral duties: First, that one should always treat humanity as an end and never a means; second, one should act according to that maxim whereby you can at the same time will that it should become a universal law.

## KANT AND MORALITY

This argument against using people as a means or treating them in any way other than what would be universally accepted appeals to the principles laid down by Immanuel Kant. To Kant, morality is achieved (in part) through consistency. There is a fundamental difference between those attitudes we happen to have toward things and our moral attitudes. For the attitude to be one of moral approval or disapproval as opposed to one of favor or disfavor, the attitude must be based in reason. Moral judgments are conceived to be judgments that are based on reason, which, unlike some preferences, cannot be persuaded or convinced. Moral principles then are the object of rational choice. Human beings, according to Kant, are rational beings capable of deliberating, deciding on and following rules, and making free (rational) choices. Individuals, being rational and free to choose what action to take, are guided by their rationality to choose morally right actions.

## THE GOOD WILL

What makes an act right or wrong is not the consequence of the act but rather the principle guiding the act. Regarding this principle, Kant wrote in *Grounding for the Metaphysic of Morality,* nothing can be called good without qualification except good will. Having good "will" means having good intentions. Kant spoke of the will as something that is within our conscious control as opposed to a wish that is not within our conscious control. What is done is consciously done out of a sense of duty to what is right and not for personal gain or for the sake of consequences. The will then is that part of an individual that reasons and decides what action to take or not take.

Actions an individual performs that bring about good consequences do not, according to Kant, constitute good will. Kant stressed that an individual may have good will and may attempt to do what is right, but because of circumstances may be unable to do so. Therefore, whether or not an individual has good will is determined not by the ability to act or the consequences of the action, but by accessing the reasons on which the person bases his or her decision to act. When an individual's will is morally good, then it is good under all conditions—its goodness does not depend on anything outside itself.

What factors then motivate an individual to act? Plato's theory of the tripartite soul (the bodily appetites, the spirited elements, and the highest, reason), helps us understand Kant's concept of the will and the human dilemma. Plato proposed that though we may know the good, this knowledge may run into conflict with bodily desires. He additionally thought that reason, the desire to reach the truth or the ideal, comes into conflict with bodily appetites, which desire immediate gratification. The intermediate element, the spirited element (emotions), serves as a mediator of such conflicts and is capable of acting on behalf of either reason or appetite. Addressing the difficulty inherent with human motivation, Kant (trans. 1963) wrote

> The greater the fight a man puts up against his natural inclinations the more it is to be imputed to his merit. Hence it is that virtue is more meritorious in us than in the angels who have fewer obstacles to overcome. (p. 63)

## MOTIVATION AND GOOD WILL

What motives characterize the actions of good-willed individuals? Kant suggests three types of reasons that might motivate one to do one's moral duty. The first is self-interest. The action itself does not bring about enjoyment or self-satisfaction, but the person obtains what is desired as a result of the action. An illustrative example might be the butcher whose products are weighed honestly. The butcher does this not out of duty to do the right thing, but to establish a reputation for honesty and thus attract more customers. Honesty is the action emanating from a motivation based on personal interest, not a sense of duty to be honest with customers. The second reason for doing one's moral duty is direct satisfaction or gratification gained as a result. Being kind to others is its own reward. Here the act of being kind to others is performed for the result attained by it and not because of the principle on which it is based. Lastly, an individual may act simply because it is the right thing to do. In doing so, the individual is acting out of a sense of duty. Clearly, it is acting out of a sense of duty that motivates the actions of people of good will.

Kant sees no difference between an action motivated by self-indulgence that brings about good and one similarly motivated that brings about evil. An individual motivated by self-indulgence may engage in any activity he or she finds enjoyable. Kant therefore concludes that reasoning based on self-interest or gratification does not provide justification for saying a person possesses good will.

To say that a person is motivated by a sense of duty implies something or some type of motivation beyond the individual person. According to Kant, that something is respect for the universal law. The universal law is one that all human beings ought to live up to regardless of whether they desire to or not. An individual acts from a sense of duty when the action taken is dictated or required by moral principles that all people ought to follow. Kant deems good will to dictate that an individual should act only on those principles he or she would be willing to have everyone else act on, thus making it a universal law. For anything to be universally binding, a universal law, it must be examined apart from empirical data (human desire or inclinations) because these vary greatly from person to person.

## HYPOTHETICAL AND CATEGORICAL IMPERATIVES

Kant spoke of imperatives, statements, or principles, expressing how or what an individual ought to do. He divided all imperatives into two groups: categorical and hypothetical. The categorical imperative is an unconditional directive that prescribes a certain action ought be taken because of the moral worth of the principle in question. Categorical imperatives require individuals to perform or not perform certain actions regardless of the outcome that is personally desired. The action is objectively required. An example of a categorical imperative is that one should not steal as a matter of principle. The hypothetical imperative is a conditional directive that advises us what ought be done if a desired goal is to be achieved. Hypothetical imperatives require an individual to perform an action or not to perform an action only if the outcome is personally desired. The action is subjectively required. A hypothetical imperative that one should not steal is in order to avoid punishment.

Imperatives can thus also be viewed as subjective or objective. Subjective imperatives or principles require individuals to act out of a desire to attain a certain end. If I work because I desire money, then money is the subjective end for which I work. Money may or may not be why other people work; therefore, money is not a source of motivation for everyone to work. Subjective principles will motivate only those who are interested in attaining that particular end. Subjective imperatives or principles cannot provide a universal motivation for action. On the other hand, objective imperatives or principles can provide motivation for everyone to act in spite of individual aspirations for particular outcomes. The objective principle is one that everybody recognizes should be followed no matter what individual desires they may have that motivate them.

The hypothetical imperative indicates that the end result desired justifies the means or action taken to achieve it. Therefore, knowing what a hypothetical imperative says does not tell the individual what to do unless one desires the end for which it indicates the means. The categorical imperative, however, indicates that the action taken is necessary in itself without reference to the end achieved. It requires the principle underlying the action to be universal and without contradiction. Thus the action taken can be applied to all individuals without contradictions and could become a natural or universal law for all to observe. Knowing the categorical imperative provides immediate direction. It states the action required and that the underlying principle for the action should be universally applicable. Kant reasoned that all imperatives of duty could be deduced from one categorical imperative: Act as if the maxim of your action by your will would become a universal natural law.

## DUTY AND MORAL LAW

Kant viewed duty from two perspectives and provided illustrations of duty to ourselves and duty to others. With the categorical imperative twofold test—requiring that maxims for moral action be universal without contradiction and that they be universal directives for action which do not produce disharmony by willing one thing for one's self and another thing for others—there are four components to consider in moral law. The following two examples illustrate failure in the maxim achieving universal application.

Duty to one's self can be seen in a situation where an individual, through blows of fate, has been reduced to despair. In this situation one contemplates suicide; but is suicide consistent with one's duty? The principle or maxim in question is: Out of self-love, I will end my life when the duration appears to hold more pain and suffering than happiness and satisfaction. Now the question is raised, "Can this principle based on self-love become a universal natural law?" It is seen at once that a law of nature that contains a law to destroy life by means of the very feeling whose function it is to sustain life would contradict itself. Therefore, such a law could not exist in nature and would be inconsistent with one's duty.

Duty to others can be illustrated by the example of a person who finds him/herself forced to borrow money. The individual knows that he/she will not be able to repay it, but also knows that no one will lend the money unless he/she promises to pay it back. Given this situation the individual is tempted to make such a promise. However, before doing so, the individual must ask whether or not this is consistent with one's duty. In answering this question, one must ask what is the maxim of the action. Is it permissible, because of need, to borrow money and promise to repay it, even though repayment is not possible? Even if this principle was personally acceptable, is it right? What if this maxim were to become a universal natural law? Immediately, one sees that this could not become a universal natural law because it contradicts itself. If everyone made promises that they never intended to keep, then promises themselves would be contradictions in terms and impossible to keep.

The next two examples illustrate failure to will for ourselves that which we would will for others. Duty to one's self can be seen in an individual who has a talent or natural ability that could be beneficial if developed. However, this individual finds comfort in circumstances that are less rigorous and prefers to indulge in pleasure rather than to take pains in cultivating natural abilities. The question here is whether the maxim of neglect of natural abilities, besides agreeing with inclination toward indulgence, agrees with what is called duty. It would not be possible for the individual to will that this should be a universal natural law or implanted in us as such by a natural instinct because, as a rational being, one necessarily wills that natural abilities be developed since they serve the individual and have been provided for all sorts of possible purposes.

One's duty to others can be seen in a situation where a prosperous individual realizes that other less prosperous persons have to put up with great wretchedness which the prosperous individual could help. What determines if one should help is how one answers the question, "What concern is it of mine?" Let everyone have whatever happiness God and their own efforts provide them; I will not steal from others, nor will I envy their fortunes. However, I do not want to add to their well-being or help them when they are in need. To each their own lot. If such a mode of thinking were to become universal natural law, humanity could survive. Indeed, it could even be better than a state in which everyone talks of sympathy and good will and occasionally practices it, but generally cheats when possible, betrays, and violates the rights of others. But one could not will the maxim to be a universal natural law without having one's will come into conflict with itself. We all know that many situations will arise in which one will need the love and concern of others. Therefore, in willing such a universal natural law, one would be depriving oneself of that very aid one needs.

Duty, according to Kant, is a meaningful concept that can validly impose authoritative law on one's action. It can be expressed only in categorical, not hypothetical, imperatives. In the above illustrations, Kant clearly shows what the categorical imperatives will require in a complete classification of duties. But there is yet more to the categorical imperative.

Consider that all objects of desire have conditional value. It is our appetite or desire for the object that gives it its conditional value; without this, it would have none. So nonrational creations of nature have relative value, as "means," and are called things. Rational beings are called persons and by their very nature have value and are "ends" in themselves and never "means to ends." Based on this, another version of the categorical imperative can be formulated as follows: Act as to treat humanity, whether in your own person or in that of any other, always as an end and never as a means. (Kant, trans. 1963) The statement, "the end justifies the means" is clearly never an acceptable basis for action.

Following from the first version of the categorical imperative (one's action should be in accordance with or conform to universal laws as if they were laws of nature) and the second version (rational beings exist as an end in themselves), one can derive a third version of the categorical imperative. This version, involving the autonomy of the will of rational beings, states, Act as though the will through its maxim were the maker of the universal law that it follows. Thus the will is not merely subject to the law, it is regarded as giving the law to itself and consequently is subject to itself. This principle is one of autonomy and shows that universal law is self-imposed. An autonomous agent, then, is seen as being the source of moral principles and not merely the recipient.

## THE CONCEPT OF A PRIORI

A valid moral principle, according to Kant, must be independent of the empirical data of morality; its foundation must be a priori. In philosophy, "a priori" means prior to and furnishing the basis of experience; innate, or based upon innate ideas. Kant believed that it is the nature of the mind to think in terms of cause and effect. Despite our ignorance of the cause of a given phenomenon, we are certain that it has a cause and that certainty is a product of our mind, not our experience. This principle of thinking causally is an a priori category of understanding.

Kant reasons that experience teaches us what actually happened but not what necessarily happens (Peterfreund & Denise, 1992). Therefore, a valid moral principle is a priori in that it is not derived from observation or experience but rather is universally applicable to experience. Regardless of how one sharpens or improves one's observational powers, the knowledge acquired through our senses tells us only how objects appear to us and not about the objects themselves. Kant conceded that all human knowledge by necessity begins with experience; however, the a priori structure of it cannot be obtained by induction from experience. Since empirical data (observations and experience) vary from individual to individual there must be a reality underlying the appearance that things present to our senses. This reality constitutes things as they really are; not merely as they are experienced. Acknowledging this, it benefits us to distinguish between the world of the senses (things as they appear) and the world of understanding (things as one understands them in reality to be).

## DEONTOLOGY

Kantian moral philosophy is deontological. The word deontological comes from the Greek root *deon,* meaning duty. In deontological theory (Kantian theory), an action is justified by showing that it is right, not by showing that the consequences of the act are good. Action is self-imposed by thinking for one's self and doing what one knows is right. Kant's deontology requires an unconditional or absolute reference point for moral behavior. This reference point Kant called "pure practical reason." Each individual, according to Kant, is rational and is able to reason and arrive at the right decision regarding his or her own actions. By our nature as rational beings, each individual can arrive at this right decision without appeal to any external authority. Each of us can decide for ourselves what it is we ought to do and ought not do.

Kant's deontology represents a firm conviction that morality is more than the rituals, customs, and ethos of a particular group, culture, or society; more than the outcome (greatest good for the greatest many), and certainly more than emotive reactions toward others. He views morality as the same for everyone everywhere, built into the structure of the human mind. This is not to say that all people everywhere accept the same moral principles. Kant argues that each human being has the faculty of rationality, though not every human being actually employs and utilizes that faculty. Reason, according to Kant, transcends all groups, cultures, and societies and dictates a set of rational principles which are to be obeyed by all.

## SUMMARY

Kant stressed that our moral attitudes must be based on reason, and that the criterion for moral action is not the outcome, but having good will and attempting to do what is right, even though circumstances may prevent it. He used imperatives to express what an individual ought to do, and he believed that all imperatives could be deduced from a single categorical imperative: Act as if the maxim of your action by your will would become universal natural law. The Kantian concept of duty requires individuals to will for themselves only that which they would be willing to will for others. Social implications derived from the categorical imperative state that rational beings (persons) by their very nature have value and therefore are "ends" in themselves and never "means to ends." Kant's final categorical imperative concludes that the will is not merely subject to universal law, but is its creator and, therefore, subject to itself. Kant stated that a valid moral principle must be independent of empirical data and thus requires an a priori foundation to be universally binding and consistent. Morality is seen as being built into the structure of the mind and is the same for everyone everywhere. Kant does not say that all people accept the same moral principles but he does say all have the faculty of rationality, though not all use what they have.

# QUESTIONS FOR ADDITIONAL
# REFLECTION AND THOUGHT

1. When, in the course of normal development, does an individual develop an intuitive sense of what is right and wrong? How does one know that this sense of what is right and wrong is not the product of early learning?

2. When there is a conflict between self-interest and a moral obligation to right a wrong or perform a morally correct act, is it inevitable that the moral obligation will prevail? How will motives affect the outcome?

3. Can anyone truly say, "I will do what I know to be right, no matter what the consequences to myself, my family, and my country? I will not compromise my integrity no matter what the cost"?

4. What would be the Kantian position on moral values in the following situations: (a) A martyr who holds her moral principles dear takes the ultimate stand, or (b) A martyr who out of fear or belief that future glory awaits (historically, eternally, or in reincarnation) takes a similar stand?

5. Describe a real or hypothetical situation where the end result achieved justifies the means used to achieve it. Defend your reasoning.

6. It has been said, "A foolish consistency is the hobgoblin of little minds . . ." (Emerson), so what, ethically speaking, is the value of consistency?

7. Define the term autonomy and compare your definition to that of Kant.

# USING THEORY FOR CONCRETE
# ETHICAL JUDGMENTS

## Ethical Dilemma

You are a counselor working independently in a private practice. Your client is a 45-year-old male who requested individual counseling because he is experiencing marital difficulties. Your client is a successful attorney, and though he is a private pay client, has no difficulty paying your fee. You have been seeing this client for approximately ten weeks, and during this time he appears to have made little progress. You suspect that he may be "using" counseling as a way to say he's working on his problems, but in reality is excusing his current behavior by this rationale. You question him about your hypothesis, and he agrees that as long as he can rationalize his working on it he does not really have to change his behavior. Further dialogue reveals that he finds the sessions stimulating, much like a chess game, but professes little desire to change his current behavior. He again states that he enjoys the sessions and desires to continue seeing you.

## The Problem

Your client has stated that he enjoys the mental stimulation provided by counseling but has no desire to change his current behavior (the reason he gave for coming to counseling). The client desires to continue counseling; however, you as a counselor see no commitment to change. Coming to counseling appears to be a rationale by which he excuses his ongoing behavior. Should you terminate the counseling relationship, refer this client, or continue to see him?

## The Case of Kantian Moral Philosophy

Kant believed that any action must be done from a sense of duty in order to have inner worth. Action performed from duty derives its moral value not from the result it achieves, but from the principle by which it is determined. The supreme principle of morality is the categorical imperative. Kant's concept of duty (to one's self and to others) is expressed through the categorical imperative. Social implications of the categorical imperative are seen in the requirement to respect all humanity and avoid exploiting anyone (including one's self) for any reason. Consistency (in the application of the categorical imperative), dictated by duty, is seen as the supreme moral principle.

## The Decision-Making Process

A Kantian approach might begin by determining if this is a therapeutic or an ethical issue. When and for what reason(s) should a counselor terminate a counseling relationship? What duty do you as a counselor have in this situation? You may wish to address the question of transgression of duty. In transgression of duty, you find that you actually do not will that your maxim should become a universal law. Recall that when you tell a lie, you do so believing that others are truthful and will believe that what you are saying is true; otherwise, your lie would not work and get you what you want. This clearly is a transgression of duty. The dilemma here entails a similar process and question involving transgression of duty. If you agree to continue to see this client, you must ask yourself if you will the principle of your action to become a universal law. Remember that an end is something that serves as a motive for acting and is valid for every rational being, or in this case, every rational counselor. A means, however, is something you can use in the actions by which you pursue the end you seek. If every counselor were to continue counseling with clients who were not desiring change but were using counseling as a mechanism by which they rationalized and continued their current behavior, would this not be enabling? What is the end that you seek in the counseling process? What is the end you seek for this client?

# 7

✳

# Natural Law Ethics: Saint Thomas Aquinas

St. Thomas Aquinas is credited with, among other things, giving us a Christian version of Aristotle's moral theory. A prodigious writer, his best known systematic treatises are the *Summa Theologica* (A Summary of Theology) and *Summa Contra Gentiles* (A Summary Against the Gentiles). *Summa Contra Gentiles* was designed to provide missionaries with a tool for converting Moslems, Jews, and other non–Christians to Christianity. *Summa Theologica* was authored to provide novices a systemic understanding of Christian theology. Aquinas' view was naturalistic and he was able to demonstrate that philosophy can provide a framework for religion. His writing is unique in that it is divided into short chapters called questions. Each question is a separate inquiry that is further subdivided into articles. In each article, Aquinas states his own view on the various questions he poses and then presents a response to the major objections that might be made. He convincingly argues that there is no real conflict between reason, faith, and philosophy because all are derived from the same ultimate source, God. God, the creator of all things, is the source of human intellect and the creator of the universe which humans study and from which they logically draw their principles. Given this line of logic, to admit that faith and reason could be contradictory would be to say that one or the other is false. According to Aquinas, this would make God the author of falsity, which he (Aquinas) rejects as impossible.

## PROOF OF THE EXISTENCE OF GOD

Aquinas views God as the source from which all things come. In doing so, he acknowledges that God's existence is not self-evident in this life, but can be established philosophically by reasoning from effect to cause. To the skeptics who question the existence of God, Aquinas, in the first part (question 2, article 3) of his work, *Summa Theologica,* offers the following five proofs:

1. Sense experience provides the first proof in the awareness that certain things in the world are moved, and whatever is moved is moved by something. To move something is to bring it from potential to actuality. Aquinas reasons that something cannot be moved from potential to actuality except by a being that is in actuality. Therefore, whatever is moved must be moved by something and nothing can be both the mover and the thing moved. Aquinas concludes that, given this logic, one must accept the existence of the first mover that is not moved by anything else. The first mover is God.

2. The second proof is based on efficient causality and the observation of an order of efficient causes among sensible things. Logically, it is impossible for something to be the efficient cause of itself because that would mean it existed prior to itself. Even an infinite series of causes have a point of origin, an uncaused efficient cause that is God.

3. The third proof contains two parts. The first part states that one experiences things as capable of existing and not existing. For anything that exists now there was a time when it failed to exist. Therefore, if all things that exist now are capable of not existing, and at some point in time nothing existed, then nothing would exist now. This demands the acknowledgment of a necessary (incorruptible, indispensable) being. Part two addresses the fact that a necessary being either derives its necessity from some causative agent or it does not. Because one cannot regress, as stated earlier, to the origin of necessary causes, Aquinas concluded that there must be a necessary being that does not depend on anything else for its necessity and that causes the necessity in all else. This being is God.

4. The fourth proof is based on the degree of perfection. In the world there are things that are more or less good, more or less true, or more or less virtuous than others. The more or less refers to the degree something differs from the ideal or from perfection. According to Aquinas, that which is ideal or perfect in a classification is the cause of everything in that class. Therefore, there is something that is the essence of, the cause of, perfection for all things, and this something is God.

5. The fifth proof is derived from the evidence for regulation that Aquinas notes among natural bodies. Certain things, natural bodies, lack knowledge, in that they act for the sake of an end. Planets, flowering plants, and other natural bodies act or usually act in the same way so that they obtain

that which is best. This, according to Aquinas, cannot be accounted for by chance; instead, it is by intention that they do what they do. Natural bodies lacking knowledge cannot tend to an end unless directed by something in possession of knowledge. Therefore, there must be some knowing being who directs and orders all natural things to their ordered end and this being is God. God is the basis of final causality.

Having established the existence of God, Aquinas moves on (Part I, questions 75–102) to prove that human beings by their distinct nature bear resemblance to God and reflect God's image.

## RELATIONSHIP OF SOUL AND BODY

Aquinas maintains that the soul is the first principle of life. In doing so he is saying that all living things have souls; however, he is not saying that plants or nonhuman animals are spiritual creatures. Simply having a soul is not enough to give a living thing a spiritual component. Viewed theoretically, the soul of a plant is the nutritive first intrinsic principle of life, and the soul of a nonhuman animal is a nutritive + sensory, and the soul of a human being is a nutritive + sensory + rational. Aquinas rejected the view of the human soul as three separate and distinct cooperating forms, preferring a single form that gives a human being its specifically human mode of existence. What is distinctively human is intellect (rationality). Intellect is defined as a spiritual rather than a bodily activity. Intellect neither is nor directly uses a bodily organ. However, intellect encompasses sensations that are bodily products. Proper objects of intellect (formation of concepts of external objects) result from sensory input. The human soul is, therefore, united with the body as a form, but can also transcend the body and other material things. Therefore, the soul's involvement with the body is not one of possession and use, but rather of union.

A nonhuman animal possesses sensory cognition and an ability to engage in goal-directed behavior. The goal is connected to a natural desire for satisfying some need or want (appetite), and is dependent on the animal's senses and what is presented to them that their senses find desirable. Aquinas differentiates between natural appetites (the desire for food) and sensory appetites (the desire for this sort of food). Sensory cognition is something that humans share with nonhuman animals. The pertinent difference between humans and nonhuman animals is that humans possess an intellective reason. Nonhuman animals with only sensory cognition are cognizant of particular governing factors only, presenting their carnal appetite with only one object that moves it determinately. In humans, rational cognition is aware of universals, presenting will with an array of particular goods allowing it to be moved by many things.

The important issue here is the distinctly human ability to utilize rational faculties (conscience), and not immediately be moved by natural and/or sensory appetites; but to wait for the command of the will (power of choice), guided by rational cognition. Aquinas acknowledges that some sensory cognitions are beyond reason's control, such as the presence or absence of some things in the environment. However, some sensory cognitions are not immediately dependent on external factors and are subject to the command of reason. Passions, for example, can be stirred up through irrational thinking and giving one's self over to sensory demands, or calmed down through rational consideration of circumstances or objections to the passions themselves. The rational soul has control over the body; however, the sensory appetites and passions that are the subjects of this rational mediation are no slaves to reason. It is because of this that conflict is experienced when sensory cognition senses something pleasant and desirable that reason forbids, or something unpleasant that reason dictates. However, human beings are rational beings and as such they act for an end. That end is what is best or good. This idea that all action is rationally ordered and naturally directed toward what is good is consistent with the view that God is the basis of final causality. Therefore, reason dictates good is the end result sought by action. Human action is then by natural inclination oriented toward good. Natural inclination is or involves those inclinations that one has but does not choose to have.

## VOLUNTARY AND INVOLUNTARY ACTS

Acknowledging that the sensory appetites and passions are no slave to reason, Aquinas (question 6, articles 1–8, part I of part II) addresses an obvious question of concern: Is moral responsibility relinquished when one is overcome by fear or consumed with desire or other passion? To answer this question one must look at what constitutes a voluntary act. Voluntary acts, according to Aquinas, require (a) perception or rational understanding of a goal or end result, (b) a natural disposition to attain goals, (c) consideration and forethought on how to attain the goal, and (d) the willful act of choosing the action. Voluntary actions result from one's natural inclinations directed by rational faculties and moved by the will (choice). Desire is what makes something voluntary rather than involuntary. Our natural inclination is to desire the good; therefore, based on the logic that something cannot at the same time be affirmed and denied, one cannot desire something bad or evil because these are the opposite of desirable. Desire, then, has reference to the good and to voluntariness. Our emotions become "humanized" insofar as they are brought under the dominion of reason or conscience and action is directed toward an end of which one has knowledge.

Knowledge is a factor in the analysis of action and a prerequisite to voluntariness. If ignorance causes involuntariness, it does so in that it deprives one of knowledge. However, not every lack of knowledge or condition of ignorance results in involuntariness.

Ignorance has a three-way relationship to the act of will (power of choice): concomitant, consequent, and antecedent. Ignorance is concomitant when there is ignorance about what one does, but one would have performed the act even if one had known the outcome. As an example, say one wills (desires) to kill an enemy, and while hunting mistakes the enemy for a deer, killing him in ignorance. The outcome is not repugnant or antagonistic to the will, but rather something sought after, so the act is not involuntary. But one cannot actually desire or will that of which one is ignorant, so neither is it voluntary. The act is therefore nonvoluntary.

Consequent ignorance is voluntary, following as a result of not wishing or choosing to know. The act of will creates the ignorance, as when one wishes not to know and thereby have an excuse. Ignorance is also called voluntary when it regards that which one can and should know. Here, not to act or not to will (choose) are said to be voluntary. Ignorance of this kind is when one does not actually consider what one can or should consider, and is called ignorance of evil choice. This may arise from some passion or habit, or when one does not take the trouble to acquire the knowledge which one should have, resulting in negligence.

Ignorance is antecedent to the act of will when it is not voluntary and yet causes an act of will that would not otherwise occur. This happens when one is ignorant of some circumstances of an act which one is not bound to know, and acts out of that ignorance, creating unforeseen results. For example, an individual, after taking proper precautions, may not know that someone is coming down the road and may discharge a gun, killing a passerby. Such ignorance results in involuntariness.

## GOOD AND BAD ACTS OF WILL

Good and evil are essential differences of the act of the will. The will is not always directed toward what is truly good (question 8, articles 1–3 & question 9, articles 1–6, part I of part II). According to Aquinas, what is good or evil about an act is what one intends and not merely the outcome or consequence that the act produces. What is intended, as was noted in the above discussion on voluntariness, includes the foreseeable consequences of the action. Therefore, action that results in consequences that one could not possibly foresee does not dictate it was an act of bad will. Likewise, a good act of will is not merely determined by the good that the act produces. It is possible for a good act to be performed for an evil end, such as leaving one's estate to charity in order to deprive one's heirs. The reverse is also possible when an evil act is committed in order to attain a good end, as when one steals from the wealthy in order to give to the poor who are in need. The goodness or badness of an act of the will cannot be derived from its end result.

Reason directs the will toward that which is good, the relationship being analogous to that of a navigator and a pilot. Human conscience (the navigator) is a function of reason and provides for the application of reason (knowledge or map) to action. The will (pilot) exercises power of choice deciding whether to follow or not to follow the direction given. There are circumstances in which the will may be unresponsive to the dictates of the conscience, resulting in bad acts of the will. Furthermore, the conscience may be in error, and if that error is voluntary, either directly or indirectly through neglect, it does not excuse the bad act of will. However, there also exists the possibility that one's conscience is not ignorant of specific facts in a situation, but simply incorrect in its dictate regarding moral action. The will, according to Aquinas, in following the dictates of an errant conscience is bad, but only accidentally so.

## ETERNAL AND NATURAL LAW

Following the five proofs of the existence of God, Aquinas' *Treatise on Law* (questions 90–114, part I of part II) is probably the most well-known part of *Summa Theologica*. Beginning with the qualities that all laws must have, Aquinas (question 90) argues first that all laws must be determined by reason. Because of this, they cannot be senseless or arbitrary. Reason dictates that laws are made to achieve some end and only by using reason can one correctly determine what the ends are and how to attain them. Whenever one determines that an end is desirable, reason dictates what should or should not be done in order to achieve it. Reason, according to Aquinas, provides the means of achieving the moral life. What is morally good and right is known through our capacity for rationality. It is understood that the will must be guided by reason. If not, the result would be iniquity rather than law. Second, Aquinas argues that all law must be based on the common good of the community. To be based on that which is good for the entire community, laws must be made by someone who has the good of the entire community in mind. Therefore, Aquinas concludes that a true law is one that is reasonable, directed toward the good of the entire community, originates from someone concerned with the community's good, and is declared openly so that everyone should know.

The following explanation is presented to clarify what Aquinas meant in reference to the quality a law must have to be a true law. Contemporary history is replete with examples of dictators or military leaders who had such power that any decree or order (regardless of contradictions or inconsistencies) issued by them automatically became law. A modern example is the "ethnic cleansing" in Bosnia. The extermination of one group by another is contradictory to the country's constitution and violates basic judicial rights established by law. The fact that the orders to kill citizens were inconsistent with established laws exposes their irrational nature. Certainly, these orders or decrees were not reasonable, and in lacking reason they were merely arbitrary expressions of will. The orders also disregarded the good of the whole society, focusing instead on the personal desires of a particular group. The individual with whom ultimate authority rested was clearly dedicated only to the interests of this particular group and not the whole society. Finally, as in most situations, many of these orders or decrees were not openly promulgated. Many of these orders had to be enacted and carried out in secret because they were grossly inhumane. Clearly, decrees or laws such as these do not have any of the characteristics outlined by Aquinas in his definition of what constitutes a true law. Therefore, anyone who committed acts detrimental to others in this or a similar situation could not hold that in following orders they were merely obeying the law.

Aquinas, in outlining his typology of laws, began at the top of the hierarchy of laws with eternal law (question 93). Eternal law is supreme divine reason that governs the entire world community. It is the order of the universe as it exists in God's plan—the order of things as determined by God and experienced in human beings as natural inclinations. All inclinations that guide us to proper actions and proper ends are the result of eternal law. Natural inclinations are those inclinations that we possess but have not chosen. By natural inclinations, Aquinas meant norms or principles that everyone is capable of recognizing. A group or society that permits practices to the contrary sows the seeds of its own dissolution.

Human beings, unlike other creatures, have reason; and it is through the use of reason that natural inclinations are understood and actions are ordered. Through the use of principled reasoning, order is imposed on our thinking similar to the order that nature imposes on the activities of all living things. This order is realized in human beings through natural inclinations that, when followed, also impose order. The existence of this order, according to Aquinas, does not depend on one's personal belief in God, as the nonbeliever will attribute this order to other causes.

The principles that govern reasoning are what Aquinas called natural law. Natural law ranks below eternal law and can be regarded as eternal law as it is realized in human beings. Natural law is about moral reasoning; the quest for proper actions and ends. Aquinas (question 94, part II of part II) defined natural law in part as principles of reasoning, and then explained exactly these principles of reasoning that constitute natural law. In addressing this issue, Aquinas distinguished between practical reasoning and theoretical reasoning. Practical reasoning involves our mental ability to reason and arrive at a decision regarding what action to take. Theoretical reasoning involves using our mental ability to reach conclusions about the nature of reality (what is and what is not). Regardless of whether one is dealing with practical or theoretical matters, certain principles must be followed if reasoning is to be correct. Aquinas suggested that the principles that make up natural law are self-evident. By self-evident he meant self-revealing—that it will be obvious to anyone who knows what these principles mean that they are true. For example, the proposition that a bachelor is unmarried is self-evident because part of the definition of bachelor is being unmarried. Theoretical reasoning employs this principle of logic in determining (theoretically) what is and what is not. Aquinas proposed this as a rule of consistency, which stated that one thing cannot be affirmed and denied at the same time. Just as there are self-evident rules of logic one follows in reasoning about theoretical matters, there are also self-evident rules that apply to practical reasoning. The idea Aquinas suggested was that whenever one reasons about what ought be done, one moves from the thought that something is good and that it might be attained through certain action to the conclusion that the action should be taken. The basic rule is that what is good ought to be pursued. Again, the rule is self-evident according to Aquinas because part of the meaning of good is that which ought be pursued. Likewise, that which is evil ought to be avoided. Ultimately, the guiding principle to which human beings refer in making moral judgments is our intuitive knowledge of natural law. This synthesis of rational endeavors Aquinas called conscience. While insisting on the moral authority of the dictates of the conscience, Aquinas never insisted on their infallibility.

Natural law does not provide one with specific laws, but does suggest that something is good for us if we are drawn to it by those natural inclinations that are part of every human being's nature, regardless of whether or not one is willing to follow them. Therefore, all people recognize the same basic goods and it is evident that these goods should be preserved. However, Aquinas cautioned that one cannot conclude that all people have the same moral beliefs. This is because different societies or cultures use the principles of practical reasoning to arrive at different conclusions about how a given good is to be attained. The logic Aquinas used was that in theoretical reasoning, conclusions that are incompatible cannot logically flow from the same premise. The end is what is sought and our intention is defined here as the achievement of this end. Practical reasoning, however, is concerned with finding a means to the end. As logic dictates, there are often many means (some incompatible) through which the same end may be achieved. An example might be the differences between a society practicing communal living and a society whose individuals have a system of private ownership. Both societies are similar in that they have common values involving respect for the individual person and an orderly society. The means employed by each society to attain these ends can be quite different. In the society practicing private ownership, theft of property is considered wrong. In the communal society, however, all property is owned in common and social order is not disturbed when one individual uses or takes something previously used by another individual. This example demonstrates two different and incompatible means for maintaining social order. Although individuals everywhere have the same basic (theoretical) moral values (what is good ought be pursued), they often differ in the particular rules or laws they adopt to achieve those moral ends. Different societies may use practical reasoning to arrive at different conclusions about what goods are to be attained. Therefore, practical reasoning differs significantly from theoretical reasoning. Aquinas did, however, maintain that some prohibitions are exceptionless (i.e., lying, theft, and adultery) and anyone is capable of recognizing these exceptions. According to Aquinas, a society that permits such practices will ultimately sow the seeds of its own destruction.

In question 95 and question 96 Aquinas explained the relationship between natural law and human law. In order for a human law to be valid, it must conform to natural law. A valid human law is then one that, in accordance with natural law, imposes an obligation of justice on the members of society. Human laws that are unjust or immoral violate the rights of human

beings and are not valid; therefore, members of society are under no obligation to obey them.

When Aquinas discussed the relationship (application) of natural law to
human law he noted several concepts that allow for more flexibility than one
might expect. Prudence and equity are two concepts Aquinas borrowed from
Aristotle's *Nicomachean Ethics*. Equity refers to the power of the lawmaker(s) to
depart from the letter of the law when its literal application would violate its
spirit. Prudence is practical wisdom that deals with or applies to particular facts.
Prudence is described as a virtue by which human beings choose the right
means for the attainment of the end identified through practical reasoning.

In his *Treatise on Justice,* (question 64, part II of part II) Aquinas addressed
the relationship of natural law to the act of killing. In doing so, he introduces
an important qualification. That qualification has come to be known in ethics
as the principle of "double effect." Beginning with the premise that it is always
wrong to take one's life, (because suicide destroys the basic value of life), natural law posits that this value must be preserved. The question continues (article 7), but is it also wrong to kill in self-defense? The answer, according to
Aquinas, is that it depends on one's intentions. An act of self-defense may have
a double effect: the preservation of one's own life and the killing of the attacker.
When an act has more than one effect, it is not immoral or wrong if the one
acting intends only the good effect (saving one's life by defending one's self),
and does not intend more harm than was necessary in order to achieve the
good effect. However, it would be wrong for one to intentionally seek to kill
the attacker. This is consistent with the natural law that states life must be preserved; therefore, it is wrong to kill intentionally. This logic has relevance and
is connected with debates such as the morality of nuclear warfare, with the de-
fenders of nuclear deterrence arguing that it is not immoral to target military
objectives that may incidentally have the unintended but real effect of killing
innocent people. Other related issues include abortion, euthanasia, and capital
punishment, to mention only a few.

## HUMAN ACTS

Aquinas (question 18, part I of part II) noted that in acting, human beings are
aware of what they are doing and why; the distinction between the theoretical
and practical is not one of knowledge and nonknowledge, but between rationally knowing and exercising through the will the power of choice. Here
Aquinas made a distinction between human acts and acts of a human being.
Acts of a human being include all acts (moral and nonmoral) attributable to
human beings. Human acts, according to Aquinas, are based on reason and will
and constitute moral order. Human beings, having been made in God's image,
have a free will that is directed to distinctive human ends. Aquinas claimed that
human actions are teleological in that they are directed toward an end, and
when achieved, a given end becomes the stepping stone by which another end
is achieved. All ends are rationally ordered toward an ultimate end in God.

Acts properly called human acts are those that proceed from a deliberate act of the power of will and reason. This implies that there is something voluntary in human acts. Human action is ordered toward an end; that is, one has a reason for action, the attainment of a given end or result. Moral responsibility is established by asking the question, "Why?" "Why did you do that?" Unlike acts of human beings, human acts are those over which one has choice.

## SUMMARY

Aquinas acknowledged that God's existence is not self-evident in this life, but was convinced that logical philosophical argument can prove that God exists. In *Summa Theologica,* he presented his five proofs for the existence of God and logically resolved the conflicts between reason, faith, and philosophy. Aquinas saw human beings as intelligent rational beings whose intellect separates them from other animals and endows them with free will. He differentiated between voluntary and nonvoluntary acts in determining whether an act is morally responsible. What is intended and the rationale providing guidance for it are of unique concern.

Aquinas defined law and distinguished between different types or levels. Eternal law is the order of things as determined by God and experienced in human beings as natural inclinations. Natural law is eternal law as it is realized by human beings. Human law as well as moral judgments is the result of interpretations and choice made through utilization of our knowledge of intuitive natural law that God provides. For human law to be valid, it must conform to natural law.

Finally, Aquinas succinctly described moral acts as human acts. Human acts are based on reason and will directed toward distinctively human ends that are consistent with a being made in the image and likeness of God.

## QUESTIONS FOR ADDITIONAL
## REFLECTION AND THOUGHT

1. What is the difference between human acts and acts of human beings?
2. What is the difference between a voluntary act and a nonvoluntary act?
3. Have you ever acted involuntarily?
4. Under what conditions or circumstances is a human being morally responsible?
5. Aquinas set out guidelines for what constitutes true law. Cite some examples of laws (either past or present) that fail to meet these criteria. What are the implications?
6. According to Aquinas, are we morally obligated to obey human law? Why? Why not?

7.  In his *Treatise on Justice,* Aquinas introduced the principle of the double ef-
    fect. Describe a situation in which action you take would have two effects,
    one good and the other bad. What would determine the moral/ethical ac-
    ceptability of your action in a case where there were two outcomes?

## USING THEORY FOR CONCRETE ETHICAL JUDGMENTS

### Ethical Dilemma

As a counselor in private practice, you have been actively involved in community service, including church work, for many years. Many of your clients
come to you as a direct result of this community service. A woman who knows
you as a result of your church involvement calls for an appointment. She and
her husband are active members in the Catholic Church (as are you), and she
was referred to you by the parish priest. In the interview, she tells you she is six
weeks pregnant. The couple is concerned because this is an unplanned pregnancy. They have three children already and she and her spouse are close to 40.
She had recently made a career change that she not only found exciting and
personally fulfilling, but that also filled a large need in the community. Her
conflict is whether to give up her new career of community service to have another child in middle age or to have an abortion. Neither she nor her husband
are thrilled at the prospect of being new parents at age 40, and she knows she
would have feelings of resentment. However, you and they are all aware of the
Catholic Church's teaching that abortion is acceptable only when necessary to
save the life of the mother. During the interview, you are acutely aware of your
own strong beliefs related to abortion and the Catholic Church's teaching.

### The Problem

You have an ethical dilemma in terms of your decision to provide professional
services. Can you competently counsel this individual without compromising
your values, or would it be better to explain your dilemma and refer? How
might either of these decisions affect your client? Your decision is further complicated by your awareness of the polarity that exists on the issue and the question of whom you would refer this client to if you determine that you cannot
see her.

### A Thomasian Approach to Ethics

Aquinas saw human beings as united in body and soul with the rational soul
being able to transcend the body and other material things. Our experience as
rational beings is traced back to our intuitive knowledge of natural law, which
represents our participation in God's eternal law. The rational soul has control
over the body; however, the outcome of conflict is by no means automatic.

Resolution is sought by way of practical wisdom through interpreting and applying intuitive knowledge, which directs the will toward proper choices. The sum of this process is what Aquinas referred to as conscience. While insisting on the moral authority of the dictates of conscience, he does not insist on its infallibility. According to Aquinas, what is good or bad about an action is not merely the outcome, but what one intends as the consequence of the action. Being no slave to reason, whether an act is voluntary or involuntary is a critical factor in determining culpability, as are desire, intent, and knowledge.

### The Decision-Making Process

Using the Thomasian approach, a possible first step for you (the counselor) is to develop and maintain an awareness of the dictates of your own conscience as well as its inherent limitations (fallibility). Additionally, you realize and accept that human beings are made by God and they bear resemblance to Him in being rational. An individual, being made in God's image, has a free will that is directed toward distinctively human ends. Knowledge is a key factor in deciding to act and is a prerequisite to voluntariness. You must therefore ask the question, "What is it I desire for this client?" What should be willed by you for your client is not that your desire or the dictate of your conscience be followed, but rather that she is assisted in the formation of her conscience and the subsequent voluntary act of her will. The process of exploration is aimed at helping her as she initiates her own decision, which she does for a rationally ascertained end. If you can resist being moved by initial strong emotion and can allow the rational will to guide your choice, a voluntary decision to work with this client can be made. This does not compromise your values; rather it acknowledges our human tendencies to act and react while possessing a natural inclination to know and choose. Remember that what is good or evil about an act is what you intend and not the consequence the act produces.

# 8

# Virtue Ethics

Aristotle's *Nicomachean Ethics* was the earliest attempt to offer a systematic treatment of ethics and the principles on which it rests. He began by asking: What is the good life? How can one attain true happiness? How is one to understand the concepts of good, bad, right, wrong, virtue, and vice? It was pondering how one might attain happiness that led Aristotle to the discussion of virtue. For Aristotle, virtue referred to the excellence of a thing and to the effective performance of its proper function. A virtuous physician, for example, is one who effectively restores the health of his/her patients. Through the investigation into and the subsequent definition of moral virtues, Aristotle attempted to give meaning to human action and to the manner in which it is judged.

Aristotle first defined virtue as a state of character, that of being a good person. A good person is one who performs the function of a person well. The critical question here was to determine what the function of a person should be. Aristotle thought it should be something that a person does better than anything else. According to Aristotle, this function is reasoning. Aristotle went on to argue that human beings flourish when they reason well. A virtuous person, then, is one who reasons well and flourishes as a result of that sound reasoning.

Further, virtue is a state of character lying in a mean with most choices. Lying in a mean refers to the avoidance of the extremes of excess and of deficiency, both of which hinder performance. Aristotle's doctrine of the mean explains that for each virtue there will be two vices—one a vice of excess and the other a vice of deficit. An example of a virtue lying at the mean might be industriousness. The vice of excess is working too much and the vice of deficit is laziness. Similarly, the self-confident individual is at the mean, with the excess being arrogance and the deficit subservience. Aristotle acknowledged that not every action warrants a mean. He stated that some acts have names that imply they are bad in themselves (i.e., murder, adultery) and not in their extremes. The morally virtuous individual chooses to act in accordance with the mean; however, Aristotle pointed out that the mean is not the same for all individuals.

## CONTEMPORARY VIRTUE ETHICS

Aristotle began the investigation, but it has by no means stopped there. Virtue ethics is about subjective qualities, traits, and habits that lead an individual to a given choice and action; ultimately addressing the question, "Whom shall I be?" Keenan (1992) states that in addressing this question one must determine whether it is the act or the one acting that ultimately determines the answer. If the act one performs is the determining factor, then the act is under appraisal and the question should be: What acts are permissible and what acts are prohibited? Therefore, acting as a virtuous person would require knowing what acts are prohibited regardless of the situation or circumstance and avoiding those actions. Another consideration might use both the actor and the act as determining factors. In this case, right action considers not only the act itself but also the state in life of the one acting. The right actions of a soldier in war would be different from those of a civilian because determining the right action requires consideration of prescribed role (vocation or relationship to others; state in life).

Contemporary virtue ethics, in addressing the abovementioned question, seeks to avoid fitting moral experience into preestablished rules or ideals (Thomas, 1996; Teehan, 1995; Keenan, 1992; Braybrooke, 1991). Virtue ethics' prescription for right action entails the individual's asking, "What action will make me a better person both now and in the future?" Inherent in this orientation is the assumption that one becomes the agent of the acts one performs and therefore self-understanding is necessary for determining the right action (Punzo, 1996; Thomas, 1996; Keenan, 1992; Braybrooke, 1991).

This type of self-understanding gives rise to the need for distinguishing between doing what is good and being a good person. Punzo (1996) suggests that according to virtue ethics, the goodness of an act is determined not by its consequence or adherence to established rules but primarily by the qualities of the agent performing the act. Moore (1912) distinguished the goodness or badness of one's motivations from the rightness or wrongness of one's actions. Moore went on to suggest that a moral atrocity is committed when one acts rightly, but with bad motivations. Kant (trans. 1963) clearly distinguishes between actions done out of duty and dutiful actions. Actions done out of duty are consistent with virtue ethics' conception of good motivations, and dutiful action is analogous to right actions. Kant argued that a dutiful action is good only if the act is done out of duty. Clearly, both Moore and Kant agree that bad people can act rightly but that it does not make them good people. This gives support to the supposition that if a person acts out of motivation to actualize right living, then that person is good despite the outcome or consequence of the act. Foot (1978) summed up this view nicely by saying that one is generally better off having a virtue than not having it owing to the fact that human beings do not get on well without them. MacIntyre (1984) argued that virtues enable one to achieve the goods internal to the characteristically human practices that strengthen traditions and the communities that sustain them. All agree that what is derived from virtues is beneficial to human beings individually as well as in community.

## COMMON FEATURES OF CONTEMPORARY VIRTUE ETHICS

There are several proposed models or structures of virtue ethics. MacIntyre (1981) saw virtue ethics as requiring answers to three clear questions: (a) who one is, (b) what one ought to become, and (c) what form of action will bring one from the present to the future. Addressing the first question, who one is, requires the virtue of self-understanding. This virtue, however, is not without prerequisite. Self-understanding requires openness, honesty, and the willingness to accept responsibility for one's life—the outcome of which is the person that one is now. Existential components of freedom and responsibility are essential if one is to be free of external constraints and responsible for defining who one is.

Having accepted the present, one must determine which possibilities exist for the future. Self-understanding continues to be essential in determining who one ought to become. Existentialism suggests that a set of psychological principles (symbolization, imagination, and judgment) direct the universal search for meaning (Kobasa & Maddi, 1977). Symbolization involves abstracting from concrete experience a representative category or idea. The more symbolization is exercised the more categories one has through which to identify and classify experience. Imagination is the combining and recombining of these ideas and categories in new and different ways that lead to the conceptualization of change. This change results in an answer to the question of who one ought to become. Judgment is the final step involving assessment of this experience with a view toward the future.

Finally, through the utilization of prudent judgment one recognizes that the transition from the person one is to the person one ought to be will be brought about by the judicious employment of virtuous acts. Prudence is a virtue through which one is able to understand the present situation and to act in a virtuous manner that will have implications in determining who one is now and also who one will (ought to) become.

In MacIntyre's model, the more one grows in self-understanding and utilizes prudent judgment, the more one will know and understand who one is and who and what one ought to be. In this way, virtues one never considered present become clear, as do vices one never thought of overcoming.

Teehan (1995) sets the following three points as characterizing virtue ethics in general: (a) It is in response to the limitations of rule-based ethical theories (such as Kant's and utilitarianism) in capturing the full significance of moral experiences, (b) it shifts the emphasis in moral philosophy from the appraisal of the act to the appraisal of the one acting, and (c) it contains both a theory of virtue and a discussion of the virtues of the one acting. He further argues that the cause of virtue ethics may be furthered by drawing on the moral philosophy of John Dewey. Teehan acknowledges that one does not find in Dewey's writings a full-blown treatise on virtue ethics; however, he contends that the seeds of contemporary virtue ethics were sown decades ago by Dewey.

Spohn (1992) reports that proponents of virtue ethics consider it more adequate than utilitarianism or neo-Kantianism theories because it provides a more comprehensive picture of moral experience and stands closer to the issues of ordinary life. Acknowledging that the exact shape of virtue ethics remains unsettled, Spohn finds that there is agreement that a virtue is a disposition to act, desire, and feel that involves the exercise of judgment and leads to a recognizable human excellence, an instance of human flourishing. Based on this agreement he proposes that discussions of virtue ethics have five common features.

1. Moral evaluations focus on the individual's character. Actions are important because they display the individual's values and commitments.

2. Good character generates practical moral judgments based on beliefs, experiences, and sensitivities more than or instead of rules and principles.

3. A moral psychology gives an account of how virtues and vices form and develop.

4. A theory of human fulfillment explains by example the goal toward which virtues lead and/or in which the virtues are components.

5. Increasingly, attention is paid to the cultural shaping of virtues and what relation, if any, exists between specific historical manifestations of virtues and more universal human traits. (p. 61)

Oakley (1996) points out that the revival of virtue ethics over the past 35 years has produced a bewildering diversity of theories. On the surface, they appear united only by their opposition to various features of Kantian and utilitarian ethical theories. Oakley (1996, pp. 129–143) presents a systematic account of the main features of virtue ethics by articulating the common ground shared by the different varieties. He sets out six specific claims made by all forms of virtue ethics.

1. An action is right if and only if it is what an individual possessing a virtuous character would do in this circumstance. Here Oakley makes claim to what appears central to any form of virtue ethics: namely, that the action is right because someone with the particular virtue in question would do the same in this situation. Foot (1978) provides an example, arguing that

based on the virtue of benevolence, it is right to save another's life when life is still a good to that person because that is what someone with that virtue would do. Virtue ethics clearly gives primacy to virtuous character and maintaining that character is fundamental in referencing a right from a wrong action.

2. Goodness is primary with rightness being defined by it. This second claim made by all varieties of virtue ethics holds that one needs a description of human goods or what human traits are admirable before a determination can be made about what is right for one to do in a given situation. This second assertion or claim is actually included in or at least implied in the first.

3. The virtues are irreducible plural intrinsic goods. Intrinsic means these virtues are valued in and of themselves as something one desires for their own worth rather than for the outcome they provide. This view is opposite to the utilitarian view of virtues as good insofar as they result in pleasure. The different virtues embody irreducibly plural values. According to Aristotle (trans. 1987), each is valuable in a way that is not reducible to a single overarching value. They are valuable for their own sake (intrinsically) and not as a means (instrumentally) of realizing some other value.

4. The virtues are objectively good. Virtues are objectively good in that their goodness is independent of specific or subjective desire. Therefore, according to Oakley, it does not matter whether the goodness of the virtues is linked to essential human characteristics such as rationality or if they derive their goodness from admirable character traits. Neither approach makes the value of any virtue contingent on the desire of the one acting (i.e., courageousness is a virtuous trait even when the individual had no desire to be courageous).

5. Some intrinsic goods are agent relative. Oakley states that some goods such as friendship and integrity are agent relative, while other virtues such as justice are agent neutral. In describing a good as agent relative, Oakley explains that a good of "mine" has additional importance (to me) as opposed to an agent-neutral good that derives no additional importance from being a good of mine. A good may be either agent relative or agent neutral; however, those goods that are agent relative are regarded as more morally relevant to the one acting than those that are agent neutral. Therefore, in situations containing both agent-relative and agent-neutral goods, one might be expected to act and be justified in acting in a way more relevant to a good of mine. If amiable acts toward a friend were to conflict with promoting friendships between others (e.g., hosting a social for a new coworker) one would be justified in acting for a friend.

6. Acting rightly does not require that one maximize the good. This final claim expands on the previous one. Virtue ethics, in rejecting the requirement of maximizing the good, demonstrates the nature of irreducible pluralistic goods by showing, for example, that one can favor an individual

friendship over promoting others' friendship. One is not required by virtue ethics to maximize one's friendships; however, either can be virtuous and good and either can be chosen.

Punzo (1996) attempts to provide a more holistic perspective of the process of virtue ethics and states that individuals discern what constitutes a morally good act through a social-cognitive-emotive process. He notes that, by itself, rationality does not make known real-world experiences and as such cannot supply (through formal determinations) knowledge of whether an act is a good or bad one. The consideration of character goes further, though it is not incompatible with having a firm disposition to do what is right or engaging in rational action. He further notes that anyone who has an understanding of the good of deep trust in an interpersonal relationship has reached such understanding not by having read a textbook account, despite the prowess of the author, but rather by having a life experience in which deep trust has been a part. Punzo suggests that moral behavior has to do with social factors such as identification, cognitive factors such as discernment of the current situation, and emotive factors such as empathy and loving kindness. Thomas (1996) notes that the real-world experiences of individuals differ dramatically and that there are subjective attributions of meaning that individuals have of their experiences. These subjective attributions represent a gulf, between individuals. Thomas believes that there is no set of formal rules that can span the gulf, but unless the gulf is bridged human beings cannot be the morally decent individuals they can and should be.

## VIRTUES AND PRINCIPLES

Addressing Thomas' comment on the need to bridge the subjective gulf of individual experience, virtues and principles may be viewed as complementary rather than competitive systems of ethics. Frankena (1973) stated that principles without traits are impotent and traits without principles are blind. He joined to this the belief that virtues do not provide concrete directives that point the way for right conduct, but rather stimulate individuals with good motivations. Frankena's statement gives rise to the consideration of virtue and principle ethics as potentially compatible systems.

Principle ethics may be seen as having as its structure a set of prima facie obligations. Ross (1930) contended that some rules or principles were self-evident. For example, he contended that some rules were known intuitively, such as that one ought to tell the truth or one ought to keep promises. These rules represent what Ross called prima facie duties. They tell one what one should do only if there are no other overriding moral considerations. However, they do not tell one what the other overriding moral concerns are or what the actual duties are in any particular situation. Principle ethics encompass five prima facie duties: nonmaleficence, fidelity, beneficence, justice, and autonomy

(Beauchamp & Childress, 1994; Bersoff & Koeppl, 1993). In moral reasoning, applying principles (flexibly) to concrete situations provides a potential array of moral choices that can apply in relation to dictates or specifics of the dilemma. Jordan and Meara (1990) posit that principle ethics typically focus on acts and choices. The question of "What shall I be?" is answered through the application of what are taken to be objective, rational standards, rules, or codes. Virtues, taking a slightly different perspective, emphasize the agents or actors. The question of "Whom shall I be?" is answered through the formation of internal qualities, traits, or mature habits. This union appears to give potency to traits and sight to otherwise blind principles.

The community has been cited as being of primary importance in the understanding of virtues (MacIntyre, 1988; Hauerwas, 1981). The community, according to MacIntyre, provides the proper context for the tripolar model. Likewise, it is the community that determines how nonmaleficence, fidelity, beneficence, justice, and autonomy are defined. However, too much reliance on tradition and the community can, as history reveals, create ethnocentric and even immoral decisions. Jordan and Meara (1991) propose that the best defense against this is an acquisition of professional virtues. Meara, Schmidt, and Day (1996) note the application of virtue ethics allows professionals to keep norms flexible and not completely relative to societal or community whim. Looking closely at the questions, "What shall I be?" and "Whom shall I be?" there appears to be a significant meaningful relationship between virtues and principles. Likewise, (flexible) moral principles and moral virtues appear to share a similar relationship. This strong complementary relationship can be imbalanced due to an overreliance on one and a lessening or exclusion of the other.

## VIRTUES AND RULES

Those who champion virtue ethics often see virtue ethics and principle ethics as conflicted. They object to the idea of giving rules an excessively prominent place so that virtues become simply dispositions to obey moral rules (MacIntyre, 1981). Other concerns regarding rules focus on the incompleteness of any account of ethics grounded in rules that neglect virtues. The excessive rigidity of such accounts leads inevitably to overformalized practical reasoning (Pincoff, 1986). Additionally, a rule system is seen as incomplete and therefore incapable of addressing novel issues as they are presented. Braybrooke (1991) proposed an intriguing thesis: no rules without virtues; no virtues without rules. Ethics is viewed as a bifurcating process where virtues and principles are two closely related branches originating from the one trunk. Braybrooke accepts St. Thomas Aquinas' logic and rhetoric that one can identify moral rules that apply to human beings; however, they do so imperfectly. But where does one look for rules? Aquinas always looked to the law, provided that the laws in question had been arrived at properly. Recall from the chapter on natural law that there are qualities a law must have before it can be considered a true law. Aquinas further noted that the body of moral rules, like the body of law, is incomplete at least to the extent that it is humanly possible for one to discover it. Braybrooke (1991, pp. 143–144) gives the following Thomasian example of the necessity of having incomplete laws or rules: The rule is that during the present siege the city gates shall be closed at sunset. This rule is one of moral significance, aimed at the security of the community and therefore the common good. Sunset arrives and it is time to close the gates; however, the gatekeeper sees in the distance a party of the city's soldiers returning from a sortie, hotly pursued by the enemy. What is the gatekeeper to do? Does she lock them out, giving them over to the enemy? The rule (properly understood) was not applied so rigidly. Proper understanding of this or any rule must in application be adjusted to the circumstances. Braybrooke uses this argument to buttress the first tenet of his thesis—no rules without virtues.

Acknowledging Aquinas' commitment to moral rules and to the laws of natural law includes recognizing his commitment to the special virtue of adjusting rules to circumstances. This special virtue, lacking an English or even Latin name, in Greek is *epieikiea.* Pincoff (1986) displayed a similar belief, stating that a virtue is a determinable disposition that will in different situations guide one in different paths; which supports the desirability of and preference for one who possesses it as opposed to one who does not. Virtues, as seen by Braybrooke, are mediating factors that allow rules to be administered with skill and prudence. It is because rules, by their very nature, are incomplete that prudence is required in their utilization.

Braybrooke (1991) acknowledges that *epieikeia,* or the idea of adjusting rules to circumstances, by itself cannot support his claim that the existence of rules implies the existence of virtues. Borrowing again from Aquinas and Aristotle, he firmly declares that justice will serve as that virtue supporting his claim. Aristotle, speaking of justice in *Nicomachean Ethics,* posited that being just is the perfection of virtue in dealing with others. Aquinas likewise believed that justice is embedded in one's concern for others. Braybrooke asserts that this concern for others manifests itself in law-abidingness. Therefore, if one accepts justice in its broadest sense as law-abidingness, then it can be seen as a virtue that is demonstrated through the observance of some rule or law. Braybrooke intimates in this logic that the existence of rules implies the prior existence of virtues. Rules (even if incomplete) are seen as the vehicle through which virtues are experienced. Flexibility or adjusting responses to varying circumstances cannot be exercised unless there is some rule or expectation with which to be flexible. Likewise, law-abidingness cannot be a virtue unless there are rules or laws to obey.

Braybrooke now moves to the second branch of his thesis, no virtues without rules. He postulates that virtues may depend for their importance on the importance of having rules. His second thesis postulates that even if an idealistic society were to exist in which everyone automatically behaved in such a manner that rules were not needed to ensure good behavior, there would still be some rules. In this perfect society, individual behavior would not be predictable or consistent without being in accordance with some rules. Likewise, virtues would be appreciated even if there were no need to worry about the goodness of individuals' actions. Actions that are appreciated would be approved of and possibly expected or at least desired. Braybrooke argues that the resulting regularities in behavior constitute a sort of informal moral rules; and, consequently, virtues are in accordance with rules that could be charged to their behavior.

There appears to be nothing in the definitions of virtue ethics that prohibits the existence of a set of principles or rules for describing actions performed by a virtuous person. An example of a principle or rule might be "Act like a virtuous person." This does not change the fact that the evaluation of the act is less important than the evaluation of the person.

Whether one precedes the other or the reverse can be debated; however, it can be seen that they do bear a strong complementary relationship to one another. It would be difficult to imagine a system of rules working if the individuals involved lacked virtues consistent in some way with established rules, formal or informal. Similarly, it would be difficult to imagine virtues that did not generate rules or expectations regarding behavior that were not consistent with them.

## MORAL EDUCATION: TEACHING VIRTUE ETHICS

Imitation, it has been said, is the most sincere form of flattery. It is also the method through which moral education occurs when one is a small child. Anyone who has children or who has spent time around them knows that small children are too young to learn and comprehend complex moral rules. Therefore, their behavior is in part a reflection or imitation of their parents and others around them. Learning by example, according to Baier (1985), can proceed through the process of setting examples rather than by formulating and communicating complex rules. Braybrooke (1991), while not denying this observation, adds that individuals learning from examples gather rules and generalize these rules to similar situations as a guide for action. Braybrooke provides the following example to demonstrate the informality of rules as well as the method of instruction used to teach them:

> Late one afternoon in a year nearly halfway through the fourth decade of this century, a small boy found himself retreating from a menacing platoon of his acquaintances; the boy launched one final round of inventive verbal abuse at the platoon and turned to open the door into his house. At just that moment his mother, standing behind the door and observing the retreat, firmly locked him out—shutting the city gates—almost as much to his enemies' consternation as to his own. (p. 152)

So what, Braybrooke asks, is the rule to be learned? His mother never explained, never again did she bring up the incident; however, the lessons that she taught him, he recalls, left the most incisive impression.

Braybrooke utilizes the above example to demonstrate how inextricable are teaching by rules and teaching by example, as well as how indistinguishably related are rules and virtues. Whether one agrees or disagrees, the strength of the relationship is again made evident.

## SUMMARY

The reawakening of interest in virtue ethics has produced a perplexing variety of theories. Despite the variations, all share a similar core that can be articulated by the question, "Who shall I be?" The central focus is on individual self-understanding and the quest for actions that will give rise to a better person now and in the future. However, doing what is good is insufficient. One must act out of motivation to actualize right living. Virtues, however, do not provide specific directives that point the way for right behavior. These directives can be found by considering virtues and principles as related and complementary as opposed to competitive systems. The question of action or "What shall I be?" provides specific directives through objective, rational standards, rules, or codes. The complementary question of "Who shall I be?" is less specific, but nonetheless important, providing specific directives through the formation of internal qualities and traits. This complementary union provides concrete direction to virtuous traits and prudence to principles and rules.

## QUESTIONS FOR ADDITIONAL
## REFLECTION AND THOUGHT

1.  Who is more virtuous? Is it the individual who struggles to maintain the proper course of action despite the tendency to be easily swayed or the individual who is by nature disposed to act properly? What is your position and why?
2.  What characteristics do you consider basic to moral virtue?
3.  What is the difference between asking "What shall I be?" and asking "Who shall I be?" How would you answer these questions about yourself?
4.  Can you describe a rule or principle that should never be broken or violated regardless of the circumstances?
5.  How would you explain the following statement: "Principles without virtues are impotent, while virtues without principles are blind"?
6.  What is meant by the phrase "overriding moral consideration"?
7.  Do you agree or disagree with the following statement regarding professional codes or the law: One has the choice of adhering to them or trying to change them, but not breaking them. Can you cite any exceptions to this statement?

8. Segregation was once the law of the land, and being the law, it was to be followed by all citizens. On December 1, 1955, Mrs. Rosa Parks, an African-American woman, violated the law by refusing to give up her seat on a bus to a white male passenger. Was the law right or was Mrs. Parks right? Is there an overriding moral concern in this situation that mediates the application of the principle of law?

# USING THEORY FOR CONCRETE ETHICAL JUDGMENTS

## Ethical Dilemma

You are a counselor working independently in private practice. Ms. G. is a client you have been seeing for approximately eight weeks. Her presenting problem had to do with a difficult adjustment she was experiencing following separation from her husband and an impending divorce. She and her husband are now divorced and she has custody of their two children. She appears to be progressing well, but now confides that she has been taking a drug prescribed by her family doctor for anxiety and is addicted. A compounding problem is that she has been forging these prescriptions for the past three months with prescription pads she had stolen from her doctor's office, since the doctor would not refill them. Your client, having been a nurse, knows she needs help to withdraw from this drug but is fearful of the potential legal consequences of her actions. She is planning to refill a forged prescription today because she is almost out and knows she cannot do without the drug. She has a plan to seek medical help for her withdrawal from the drug, and she asks you to help her but not to inform anyone about the forgeries, as this would jeopardize her keeping custody of her two children.

## The Problem

Your client confides her illegal actions to you and asks for your help and support in making changes. Should you notify the authorities of your knowledge of the commission of a crime? What about Ms. G's well-being and the children's? What do you do? More importantly, why do you do it?

## A Case for Virtue Ethics

Virtue ethics can be used as a bridge between principles and values. There are certain principles that provide good reasons for value judgments. Likewise, certain virtues can provide guidance in the application of principles to specific situations. Prudence also plays an important role in virtue ethics. The prudent individual knows the means or principles that guide one to certain good ends; this individual also knows how much particular ends are to be valued.

## The Decision-Making Process

The rules of law are clear regarding situations in which you have knowledge of the commission of a crime. They state that the authorities should be notified. Should you notify the authorities out of fear of being culpable later, or is there other rationale that determines your actions? Are there other possible courses of action? If so, what rationale exists for them? Prima facie duties may help by telling you what should be done if there were no overriding moral considerations. What are the prima facie duties that exist in this situation, and do you see any overriding moral considerations? Beneficence, nonmaleficence, and fidelity all appear to vie for attention. These concerns appeal to the flexible application of the rules. Action should be guided by beneficence toward your client's children. The effect any action may have on them should be considered. Additionally, nonmaleficence (do no harm) should factor into the decision-making process as should fidelity (faithfulness to your client and your profession). The question of harm is two-sided with respect to taking too little or too much action. Address the questions of what shall I be and whom shall I be as you consider these factors and determine your course of action.

# 9

*

# Moral and
# Ethical Development

Morality has to do with the conscious adoption of standards related to right and wrong. These standards are established when certain behaviors are labeled as good and others are labeled as bad, beginning in childhood. With age and experience these standards of morality come to include complex ideas, values, and beliefs (Carroll & Rest, 1982).

The process of moral ethical development is analogous to Hegel's theory of Dialectic with each stage, its conflicts, and its resolutions forming the cornerstone for the next developmental progression. Hegel's theory of Dialectic is triadic, consisting of three stages. The first involves the formation of a thesis, or in the case of moral ethical development, a principle based on a paradigm. This is followed by a second (developmental) stage where the first principle is challenged, opposed, or negated by the formation of a new opposing principle, or antithesis. This new principle or paradigm formation causes cognitive dissension leading to the third stage, synthesis. Here a new concept (paradigm) or principle emerges which transcends the two previous theses. Synthesis, or the resolution of this developmental conflict, has three functions: (a) It cancels or resolves the conflict between the original thesis and its antithesis, (b) it preserves and maintains the elements of truth within each of the conflicting views, and (c) it transcends the opposition and raises up or sublimates the conflict into a higher level understanding or truth.

Both Piaget and Kohlberg recognized that human life involves conflict within the individual person and between the individual and the group. Moral judgments pertaining to the resolution of these conflicts are a given part of life.

At what level of understanding is each situation viewed, and how does this impact moral conflict and choice of solution?

## MODELS OF MORAL DEVELOPMENT

To understand how morality is shaped by cognitive awareness, Piaget created pairs of stories and asked children to decide which of the two were naughty. Piaget's conversations with the children led him to a three-stage theory of moral development. The three stages were

Stage 1. Premoral: In this stage awareness of rules and reasons for them is limited if it exists at all.

Stage 2. Moral Realism: This stage demonstrates an increased awareness that rules exist as they are learned from parents. Obedience is based on submission to external authority.

Stage 3. Moral Relativism: Here an awareness of the meaning of rules and the reasons for them exists. Rules become regarded as products of mutual consent and respect, and are understood in relation to the principles they uphold.

Moral development emerges from the interaction between cognitive structures (cognitive development and social experiences). Therefore, to understand the concept of morality, it is necessary not only to understand the logic of the individual but also the experience he/she is attempting to make sense of.

Kohlberg offers a detailed explanation of the development of morality. Like Piaget, he maintains that morality is achieved in a series of stages. Also like Piaget, Kohlberg was interested in understanding moral conflicts and in the process involved in resolution of such conflicts and arriving at decisions about right and wrong. Kohlberg (1969) found that although children might come up with the same answer to moral dilemmas as adults (believing that it is not right to lie or steal), the logic of the children's thinking about values was distinctively different from that of adults. Children's thinking, it was found, was less complex but in its own terms no less logical.

According to Gilligan (1980), Kohlberg's six stages of moral development represent increasingly adequate conceptions of justice and reflect an expanding capacity to take the role or perspective of the other person. In the end, she sees these two as the same because the claims of all are accounted for in one just solution. The explanation of moral perspective, according to Gilligan, signifies an extension of the social universe to which the moral considerations pertain. This expansion in perspective defines the three levels of moral judgment into which Kohlberg's six stages fall.

**Level 1. Preconventional**  At this level an individual's moral reasoning results from the consequences of action (punishment, reward, exchange of favor) and from the physical power of those in authority. Moral dilemmas are seen as conflicts between the individual needs of the people involved.

Stage 1. Decisions result from a blind obedience to power, an attempt to avoid punishment, or an attempt to seek rewards.

Stage 2. Decisions result from a desire to satisfy one's own needs and occasionally the needs of others. Individuals view reciprocity as a matter of "you scratch my back and I'll scratch yours." Reasoning involves little consideration of loyalty, gratitude, or justice.

**Level 2. Conventional** At this level an individual's moral reasoning involves consideration of the interests of others (family and peers), a desire to maintain respect and support, and to justify the existing social order. Moral judgments always appeal to authority, but the authority derives its moral claim not from greater power but from its consensual validation or legitimate traditional base.

Stage 3. At this stage decisions result from a desire to please and help others and receive their approval in return. Behavior is frequently judged by intention—he or she "means well" becomes important for the first time.

Stage 4. Decisions made here result from a desire to maintain the existing authority, rules, and social order. Right behavior consists of doing one's duty.

**Level 3. Post-Conventional** At this level an individual's moral reasoning incorporates moral values and principles with validity and application beyond the authority of groups. Moral reasoning becomes comprehensive and reflects universal principles.

Stage 5. Here decisions result from recognition of an individual's right within a society that has a social contract. As a result, the individual's reasoning emphasizes the legal point of view but with the emphasis on the possibility of changing laws.

Stage 6. In this, the highest stage, decisions result from an obligation to universal ethical principles that apply to all humankind. The universal principles of justice, reciprocity, quality of human rights, and respect for the dignity of human beings as individuals serve as a basis for individual reasoning.

Kohlberg's third post-conventional level of morality has been labeled by Smith (in his commentary on Gilligan, 1980), as a twentieth-century categorical imperative. Kohlberg encapsulated moral development as a process involving the restructuring of the concept of the self in its relationship to the concept of other people. This takes place in a common social world with social standards.

Van Hoose and Paradise (1979) proposed the ethical orientation could be viewed from a model of five qualitatively different stages of ethical reasoning. The stages are as follows:

Stage 1. Punishment Orientation:  In this stage, individual ethical orientation is guided by and relies exclusively upon external resources and strict adherence to rules and standards. Motivation is influenced by awareness of consequences of behavior.

Stage 2. Institutional Orientation: As in the first stage, ethical orientation is externally oriented. The institution with which the individual is associated provides the rationale for ethical decisions. There is strict obedience and compliance with higher authorities within the institution.

Stage 3. Societal Orientation: At this stage, there is an ethical orientation toward adherence to the law. The law reflects the societal goal of the greatest good for the greatest many. Where there is a conflict between the individual and the society, the individual is expected to yield to the societal interests.

Stage 4. Individual Orientation: In this stage, the locus of control (ethical orientation) shifts from external to internal. Concern is now for the needs of the individual while not violating the laws of society or the rights of others. The individual is of primary concern with the societal context being second.

Stage 5. Principle or Conscious Orientation. This is the highest stage of ethical/moral orientation. Concern here is for the individual regardless of the legal, professional, or societal consequences, or situational factors. The individual operating in this stage has defined an internal code of ethics that guides behavior regardless of external pressure or situational factors. (p. 38)

Learning patterns of social interaction is the beginning process whereby moral orientation is organized at the individual level (Youniss, 1978; Kohlberg, 1969; Whitehead, 1929). Individuals interact with other individuals and, as a result of many factors, form groups. Moral bias exists and is in part related to an individual's position in a socially structured environment or group (Douglas, 1982). Paradigms are used by individuals to organize related concepts. Paradigms provide approaches for organizing, interpreting, and evaluating information for decision making. Groups interacting with other groups combine to form social institutions. Gilligan (1980) believed that social institutions influence moral development. She further asserted that social institutions impede or foster moral development by the concept of justice they embody. A conceptual framework for understanding social justice begins with the individual, moves to the group, then to the larger society before reverting again to the individual.

This process is circular, not linear. Individuals interacting with and reacting to other individuals combine to form groups with similar goals, beliefs, or values. These groups exert some potential influence on their members as well as on members of other groups. Multiple groups combine to form institutions that exert influence on the groups that make them up as well as on the individuals who make up the groups. An event begins with the individual affecting the group; the group affecting the institution; the institution affecting the individual; and so on. Different levels of moral understanding are related to group or societal position and paradigm structure. These factors impact the understanding of moral conflicts and the process of resolving moral dilemmas, including principles utilized.

## INDIVIDUAL MORAL DEVELOPMENT

Individuals innately struggle to make sense of their experiences both within themselves and in the outside world in which they live. One struggles to know what is good. Piaget's (1932) view of the child making sense of his or her world is coupled with the conception of knowledge as residing neither in the child nor the world but rather in the interaction between them. Piaget saw knowledge of morality as emerging from the interaction between cognitive structures and social experience. Therefore, to understand the individual's concept of morality it is necessary to understand not only the logic used but also the social interactions and experiences of which the individual is attempting to make sense. Piaget's work on the moral judgment of the child suggests that a shift in the child's social position from the hierarchical world of the family to the often more democratic world of peers can lead to a concomitant change in the child's view and practice of rules. To understand this transition is to become aware of the region between the event and the reaction to the event—the region where meaning of the experience is determined. The attention is not on what is believed or seen as being true or even on uncovering the why, but rather on the process by which the individual arrives at those views and practices.

Gilligan (1980), in asserting that social institutions impede or foster moral development by the concept of justice they embody, adds three supporting propositions: (a) moral judgment is advanced by an environment that provides moral stimulation and reasoning one stage above the individual's own; (b) moral judgment is advanced by an environment that exposes the individual to conflicts of value and to attempts at integrating these conflicts; and (c) moral judgment is advanced by a social class and peer environment that provide the individual with the opportunity to take the role of others and with the experience of social membership and participation. Even if these propositions have nothing else, they have a high degree of face validity.

The failure of morality signals a breakdown in the process of interaction through which the individual comes, through experience, to replace more primitive concepts of morality with the understanding of cooperation manifested in the notion of justice (Gilligan, 1980). John Dewey (1916/1966) described the democratic community as possessing a variety of commonly shared interests in a group and a certain amount of interaction and cooperative interchange with other groups. Dewey posited that democracy in the school is the bridge between the family and the outside society that is necessary for providing experiences of democratic participation and community and leads to the development of social responsibility. Ironically, for most adult individuals there seems to be a cessation of the further development of moral judgment beginning around the time they leave school. Rest (1980) suggested that development continues as long as individuals are in school, but plateaus when they leave.

While one must be free to choose for morality to make any sense at all, an action does not become right merely because it is chosen. So what factors influence what one chooses and ultimately does?

## VALUES, BELIEFS, AND ATTITUDES

Values, beliefs, and attitudes are a triad that influence choice and behavior. Values are prescriptive beliefs that a certain mode of conduct or way of being is preferable to others. They serve as guides in daily activities. Values are positive and idealistic in character and have similar properties to goals (Schwartz, 1994; Feather, 1994). While seen as enduring and stable over time, values may vary in importance at any given time depending on the context (Schwartz, 1992; Feather, 1994; Braithwaite & Scott, 1991; Braithwaite, 1994). This prioritization suggests that values are dynamic rather than static and change in the level of importance according to contextual scrutiny. Beliefs, on the other hand, can be viewed as information individuals have about other individuals, groups, or situations that are either fact or opinion (Braithwaite, 1994). Attitudes involve evaluations of other individuals, groups, or situations in a direct way often requiring interaction (Fishbein & Ajzen, 1975; Petty & Cacioppo, 1981). Attitudes are relatively peripheral in the belief system and they may change, even with similar objects in different situations (Grube, Mayton & Ball-Rokeach, 1994). Attitudes are instrumental for and serve more central values. Therefore, while individuals may possess a plethora of attitudes, there are but a few core values that underpin them.

Attempts to change the attitudes of an individual have limited success if they are not congruent with the more enduring underlying values that support the attitudes and behavior. It is precisely for this reason that a change in one value may precipitate numerous changes in functionally related values, attitudes, and behaviors (Grube et al., 1994). Rokeach (cited in Braithwaite & Scott, 1991) differentiated between values that encompassed ideal end states and values that are concerned with modes of conduct. In doing so, he distinguished between goals of thought and goals of action. It is viewed as being most likely that individuals will act in accordance with their underlying values but not always. Schwartz (1994) provides an example of pursuit of achievement values as a personal value conflicting with values relating to cooperation and benevolence, an institutional requirement. Value conflicts can be seen as potentially existing between the individual and the group or institution within which the individual must function, with the resolution being unpredictable.

Social institutions have a profound impact on individuals' values and view of morality, as do environmental factors. Some of those are briefly examined in the next section.

## SOCIAL ENVIRONMENTAL FACTORS

It has been said that where you stand determines what you see, and what you see determines where you stand. Applying a pragmatic interpretation, Douglas (1982) suggests that specific dimensions of social environments are important in determining an individual's moral reasoning. Her concept of grid/group analysis identifies specific social environments in which each of the various types of moral reasoning are most likely to occur. According to Douglas, grid describes the extent of regulation or constraint imposed on an individual, while group refers to the individual's degree of commitment or allegiance to a given group (p. 5). She links alternative visions of a just society and moral bias directly to an individual's position in a socially structured environment.

Douglas analyzed four social relationships as defined by grid/group analysis, which she labeled A, B, C, and D. Type A, the low grid; low group environment, is characterized by individualism. Here individuals often feel little commitment to the group and the pursuit of individual freedoms is seen as unconstrained. Self-motivated entrepreneurial types are examples of Type A. Type B, the high grid; low group, is an environment where individual behavior is highly limited by those in power. In this environment certain individuals are in positions not necessarily of their choice and must do as they are told. Douglas conjectures that in a highly competitive society most women and children (and possibly minorities) are in such positions. Type C, the high grid; high group, is viewed as an ascribed hierarchy. This is similar to the environment of large institutions or the military, where loyalty to the group and its rules are rewarded and the hierarchy respected. The orientation here is toward authority, fixed rules, and the maintenance of social order for its own sake. Type D, the low grid; high group, is composed of small groups formed in disagreement with, and withdrawal from, the larger society. Egalitarianism is expounded while at the same time there is exclusive commitment to the group above all else. Radical groups and cults are examples of Type D.

Feather (1994) appears to agree with Douglas and argues that some research suggests that moral judgments and value preferences are the outcome of socialization experiences rather than the product of developmental sequence. This research suggests that moral decision making involves more complex processes than an attribution to a developmental stage would allow.

As society has grown in size, it has grown in complexity of its organizations. Any organization, regardless of its size or purpose, is similar in that it involves the cooperative endeavor of several people acting to influence and direct other people. All involved have a similar focus and goal, that being the one provided by the group or organization. That which would be quickly abandoned or identified as wrong if done by a single individual can be carried out by the group without hesitation or apparent culpability. Isolation is thought to encourage the development of groupthink as a result of decreased interaction and cooperative interchange with other groups.

Additionally, these factors, to a greater or lesser degree, make it difficult for individuals in various groups to see the same issues and dilemmas in complex real-life situations or events. This is especially true when the issue or dilemma is one in which they all participate, but do so from different group perspectives. Cooperative interchanges may be possible for some individuals depending on their perspective, but not for others because they do not identify the situation or event as important or even controversial. How and if the group or organization allows participation in decision making or legislates to its members is a potent factor in determining the process outcome of moral judgments.

Grid/group analysis is consistent with the idea that moral development plateaus after leaving school (Rest, 1980). According to grid/group analysis, moral judgment does not result from an advance in reasoning to a qualitatively higher, more complex structuring of the content of moral knowledge. Instead, it occurs as a strategic response by the individual who realizes that others in a given environment find this type of justification appropriate under the circumstances. Changes in moral orientation, according to Douglas, are therefore not a result of logic, but the result of movement to a new grid/group position. Acceptance or nonacceptance of a particular moral view is dictated by association rather than logical reasoning. Opportunities for groups or organizations to "cause the effect" or "effect the cause" regarding moral judgments are vividly clear.

Let us return to Dewey's idea that democracy in the school is the necessary bridge to provide the experience that leads to the development of social responsibility, and let us substitute groups or organizations for school. Facilitation of cooperative interchange with and among different groups on a variety of social and moral issues allows for individual participation in the exchange of ideas. This participation and the differing roles, much as in school, discourage isolation and tendencies toward groupthink. Groups and organizations become sources of stimulation and interchange instead of static havens where one finds others in this environment accepting, without question, a particular justification appropriate under the circumstances. Isolating and compartmentalizing groups allows for and encourages groupthink and similar phenomena that contribute to the effect.

However, the problem of agreement (not groupthink) remains and can still be heard in the echo of Aristotle's comment that there is no agreement as to what young people [or adults] should learn . . . all people do not appreciate the same kind of goodness, so it is expected that they would differ (Burnet, 1903).

To understand more fully how these social environmental factors, groups, and organizations go about the process of influencing the perception of social justice one must explore the paradigm(s) by which they work.

# THE PARADIGM OF PRINCIPLES

Gilligan (1980) returns to the individual by stating that moral judgment is related to [individual] moral action. Smith (1980) stated in his commentary on Gilligan that he heard her message as saying adults influence the moral judgments of children, for better or worse. However, those adults who are themselves adrift in a sea of moral relativism are without maps by which their offspring can chart a course toward what is right and good in human life. This statement, especially the importance of a map, can be generalized to our discussion of the process of social justice. Individuals, groups, and organizations all possess knowledge of principles of morality they believe to be correct. The map or principles of morality that are transmitted or taught, regardless of their correctness, are based or constructed on paradigms.

Paradigms provide approaches for organizing, interpreting, and evaluating information for the purpose of making decisions. These are expressed as principles, rules, or laws. Individuals often act as though moral rules or principles are exhaustive and justice requires only an understanding of and adherence to some code of ethics or rules. In given environments or situations a behavior is judged appropriate under the circumstances based on the principles or rules derived from the paradigm. Moral orientation, as viewed by Douglas (1982), is a strategic move to a new grid/group position whose principles support or justify a given action.

The public rhetoric on various aspects of social justice, (e.g., affirmative action, equal rights, abortion, and similar issues) has increasingly become discourse that focuses on matters of principle. Jonsen and Toulmin (1988) have described discourse involving matters of principle as often ending up in a head-butting that pits unqualified and unconditional rights against unqualified and unconditional rights. The very process employed (arguing on high-level theory and general principles) assures that on a practical level no resolution is possible. The more that principles become mottos and slogans, eventually evolving into battle cries, the more the fervent devotees on both sides are driven to frustration and even violence. Pitting contradictory and/or incompatible ethical principles against one another guarantees deadlock. Therefore, solutions must be sought elsewhere. In looking for a pragmatic solution, one must acknowledge that in accepting [universal] rules and principles as the basis for ethics, little if any middle ground can be found between absolutism and relativism (Jonsen & Toulmin). In dealing with real-life ethical dilemmas, one finds that rules and principles apply to some situations without ambiguity but only apply marginally to others. This makes the marginal situation just as problematic as the situations in which different rules or principles conflict with each other.

As we have seen, a given paradigm results in the establishment of rules and principles associated with a certain reference point, often that of the group or organization. The adherence to rules and principles as unchallengable results in what Jonsen and Toulmin have called a principled tyranny. The principle itself, rather than the reason for it, is the treatise on which action is taken. The principle then becomes more important than its underlying rationale. The problems that principled tyranny brings about are not confined to the theoretical level but permeate functioning at all levels. In part, the inability to engage in cooperative interchange is due to a groupthink-type skewed perception of moral problems and/or the inability to identify the situation as important or controversial. The resulting behavior is a "head in the sand" type of denial of the opposing view that further polarizes already differing groups. Another view of this type of situation might be framed as the rigidly dogmatic versus the overly flexible tolerant permissive. The problem again is not as it appears, rigid versus permissive; rather, it lies in the inability to make a paradigm shift to see how, if, and under what conditions justice is served by tolerance of exception. In situations like this, if remediation is possible, one is forced to go beyond the principle or rule and examine the process that underlies it.

## DEVELOPMENT OF PRUDENCE

In the application of principles to the process of moral decision making the question remains, "What kind of understanding of human conduct does ethics provide?" Aristotle (trans. 1987) declared ethics is not and could not be a science; therefore, it cannot provide universal principles for particular judgments. Rather, ethics is a field of experience that calls for prudence; prudence being practical experience that cannot be gained in social isolation. Practical wisdom is born of experience and deals with the particulars of a given situation and also with universally applicable concepts. The experience and resulting moral ethical development is analogous to a major part of Smith's moral map. Principles derived from the paradigm are used to judge appropriate behaviors under the circumstances. Granting that some general principles are universal and are to be taken as ethically binding, no matter what their source, one must learn (through the process of moral development) to fit them to particular cases (Arras, 1986, 1994; Kuczewski, 1994).

For pragmatic judgments regarding ethics and social justice, practical wisdom is a prerequisite. Aristotle (trans. 1987), explaining practical wisdom argued, "While the young become geometricians and mathematicians, and wise in matters of that sort, they do not seem to be prudent. The reason is that prudence applies to particular cases, and these cases become known by experience" (p. 198). Jonsen and Toulmin (1988, pp. 34–35) distinguish two approaches in dealing with moral ethical dilemmas. One, the theoretical, is concerned with principles, rules, and other general ideas that posit universal rules [axioms] from which particular moral/ethical judgments are deduced. The second, more practical, focuses on specific features of the particular kinds of moral cases, with moral rules serving as maxims that can be understood only in terms of the paradigmatic cases that define their meaning and force. Theoretical arguments are not dependent on the circumstances of their presentation. The argument is a chain of propositions, linked together in such a way as to guarantee its conclusion. Conclusions are deduced from initial axioms or universal principles.

These truths flow downward to provide resolution for the questions at hand. Practical arguments draw on the outcomes of previous experience, carrying over procedures used to resolve earlier problems and reapplying them in new problematic situations. Their validity depends on how closely the present situation resembles those of the earlier precedent cases for which this particular type of argument was originally devised. The task at hand is not about showing what makes one particular ethical view more correct by referring to rules or laws that are held as true with great certainty by various groups or organizations. Rather, resolution may be sought in the manner ascribed:

> The analysis and resolution of moral issues utilizes procedures of reasoning based on paradigms and analogies, leading to the formulation of opinions about the existence and stringency of particular moral obligations, framed in terms of principles that are general but not universal or invariable, since they hold good with certainty only in the special conditions of the agent and circumstances of action. (Jonsen & Toulmin, p. 257)

The process of moral development requires one to understand not only the general principles of morality, but also in what circumstances and situations they do and do not apply. This requires a paradigm shift from traditional inductive (generalizing or drawing conclusions from particular facts) and deductive (generalizing from a known principle to an unknown) reasoning to a more practical problem-solving approach. This approach views principles as general in form but limited in scope of practical application and understanding arrived at through varied experience. The commitment is not to the principles or views of a particular group, institution, or race, but rather to the understanding of human needs. The practical task is to identify and apply general moral rules and other ethical factors relating to the concept of justice to new and increasingly complex circumstances in ways that respect human needs. Concomitantly, this entails a review and redefining of concepts such as autonomy. Autonomy moves from simply a right to self-determination to a broader independence, meaning that an autonomous agent is the source of moral principles and not merely the recipient. This requires individuals, their groups, and institutions, to facilitate cooperative interchange with and among other groups and institutions allowing for varied human experiences, exchange of ideas, and roles leading to the development of prudence. The key to practical wisdom is embodied in the knowledge of the process; application of this knowledge entails education through cooperative human interchange and transmission of knowledge to others through respectful dialogue. Kung (1991) in his book *Global Responsibility* wrote

> . . . the world in which we live has a chance for survival only if there is no longer any room in it for spheres of differing, contradictory and even antagonistic ethics . . . it needs some norms, values, ideals and goals to bring it together and to be binding on it. The obligation is to the whole not to any part. (p. xvi)

# SUMMARY

Moral ethical development is a complex process involving interaction of the individual with one's self and with others. The level of cognitive understanding at which a situation is viewed impacts the conflict as well as the solution. Various models of moral development have been proposed, all of which involve cognitive development and social experiences. Each model views development as a tiered or staged progression, with each stage possessing its own unique logical approach to problem solving. Each stage represents an increasingly adequate conception of fairness or justice. Interaction between the society and the individual leads to the establishment of values, beliefs, and attitudes that influence individual choice and behavior.

Paradigms provide approaches for organizing, interpreting, and evaluating information for the purpose of decision making. Expressed as principles, they are transmitted through the interactional process of moral ethical development. Based on developmental levels, group, or societal position, all individuals, their groups, and organizations possess knowledge of principles of morality that they believe to be true, regardless of their actual correctness.

Moral ethical dilemmas involving matters of principle often reflect a given paradigm, which results in rules or principles associated with a certain inflexible reference point. The inflexibility reflects a lower level of moral ethical development, (e.g., the inability to take another's point of view or to see how principles might apply differently in different situations).

Moral ethical development is a process that involves both the individual and the environment, to include other individuals. The process is seen as interactive and circular, not linear. The sum of the products of this interaction is the development of Aristotelian prudence or what one may call moral ethical maturity.

# QUESTIONS FOR ADDITIONAL REFLECTION AND THOUGHT

1. Using the information presented in this chapter, respond to the following statement: What you see depends upon where you stand and where you stand depends upon what you see.

2. Can groups or organizations function autonomously apart from the individuals that comprise them? If so, what are the implications for the moral and ethical functioning of these groups?

3. List some of the groups or institutions in which you have or have had affiliation (e.g., church, school, social organization). How influential have they been in your moral/ethical development? Do the same for significant others in your life. In the process of moral/ethical development which comes first, the individual or the group?

4. List some of the groups or institutions that hold different moral/ethical beliefs from yours. How have these influenced your moral/ethical development?

5. Are your values dynamic or static? Do they change in relative importance depending on situational context?

6. Describe the relationship between values, beliefs, and attitudes.

7. Do females and males differ in their moral development? If so, can you explain the differences and their possible sources?

# USING THEORY FOR CONCRETE ETHICAL JUDGMENTS

## Ethical Dilemma

You are a nontraditional counseling student who is in the final stages of her program and is taking a practicum in counseling. Before returning to graduate school to become a school counselor you were a social worker (CSW–ACP) and are still licensed to practice in your state. You had worked in a psychiatric hospital for a number of years but after marriage and children you made a career change to teaching. After several years of teaching, you decided to return to your original field and began working on certification as a school counselor. You have completed all your required course work and are seeking a school site to do your practicum. You approach your school district about placement at a local school and they are elated. They inform you that they want to place you in a school where they need experienced counselors, especially licensed counselors. The district has devised a plan by which the licensed counselors (or in this case a social worker) can bill for third-party reimbursement of counseling services rendered to students. Even though you are technically a student, you are a licensed social worker with advanced clinical practitioner certification and experience. The principal and other counselors at the school are excited about having you as a practicum student and desire to know how soon you can begin. The reception you have received is flattering. You are now expected to give them a date when you can begin.

## The Problem

As a student, are you agreeable to the practicum placement and the staff's expectations? As a licensed professional, should you agree to the billing of your services for third-party reimbursement? When does a student stop being a student, or when does a professional stop being a professional and become a student? Is it ethical, when working in the role of a student, to bill for services rendered even if you are competent and licensed to do so legally?

## The Decision-Making Process

In the current situation a critical question that emerges is how much responsibility for ethical behavior is borne by the institution and how much by you? Who makes the decision? Many actions later shown or acknowledged to be unethical have been defended by the statement: I was only doing what I was told to do by my superior. This statement, considered a rationalization, makes it clear who has the final responsibility. Are your beliefs about what is right and ethical consistent with what you value in this situation? What, if any, effect is your school district's response to you and to this situation having on you and your thoughts about what to do? Is this situation a special one in which the existing principles do not apply?

What are your college's or university's rules regarding practicum students? What are the school district's rules? Imagine yourself belonging to another group and looking in at this situation—what would you see? How would you assess the situation? Is it different from the way you see it currently?

# 10

＊

# Feminist Ethics:
# A Different Voice

arol Gilligan's (1982) book, *In a Different Voice*, exposed us to the fact that women bring considerations of care to ethical issues. Their moral decisions are frequently made in context of concern for preserving and nurturing relationships. Gilligan's work represents an objection to the methods and conclusions of Lawrence Kohlberg in the area of moral development and moral reasoning. Kohlberg's work was seen as denigrating females' responses to moral dilemmas in comparison to the responses of males. Over the past two–plus decades, research on women's development has led to a reconsideration of many of the fundamental questions regarding the development of morality, identity, and human relationships. Given these changes and their intensity, no introduction to the subject of ethics and moral theory would be considered complete without giving attention to the ever-growing body of work known as feminist ethics.

## CARING: THE MORAL IMPERATIVE

Annette Baier (1986), reflecting on the issue of traditional ethics from a feminist perspective, wrote;

> The recent research of Carol Gilligan has shown us how intelligent and reflective twentieth-century women see morality, and how different their

picture of it is from that of men, particularly the men who eagerly assent to the claims of current orthodox contractarian–Kantian moral theories. Women cannot now, any more than they could when oppressed, ignore that part of morality and those forms of trust which cannot easily be forced into the liberal and particularly the contractarian mold. Men may but women cannot see that morality as essentially a matter of keeping to the minimal moral traffic rules, designed to restrict close encounters between autonomous persons to self-chosen ones. (p. 249)

The current body of work in feminist ethics can be seen as dividing into two streams. One stream focuses on exposing and incriminating patriarchal male-dominated societal institutions and traditional value systems as instruments of bias used by men to subordinate women. The other stream directs interests toward the examination of women as moral agents. Unifying these two streams is the underlying insight that women and men see things differently and, according to Gilligan (1982), this difference is gender related. This is especially true when the view is of human relationships and moral development. Gilligan (1988) maintained that there are two distinct modes of moral judgment—justice and care. Both are gender related and, according to Gilligan, are also related to modes of self-definition. A principal proposition of feminist ethics is that men tend to see human relationships and problems of moral behavior in terms of justice. Justice requires a solution be found that allows for the resolution of differences in an equitable manner. Women, on the other hand, tend to see human relationships and related problems in terms of care. Care is the need to protect others from hurt or harm regardless of the formal equity involved. According to Gilligan (1982),

> The moral imperative that emerges repeatedly in interviews with women is an injunction to care, a responsibility to discern and alleviate the real and recognizable trouble of this world. For men, the moral imperative appears rather as an injunction to protect the rights of others and thus to protect from interference the rights to life and self-fulfillment. Women's insistence on care is at first self-critical rather than self-protective, while men initially conceive obligation to others negatively in terms of non-interference. (p. 100)

The justice-oriented thinker conceives relationships in terms of equality. Moral concerns focus on the problems of oppression or inequality, with the moral ideal involving reciprocity and mutual respect. To the care-oriented thinker, relationship paradigms are organized in terms of connectedness. Moral concerns focus on the problems of detachment and abandonment. The moral ideal is one of attention and responsiveness. Gilligan makes a case for female moral reasoning based on relationships rather than individuality, attachment rather than autonomy, and the injunction to care versus the injunction to restore the rights of others.

# MORAL SENTIMENTS

Most of the approaches to ethics and morality covered in previous chapters have not been compatible with feminist views. For example, Kant's moral rationalism stresses abstract rules and a view that moral worth is attached to an act; that product is the result of duty as dictated by reason. Actions dictated by care, love, and compassion, while praiseworthy, are viewed as morally irrelevant. Kant was reacting against and seeking to correct Hume's substantial arguments against rationalism and for sentiment. Baier (1985) notes that Hume's nonprinciple-based ethical theory of sentiment and morality provides a foundation that can accommodate feminists' insights.

A summary of Hume's moral theory may be gleaned from the following:

> Take any action allowed to be vicious: willful murder, for instance. Examine it in all its lights, and you will see if you can find that matter of fact, or real existence which you call vice. . . . You never can find it, until you turn your attention into your own breast, and find a sentiment of disapprobation, which arises in you, towards this action. Here is a matter of fact, but it is the object of feeling, not of reason. It lies in your self, not in the object. So that when you pronounce any action or character to be vicious, you mean nothing, but that from the constitution of your nature you have a feeling or sentiment of blame from the contemplation of it. (Hume, 1739/1956, p. 177)

From the above summary, one can see that Hume viewed individuals as being psychologically constituted to attribute a moral quality to external actions in concert with their feelings of approval or disapproval. Hume considered the individual's feelings of approval and disapproval to be more than idiosyncratic responses. He thought that people in general have the same psychological makeup and therefore their moral responses for the most part are comparable. He did not say that everyone will agree on the moral value of a given act; rather, he said that if everyone is given the same information, they will tend to respond similarly. Additionally, Hume, observing individual moral assessments, concluded that socially useful actions are generally approved of while actions that are socially detrimental find disapproval. He concluded that an individual's acts are generally judged by their social contribution and conformity, rather than by immediate personal gratification, indicating that impartiality prevails when making moral judgments. Underlying Hume's argument is the idea (observation) that ethical disagreements do not originate from our passionate nature but rather from misunderstandings about the actual circumstances accruing from the act. Individual morality, according to Hume, is based on sentiments having their bases in social contribution or concern for others. These sentiments, Hume observed, are natural and universally shared and serve as the basis for our shared moral views.

Feminists remind us of the important role of moral sentiments and relationships in ethics. Gilligan (1982) suggested that moral behavior focuses more on responsibilities within context, often within the context of special relationships, opposing Kohlberg's (1984) contention that moral behavior emanates from the construct of justice. Kitchener (1984) acknowledged that a care perspective emphasizes the importance of virtue rather than justice in moral life. Nell Noddings (1984) wrote

> One of the saddest features of this picture of violence [in the world today] is that the deeds are so often done in the name of principle. . . . This approach through law and principle is not, I suggest, the approach of the mother. It is the approach of the detached one, of the other. The view to be expressed here is the feminist view. . . . It is feminine in the deep classical sense—rooted in receptivity, relatedness and responsiveness. (pp. 1–2)

Noddings succinctly exposes what is problematic about the detachment involved in the abstract deductive reasoning approach to ethics. Moral sentiments, it appears, allow for more flexibility in moral decision making but do not, as Hume noted, allow for relatively whimsical individual or societal decisions.

## VIRTUES: COMPASSION, FRIENDSHIP, AND LOVE

Humean ethical theory appears compatible with feminists' views, but it may not be the only natural ally. Virtue ethics may also to some degree be seen as compatible with the feminist view. Just as there are different versions of feminist ethics, there are different versions of virtue ethics, and the compatibility seen here is general. The virtue described in the feminist ethic is one of caring, which is built up in relations; one reaching out to the other and growing in response to the other. Solomon (1993) suggested that an admirable person would be a passionate person who possesses the virtue of caring concern. Using Hume, Rousseau, and Aristotle as his philosophical base, Solomon finds agreement with the feminist perspective that moral sentiments (virtues) and intimate relationships have a pivotal role in ethical behavior. Acknowledging the philosophical agreement that sentiments are unlearned and exist for everyone, Solomon concedes they can be destroyed by the wrong upbringing, or, as Rousseau states, by the corruption of competitive society. The following is taken from Solomon's discussion on the connectedness of the feminist perspective and the moral sentiments or virtues of compassion, friendship, and love.

> The sentiment or virtue of compassion literally means to feel with and is the most basic of our social feelings. It is seen as the basis from which moral behavior is spawned and is the mortar that cements the bricks of emotional attachment together that make up society and ultimately humanity. Compassion as an emotion can spur us to act spontaneously without thought for ourselves. The point of compassion is always another person's interest or well-being as opposed to our own. The point here is that spontaneous behavior is not always selfish; it is capable of being

concerned with another's well-being and is an aspect of morality and not merely a personal impulse. (p. 133)

Friendship, as sentiment or virtue, is also seen as essential to ethics and behavior. The origin of friendship, according to Aristotle (trans. 1987), lies in our relation to ourselves. As social beings we live in families and communities not because we have to but rather because we want to. Aristotle viewed friendship as being a basic law of human nature and an innate and indispensable component of both virtue and happiness. Friendship is also seen as a variety of love. Love is a specialized form of friendship, often limited to one individual as exemplified in the social institution of marriage or in a parent's love for her or his child or family; however, love may also be viewed as universal applying to everyone everywhere. A variety of this type of love is called *agape,* which in Christian theology means spontaneous altruistic love that applies to everyone everywhere, without discrimination.

Love and friendship do have their limits, as does compassion. Solomon (1993) points out that it is almost impossible not to feel compassion for those who suffer on our doorstep, but our reaction to those whose suffering is on the other side of the world is seldom as acute. When we are dealing with others whom we do not know or do not like or whose numbers we find overwhelming, it is clear that we may need some guide beyond our sentiment. Aristotle (trans. 1987), identifying where friendship and compassion end, addressed the need for justice, a key virtue and an essential ingredient in morality. Solomon (1993) identifies Hume as also arguing for the importance of what he called an artificial, calculated virtue—justice. Justice according to Hume, one could argue, is the natural sentiments of care and concern for others extended from the sphere of personal relationships to the greater sphere of society and humanity as a whole.

Anderson (1990) wrote of the dilemma facing feminist theorists,

> Feminist theory appears to be caught between the seemingly mutually exclusive and exhaustive alternatives of seeking equality with men, on the one hand, and seeking respect and space for difference from men, on the other. Each alternative poses its own characteristic difficulties. . . . In practice, the equality view calls upon women to be more like men . . . [while] the difference perspective . . . encourages women to opt out of activities that challenge men's domination. (pp. 1792–1793)

Baier (1985) accepted the philosophical challenge of Gilligan's seminal work, *In a Different Voice,* in which she describes what is distinctive about the moral attitudes and the moral development of women. In response, she undertook the task of constructing a proper comprehensive theory. In the light of Gilligan's work and the historical development of ethical theory, Baier concluded that a proper theory

> . . . must accommodate both the insights men have easier than women, and those women have more easily than men. It should swallow its predecessor theories. Women moral theorists, if any, will have this very great

advantage . . . they can stand on the shoulders of the men theorists. . . . So women theorists will need to connect their ethics of love with what has been the men theorists' preoccupation, namely obligation. (p. 56)

## BAIER: TRUSTING IN TRUST

Responding to the quest for a proper theory, Baier (1985) developed the concept of "appropriate trust in trust" which is to mediate between and supplement the moral insights of women and men. Central to this concept is the acknowledgment that trust relationships permeate human life, and awareness of them is a basic source of moral principles. Baier notes that our natural response to this concept is twofold. First, we recognize that some trusts are moral and others are immoral; second, we feel obligated to trust those that are moral and to distrust those that are immoral. Baier's stated goal was "to show or begin to show how [the appropriate trust in trust] would include obligation, indeed shed light on obligations and shed light on their justification, as well as love . . ." (p. 57).

Entering into a trust relationship, according to Baier (1986), requires reliance on others—specifically, reliance on others' competence and willingness to look after and not harm those things that are entrusted to their care. This reliance, Baier acknowledges, is true for immoral as well as moral relationships. She notes that to be effective in a crime spree, a pair of criminals requires, among other things, a mutual climate of trust between them. The same climate of trust is required of a pair of police officers working together to apprehend the criminals.

Baier's thesis includes the idea that many trust relationships are asymmetrical rather than symmetrical in the area of responsibility borne by each participant. The trust relationship binding a counselor or therapist and client is also asymmetrical. Both participants mutually trust; however, the relationship is seen as asymmetrical when the consequences resulting from a violation of trust are weighed. The nonjudicious or exploitive use of power by the counselor in the relationship is potentially more detrimental to the client than to the counselor. Though the counselor could lose the license to practice, the client emotionally stands to lose much more. Therefore, the counselor is seen as having more power to affect the well-being of the client, and that power translates into a greater burden of responsibility.

Baier continues this line of logic, adding that modern moral philosophy has concentrated on reason-guided (contractarian) moral symmetrical relationships. These are relationships between those who are deemed to be roughly equal in power. These near-equals attempt to determine the rules and to instigate sanctions against those who break the rules. The main form of trust receiving attention has been the trust in governments and in parties to voluntary agreements to do what they have agreed to do (Baier, 1986). Baier acknowledges that historically the focus on symmetrical trust relationships was responsive to the repressive asymmetrical relationships (e.g., master to slave) that had long prevailed. However, she regards this focus on willfully accepted reason-guided symmetrical trusts as ignoring primal moral trusts that are asymmetrical in form and which women are more aware of than men.

Given the premise that trust relationships permeate life, human beings can prosper only where there is a climate of trust. Without trust, what is important to one would be unsafe and might not prosper. To this must be added the idea that not all things that matter and prosper in a climate of trust should be encouraged to do so. As noted earlier, there are immoral as well as moral trust relationships; exploitation as much as justice flourishes better in a climate of trust. Given this, it is expedient to be able to tell when morality requires the preservation of trust and when it requires the dissolution of trust. This cannot be done without the ability to distinguish different forms of trust, and to observe for some morally relevant features they may possess. This is the theoretical task on which Baier embarks.

The general topic of the morality of trust relationships has, according to Baier, been conspicuously absent in discourse on moral philosophy. The questions of whom to trust, in what way, and why have not been important. If, however, trust permeates life and morality requires trust to prosper, it seems obvious that moral philosophers should look into it. They must determine what forms of trust are needed for the version of morality we endorse to thrive (Baier, 1986). Then they must determine how to judge trust relationships from a moral point of view. Historically, traditional moral philosophy has been interested in cooperation between people, but from a formal contractarian reason-oriented perspective rather than from a moral theory of trust. This difference appears to underscore the moral insight into trust that women are more open to than men and that Baier attempts to begin to flesh out.

What is the difference between trusting others and merely relying on them? Relying on others is not the same as trusting them. The acceptance of another as reliable depends on the assessment of that person's attitudes, habits, motives incompatible with ill will, and other factors (e.g., anger, deceit). An example might be relying on the butcher's concern for her profits to motivate her to take proper precautions against selling tainted meats. At the same time, we might also trust her to want her customers not to be harmed by her products. Trust and reliance are often mixed. When one decides to trust another, one depends on the other's good will toward them. In other words, when one trusts, one is vulnerable to the limits of the other's good will. In allowing the vulnerability incurred by depending on another's good will, one also displays confidence that the advantage will not be used for harm. The first prerequisite of trust is accepted vulnerability to another's possible, but not anticipated, lack of good will (Baier, 1986).

Relationships are a necessary part of human existence; therefore, others whom one trusts will have certain discretionary power in various circumstances and will (we trust) use it wisely. Many, possibly most, trust relationships according to Baier's thesis are asymmetrical rather than symmetrical in terms of the responsibility borne by the participants. Trust, then, can be seen as embedded in the connectedness of the human condition, defined here as mutuality and caring, rather than control.

## PRINCIPLE OR PERSON

Noddings (1984) wrote "whatever I do in life, whomever I meet, I am first and always the one-caring or one cared-for. I do not assume roles unless I become an actor . . . when ever encounter occurs, I must meet the other as one-caring" (pp. 176–177). The emphasis here is on caring and doing no harm as opposed to acting for the sake of a principle, justice. The individual (and her/his well being) is always considered to be the end and never the means. Martin Buber's (1923/1970) existential encounter of the I and Thou fits well into this concept of caring. Buber acknowledged the paradox inherent in every relationship— one party remains herself even as she draws close to the other. In genuine relationships, one accepts and affirms others in their personhood. Noddings (1984) speaks of the caring-one as the I and the cared-for as the Thou. The Thou is a subject, and not an It, an object of analysis.

As part of the human condition, we want to care for and be cared for. Noddings acknowledges that there are situations in which one cares quite naturally and in those encounters no ethical effort is required. She notes in these cases that the concepts of I want to do and what I and/or others judge I ought to do are indistinguishable. While conceding that one cannot conjure up the feeling response or inner voice that says "I must do something" in response to the need of another, she asks if there is also an obligation to care. She believes that though there exists no demand requirement on an emotion related to caring, we consider those totally devoid of empathy or care to be beyond the realm of normalcy, and to be avoided. Noddings says that we cannot require but can accept the natural impulse to act on behalf of another, as this is part of the human condition. While acknowledging the feeling and associated impulse to act, we have a choice; and that is to accept what is felt and act or to reject it and not act. Caring requires action in that one commits either to act or to thought about action taken on behalf of the other in need.

Noddings suggests that acknowledgment that the I must, should, or ought do something, arises directly and prior to considering exactly what it is I should do. When this "I must" is congruent with the "I want," the caring response is natural and proceeds easily out of desire. However, when conflicted, as when one cares for oneself but does not care naturally for the person in need, a second sentiment is required if a caring response is to ensue. This sentiment is the "I ought," that sentiment to which I have committed myself; what Noddings refers to as the moral imperative.

The sentiment I ought has its origin in natural caring where what I want to do and what I and others judge I ought to do are indistinguishable. Noddings gives the example, when my infant cries at night, I not only feel that I must do something but I want to do something. The I must is not a dutiful imperative, not yet a moral/ethical ought, but follows the I want and is based on love and caring. Taking care of one's child is first a natural act and from this connection it derives its morality. This premise serves to support Noddings' suggestion that our inclination toward and attention to that which is moral derives from caring. She believes the impulse to act on behalf of another in need is itself innate, and in caring, one accepts the natural impulse to act on behalf of the other. Again, one has a choice to accept what is felt or reject it. A strong desire toward morality precipitates acceptance and is derived from the innate desire to relate and remain related to others.

In situations where dislike, distrust, or similar ill feelings overshadow the I must the question arises, "Why should I act morally toward the object of my dislike?" (Recall Buber's existential concept of the I Thou and its relationship to caring.) Why should I not reject the faint and fleeting impulse to act on behalf of another and accept the other more intense ill feelings. The answer, according to Noddings, is that genuine moral sentiment (one's second sentiment, the I ought) arises from an evaluation of the caring relation as better than and superior to other forms of relatedness. In recognizing that one's choice will either increase or decrease the likelihood of genuine caring, there is a loud resounding ring of the I ought. It is here that the I must becomes a dutiful moral imperative. It is the value one places on the relatedness of caring that is the source of obligation.

After the decision has been made about one's obligation to do something, what exactly is it that one should do? To this point it appears that the obligation is to maintenance of the caring relation. Paradoxically, the ethic of caring imposes a limit on our obligation. Noddings (1984) explains that one's obligation is limited and delimited by relation. We are never free to abandon our preparedness to care for others; but pragmatically, our obligation is limited by our ability to adequately care for those in closest proximity and formal relation to us. We cannot possibly care for everyone. So what shall one say is the rule regarding obligations? According to Noddings, there are two rules. The first has to do with the existence of or potential for present relations. When one encounters in relation another who has imparted to us a need and has the capacity or is capable of receiving that which is given (caring), then here the obligation is absolute. Therefore, when one is in relation or when one is called upon by another with the potential for relation, we must respond. The imperative, according to Noddings, is categorical. The second rule involves the dynamic potential for growth in relations. Here it is the nature of potential relations and the capacity or capability of the other to receive that which is given and to respond that is scrutinized. If the relation has the potential for growth with respect to reciprocity (responsiveness from the cared for), then so does the potential degree of obligation. Noddings points out that it is the second rule that helps in distinguishing one's obligation to the nonhuman animal world and the human fetus. Also, she reminds us that relation itself is fundamental in obligation and that the second rule binds us in proportion to the probability of increased response and to the imminence of that response.

The next question Noddings addresses is how we are to make judgments of right and wrong under this ethic. Cautiously, she notes that the task is not primarily to judge; but rather, to heighten moral sensitivity and perception. While not ignoring the principles and rules associated with judgments of right and wrong, the focus is to consider them in the light of caring.

Take as an example the rule that stealing is wrong. Rather than simply applying some principle associated with stealing being wrong, under this ethic one must ask why is it or may it be wrong in this case to steal? Because no rule is immutable or without exception, setting up such a principle or rule also implies there are exceptions, but fails to succinctly state them. In this case, it might also be too easy to act on authorized exceptions once one determines what they are. Under this ethic one must consider the act in its full context before any decision regarding the morality or rightness of the act can be determined. Noddings' view is that the world may not depend on us to obey its rules or fulfill its wishes; however, the ones that we encounter may depend on us to meet them as one-caring.

The why of an act refers to the justification or motivation for the act. When the why refers to motivation, the one-caring acts on behalf of the other as one would for oneself. Motivation is not simply obeying a given rule because of fear of punishment for not obeying it. Instead, its origin is the self-ideal fashioned out of the memory of caring and being cared for. For an ethic of caring there is no justification, rather there is obligation. The obligation, Noddings says, is to do what is required to maintain and enhance caring.

Deciding what action is morally correct in a given situation is approached differently by men and women. Feminists view men as placing emphasis on moral judgments, needing to derive justifications from abstract reasoning, and then applying the logically correct solution to concrete situations. Women, on the other hand, approach moral dilemmas not as intellectual problems in need of logic-based abstract reasoning for solutions, but as real-life human encounters whose resolution lies in living relationships. This approach is based in caring. Carol Gilligan (1979) wrote of this difference between men and women.

> . . . women not only define themselves in a context of human relationship but also judge themselves in their ability to care. Woman's place in a man's life cycle has been that of nurturer, caretaker, and helpmate, the weaver of those networks of relationship on which she in turn relies. (p. 440)

This difference in relationship to an ethic of caring does not exclude men; nor, as has been noted, does it speak for all women. There is, according to Chadrow (1978), however, support to be gleaned from a developmental perspective that women may be more naturally disposed than men to relation and caring. A girl can identify with the mother, the one caring for her, and maintain relation while establishing identity. A boy, however, identifies with his father, the one more often absent, and consequently disengages himself from the intimate relation of caring.

An ethic of caring requires a natural sentiment of caring having its origin in the mother–child relationship. However, the ethic is pragmatic and tough. Caring is, as we have seen, both self-serving and other-serving. As such, if caring is to be maintained there must be care for the caregiver. The obligation again is to the maintenance of the caring relation and the caregiver is the primary mechanism of action on which everything depends.

## SUMMARY

Carol Gilligan's (1982) book, *In A Different Voice,* exposed the fact that men and women think very differently about ethics and the related process of moral decision making. Men think in terms of justice, women in terms of care. Annette Baier, after reading Gilligan's work, undertook the task of constructing or beginning to construct a comprehensive theory and developed the concept of appropriate trust in trust. Nell Noddings described the essence of the I, Thou relationship as first and always identifying oneself with the caring one or one cared for. The one that we encounter may depend on us to meet them as one-caring.

## QUESTIONS FOR ADDITIONAL
## REFLECTION AND THOUGHT

1. What are the basic differences that you see in the way women and men view morality?

2. Is there a basic gender-based difference with respect to morality?

3. Reflecting on this chapter, answer this question regarding altruism: Can human beings act genuinely for the benefit of each other?

4. Consideration of trust and trustworthiness requires attention to a multiplicity of perspectives. Discuss from the viewpoint of trusted party the trusting one's need for attention, concern, fairness, and honesty.

5. Is there a difference between trusting and merely relying on someone? Explain your answer.

6. Trust is naive if not well-founded. Under what conditions is a trust relationship morally sound? Under what conditions is a trust relationship morally unsound?

7. Traditional approaches to ethics have been male dominated and have not included the female perspective. Have feminist ethicists made a similar error, or can males also be accounted for in this approach?

8. What similarity, if any, do you see between feminist ethics and virtue ethics?

## USING THEORY FOR CONCRETE
## ETHICAL JUDGMENTS

### Ethical Dilemma

You are a high school counselor working primarily with juniors and seniors. A student you recognize from previous work together asks to see you. You remember him as a good student active in various sports and academic and social clubs. During your meeting, he announces to you that he is gay and has recently become sexually active. He is now concerned because an older male with whom he has had sexual contact has been identified as having AIDS. This older male no longer resides in the area and your student heard about the supposed diagnosis through the rumor mill. He has been unable to contact this person with whom he had sexual contact and cannot verify or deny the rumor. He says he has been sexually active only infrequently since the encounter, and then only with two people. Since hearing the rumor, he has had no further sexual contacts, but he has not told his partners that he may have been exposed to AIDS. He verbalizes to you his ambivalence about being tested for HIV and also the fact that he may have to tell his parents he is gay. He has continued to be active in contact sports as well as other activities and is again unsure of what to do or how to do it. After talking to you, he says he feels somewhat relieved, though no less ambivalent, and says he knows you will keep this information confidential.

## The Problem

The information you have could have serious medical implications, not only for your client, but for others as well. You do not know if the rumor is true, or if your student is carrying HIV. Some action may be warranted, but what?

## A Case for Feminist Ethics

Feminist ethics sees caring as the moral imperative. Neither law nor principle is the overseer of morality. Moral behavior is established as the result of responsibility recognized within the context of special caring relationships. The world does not depend upon us obeying its rules; however, the one we encounter does depends upon us to meet them as one-caring.

## The Decision-Making Process

When there is information disclosed in a counseling session that may (or may not) involve potential harm to others, what action is required on the part of the counselor? What about the lack of certainty and the questions of privacy and confidentiality? Is there a duty to warn? What about your client? Feminist ethicists view ethical dilemmas not as dichotomous, black or white, but rather as a spectrum of gray having the potential for multiple responses and solutions. The current dilemma involves the person, the relationship, trust, and trustworthiness. You must first determine what your obligation is to this client. This is done by examining the relationship or potential for a relationship. You must ascertain whether or not the client who expresses to you a need has the capability of receiving what it is you have to offer. This involves evaluating your client on various factors (e.g., age, psychological status, level of maturity, family, and social situations). The next question addresses the growth potential for the relationship. You must ask yourself if there is receptivity on the part of the client for what counseling has to offer. The final task involves heightening your moral perception of and sensitivity to this dilemma. Your motivation to act has its origins in acting on behalf of the client as you would act for yourself. In dialogue with your client, as well as yourself, a question to be asked is, "What reasons does your client have for confident reliance on you and you on him?" Mutual reliance requires knowledge of the conditions for the reliance. This means acknowledging on your part that you, the counselor, have discretionary power and will not use it for harm. Contemplate the various options open to you and your client that move the dilemma toward resolution without harming either your client or any other parties.

# 11

✳

# The New Casuistry

The terms "ethics" and "morals" are frequently used interchangeably in the vernacular despite their different foci. Ethics has been variously defined as the study of morality (Holmes, 1993), attempts to identify and discuss theories of morality, or as a systematic explanation for human conduct. A common misconception is that ethics demands adherence to a particular code of rules or subscription to a set of principles essential to moral understanding. By contrast, morals generally reference actions or activities for which a certain kind of praise or blame is awarded. We all make judgments of good or bad in a multitude of daily activities, illustrating the recursion (often unconscious) between thought (ethics) processes and choice of action (morality).

Among approaches to differentiating bad from good are utilitarian and deontological theories. Each posits a fundamental test of moral rightness, but they differ in their focus. Utilitarians, also known as consequentialists, judge moral good in terms of value outcomes; deontologists judge moral good according to fidelity to one's duties to others, both positive (thou shalt) and negative (thou shalt not). Because no perfect system for decision making in any enterprise exists, employment of one or the other of these principle-driven approaches is usually elected. Regardless of which theory is embraced, Francouer (1983) asserted that six basic principles combine in a foundation for medical codes of ethics, and that these principles are applicable to other areas of human endeavor as well. Beauchamp and Childress (1983) enumerated the six principles as follows: autonomy, veracity, nonmaleficence, beneficence, confidentiality, and justice. The authors propose that a four-level hierarchy for ethical thought includes

**127**

ethical theories or systems, principles, rules, and individual judgments. Each level is analyzed with reference to the levels above in the analytical process. Ethical dilemmas within any system are created when moral principles can be cited for both opposing actions with neither side presenting the obvious, right course to follow. Thus, principle-driven decision making designed to facilitate deliberation and justification of decisions has its limitations irrespective of theoretical basis.

Casuistry presents an alternative system for making ethical decisions. Principles in this approach are neither discarded nor ignored; they serve as general statements describing human behavior, out of which come "'paradigm cases' illustrating the most manifest breaches of the general principle" (Jonsen & Toulmin, 1988) for the casuist. Scrutinization of a series of cases from the simplest to the most complex is undertaken to resolve the doubt inherent in ethical dilemmas. Reasonable expectations are discovered in subsequent cases, driving the search until resolution is reached. The casuist sets out to join unique individual cases with general principles without discounting the validity of either, all the while determining how exactly to act in a particular situation (case).

There exist, according to Jonsen and Toulmin (1988), two distinct approaches in dealing with moral ethical dilemmas. One, the theoretical, is concerned with principles, rules, and other general ideas positing universal rules (axioms) from which particular moral/ethical judgments are deduced. The second, more practical, focuses on the specific features of the particular kinds of moral cases with moral rules serving as maxims which can be understood only in terms of the paradigmatic cases that define their meaning and force (p. 1).

## THEORETICAL ARGUMENTS

Theoretical arguments are not dependent on the circumstances of their presentation. The argument is a chain of propositions, linked together in such a way as to guarantee its conclusion. Their validity is not affected by the practical context of their use. Conclusions are deduced from initial axioms or universal principles. These truths flow downward to provide resolution for questions at hand.

### The universal starting point . . .

universal major premises
taken as known for the purpose
of the present argument

particular minor
premises specifying
the present instance

so, necessarily conclusions
about the present instance

### . . . underpins the particular end point

(Jonsen & Toulmin, 1988, p. 34)

## PRACTICAL ARGUMENTS

Practical arguments draw on the outcomes of previous experience, carrying over procedures used to resolve earlier problems and reapplying them in new problematic situations. Their validity depends on how closely the present situation resembles those of the earlier precedent cases for which this particular type of argument was originally devised. Truths are passed sideways, to provide resolution for new problems.

### The outcome of experience . . .

general warrant based
on similar precedents

present fact situation                                          provisional conclusion
(particulars of the case)                                   about the present case
                                                                              (presumably so)

absent exceptional
circumstances
(rebuttals)

### . . . serving to guide future action

(Jonsen & Toulmin, 1988, p. 35)

Real-life problems are often quick to show the limitations of many theoretical as well as practical approaches. Real situations are often more complex than typical examples reveal. In looking for solutions to real-life problems, certainly one would agree that an absolutist approach is too rigid and a relativist approach is overly flexible. However, the rigidity of the absolutist as well as the overflexibility of the relativist are grounded in the individual's belief about the situation. Belief is an absolute necessity for practical existence, as well as for problem solving. The logical inquiry that follows is, "What differentiates the belief of rational thinkers from irrational thinkers?" The answer lies not in the presence or absence of belief, but in the grounds on which the belief is based. So what are legitimate sources of belief? In the arena of scientific investigation, the source is evidence or investigation. Accepting the fact that there are beliefs that cannot be investigated or proven by evidence, we will proceed to view some theoretical and practical approaches to the question of beliefs.

## INDUCTION

Induction is the process by which one generalizes from particulars; this involves the assumption that particular events in the future will be similar to those encountered in the past. At the same time, one allows for the possibility of exceptions and even the possibility of changing circumstances that may invalidate the whole generalization. Inductive generalizations are accepted as probable rather than as certain truth. However, the propositions of science often seem to be not merely probable, but in some cases, absolutely certain. This certainty is based on laws or principles that have been found to be immutable. Who would question the boiling point of water? At what altitude, you ask? For practical purposes, statements (scientific as well as ethical) possess only a degree (more or less) of probability, and not absolute certainty.

Induction is generalization from evidence. The main question here is whether or not the evidence is authentic and in sufficient quantity or quality to warrant generalization. Evidence is amassed through observations that are either casual or systematic. Having been pleased with the work performed at a local garage, one infers that future work will be satisfactory. This is a causal or commonsense inference.

Scientific inferences differ from commonsense inferences in that evidence is systematically collected through careful elaborate repeatable methods and tested. Here, observation is an art requiring demonstration that the evidence has been gathered in such a way as not to affect the outcome. From here, we move to the question of adequacy of evidence. Proving the adequacy of evidence is complicated. The question of adequacy varies according to the particular problem under study. Some situations might require only a single piece of evidence to establish generalizability. However, the more evidence that is available and included, the more sound in terms of probability the conclusions. Mere quantity, however, is not sufficient for acceptance of probable proof. It is of paramount importance to show that the evidence provided is typical and representative of the entire domain under study. From here we progress to analyzing the evidence. Evidence can be categorized as either descriptive or causal. Descriptive evidence is exactly that—descriptive; an accumulation of positive and negative instances that serve to paint a picture of a given circumstance. The differences that are described obviously mean something, but what? To answer requires analysis and interpretation. Induction may go beyond simple description to consider causal relationships. The term "cause" has some inherent problems, not the least that it is ambiguous, particularly when viewed in light of scientific probability and immutability. The fact that two phenomena constantly appear together does not necessarily indicate that one is the cause of the other. Complex phenomena may not be the result of any one single cause but may have arisen from a combination of factors.

Part of the art of induction lies in the accurate statement of conclusions, mainly in distinguishing between generalizations supposed to be universally true and those intended to be just generally true. It may be said that in the physical sciences, most generalizations are of the universal type; but in the social sciences, and certainly in everyday life, they are only generally true. The discovery of an exception has a markedly different outcome depending on the type. A universal generalization would be rejected by the discovery of a single exception, whereas one that is only generally true would continue to be accepted as long as it proved true more often than not.

# DEDUCTION

Deduction is a form of reasoning that puts ideas together to see what can be inferred from them without further investigation. Reasoning is from premise to conclusion, not from facts to generalizations. Reasoning is from a known principle to an unknown, from the general to the specific, or from a premise to a logical conclusion. This argument tries to establish the truth of a proposition, not by offering factual evidence, but rather by showing that it naturally follows from some other proposition whose truth supposedly has already been established. A deductive argument is valid if it conforms to the rules of deductive reasoning. If these rules are followed and if the premises are true, then the conclusions are true. An example may be taken from geometry. In geometry one begins with general statements. The two accepted statements must be such that one is a general statement which tells you that a certain set of conditions imply a certain conclusion. The other is a statement which tells you of a particular situation in which all the conditions specified in the general statement are met. When you accept a general statement and reason from it to a conclusion in a particular situation, you are reasoning deductively. The conclusions reached by deduction are regarded as being not merely probable, as in the conclusions of inductive reasoning, but certainly true, provided that the premises are true and that the rules have been followed. This, however, does not ensure that all valid deductive arguments arrive at the truth, because such arguments may be based on false premises.

The syllogism is a form of deductive argument that leads from two premises to a conclusion. The first premise can be viewed as the main premise (initial axioms or universal principles), and the second or minor premise as introducing a new idea or independent proposition specifying the present circumstance. A syllogism relates two things, situations, or circumstances to a conclusion in order to show their relationship to each other. The following are examples:

Some books are written in French.

This is a book.

Therefore, this book is written in French.

In the first example, "books" has become distributed between the premise and the conclusion. What was stated as being true about some books is now applied to a specific book. The point is that what applies to some books cannot be generalized to all books; therefore, this particular book may or may not be written in French.

All people who cause pain to others are wicked.

Surgeons are people who cause pain to others.

Therefore, surgeons are wicked.

The second example is formally correct but logically absurd. This is because the main premise is inexact. All people is inexact in that it includes classes of people who cause pain to bring about good or benefits to those they treat.

Quinine is good for a fever.

This medicine is quinine.

Therefore, this medicine is good for a fever.

The third example shows the possibility of a correct conclusion being arrived at despite the fact that the minor premise is false (if in this case the medicine is not really quinine, but is still good for a fever).

The analogy is a combination of the inductive and deductive processes. In analogy, reasoning is from parallel cases; that is, because two things are known to be alike in certain respects, they will be alike in other respects. The inference is that certain admitted resemblances imply probable further similarities. An example of this logic can be seen in the current political debate over a balanced budget. The analogy goes something like this: Logically, we know that all budgets must be made to balance; the nation's budget, though large, is still a budget; therefore, the national budget must be made to balance. Taking one member of a class, household budgets, one can conclude inductively that budgets must be balanced. Furthermore, using this conclusion as a premise, one can reason deductively that our nation's budget must be balanced. (The weaknesses of both arguments are acknowledged.) Often, however, the function of an analogy is merely explanatory rather than argumentative.

## PRACTICAL WISDOM

In applying principles to the process of moral/ethical decision making, we must ask "What kind of understanding of human conduct does ethics provide?" Aristotle (1987) declared ethics is not and could not be a science; therefore, it cannot provide universal principles for particular judgments. Rather, ethics is a practical field that calls for practical wisdom. Practical wisdom, according to Aristotle, was the joining of wisdom with prudence. Wisdom has to do with scientific knowledge and prudence has to do with knowledge applied to particular cases derived from experience. Aristotle, in *The Nicomachean Ethics,* argues

> . . . why is it that a boy can become a mathematician but not a philosopher and the answer is probably that mathematics is an abstract science, but the first principles of philosophy are derived from experience, and thus the young do not believe, although they may repeat philosophical truths, but they easily comprehend the meaning of mathematical truths (pp. 198–199).

Jonsen and Toulmin (1988) note that in practical fields we grasp particular facts of experience more clearly, and have more certainty of their truth, than we ever do about the general principles that we may use to account for them.

This does not mean that discussions about moral/ethical theory are fruitless. What it does imply is that the movement from the theoretical to the practical is more than a matter of application.

# THE PRINCIPLE OF DOUBLE EFFECT

With great frequency, moral dilemmas have prompted ethicists to turn to the principle of double effect. Beauchamp and Childress (1983) in *Principles of Biomedical Ethics* note

> Through a long history . . . the principle of double effect has long been invoked to support claims that an act having a harmful effect, such as death, does not always fall under moral prohibitions, such as murder, suicide, or abortion. The harmful effect is seen as an indirect, unintended, or merely foreseen effect, not as the direct and intended effect of the action. (p. 113)

The principle of double effect involves four conditions: Object of activity, intention, material cause, and proportionate reason. Object of activity means the action in itself must be good or at least morally indifferent. Intention requires the agent to intend only the good effect and not the evil effect. Material cause declares that the evil effect cannot be a means to the good effect and proportionate reason means there must be a favorable balance between the good and evil effects of the action. Cases are required to meet the conditions outlined. Conformity to the four conditions or principles legitimizes the action taken as a solution to the dilemma. While more generally appealing when obligations or values conflict, this approach has, according to Beauchamp and Childress, come under considerable attack.

One such attack comes from Kekes (1988), who argues that principles are not the guide of moral conduct. He explains that principles are an expression of currently accepted conduct and are revised so that they conform to prevailing social practices. The validity of the principle depends on the acceptance of the practice. Hence, principles result from dominant social practices: Practice is first and principles are derived from them.

Jonsen and Toulmin (1988) differentiate two methods for deliberating ethical issues. The first method approaches issues theoretically using principles and derived rules. Its arguments are universal and idealized and involve relating general ethical rules to specific moral cases in a theoretical manner that fits the principles to the cases. A syllogism is an example of this process and utilizes geometric logic. The other method uses practical reasoning and focuses on specific features of particular kinds of moral cases. It utilizes richly detailed methodological comparisons of likenesses and differences between related cases. Jonsen and Toulmin state that the application of principles to cases (i.e., principle of double effect) is geometric, while the second approach stresses experience gathered from a variety of similar cases as a guide for action and is casuistic.

Keenan (1993), using the work of Jonsen and Tomlin as his base, questioned whether or not the principle of double effect has a justifying function. He argued that when the principle of double effect is invoked to see whether or not a case and the proposed solution conform to the four stipulated conditions, to that extent it is being used geometrically. He further argued that applying principles to cases in a geometric fashion vests the principle with unwarranted authority which provides justification for the action taken.

Experience, it has been said, is the best teacher. One can always apply the results of previous ethical quests to novel problems; however, one solution or set of solutions will not fit all future problems. Aristotle (trans. 1987) reminds us that ethics is not a science and as a theory does not easily provide a sure method of application. Toulmin (1981), citing Aristotle and Dewey, argues that the pursuit of rigorous theory is detached from the substance of moral life and animated by a deceptive search for immutable truths.

# CASUISTRY:
## A CASE APPROACH TO ETHICS

In genuinely marginal cases, all that any arbitrator can do is take the detailed circumstances of the dispute under advisement and then decide if, all in all, it is more equitable (i.e., fairer) to tilt the scale to one party rather than the other. The decision is one of equity rather than issues of law in the strict sense. Recalling Aristotle's concept of practical wisdom, it is acknowledged that such rulings do not require one to merely apply general legal rules, since in truly marginal cases the available rules are not decisive. Rather, it relies on the exercise of judicial discrimination in assessing the delicate balance of facts at issue in a particular case.

Casuistry is defined in the Oxford English Dictionary as that part of ethics which resolves cases of conscience, applying the general rules of religion and morality to particular instances in which circumstances alter cases or in which there appears to be a conflict of duties. Jonsen and Toulmin (1988) offer a slightly more embellished definition of casuistry:

> The analysis of moral issues, using procedures of reasoning based on paradigms and analogies, leading to the formation of expert opinions about the existence and stringency of particular moral obligations, framed in terms of rules or maxims that are general but not universal or invariable, since they hold good with certainty only in the typical conditions of the agent and circumstances of action. (p. 257)

In advocating a casuistic approach, Jonsen and Toulmin state that one indispensable instrument for helping to resolve moral problems in practice is a methodological map detailing significant likenesses and differences, which they have called a moral taxonomy. This is opposed to theory-driven approaches that apply principles to cases. Casuistry is a case-driven method that derives moral knowledge developed progressively through the detailed analysis of concrete cases. These cases Jonsen and Toulmin call paradigm cases. These well-analyzed cases serve as objects of comparison or paradigms in dealing with novel and more perplexing cases. This practice, according to Jonsen and Toulmin, is consistent with good Aristotelian reasoning and gives priority to concrete issues of practice rather than to abstract matters of theory.

# PRINCIPLES AND THEIR
# ROLE IN CASUISTRY

Theory-driven approaches to ethics appeal to a particular philosophical theory judged to be the most comprehensive, and from this principles are developed. These principles are then to be applied to real-life situations as a guide to resolving moral dilemmas. This approach posits the existence of objective, universal principles that ought to govern moral behavior (Beauchamp & Childress, 1979). This process has ultimately led to the acknowledgment and acceptance of a small cluster of axiomatic values or principles: autonomy, beneficence, nonmalificence, and justice. Moral judgments can now be made by appealing to these governing principles. The orientation is from the top down, applying the principles to the situational aspects of particular cases. The appeal of principled ethics is the principle itself, which aligns ethics more with objectivity and science.

Jonsen and Toulmin (1988) expose a tendency of many to think of ethical principles or moral rules as though they were exhaustive of ethics. All that is required is commitment to some principle or code of rules, which can be accepted as authoritative. Principles, however, require definitions; the definitions require interpretation, and more often than not, principles require some type of rank ordering as the case contains more than one principle that is in question. The reality is that situations involving moral conflicts are often too complex to avoid the additional reality that principles can and do conflict with one another. In this situation, one might appeal to a higher-level principle derived from a higher-level theory (Clouser & Bernard, 1990). However, even here the same problem may arise, resulting in a similar dilemma. The implication is fairly clear: The application of principles derived directly from theory is limited in its pragmatic application to the resolution of real-life moral dilemmas.

The application of principles to cases does make good sense; however, the question of where principles are a priori or post hoc must be addressed. Aristotle (trans. 1987), addressing morality, has argued for practical wisdom that requires experience with particulars. Contrary to principled or theory-driven methodologies that approach moral dilemmas with established principles ready to be applied, the new casuistry operationalizes ethics as case driven (Jonsen & Toulmin, 1988; Strong, 1988; Arras, 1991). Case driven means that ethical principles are discovered through the cases themselves. Agreeing with Aristotle, casuists believe that moral knowledge (ethical principle) is embedded in the particulars of the situation (Jonsen and Toulmin, 1988). Clearly one can always learn from mistakes, as well as successes, that entail applying the results of previous ethical inquiries and experiences to novel problems.

This does not mean that casuistry is atheoretical and that cases simply speak for themselves. Strong (1988) argued that the revival of casuistry resulted from the failure of [principled] theoretical ethics to provide plausible remedies for particular ethical quandaries, rather than from a theoretical rejection of moral philosophy. Rather than throwing the baby out with the bathwater, Jonsen and Toulmin (1988) concede an indisputable role for principles and maxims drawn from a variety of sources including theology, common law, historical tradition, and ethical theories. Arras (1991) speaks of casuistry as a search engine of thought that receives its direction from values, concepts, and theories outside itself. The role of theory and principles in casuistry is to provide knowledge of general principles, values, and direction; the individual cases determine which of those values are present, what principles apply (in what order), and how they are affected by other considerations defining the particular set of circumstances. The integration of these considerations is accomplished through the systematic comparison of cases (Jonsen & Toulmin, 1988).

## PARADIGMS AND CASE COMPARISONS

According to Jonsen and Toulmin, bioethical principles are best learned by the casuistic case method of discovery. This logic holds true for other areas involving ethics and related principles. Jonsen (1990b) noted that casuistic reasoning is prudent reasoning that displays an appreciation of relationships. The method of case discovery proceeds through a series of steps (Strong, 1988), beginning with a typology or grouping of cases around a paradigm of a moral rule or principle, and involving concrete pedagogical implications (Arras, 1994). First, one must identify the principles that apply to the case and note the relevant duties or actions required. In doing this, a casuistic approach encourages the use of real rather than hypothetical cases. This is because the orientation of most hypothetical cases is designed to coincide with some theoretical point. Real cases, on the other hand, display more often than not a moral complexity and untidiness demanding a practical approach to judgments. Second, the potential course of action must be identified. This requires a lengthy detailed case study, for casuistry states that truth resides in details. The orientation is from the bottom to the top. Third and fourth, the case at hand is compared to other similar cases; for each possible course of action, one should identify a case in which the option in question is justifiable. These justifiable cases serve as paradigms and also give emphasis to what the case is actually about, what Arras refers to as the moral diagnosis. A casuistic pedagogy would encourage the use of multiple cases bearing on a related principle. Here interpretation is valued over simple illustration. Interpretation of a sequence of cases allows the process of reasoning by paradigm and analogy to be experienced firsthand. The process effectively shows how the principles of biomedical ethics are actually shaped by the details of successive cases and their relevant moral diagnosis.

The paradigm case is paramount to the application of the process of casuistry. In a given case, the action to be taken is clear and can be agreed upon by virtually all participants familiar with the details of the case. Jonsen (1991a) defines a paradigm case as

> . . . a case in which the circumstances were clear, the relevant maxim unambiguous, and the rebuttals weak, in the minds of almost all observers. The claim that this action is wrong (or right) is widely persuasive. There

is little need to present arguments for the rightness (or wrongness) of the case and it is very hard to argue against its rightness (or wrongness). (p. 301)

Once a set of paradigm cases is identified, new cases are juxtaposed and the paradigm similar to the new case in question is located. Possible courses of action are judged against the paradigm case. Decisions regarding courses of action are thus achieved by seeking agreement on the justified response to a particular case rather than by applying agreed-upon principles. Strong (1988, pp. 195–204) provides examples of mid-level principles (autonomy, beneficence, nonmalificence, and justice), conflicting in paradigm cases. He also illustrates how, through comparing problem cases with relevant paradigms, the paradigm closest to the problem case is identified along with the mid-level principle that should prevail in the resolution. Examples involve elucidation of the problem case through variable manipulation of the circumstances until two paradigms emerge. In the first, action is guided by beneficence to third parties; the other is guided by respect for autonomy.

The example cases involve the refusal of blood transfusion by Jehovah's Witness patients. In the first case, a 38-year-old mother of six gives birth to her seventh child and experiences complications. Her blood ceases clotting, creating the need for an emergency transfusion. History reveals that her husband is an unskilled laborer earning a modest income and the family receives welfare assistance. Should the patient die, the husband would be left to care for the seven children alone. The values in conflict are respect for the patient's autonomy and beneficence toward certain third parties, the children.

The first paradigm case involves a 39-year-old man admitted to the hospital for a bleeding ulcer. Treating physicians believe that death is imminent without transfusions. History reveals the patient is married and has three children ages 3, 6, and 7. He is an unskilled worker who earns a modest income, his wife has never worked, and there is no available support from extended family. A court order for treatment is sought and obtained, allowing the lifesaving transfusion.

The action taken, according to Strong, is supposedly justified by beneficence toward certain third parties. The expected harm (based on history) to the children, financially and emotionally, justifies overriding the patient's wishes (autonomy). However, the circumstances of this case can be manipulated to produce a paradigm in which autonomy outweighs beneficence.

In the second example, a 34-year-old man is admitted to the hospital with bleeding and internal injuries. The patient refuses necessary life-saving transfusions on religious grounds. History reveals that the patient is married and has two children. The family is financially secure, the patient owns a prosperous business, and support from family members is readily available should the patient's wife need help running the business. A court order for treatment was sought but not granted. In this case, Strong contends that the circumstances reflect insufficient harm resulting from the refusal of treatment and autonomy overrides beneficence.

In comparing the first case to each of the case paradigms, one can see that it is more like the first than the second. The degree of harm caused by allowing the mother to die seems robust enough to justify overriding autonomy on the basis of beneficence toward the children. The greater the degree of similarity to the paradigm, the more appropriate is similar action. For the purpose of example, only two paradigm cases were used, but in actual practice many more cases would be utilized with multiple comparisons being made.

Strong (1988) argues for the importance of paradigms as they define the proper use of mid-level principles, which he believes to be quintessential to morality. Jonsen and Toulmin (1988) take an opposing view, seeing mid-level principles as post hoc and less important than the particular actions themselves. Viewed either way, to the casuist there is agreement that there is no further justification in an absolute basis of morality. Mid-level principles are viewed by casuists through the glasses of human need, providing summaries of one's intuitive (prudent) responses to paradigm cases.

These extreme cases exemplify the complexity of situations encountered by today's practitioners. Using the concepts of casuistry, the facts from these contextually complex cases were logically and systematically organized, adding depth and meaning to the analysis.

## SUMMARY

Ethical dilemmas are seldom simple and often present conflicts involving moral obligations or duties. The casuistic approach is a case-driven approach that seeks out the principles unique to each case, given the individual circumstances. The analysis of moral issues is guided by reasoning based on paradigms and analogies. It has been described as a methodological map detailing significant likenesses and differences developed through progressive detailed analysis of concrete cases. These well-analyzed cases serve as paradigms used for comparison with novel or more complex cases. In practice, casuistry is a utility search engine that gives priority to concrete issues (of practice) rather than to abstract theory. However, casuistry is not an alternative to principles, but rather as Jonsen (1995) suggests, a complement. Ethical principles originate within the concrete details of the case itself and are ferreted out through the method of paradigm case comparisons and analogy, which is the casuistic method.

## ADDITIONAL QUESTIONS FOR
## REFLECTION AND THOUGHT

1. What purpose(s) do principles or rules have in morality? Where do they get their power?
2. Explain what is meant by the tyranny of principles.

3. In an earlier chapter it was said: Principles without virtues are blind and virtues without principles are impotent. Relate this statement to the practice of casuistry.

4. Describe a dialogue in which two sides butt absolute categorical rights against absolute categorical rights. Does this hard-line commitment to principles contribute to moral blindness? Why?

5. Jewish tradition has a story that a student once asked Rabbi Hillel if it were possible to recite the whole of the Law while standing on one leg. The Rabbi replied with the golden rule, "Do unto others as you would have them do unto you" and then said, "All the rest is commentary." His final statement to the student was, "Now go study the commentary." Explain how this fits casuistry.

6. How does casuistry differ from the principle of the double effect?

7. Historically, the casuistic method has been misused. Can you see any obvious characteristics that would lead to its potential misuse?

## USING THEORY FOR CONCRETE ETHICAL JUDGMENTS

### Ethical Dilemma

You are a popular high school counselor. Before becoming a counselor you were a teacher at this school, and the students nominated you for teacher of the year honors. Since becoming a counselor, your reputation has increased. The students feel that you are fair and that you listen to them and their concerns. You do not always agree, but you treat them with respect.

During the past few weeks, tension has been building at your school between the administration and the students over whether or not a controversial public debate should be allowed at the school. Several of the student leaders have come to talk with you about the situation. Though the students consider you to be technically one of "them," they trust you and seek your guidance. Personally, you side with the students; publicly, you have remained neutral.

Today one of the student leaders comes to you and relates that the students are planning a peaceful demonstration for tomorrow, which will disrupt classes. The purpose of this is to draw attention to this pressing issue, one the students feel the administration would rather ignore because of its political sensitivity. You personally think the students are right and the discussion/debate should be allowed; however, as a faculty member you find yourself torn on what action, if any, to take.

### The Problem

You have knowledge of a situation that will violate school policy. Should you inform the administration, or should you keep silent in support of the students?

## A Case for the Casuists

Casuistry posits that principles are embedded in the dilemma or case, and the first action is to identify the principles that apply to the dilemma. Second, a course of action is identified. Third, other similar situations are identified that contain similar principles. Fourth, the dilemma at hand is compared to the other cases, and the quest begins for similar situations in which the guiding principle(s) justify the option in question. Interpreting the sequences of cases allows the counselor to determine which one(s) most resemble the current dilemma and to arrive at an appropriate course of action.

## The Decision-Making Process

Personally, you feel the students are right. Professionally, you are an employee of the school and policy states you should notify the administration. The student has confided in you because of your previous understanding and support, and the belief that you would not release the plan. Only one of the student leaders revealed the plan to you, so if you do not inform the administration it is unlikely anyone will know that you knew of the plan and did not report it.

Addressing your dilemma, you note the principles of autonomy and nonmaleficence apply. In evaluating possible courses of action, you observe significant limitations due to the students' refusal to consider alternative courses of action. Your options are basically reduced to two—somehow tell the administration of the students' plan, or remain silent and allow the student demonstration to take place.

You now need similar cases or situations for comparison. Cases can be real life (preferable) or, in the absence of actual cases, hypothetical. Two hypothetical cases will be used for comparison. The first involved a faculty member's knowledge of a planned student demonstration. Students were deeply divided over the issue of affirmative action. The groups had been confrontational in the past, and on several occasions had engaged in violent clashes requiring police intervention. The faculty member notified the administration of the intended protest and security measures were taken to avert the protest and the likelihood of violence. The justification for the intervention rests on the principle of nonmaleficence, the principle that your action should do no harm, or that you ought to prevent harm to others. The faculty member was justified in intervening and preventing the students from demonstrating because considerable harm would reasonably be expected to occur as a result of the demonstration. The principle of nonmaleficence outweighs or supersedes the principle of autonomy in this case.

The second comparison case involved a faculty member's knowledge of a planned peaceful demonstration by students over administration policies students deemed unfair. There was no organized opposition to the demonstration, and student organizers planned a noisy but peaceful demonstration. No countermeasures were taken and the student demonstration took place as planned. Classes were disrupted by the noise, but no confrontations occurred. The student protest occurred as planned and students dispersed peacefully following the

two-hour demonstration. The faculty member was justified in her noninterven-
tion based on the lack of harm presented by the circumstances. The principle of
autonomy in this case supersedes or outweighs the principle of nonmaleficence.
These cases will serve as paradigm cases for purposes of comparison.

The final element is a comparison of the current dilemma with the paradigm cases. Attempt to determine which of the paradigm cases it is closer to in
terms of the morally relevant factors. Choice of a course of action is based on
this comparison. When the dilemma in question is closer to one paradigm case
than to others, the course of action justifiable in that paradigm case is also justifiable in the one at hand. Should the case dilemma under consideration fall
between two paradigms (in the gray), then more than one option would be
considered ethical. In this process you are not simply weighing the principle of
autonomy in general against nonmaleficence in general; you are assessing the
degree to which morally relevant factors are present in the current situation.

✳

# PART III

# Ethical and Legal Issues

That which is legal is not always ethical and that
which is ethical is not always legal

# 12

✳

# Ethics and the Law

## INFORMED CONSENT

**B**efore a person becomes a client, he or she must consent to treatment. Obtaining consent precedes any treatment and recordkeeping. In order to consent to treatment, the client must first be made aware of what he or she is agreeing to become a participant in. Minimally, the client should be made aware of the who, what, when, and how. The qualifications of the professional counselor who will be treating the client should be clearly acknowledged. The particular goals of counseling must be identified, as well as the risks and benefits associated with counseling. When results, if any, may be expected and how financial considerations are arranged should be specified.

A client's consent to treatment can occur only after certain requirements are met, defined as the elements of informed consent (Bray, Shepard, & Hays, 1985; Schwitzgebel & Schwitzgebel, 1980). The elements of informed consent are competence, voluntariness, full information, and comprehension. Competence is the client's ability to make a rational decision with regard to participation in treatment. Voluntariness means that the client is free to make the decision to participate or not to participate in treatment. Full information is provided to the client regarding the probable risks and the potential rewards of participation in treatment. Comprehension means that all information provided is expressed in simple language the average person would be expected to easily understand. The actual amount of information to give a client continues to be a subject of controversy. Professional judgment must be used when seeking a balance between the client's desires and right to make an informed decision about treatment and the potential therapeutic compromise resulting from overdisclosure.

## CONFIDENTIALITY

The obligation of practitioners to maintain the confidentiality of their relationships with their clients is a cornerstone of the therapeutic process and an essential prerequisite for the therapeutic relationship. Confidentiality, according to Siegel (1979), involves professional ethics rather than legalism and expresses a promise or contract to reveal nothing about an individual except under certain conditions agreed to by the client. Confidentiality may also be based in statute or case law (Swoboda et al., 1978). Confidentiality is thought of as being similar to, but not interchangeable with, privileged communication and privacy because they have different meanings. Distinguishing between confidentiality, privilege, and privacy is critical in understanding a variety of legal/ethical problems. Confidentiality, as defined by Shah (1969), relates to matters of professional ethics. Confidentiality protects the client from unauthorized disclosures of any sort by the practitioner without informed consent of the client. Confidentiality, however, is not absolute. State and federal regulations and court decisions have mandated the disclosure of information in certain situations, even if it means breaking confidentiality. Understanding the concepts of privilege and privacy will better enable practitioners to maintain confidentiality.

## PRIVILEGED COMMUNICATION

Privileged communication is "a legal right which exists by statute and which protects [clients] from having [their] confidences revealed publicly from the witness stand during legal proceedings without [their] permission" (Shah, 1969, p. 57). Siegel (1979) defines privileged communication as

> . . . a legal term involving the right not to reveal confidential information in a legal procedure. Privilege is granted by statute, protects the client from having his/her communications revealed in a judicial setting without explicit permission, and is vested in the client by legislative authority. (p. 251)

Privileged communication, then, is a legal concept and refers to the right of the client not to have his or her confidential communications revealed without his or her consent. If the client waives this privilege, then the information must be revealed. Privilege belongs to the client and is meant for the protection of the client. Privilege may be claimed by the client or by a representative of the client acting on the client's behalf. A professional may claim privilege only on behalf of the client, not himself. However, it is important to note that the privileged communication for the counselor–client relationship is not legally supported in many states. This means that privileged communication only exists for clients of professionals specifically enumerated in the statute. In other words, only those "professionals" (e.g., physicians or psychiatrists) specifically defined are included. In the absence of specific enumeration in the statute, inclusion may be provided by meeting the qualifications of one who is defined as a professional. Texas, for example, uses the following definition of professional to determine where privilege applies:

> (1) A professional means any person . . . licensed or certified by the State of Texas in the diagnosis, evaluation, or treatment of any mental or emotional disorder, or involved in the treatment or examination of drug abusers; or reasonably believed by the patient to be included in any of the preceding categories. (2) A patient means any person who consults, or is interviewed by a professional for the purpose of diagnosis, evaluation, or treatment of any mental or emotional disorder, including alcoholism, and drug addiction; or is being treated voluntarily or being examined for admission to voluntary treatment for drug abuse (Rule 510, Texas Rules of Civil Evidence).

## PRIVACY

Privacy, with regard to counseling and psychotherapy, has been defined as "freedom of individuals to choose for themselves the time and the circumstances under which the extent to which their beliefs, behaviors, and opinions are to be shared or withheld from others" (Siegel, 1979, p. 251). The concept of privacy is addressed by the Fourth Amendment to the United States Constitution, which offers protection against invasion of privacy by the government. Everstine et al. (1980) raise some important questions pertaining to privacy: To what extent should beliefs and opinions be protected from the scrutiny of others? Who may intrude on a person's privacy and how and under what circumstances is this decided? These questions are of particular importance when they include a prospective employer's access to an applicant's psychological tests, parental access to a child's school records, or insurance company or other third-party payer access to information regarding counseling or psychotherapy, or when counseling professionals are bound by law or professional codes of ethics to break confidentiality.

Of central issue here is the question of whose behalf the counselor or therapist is acting on as agent. Shah (1970) notes that in some governmental agencies and institutions the counselor or therapist is not primarily the client's agent. In these situations, counselors or therapists are faced with conflicts between their obligations to their clients and their obligations to their agency or institution. Shah maintains that any potential conflicts should be clarified before entering into a diagnostic or therapeutic relationship with the client. Denkowski and Denkowski (1982), in support of Shah's position, contend that counseling professionals should inform clients of potential breaches of confidentiality. Furthermore, they note that it is ethically incumbent on counseling professionals that all reasonable steps be taken to restrict the legally sanctioned dissemination of confidential client information to its bare minimum (p. 374).

## DUTY TO WARN

Because confidentiality is not absolute, it is essential that the counseling professional determine under what circumstances it cannot be maintained. Ethical guidelines (ACA, AMA, APA and others) maintain that disclosure of information is necessary or required in order to protect the welfare of the individual or the community, or where there is a clear and imminent danger to the individual or to the community. What represents a need to protect or clear and imminent danger is usually left to the discretion of the counseling professional. The best-known case regarding clear and imminent danger and duty to warn is the Tarasoff case (*Tarasoff v. Regents of the University of California*, 1976). The facts of the case are as follows:

In the fall of 1969, Prosenjit Poddar, a citizen of India and a naval architecture student at the University of California's Berkeley campus, shot and stabbed to death Tatiana Tarasoff, a young woman who had spurned his affections. Poddar, prior to killing Tarasoff, was seeing a psychologist as an outpatient at the student health service on the Berkeley campus of the university. Poddar had confided to the psychologist that he intended to kill an unnamed woman (who was readily identifiable as Tatiana Tarasoff) when she returned from a trip out of the country. The psychologist consulted with colleagues and then made the assessment that Poddar was dangerous and should be evaluated for civil commitment. The psychologist called the campus police and told them of the death threat and of his conclusion that Poddar was dangerous. The campus police did take Poddar into custody for questioning, but after finding him rational and obtaining a promise that he would stay away from Tarasoff, they concluded he was not dangerous and released him. Poddar never returned to the student health service center, and two months later, killed Tarasoff.

Tarasoff's family filed suit against the University of California Board of Regents, the student health center staff members involved, and the police for failing to notify the intended victim of the threat. A lower court dismissed the suit, and the family appealed to the Supreme Court of California, who in 1976 ruled in favor of the parents, holding that the psychologist did indeed have a duty to warn the victim or her family of the danger. The court's ruling requires that counseling professionals breach confidentiality in cases where the general welfare or safety of others is involved. This was a California case, so counseling professionals in other states are not bound by this court ruling.

Differing opinions, however, do exist. Siegel (1979) contends that "this was a day in court for the law and not for the mental health professions" (p. 253). He contends that, if Poddar's psychologist had accepted the absolute and inviolate confidentiality position, Poddar might well have been kept in psychotherapy and the life of Tatiana Tarasoff might have been saved. Other professionals (Everstine et al., 1980) accept the duty to warn, seeing that there are certain conditions under which counseling professionals must exchange their professional role for the role of a concerned citizen.

Corey, Corey, and Callanan (1984) offer guidelines for counseling professionals to follow if they determine a client poses a serious threat of violence to others.

1. The counseling professional should inform the client of the possible action they must take to protect a third party in situations where there is a threat of violence.

2. When a client makes a threat against others, the counseling professional should document everything observed and stated in the session.

3. If the counseling professional is under supervision, he or she should notify the supervisor verbally and in writing of the threat.

4. The counseling professional should seek professional consultation on how to proceed, and document the consultation.

5. The appropriate authorities should be notified.

6. The intended victim must be notified; in the case of a minor, the minor's parents should be notified also.

## SUICIDE AND DUTY TO PROTECT

Clients can pose not only a danger to others, but also to themselves. Most professional counselors inform their clients that they have an ethical and legal responsibility to break confidentiality when they have valid reason to suspect active suicidal intent on the part of the client. In the previous discussion, it was emphasized that professional counselors have a duty to warn and to protect others; these principles also apply to the client. Despite the argument that states, "It's my life and I have a right to do as I desire, including ending it," professional counselors have an ethical duty to protect their clients as well as others.

The debate over individual rights, including the right to take one's own life, has intensified in recent years. Szasz (1986) challenges the position that mental health professionals have an absolute duty to try and prevent suicide. He argues that suicide is the act of a moral agent who is ultimately responsible, and opposes coercive methods of suicide prevention, such as involuntary commitment to a psychiatric hospital. Guided by the principle of autonomy, Szasz takes the stance that it is the client's responsibility to choose to live or die. Szasz contends that if the client seeks professional help for suicidal tendencies, then the professional has an ethical obligation to provide the help being sought. However, according to Szasz, if the client does not seek such help or actively rejects it, then the professional's duty is either to persuade the client to accept help or to leave the client alone. The core of his argument is seen in the following:

Because I value individual liberty highly and am convinced that liberty and responsibility are indivisible, I want to enlarge the scope of liberty and responsibility. In the present instance, this means opposing policies of suicide prevention that minimize the responsibility of the individual for killing themselves and supporting policies that maximize their responsibility for doing so. In other words, we should make it more difficult for suicidal persons to reject responsibility for deliberately taking their own lives and for mental health professionals to assume responsibility for keeping such persons alive. (p. 810)

Szasz is not stating that suicide is always a good or moral option; rather he is insisting that the individual and not the government be responsible for the decision to take one's own life. The right to suicide implies that individual rights supersede the power or right of the government to coercively prevent it.

In an opposing view, this author (Freeman, 1993) also sees responsibility and choice as central concepts; however, responsible rational choice and therefore autonomy is not possible when the individual feels compelled to make one choice over another, often out of desperation, as in the case of suicide. The option of suicide is necessitated by a constricted narrowing of choices that an individual sees as open to them. The goal is not death, but freedom or escape from that which is oppressive or undesirable. A responsible choice is seen here as severely limited at best and, in the worst case, not available as the need to escape is overwhelming. The option of surrender or suicide presents a struggle, a dilemma. The question is to die or not to die (not how to address the overwhelming or insurmountable oppressive problem that has driven the individual to the point of desperation). If suicide is an option in resolving a conflict, then the individual must guard against it, watching with one eye, so that the back is never completely turned. To turn away might result in unwillingly becoming a victim of one's own hand. However, dealing with the problem requires the individual's full attention and energy, which cannot be given up because of the vigil required over one's own death impulse. Intervention, then, is seen as an ethical requirement, not to take away from but to return to the individual the task of responsible choice. Utilizing Schneidman's (1984, p. 310) succinct statement that "suicide is not a 'right' any more than is the right to belch, but if compelled to the individual will do it," the point is made that if forced or compelled to do it, suicide will be the choice regardless of interventions. This author does not say that suicide is never an acceptable option, but an individual should be given the time and resources whereby he or she may be allowed to give up the option of suicide and not be compelled to automatically accept it. I agree with Schneidman that the election of suicide by the individual cannot be taken away, for if driven to take their lives, many will. Many times, with appropriate intervention and help, other options are found.

When faced with the risk of potential suicide by a client, the professional counselor is immediately placed in a precarious situation. The conservative response might be to safeguard the client through hospitalization. The less conservative approach might be to continue to do outpatient work, but on a more frequent basis. Regardless of which approach one chooses, it should be based on a clear and thorough understanding of one's own values underlying the counselor's role and responsibility in preventing suicide. Additionally, counseling professionals should have knowledge and understanding of legal obligations that require action on their part. A determination of lethality should also be made, because what may appear on the surface as a mild suicidal risk, when assessed, could actually be much more serious. Readers are referred to Schneidman's work on assessing suicidal lethality.

Counseling professionals have an obligation to inform clients that the duty to protect exists. Additionally, clients should be told that the counseling professional has a duty to report suspected or substantiated instances of child abuse, incest, and/or other actions that constitute a threat to others or to the clients themselves. These conditions or limitations should be made clear to the client at the beginning of the therapeutic relationship.

## ACCESS TO RECORDS

Professional counselors maintain records on clients for various reasons, such as legal obligation, documentation of service, communication to other professionals, and maintenance of a chronological therapeutic history. These records, by their very nature, will contain confidential information; and as long as they exist, someone other than the professional counselor who collected the material may seek access to them.

Requirements for retaining records will vary as a function of the applicable state and or federal regulations, age of the client, and whether the file or record is considered a business record, medical record, school record, or research record. The legal requirements regarding retention of medical, school, and research records are usually more available and specific than those regarding a mental health practitioner's records. Many states do not specifically mention counseling or mental health records, making the requirements unclear. In the absence of clearly defined retention guidelines, the U.S. Internal Revenue Service (IRS) requirements on record retention for professional businesses may provide an alternative and defendable guideline. The IRS requires that professional businesses retain bookkeeping records for seven years. Following this guideline, the counseling professional can show a good faith effort in following established criteria for retention of records.

Time of retention of records begins with the termination of professional services to the client. In the case of a minor client, the retention clock begins when they have attained their legal majority. This means that in the case of a minor the record may need to be kept much longer than seven years.

Disposal of confidential records after the mandatory retention time should be performed in a manner consistent with their confidential nature. Shredding of records is a common method of disposing of confidential material. Other methods such as incineration are equally common and acceptable. The disposal of confidential records in any way that compromises their confidentiality must be avoided at any cost. An example of potential compromise might be placing records in plastic bags and depositing them in a Dumpster. This exposes the records to unauthorized examination and culling by third parties, as well as accidental exposure due to various traumas while in route to a final disposal point.

While records exist, the obvious points to consider are how, under what circumstances, and to whom should access to client records be allowed? To begin, the professional counselor must decide how to obtain the client's informed consent for the release of confidential information. Second, the circumstances under which the information is being sought by a third party or parties and the purpose for which it is sought must also be determined. Finally, who is going to be the recipient of the information, and is the information appropriate for disclosure to them?

## INFORMED CONSENT AND THE RELEASES OF RECORDS

The elements of informed consent have been identified as competence, voluntariness, full information, and comprehension. The client's informed consent for the release of confidential information should meet those criteria and also follow the guidelines outlined in the Code of Federal Regulations (42 C.F.R, Part 2). A consent or release of information form should contain the following information: the name of the person, persons, or agency to whom the records will be released; specific description of which records, containing what information about the client (psychological or other testing, diagnosis, prognosis, treatment, or case notes) and the intended use of the information; the date the release was signed; the date the release expires, as well as a statement that the consent may be revoked at any time by the client (except when action has already been taken); any limitations on the information provided; the name and signature of the individual providing authorization to release the information (identify the individual's relationship to the client if not the client him/herself); and the signature of at least one witness. Furthermore, a disclaimer is usually included stating that this information is confidential and further disclosure or release of this information to anyone other than the identified recipient may be a violation of confidentiality.

Access of client records by the court is yet another issue to be considered. It is not unusual for a subpoena duces tecum to be issued requiring the professional counselor to appear in court and bring "any and all files, case notes, tests and reports generated, billing records and correspondence" regarding the case in question. In such cases the practitioner is wise to seek consultation with legal counsel regarding the law and any resulting obligations. Should it be ultimately determined that the demand for records has been appropriately issued, the professional counselor may be in an awkward position, especially if disclosure is viewed by the practitioner as potentially detrimental to the client's well-being or if the client does not wish the information disclosed. There are times when ethical behavior will be at odds with legal requirements. In such cases, the professional counselor may be accused of breaking the law should the disclosure not be made as demanded. A counselor could be fined or jailed for contempt. On the other hand, allowing access to the client's confidential information may be an ethical violation. In the absence of clear guidelines provided by the ethical codes, one must rely on a thorough knowledge of professional ethics and the process as it is applied to a given situation. As Cervantes advised, "Forewarned is forearmed." Consultation with and representation by legal counsel is strongly recommended.

## CLIENT ACCESS TO RECORDS

Clients' rights to access their mental health records remain a potential area of conflict that is not directly addressed in the various ethical codes. This is further compounded by the type of records sought, as well as open-records laws governing public and private information. Legislative, ethical, and other practice guidelines regarding clients' rights to access their files have fueled debate and opposing views. Given the recurrence of legal and ethical debate regarding client access, the right of clients to have access to their files merits attention.

Access to institutional or agency records is usually governed by institutional or governmental policy. Federal law such as The Family Educational Rights and Privacy Act of 1974 (The Buckley Amendment) and other federal and state legislation specify a right to access institutional or agency records. The way records are defined will often determine their accessibility. Records can be categorized in three basic types: institutional (e.g., school, agency/clinic, or hospital), testing (scored standardized tests requiring test security), and working or case notes. It is this latter category, working notes or case notes, that causes the greatest concern.

Advocates of more open access to records cite improved client knowledge as helpful and claim improving consumer rights aids in consumer behavior (Roth et al., 1980). Mappes, Robb and Engels (1985) provide the following:

> Feedback provided by such access may be valuable to both the client and the practitioner. It seems logical that counselors who are not willing to explain and to be open and honest with clients, to the extent of allowing clients to see their own files, cannot be expected to create an atmosphere and relationship of trust and safety sufficient to allow the clients to examine their problems openly and experiment with new ways of handling their lives. Preventing client's access to their own counseling files risks limiting potential for growth and strength and may suggest a lack of therapist confidence in the client's self-help abilities. (p. 251)

Previous studies performed at the University of Vermont and Pittsburgh's Western Psychiatric Institute suggest that a more open records policy may reduce clients' anxiety and improve cooperation, while no adverse effects were noted (Roth et al., 1980).

Those who oppose clients' rights to openly access their files note that the information contained may be unintelligible to the client or may be misleading and possibly detrimental if taken out of context (Strassburger, 1975). When a professional denies a client's request for release of mental health records, he or she should provide the client a reason for the refusal in writing and file a copy in the client's file. The statement should specify what part or parts of the file access is being denied, the reason, and duration of rejection.

An additional concern with regard to access of a client's records occurs when the client is a child or has been deemed legally incompetent, and a parent or guardian has been appointed and may be entitled to legal access. The professional counselor must recognize the potential uniqueness of this situation with regard to the individual client's right to privacy and confidentiality. From the onset, all parties should be informed about the confidential nature of the therapeutic relationship. Discussion and subsequent agreement regarding what type of information might be shared and with whom should be made. Information such as imminent danger to self or others or the general progress or course of treatment would be appropriate to disclose.

Third-party insurers represent yet another group that may seek access to confidential client records. Clients sometimes authorize the release of information to third parties without realizing the full implications of their actions. Clients often do not realize that submitting a claim for mental health service benefits to their insurance company may authorize (or require) the professional counselor who provides the services to disclose certain information (e.g., diagnosis, type and duration of treatment, and other data). In some situations, the insurer may require a chart review or audit that requires a peer review group or person to access detailed information from the case file. This information may include detailed case notes, psychological test results, treatment plan, diagnosis, and prognosis. Some insurance companies share certain data obtained on their insured individuals with other insurance companies to aid in determining future insurability (or denial of insurance). Clients are not always aware that they are authorizing the potential release of such information when signing a claim form for submission of benefits. The potential implications of using third-party insurance for payment of mental health services should be made clear to clients, as it involves access to confidential information.

Professional Review Committees (e.g., state boards and professional associations' ethics committees) constitute another type of third party that may request access to a client's confidential information. This type of request usually involves a complaint filed against the practitioner by a client or other party. When asked to respond by such a committee, the professional counselor should first determine if a consent to release information has been obtained. It is unethical for any committee to institute an inquiry about a client without first obtaining written consent by the client to the practitioner for the release of information. When a complaint is made to an ethical committee by a client or a client's representative, the professional counselor against whom the complaint is being made must be allowed sufficient response; therefore, a consent to release confidential information must be made in order for the practitioner to defend himself or herself. The same principle applies in malpractice litigation. Confidentiality must be waived in order for the practitioner to defend himself or herself.

In the final analysis of the ethical and legal provisions regarding confidentiality and access to client mental health records, it is important to remember that ethical requirements and laws applicable to confidentiality of records are constantly changing. Answers that may have been correct in the past may now be incorrect. Continued vigilance on the part of the counseling professional is required to remain informed and updated on this keenly important and constantly changing issue.

## CLIENTS' RIGHTS

Ethical practice requires that professional counselors acknowledge the legitimate rights of the individuals they serve and have an awareness and understanding of the subsequent duties involved. In the past, those who sought mental health services have enjoyed few if any rights. Initially thought to be possessed by evil spirits, they were isolated and exposed to cruel and often inhumane conditions. Though individuals such as Phillippe Pinel, Dorothea Dix, and others were able to improve the treatment of the mentally ill, it was not until the 1960s that legal reform began to take place in the mental health arena.

The client's right to confidentiality and informed consent was discussed previously. This section is intended to provide a brief overview of the subject of client rights, such as the right to treatment, the right to refuse treatment, commitment, confinement and release from confinement, and related issues. While legislation enacted at both the federal and state levels has recognized, supported, and regulated mental health services, the courts have also rendered numerous decisions with direct influence on the actions of counseling professionals.

## THE RIGHT TO TREATMENT

Treatment may be defined as a course of planned intervention designed to bring about behavioral changes in an individual considered aberrant or dangerous (Brent, 1984; Schwitzgebel & Schwitzgebel, 1980). Treatment, by this definition, may include a variety of possible procedures (e.g., psychological [counseling or psychotherapy], sociological, or medical). Medical procedures (such as electroconvulsive therapy) can also be integrated with psychological and sociological treatments at the direction of the attending physician. Additionally, the development of major tranquilizers and other psychotropic drugs beginning in the 1950s has had and continues to have a profound effect on the treatment of the mentally ill.

The right to treatment was significantly influenced by the 1966 landmark case of *Rouse v. Cameron.* The Federal Court of Appeals in the District of Columbia held that Rouse—charged with a misdemeanor, found not guilty by reason of insanity, and involuntarily committed—had a statutory right to treatment, which he had not received in four years of confinement. Although this decision was based on a state statute, the judge deciding the case discussed a constitutional right to treatment under the Eighth Amendment (forbidding cruel and unusual punishment) and the Fourteenth Amendment (providing for due process and equal protection rights). In the 1971 case, *Wyatt v. Strickney,* a federal district court and a federal court of appeals ruled that the mentally ill have a constitutional right to treatment and that not to provide treatment would be a violation of the mentally ill person's due process under the Fourteenth Amendment. The ruling, which applied to the Alabama State School for the Mentally Retarded, has had far-reaching effects on treatment institutions across the United States. Individualized treatment plans and the least restrictive setting for treatment were two of the most significant and far-reaching results of the court ruling. In addition, addressing the mental patient's right to be free from harm, the Wyatt decision discussed the use of restraints and/or seclusion in the treatment of mental patients. The court mandated certain guidelines, many of which have been incorporated in other state statutes. These specify who can institute restraint or seclusion procedures; how long an individual can be kept in restraint and/or seclusion; what documentation is required before, during, and after; and what the individual's rights are while in restraint and/or seclusion.

In the case of *O'Conner v. Donaldson* (1975), the U.S. Supreme Court recognized for the first time a constitutional right to treatment for the nondangerous, mentally ill person. The court ruled that the state could not confine or otherwise commit a mentally ill person unless treatment was provided. The civilly committed mentally ill person has a constitutional right to be released if he is not dangerous to himself or others, is capable of surviving in the community with help, and is receiving only custodial care. In addition to addressing a mentally ill person's right to treatment, this ruling provided for an alternative or least restrictive placement of mentally ill persons who are judged not to be a danger to themselves or others.

It is clear that the right to treatment and to the least restrictive environment has been assured by the courts. The reality, however, can be different. These rights are not always consistently enforced due to many factors including a lack of financing, inadequate staff, and inadequate monitoring of these rights. Professional counselors should consult state statutes and determine which of these rights discussed have been incorporated into those statutes. They should work with other mental health professionals in assuring and providing these rights. Participation in and documentation of treatment plans, actual practices, and procedures is one way of concretely contributing to and helping to assure the rights of clients.

# RIGHT TO REFUSE TREATMENT

There are instances in which institutionalized clients, though guaranteed by law the right to treatment, have refused it. This may include not only medical treatment but also psychological treatment (counseling or psychotherapy). In recent years, this right of the individual to refuse treatment has received increasing attention. The issue of an individual's right to refuse treatment is a multifaceted one. To begin with, the commitment or labeling of an individual as mentally ill does not automatically mean legal incompetence. Therefore, generally speaking, a mentally ill individual can refuse treatment if there is no court document determining that the individual is incompetent. Swenson (1997) and Schwitzgebel and Schwitzgebel (1980) note that some obvious legal problems are the patient's competency to decide to refuse treatment, procedures for obtaining informed consent of a legally competent but severely disturbed individual, handling of objections on religious grounds, and potential liability if a client who refused treatment injures himself or herself or others.

Obtaining consent to treatment from a minor presents another unique set of issues. Usually a parent's consent is required to undertake counseling or psychotherapy with a client who is a minor. According to Melton (1981), when a child wishes to refuse treatment, even if the proposed treatment involves inpatient hospitalization, no legal recourse exists under most circumstances. In the past, the assumption appears to have been that the mental health professional contracted to treat the child at the parent's request was an unbiased third party who could assess what would be in the best interest of the child.

Refusal of treatment may also include refusing medication. The Wyatt ruling stated that no medication may be administered without a written order of a physician. Furthermore, medication cannot be used as a punishment or as a substitute for a treatment program, or merely for the convenience of the staff or facility. In the case of *Winters v. Miller* (1971), medication was administered to a patient in violation of her religious beliefs (Christian Science). The court held that, absent a finding of special incompetence (mere mental illness was not considered a special incompetence), a mental patient retains the right to refuse medication on First Amendment grounds.

The right to refuse treatment, including medication, is a complex issue. In the event of an emergency where the individual is judged to be a danger to self or others, most state mental health codes provide for the assessment and/or treatment of the individual even though he or she may refuse it. At this point, the distinction between voluntary and involuntary confinement may be appropriate.

# CIVIL COMMITMENTS: VOLUNTARY, INVOLUNTARY AND COURT ORDERED

An individual may be admitted to a mental health facility in several ways. One way is through the criminal justice system, as when one is charged and found not guilty of a crime by reason of insanity and is required to have treatment for the illness. Another way that an individual can become admitted to a mental health facility is through civil commitment proceedings. Most states have two categories of admissions: voluntary and involuntary (Swenson, 1997; Brent, 1984; Schwitzgebel & Schwitzgebel, 1980).

## Voluntary Commitment

Although voluntary admissions are included as a type of civil commitment category, it is the individual and not the civil authority that determines the need for treatment. It is also the individual who signs himself or herself into the facility (at least in theory). As in general hospitals, the individual who voluntarily admits himself or herself to a mental health facility is free to leave at any time. In either case, the individual may be required to sign a statement that he or she is leaving against medical advice if the attending physician disagrees with the discharge of the individual for medical reasons. The time required for a mental hospital to physically release an individual after request for discharge has been made varies, and during that time commitment proceedings to challenge the individual's release may be instigated. In actual practice, voluntary admission and release may not be as benign as they appear.

## Involuntary Commitment

The second category of civil commitment procedure in most states is involuntary commitment. There are usually two types of involuntary detention and/or commitment: emergency and court ordered. Procedures and terminology can vary greatly from state to state and even county to county within some states. Emergency detention or temporary commitment of another individual may be sought by a concerned party (police, mental health professional, or other third party) by alleging that the individual is in need of treatment and is a danger to self or others. Usually the requirements for emergency detention or commitment include having the person examined within a specified amount of time by one or two physicians who certify that there is a need for emergency hospitalization. In addition, the individual may only be held for a limited amount of time under an emergency commitment prior to a preliminary hearing. The preliminary hearing is required to determine whether there is probable cause for the continued detention of the individual. Prior to the hearing, the detained individual must be given notice of his or her rights under the law. The individual has the right to legal counsel; however, other procedural details vary from state to state.

## Commitment by Court Order

The second type of involuntary commitment is court ordered. The courts have ruled that mental illness alone is not a sufficient condition for involuntary civil commitment. Most state statutes typically require that a person be mentally ill and meet at least one of the following minimum conditions: (a) represent a danger to self or others if allowed to remain at liberty; (b) present a probability or likelihood of serious harm to self or others; (c) be gravely disabled so as to be unable to provide for his or her basic physical needs; (d) lack sufficient insight or capacity to make responsible decisions regarding hospitalization; and/or (e) be in need of care and treatment in a hospital.

Formal commitment procedures (Brent, 1984; Schwitzgebel and Schwitzgebel, 1980; Swenson, 1997) usually begin with a concerned person other than the individual in question petitioning the court for an examination of a supposedly mentally ill person. The supposedly mentally ill individual must physically be in the county where the petition is signed, but neither the petitioner nor the individual in question need be a resident of the county. The petition goes to a judge who determines if the individual in question is possibly mentally ill and in need of intervention of some type. A court-ordered examination need not result in immediate detention of the allegedly mentally ill individual. The court's options are basically two: one is to notify the individual of an order of examination; the other option is to issue an order of protective custody. Individuals not judged to be a danger to self or others and capable of providing for their physical needs may be allowed to stay at home until a determination is made as to their need for hospitalization. However, if the individual is judged a danger to self or others and/or unable to provide for their physical needs then an order for protective custody and emergency admission may be ordered.

A police officer, sheriff's deputy, or mental health worker must personally serve the individual with the petition and court order. Within a specified amount of time, the individual must be examined and determination made as to their need for treatment. The court then holds a hearing to determine whether or not the individual is in need of treatment and/or involuntary hospitalization.

## RELEASE FROM CONFINEMENT
## OR DISCHARGE

When the mentally ill individual recovers from the illness, he or she has the right to be released. These rights are usually described in the state's mental health statutes that cover patient's rights to release or discharge in voluntary and involuntary situations. Recall that individuals admitted under voluntary conditions must also be released upon request within the time period provided by state statute. Individuals who are involuntarily admitted have more restrictions placed on them in terms of discharge. It is up to the court to determine whether or not the individual is in need of continued confinement. This determination is made based on feedback from the treating physician.

Individuals involuntarily confined may contest their confinement legally through a Writ of Habeas Corpus (Swenson, 1997; Schwitzgebel & Schwitzgebel, 1980). The writ is used to obtain a judicial determination of the legal grounds of continued treatment. It requires immediate review and determination by the court, and if support for continued confinement is not substantiated, the individual must be released.

Counseling professionals have both an ethical and legal obligation to protect the rights of clients they serve. Often the client will not be fully aware of his or her rights and therefore is particularly vulnerable. As a professional, one has the responsibility to make appropriate disclosures to clients with regard to their rights. Failure to act judiciously with regard to clients' rights may result in liability for negligence or malpractice.

## MALPRACTICE

Malpractice may be defined as the negligent (or otherwise improper) performance, by a professional person, of the duties that are incumbent upon him or her by reason of a professional relationship with a client (*Cochran's Law Lexicon,* 1973, p. 189). Negligence may be defined as conduct that falls below the standard established by law for the protection of others against unreasonably great risk or harm. Four elements must be present to constitute malpractice litigation: (a) a duty on the part of the practitioner, (b) a breach of that duty, (c) actual loss or injury, and (d) a causal relationship between the breach of duty and the resultant injury (Swenson, 1997; Schwitzgebel & Schwitzgebel, 1980).

Additionally, there must be an expressed or implied professional relationship between the counseling professional and the client resulting in the counselor having a duty to the client. The conduct or behavior of the counseling professional must fall below the acceptable general professional standards resulting in a breach of duty. Some examples of breach of duty are improper diagnosis, violation of confidentiality, liability for suicide or homicide, and failure to supervise properly. Negative effects or injury resulting from the practitioner's neglect may include exacerbation of symptoms (depression), appearance of new symptoms, or other related maladies. The injury or loss incurred by the client must be a direct result of the practitioner's action or inaction.

Ethical responsibilities and legal responsibilities often intertwine and neither can be ignored. One of the best and most effective ways to protect yourself against malpractice is to practice ethically and keep informed about changes in the law that affect your discipline.

## SUMMARY

As professions come forth and develop, they take on certain responsibilities designed to safeguard and strengthen their service to the public and at the same time protect and amplify the profession itself. Ethical and legal guidelines are prerequisites to credibility and are central to deserving the public trust. The ethical and legal issues and responsibilities are complex and intertwined. What is ethical may not always be lawful and what is lawful may not always be ethical. However, laws may become necessary in order to give [enforceable] status to professional ethical standards. As is most often the case, ethical responsibilities equate with legal responsibilities; neither can be ignored.

## QUESTIONS FOR ADDITIONAL
## REFLECTION AND THOUGHT

1. Informed consent is extremely important; however, is it possible to give too much information? How much information is sufficient to establish informed consent?

2. Describe a situation in which ethics and law come into conflict. In this situation, which one takes precedence? What is the rationale for your answer?

3. Respond to this statement: It's my life and I can do with it as I choose, including ending it.

4. In keeping with how you answered the above question, answer this one: Am I my brother's keeper?

5. Personal rights are what our country was built on, but how far do our personal rights extend (e.g., how much privacy or confidentiality do you have a right to)?

6. Whose job is it to decide what is in the best interest of a client?

7. Some sectors of the mental health profession are debating if mental illness is a fact or a myth. How would you respond to this question, and what implications does your answer have?

8. It has been said that what is legal is not always ethical and what is ethical is not always legal. Given a situation in which a difference exists, which is more important, ethics or the law?

## USING THEORY FOR CONCRETE
## ETHICAL JUDGMENTS

### Ethical Dilemma

You are a counselor working independently in private practice. Mr. S. is a self-referred new client. During your initial intake, Mr. S. relates that he suffers from severe bipolar disorder, which is currently controlled by medication. He reports terrifying and tormenting episodes of depressive psychosis before starting his current medication. His presenting problem has to do with feelings of helplessness and hopelessness related to his mental illness. Mr. S. acknowledges that his illness is not "curable" and that there is a high probability that he will experience psychotic breaks in the future. The thought of future episodes of psychosis is overwhelming, and he is unsure he could or even would want to survive another episode. Through the course of treatment, Mr. S. begins to experience symptoms, which in the past have been precursors to psychotic episodes. Medication adjustments by his psychiatrist have failed to alleviate the advancing symptoms. He announces in session that, after significant reflection, he has decided to commit suicide rather than fight his recurrent mental illness and will refuse further intervention or hospitalization. He goes on to say that his quality of life is so compromised by his illness that he logically and rationally chooses suicide, and asks that you not interfere.

## The Problem

Your client confides in you that he is planning to commit suicide rather than face another psychotic episode. Should you notify Mr. S.'s psychiatrist and attempt to have him committed against his will, or is there a case here for individual autonomy and self-determination and/or other factors?

## The Decision-Making Process

Utilizing any of the various ethical approaches you have learned and the information contained in this chapter on ethics and the law, determine your course of action and the appropriate rationale that effectively supports it.

# 13

☀

# Ethical and Legal Issues in School Counseling

As with other counseling professionals, school counselors must practice according to standards, regulations, laws, and codes established by federal, state, and local authorities, and professional organizations. Confidentiality, use of school records, testing procedures, and referrals are some of the critical issues facing counseling professionals in the school setting. Given these critical issues, the school counselor must develop an awareness of the ethical guidelines, legal requirements, and constraints affecting the practice of school counseling. Ferris and Linville (1985) reiterate this point, stating that

> Many of the ethical dilemmas a counselor confronts are associated with when and how to report child abuse, the use and reporting of test scores, and the informal communications within the school community. Concern and caring for the student is not enough. Professional organization standards and public law, integrated with the counselor's beliefs concerning the welfare of the student and the family, are essential to the process of ethical resolution of the dilemmas counselors face in the schools. (p. 175)

Although school counselors have as their primary responsibility developing comprehensive programs, this task cannot be accomplished without assistance and support from other professionals within the school system, parents, and the greater community. For this reason, school counselors must develop and maintain collegial relationships with a variety of individuals from the educational and professional sectors who provide services to the school population. Forming successful alliances requires a clear understanding of the needs that exist, as well as a clear understanding of professional standards and knowledge of local, state, and federal legislation that governs schools and counseling practices.

Counseling professionals in the schools have the task of serving four major populations: students, parents, teachers, and community. Additionally, assignments may be delegated to them by the school principal. Performance of these functions places the school counselor in contact with professionals from various other disciplines both in and outside of the school setting. This broad scope of function in such differing areas can make accountability and ethical decision making difficult. For this reason, a review and discussion of legal requirements and the ethical standards of the American School Counseling Association (ASCA) in the areas of responsibility with students, parents, teachers, and the community might be helpful.

## RESPONSIBILITIES TO STUDENTS

Counseling professionals in the schools have a primary responsibility to ensure that counseling services and the educational program of the school consider the total development of every student, including the student's educational, vocational, personal, and social development. In conjunction with the above-noted responsibilities comes the requirement that counseling professionals protect the confidentiality of students' records and information received from students in counseling relationships. One of the most difficult areas for school counselors concerns the disclosure of information obtained in counseling sessions. As an example, should a counselor disclose to a teacher or administrator that a student exhibiting poor academic performance has recently been treated for an emotional condition or is having significant family difficulties? When does the student's right to confidentiality outweigh the school official's need to know? Conversely, when should others be notified and confidentiality be waived? The answers to these and other related questions lie in a labyrinth of ethical as well as legal considerations. Addressing these and other related questions requires school counselors to be aware not only of their professional code of ethics, but also of their legal responsibilities regarding confidentiality and privilege.

Few issues in the counseling profession are so repetitive and complex as confidentiality and privilege. Confidentiality, as was noted in a previous discussion, is both a legal and ethical term that describes if and when a professional may disclose information outside the courtroom setting. Remley (1985) suggests the following as useful guidelines for counselors in fulfilling their confidentiality responsibilities with children:

1. Always inform the child before another person is consulted regarding the child's problem. The child's consent is desirable but not always necessary.

2. Try to involve the child in the decision-making process once adults are contacted. Avoid taking action that may create for the child a feeling of betrayal by the counselor or other adults involved.

3. Keep the child involved in decisions as they are made. (p. 183)

Privilege is a legal term referring to the protection extended to an individual (or their representative) protecting them from having confidential information disclosed in a public hearing or court. Today at least 20 states recognize a privilege specifically for school counselors (Sheely & Herlihy, 1987). In those states that have recognized a privilege for school counselors, the degree of protection varies. Fischer and Sorenson (1991) cite four criteria as useful in establishing guidelines for what may qualify as privileged communication.

1. The communication must originate in confidence that it will not be disclosed.

2. The confidentiality must be essential to full and satisfactory maintenance of the relationship between parties.

3. The relationship must be one that, in the opinion of the community, should be seriously fostered.

4. The injury to that relation, caused by disclosure, would be greater than the benefit gained to the process of litigation. (p. 16)

The counseling professional is reminded that privileged communication is the client's right, and if the client waives this right, the counselor has no legal grounds for withholding the information.

A final note on confidentiality is provided by Remley (1985), emphasizing that

> Counselors in elementary schools and middle schools often must involve adults in the problems of their clients who are minors. As a result, the child's expectation of privacy sometimes is outweighed by the need to inform the parents, guardians, or other adults. On the other hand, school counselors should keep as confidential as possible details of interactions with their clients who are minors. They should also recognize that some adults involved in a child's problem have expectations of privacy identical to those of the client. Although the child's rights are the primary concern, it is important for counselors to make sure that no person's right to confidentiality is totally disregarded. In fact, because situations requiring disclosure of confidential information are rare, it is essential that the child's consent to disclose be secured whenever possible. (pp. 184–185)

## RESPONSIBILITIES TO PARENTS

Section B of the ASCA ethical standards for school counselors pertains specifically to counselors' responsibilities for informing parents about available services for students and involving parents when appropriate. In doing this, the school counselor must become involved with and learn about the families served. They must determine the needs of the parents by assessing the role they expect to play in the educational process. When consulting with parents, school counselors have many avenues through which to provide direct and indirect services. Frequently, counselors contact parents directly about such things as a student's progress in school and discuss with the parents ways to support the student's educational process at home. Parental contact may be necessitated by other conditions or situations besides the student's educational process. In situations such as this, ethical and legal considerations are paramount. The ethical responsibility for maintaining confidentiality between counselor and student may be understood, but deciding if and when to involve parents can be a very unclear situation. Here the differences between ethical and legal responsibilities or requirements often confuse and overwhelm counselors as they struggle to decide whether to protect children's rights or respond to the legal rights of parents.

Advising minors without parental consent is a particularly vague and troublesome area for counselors. Viewed from an ethical standpoint, adherence to the requirements of confidentiality requires counselors to keep what minors disclose during counseling sessions confidential. An example of some issues that make this requirement less clear are when a minor requests information and/or birth control counseling or discloses that she is pregnant and includes her plans to have an abortion. The very fact that the client is a minor creates for the school counselor a dual and often contradictory dilemma of having ethical and legal responsibilities to both the student and the student's parents. Whether or not the parents should be informed that the child is pregnant and has decided to obtain an abortion is, according to Remley (1985), a conflict of confidentiality and duty to warn. Remley states that counselors have no legal obligation to inform parents when their clients who are minors indicate their use of birth control, disclose a pregnancy, or discuss an abortion decision. If they do not disclose these situations to parents or guardians, however, these counselors must be ready to defend their decisions that their clients were mature enough to make such decisions without parental involvement and that no clear danger existed for the minors (p. 184). A more conservative response, but one that not all counselors would agree with, would be to encourage students to discuss birth control and pregnancy with their parents. In addition, counselors, when dealing with such controversial and potentially volatile issues, must be careful not to impose their personal values on others and be cautious not to go beyond their professional skill and training in providing information to students.

Professional counselors in the schools can best serve the students they counsel, the parents of these students, and the institutions they are employed by if they take responsibility for knowing state and federal law pertaining to issues such as birth control and abortion and becoming familiar with their school district's policies on these issues. Some potential problems may require interventions before they become actual problems. A potential problem requiring an intervention by the counselor before it becomes an actual problem may be a school district's not having developed sufficient guidelines in these areas. In this situation, involvement by the professional counselor in helping to address this need before problems arise is imperative.

## RESPONSIBILITIES TO TEACHERS AND OTHER COLLEAGUES

No school counseling program can be successful without the support and co-operation of the teachers in that school. Counselors and teachers work together in a process similar to that described for counselors and parents. Teachers and counselors consult each other to identify the needs of individual students, gather data to assess these needs, make strategic decisions, and evaluate out-comes. Counselors consult with teachers in group sessions, such as team meetings, and also individually by invitation of either party. This collegial rela-tionship may at times make unclear or difficult the ethical and/or legal respon-sibilities the counselor has for maintaining confidentiality. Responding to the student's rights while responding to the needs of the teacher who is also ad-dressing the needs of the student can be perplexing.

School principals have the administrative responsibility for ensuring an ad-equate environment and overall delivery of school services. Counselors have the responsibility of assessing the school's environment and informing adminis-trators of potential dangers to students' welfare. In carrying out this responsi-bility, counseling professionals in the schools need to have an awareness as well as an understanding of the ethical standards. These address the importance of counselors, defining and describing their roles and functions in the schools, and performing systematic evaluation of these services. Principals should be noti-fied, and, if necessary, made aware of the above standards that require the coun-selor to notify them when conditions in the school limit their effectiveness in providing services.

Ethical counselors keep the lines of communication open, and keep teach-ers and other colleagues within the school apprised of information they need in providing services to students. This information exchange occurs within the framework set by confidentiality and privileged communication guidelines. Through this continuous process of relational and informational flow, school counselors are better able to address and overcome problems they encounter in developing comprehensive programs of service.

## RESPONSIBILITIES TO THE COMMUNITY

Teachers and principals assist school counselors in developing and providing services, but others in the community also cooperate with school counselors. The services offered by specialists and other community agencies expand and complement the services of the school. School counselors have an ethical responsibility to be aware of the availability of these services, judge their effectiveness, and use these resources judiciously for the students, parents, and teachers who require assistance beyond what the counselor is able to offer. School counselors have the responsibility to establish relationships with other professionals and agencies in the community for the benefit of students, parents, and teachers without regard for their own benefit or interests. Therefore, counselors do not accept reward or remuneration beyond the contracts they negotiate with their school system for services, direct or indirect, provided to the school populations.

In relationships with community agencies and other professionals, the school counselor must abide by the ethical and/or legal guidelines of confidentiality and privileged communication. This applies to information that the counselor shares with the community agency or professional, as well as to information that is in return shared with the counselor.

The responsibilities associated with professional counseling in the schools and serving such a wide range of clients (students, parents, teachers, and other professionals) make it necessary to outline ethical guidelines according to different areas of responsibility (accountability) and service. The counseling professional, by being aware of the ethical standards put forth by the ASCA and aligning these different areas of responsibility with guidelines from other ethical standards such as the ACA, can develop a broader and more in-depth understanding of how the profession views ethical behavior and professional practice.

## CHILD ABUSE

The school counselor is often in a unique position to identify and report suspected cases of child abuse. Abuse can cover a variety of actions. Included in the professional literature as child abuse are inadequate supervision that leads to failure of the child to thrive, emotional neglect, abandonment, psychological bullying by classmates (Neese, 1989), physical, verbal, and sexual abuse. Those required to report suspected child abuse (including counselors) are immune from civil or criminal liability in all fifty states and the District of Columbia if they have reported in good faith (Camblin & Prout, 1983). Yet for one or another reason, it is noted that most cases go unreported (Camblin & Prout). A survey of elementary and middle school counselors concluded that the majority of respondents thought that the problem was more serious elsewhere than in their own communities. The respondents also reported that they believed they were adequately aware of the signs of child abuse to identify it (Wilson, Thomas, & Schuette, 1983).

According to Remley (1985), many states mandate disclosing suspected child abuse yet fail to clearly define it and/or provide examples. The following are examples taken from "The School Counselor and Child Abuse/Neglect

Prevention" (American School Counselors Association, 1988, Elementary School Guidance and Counseling, 22, pp. 261–263):

> Examples of child abuse include: extensive bruises or patterns of bruises; burns or burn patterns; lacerations, welts, or abrasions; injuries inconsistent with information offered; sexual abuse; and emotional disturbances caused by continuous friction in the home, marital discord, or mentally ill person. Examples of neglected children include: malnourished, ill-clad, dirty, without proper shelter or sleeping arrangements, unattended, lacking appropriate health care, ill and lacking appropriate medical attention, irregular/illegal absences from school, exploited, overworked, lacking essential psychological/emotional nurturance, abandonment (by counseling professional in the schools).

Wilson et al. (1983) view prevention programs by school counselors as part of their proactive child advocacy role. The initiation of these programs and the involvement of others is consistent with the responsibilities school counselors have to the various populations they serve.

## SUPERVISION: ETHICAL AND LEGAL RESPONSIBILITIES

Before being licensed or certified, candidates are mandated by law to meet minimal standards of education and experience. The experiential part of the process is done under supervision. An individual who possesses a limited amount of experience and/or training in a given area usually is directed by another individual who possesses competence in the area of question. The supervisor is the one identified as having achieved competence and is therefore responsible for the actions of the supervised. Said another way, supervisors are responsible for the welfare of the clients seen by those that they supervise.

There are a number of implications associated with the above-noted responsibilities. The first is that supervisors must physically meet with their supervised trainees and be familiar with all clients they (trainees) are charged with seeing. Supervisors are warned not to delegate too much to their supervised counselors, as this can result in negligence. Van Hoose and Kottler (1985) noted that a supervisor's failure to supervise a trainee working with a disturbed client is one of the leading causes of malpractice suits. This illustrates the requirement of the supervisor to know when those under their supervision are insufficiently prepared to deal with certain clients or circumstances and need assistance, including client referral or reassignment to a more experienced person. Cormier and Bernard (1982) addressed the issue of competence and recommended that if a supervisor has reservations about a trainee's abilities, supervision should not be agreed to until remedial activities result in an adequate increase of skill to minimal performance levels.

Competence is not only an issue for the supervised, but for the supervisor as well. Of concern here is the supervisory training and competency of the supervisor. Hess and Hess (1983) noted that many supervisors have little or no formal training in supervision. Familiarity with supervisory methods and models is essential in order to perform the functions of a supervisor and to ethically and legally support one's claim to be competent. It follows, then, that formal training in the practice of supervision should be a requirement of all supervisors.

## FEDERAL LEGISLATION

School counselors are faced with literally hundreds of decisions each week concerning whether or not to disclose information about students to parents, teachers, administrators, and other nonschool personnel. If the information requested of the school counselor pertains to a student's record, and the school district receives federal funds of any kind, then the Family Educational Rights and Privacy Act of 1974 (FERPA), also known as the Buckley Amendment, will govern the counselor's decision regarding access to the records.

There are four major parts to FERPA. Part I states that federal funds will be denied to any educational institution that prevents authorized access to school records by students who are over 18 years of age or by a parent of a student under 18 years of age.

Part II of FERPA states that parental consent, if the student is under 18 years of age, or the student's consent, if the student is over 18, is required before a student undergoes medical, psychological, or psychiatric examination, testing, or treatment, or participates in any school program designed to affect or change the personal behavior or values of a student.

Part III of FERPA forbids schools to allow any individuals other than those directly involved in the student's education to have access to the records or to any information from those records without written consent of the student, if over 18 years of age, or the parent if the student is under 18 years of age.

Part IV of FERPA states that the Secretary of Health, Education and Welfare (HEW) is required to develop regulations to ensure the privacy of students with regard to federally sponsored surveys.

Since its introduction, FERPA guidelines have been amended several times with the intention of clarifying implementation. The Buckley/Pell Amendment was one such attempt to address omissions in the original provisions and clarify others. Several important points of clarification were

1. Education records are defined as those records and materials directly related to a student, which are maintained by a school or one of its agents.
2. Private notes or confidential notes are exempt, provided they are not revealed to another qualified person.
3. Certain law enforcement records are excluded.

4. FERPA does not alter the confidentiality of communication otherwise protected by law.

5. Several exceptions to the need for written consent requirement for allowing access to information were listed: state and local officials where state laws are more liberal than the FERPA, organizations giving entrance or selection examinations, accrediting agencies, parents of students over 18 years of age if the students are still dependents according to the Internal Revenue Service, and in the case of health and safety emergencies.

Further clarification regarding the institution's right to records disposal and the individual's right to have access to the records appeared in the Federal Register, January 6, 1975. Students or their parents have the right to access information contained in the records as long as the information was in the records at the time the request was made. When there exists a request for information, the institution may not destroy information until after the student or parent requesting the information has obtained it. Should no request for information be noted, the institution may dispose of information contained in the record unless required by law to maintain it.

Other federal legislation that pertains to professional counselors in the schools is Title IX of the Education Amendment Act of 1972. This legislation provides that no one shall be excluded from participation in, denied the benefit of, or subjected to discrimination on the basis of gender under any educational program receiving federal funding. Specific prohibition against discrimination on the basis of gender in counseling and guidance of students is addressed (45 C.F.R. 586.36). This legislation reminds school counselors to be aware of gender biases and not to treat students of one gender differently from the other so as to place them at a disadvantage. An example of differing treatment can be seen in the use of older psychometric test instruments such as interest inventories. Used in career and educational planning, these inventories restricted females to considering only careers traditionally occupied by women. However, gender biases in counseling and guidance of students often has more to do with attitudes than instruments. Differences do exist between individuals of the same gender and also between individuals of different genders. The focus of this legislation does not appear to be on eliminating differences, because they do exist, but on reminding us to treat each other as individuals who deserve equal opportunities.

Public Law 94–142, formerly known as the Education for All Handicapped Children Act and changed in 1990 to Individuals with Disabilities Act, requires that all children with disabilities be given access to public education. When possible, they are to be educated with nondisabled students in the least restrictive environment. Professional counselors in the school are an important element in the program planning, monitoring, and counseling of mainstreamed students. As such, they are often involved with other school personnel in the development and monitoring of individual education plans (IEP's). This legislation is yet another reminder of the requirement of equal opportunity under the law and the contribution expected of school counselors.

# SUMMARY

Care and concern for those students entrusted to you may have once been the major criteria for the job, but that was a long time ago. Today's school counselors must meet a far more stringent criteria because of the requirements of comprehensive programming. Effective comprehensive programming requires an alliance with other professionals in the school system, parents, and resources in the community. This alliance requires school counselors to have a clear knowledge of the needs of the students they serve and of the various entities with which they interface. Additionally, ethical functioning requires knowledge of professional standards and the ability to effectively communicate these conditions to others. Faced with literally hundreds of decisions on a weekly basis concerning the care and welfare of students, school counselors must respond within appropriate local, state, and federal guidelines. It has been said that knowledge is power, and in the case of an ethically effective school counselor, this is most assuredly true.

# QUESTIONS FOR ADDITIONAL REFLECTION AND THOUGHT

1. Freud stated that the ego had a dilemma in that it served three masters. How many masters does the school counselor serve and what potential dilemmas does this create?

2. How do the legal and professional mandates regarding issues such as informed consent, confidentiality, records, retention of records, and other relevant issues differ for professionals counseling in the schools and those in agencies or other settings?

3. Describe a situation where there is a conflict between the welfare of a student and the policies of a school. If you were the counselor, which would take precedence? Why?

4. Describe a situation in which there is a conflict in the counselor's duty to the parent and to the child. In such a situation, what would you do?

5. Forming a collegial relationship with others in the school setting is a necessary function of a school counselor. What conflicts, if any, do you see existing if a teacher comes to you seeking counseling?

6. School counselors are often licensed as professional counselors and may practice privately in addition to working in the school. As a counselor in this situation, are there potential conflicts for you to consider?

# USING THEORY FOR CONCRETE ETHICAL JUDGMENTS

## Ethical Dilemma

You are a school counselor in an elementary school, and have been working with ten-year-old J. for about four weeks. J. is an only child, his parents are divorced, and he lives with his mother. He was referred for counseling because of acting-out behaviors that are of recent onset. You have developed a good therapeutic relationship with J., and counseling is progressing. During your fifth session with J., he expresses anger toward his mother and says at times he thinks about killing her. This past summer he even tried to poison her by putting Clorox in her drinks. He acknowledges that was wrong and states that he does not do that any more. Though he is angry, he expresses no current desire to harm his mother.

## The Problem

Your client has acknowledged to you that in the past he has tried to poison his mother. Should you warn J.'s mother about his previous attempt to poison her? Or, since he has no intent currently, should you maintain confidentiality and attempt to work this issue out in counseling without his mother's knowledge? This dilemma includes aspects of confidentiality as well as duty to warn.

## The Decision-Making Process

Utilizing the various ethical approaches you have learned and the information in this chapter on ethical and legal issues in school counseling, determine your course of action and the appropriate rationale that effectively supports it.

# 14

※

# Ethics: Research with Human Subjects

Probably every student in the field of behavioral science is familiar with the story of "Little Albert," the child who was the subject of an experiment conducted by the behaviorist John B. Watson. Little Albert, a patient in the hospital, unwittingly and without consent became the subject of an experiment on classical conditioning. The experiment was extremely successful; and Watson, through classical conditioning, was able to induce in little Albert a phobic response—a fear of white animals. Watson did have several protocols by which he intended to extinguish the phobia; however, little Albert left the hospital before this could be done. This classic experiment raises many complex ethical as well as legal questions including informed consent, issues of special populations, confidentiality, risk to benefit, and the right of subjects to withdraw.

## THE NUREMBERG CODE

Protection of human subjects and the obligation of researchers to obtain informed consent of subjects was for the first time clearly stated in the Nuremberg Code, which was first published in *The Journal of the American Medical Association,* 1946. The code was the product of the Nuremberg war trials of Nazi physicians accused of experimentation with human subjects that constituted crimes against humanity. The code clearly outlines the consent and other requirements for investigators involved in human subject research.

The voluntary consent of the human subject is absolutely essential. This means that the person involved should have legal capacity to give consent; should be so situated as to be able to exercise free power of choice, without the intervention of any element of force, fraud, deceit, duress, over-reaching. or other ulterior form of constraint or coercion; and should have sufficient knowledge and comprehension of the elements of the subject matter involved as to enable him to make an understanding and enlightened decision. The latter element requires that before the acceptance of an affirmative decision by the experimental subject there should be made known to him the nature, duration, and purpose of the experiment; the method and means by which it is to be conducted; all inconveniences and hazards reasonably to be expected; and the effects upon his health or person which may possibly come from his participation in the experiment. The duty and responsibility for asserting the quality of the consent rests upon each individual who initiates, directs, or engages in the experiment. It is a personal duty and responsibility which may not be delegated to another without impunity.

The experiment should be such as to yield fruitful results for the good of society, unprocurable by other methods or means of study, and not random and unnecessary in nature. The experiment should be so designed and based on the result of animal experimentation and a knowledge of the natural history of the disease or other problem under study that the anticipated results will justify the performance of the experiment.

The experiment should be so conducted as to avoid all unnecessary physical and mental suffering and injury. No experiment should be conducted where there is a priori reason to believe that death or disabling injury will occur; except perhaps, in those experiments where the experimental physicians also serve as subjects. The degree of risk to be taken should never exceed that determined by the humanitarian importance of the problem to be solved by the experiment. Proper preparations should be made and adequate facilities provided to protect the experimental subjects against even the remote possibilities of injury, disability, or death.

The experiment should be conducted by scientifically qualified persons. The highest degree of skill and care should be required through all stages of the experiment of those who conduct or engage in the experiment.

During the course of the experiment the human subject should be at liberty to bring the experiment to an end if he has reached the physical or mental state where continuation of the experiment seems to him to be impossible. During the course of the experiment the scientist in charge must be prepared to terminate the experiment at any stage, if he has probable cause to believe, in the exercise of the good faith, superior skill and careful judgment required of him that a continuation of the experiment is likely to result in injury, disability, or death to the experimental subject. (From Trials Of War Criminals before the Nuremberg Military Tribunals under Control Council Law No. 10, vol. 2 (Washington, DC.: U.S. Government Printing Office, 1949) pp. 181–182).

The Nuremberg Code appears to have been the prototype for the development of subsequent codes and policies concerning human subject research. The code establishes the minimal requirements of voluntary informed consent without constraint or coercion and requires that the subject have sufficient knowledge and comprehension of the procedure(s) to allow for an informed decision. Additionally, the code makes clear that the responsibility for ethical research practice lies with the individual researcher; while others involved in the research activities share ethical obligations and full responsibility for their own actions.

## VOLUNTARY CONSENT TO PARTICIPATE

Voluntary informed consent may be defined as the participant's voluntary assent to being involved in a research study after having been fully informed about the procedure(s) and related risks and benefits. Though the above definition sounds straightforward and easy to follow, voluntary and informed consent is fraught with potentially complicating factors.

The term voluntary is generally accepted to mean having the power of free choice; however, many factors contribute to making free choice difficult at best and impossible at worst. Coercion means to cause under duress and can take various forms, some being very subtle. The explicit offer of rewards or monetary compensation is controversial and may be defined as coercion. The complicating factors get larger when one considers the population to whom the offer is made. Participants with limited means or special needs may be more easily influenced or attracted to offers made by researchers than participants with "adequate means." This should not be confused with compensating participants for travel expenses or inconvenience, which is generally accepted as not being coercive. Another form of coercion, even more subtle, is to appeal to the potential participant's sense of altruism. Nonparticipation is likely to evoke a sense of guilt or selfishness, thus making "free" choice on the part of the potential participant difficult at best.

Freedom to withdraw from continued participation is an integral component of voluntariness. Freedom from coercion or other forms of pressure to participate does not end when the experiment or research study begins. Researchers have the continued responsibility to remain sensitive to participants' needs and overall well-being throughout the course of the study. Despite the complications that may arise, participants have the right to change their minds and withdraw at any time during the study. Exceptions may be allowed to this rule when the participant is legally or mentally incompetent and the experimental intervention may provide significant benefit to the individual's health and welfare, if the intervention is only available in a research context, and other alternatives have been tried or are not currently available (National Commission for the Protection of Human Subjects in Biomedical Research, 1977).

Voluntary informed consent also requires that participants be made aware of the procedures, including the benefits and risks. Procedures include the nature and purpose of the research, how long the research project and/or the participant's involvement in the project will last, and what the participant will be exposed to or what they will be required to undergo. This includes any and all inconveniences and hazards reasonably to be expected; and the effects upon one's health or person that may possibly come from participation in the experiment. Many potential factors complicate the above requirements. To begin, all participants must be informed of the purpose and procedures involved in the research except when withholding information is essential to the investigation. In such cases it may be sufficient to indicate to participants that they are being invited to participate in research that has some features which will not be revealed until the research is completed. In such research, the researcher is responsible for taking corrective action as soon as possible following completion of the research. Giving assent further requires that the participant comprehends or understands all that has been conveyed to include purpose, procedures, benefits, and risks. This implies that information provided is in language and terms that can be understood by most people. Failure to provide adequate information either through omission, concealment, or other form constitutes an ethical violation on the part of the researcher.

The purpose and procedures involved in research are often more describable and quantifiable than benefits, which may not be fully known at the time of the research investigation. This can complicate the required disclosure of benefits. To the degree possible, the potential participant should be made aware of who or what may be the recipient of the benefits from the research. Direct benefits may not apply to the participant; however, indirect benefits derived from participation such as feeling good about contributing to science, enjoying the procedure, or learning through discussion and/or feedback from the researchers may be considered (Bower & de Gasparis, 1978). Assessing benefits is important, as the acceptability of risk varies with the potential of benefits.

Referring to the ethical codes (APA, Ethical Principles in the Conduct of Research with Human Subjects; ACA, Ethical Standards, Section D: Research & Publication) and principles and regulations of the various organizations and federal regulations (45 C.F.R, part 46; FERPA), all agree explicitly or implicitly that researchers have a responsibility to assess the potential risk to participants, to protect them from physical or mental discomfort, and to detect and alleviate any negative consequences associated with participation. Among the risks associated with participation in behavioral science research are invasion of privacy, breach of confidentiality, stress, physical or psychological discomfort, lowered self-esteem, or other risks not mentioned.

## PRIVACY AND CONFIDENTIALITY

Confidentiality was noted earlier as being the cornerstone of the therapeutic process. This cornerstone also applies to research with human subjects, as none of the ethical codes excludes research. There are, however, differences between counseling and related therapeutic activities and research activities with regard to the issue of confidentiality. Counseling is a service delivered to the client who has usually, on his or her own, sought it out. The goal of the activity is the process of counseling itself. Research, on the other hand, is not an end in itself, but rather a means to an end. The direct beneficiary is generally not the participant. The relationship of the researcher to the participant is, therefore, significantly different than that of the counseling professional to the client. This difference is seen as a source of potential difficulties for the researcher in adhering to the mandates of confidentiality. Protecting the privacy of the participant and maintaining the confidentiality of data are usually routine matters of research protocol. In most cases, the job of the researcher is much simpler than that of the counseling practitioner. Complications arise in the collection of "touchy" data such as information on active users of illicit drugs or other subjects who could be in violation of state or federal laws. Seldom do researchers think about the possibility of their data or records being subpoenaed. As noted earlier, the issues involved in confidentiality and privilege can at times be vague and potentially troublesome. Researchers who anticipate problems in this area are wise to seek legal counsel at the onset of the research.

The researcher may unintentionally glean information about the participants that is not part of the research design. The information obtained may pose the question of how duty to warn applies in the research setting. During data collection, the researcher may become aware that a participant may be judged to be a danger to self or others. For example, a participant may disclose that he or she sells tainted drugs that could be lethal. In the case of research in the school, a student may disclose sexual abuse or contemplation of suicide. It was noted earlier that in practice it is often difficult and unclear what action to take in these situations. In research, the difficulty is compounded in that the ethical guidelines apply more generally and the legal obligations are even less clear. As has been suggested previously, it is judicious to notify the (client) participant of the intent to disclose information to others.

It should be obvious that ethical problems in research (as in practice) cannot be solved by simply referring to the ethical principles of right and wrong as espoused in the various professional codes. The clearest guidelines for ethically conducting research with human subjects taken from the ethical principles available are that the risks to the participants must be minimal; they (the participants) must give full and voluntary consent to participation; and they must emerge from the experience unharmed.

## FORMULATION OF ETHICAL PRINCIPLES

Though not all readers of this book will be psychology students, the American Psychological Association has provided leadership in formulating ethical principles and standards for research. *The Ethical Principles of Psychologists* and *Code of Conduct and Ethical Principles in the Conduct of Research With Human Participants* are regarded as primary sources. Therefore, the following was included to serve as a guide for all who participate in research involving human subjects. The preamble to the Ethics Code states

Psychologists work to develop a valid and reliable body of scientific knowledge based on research. They may apply that knowledge to human behavior in a variety of contexts. . . . Their goal is to broaden knowledge of human behavior and, where appropriate, to apply it pragmatically to improve the conditions of both the individual and society. Psychologists respect the central importance of freedom of inquiry and expression in research, teaching, and publication. They also strive to help the public in developing informed judgments and choices concerning human behavior. . . . It is the individual responsibility of each psychologist to aspire to the highest possible standards of conduct. Psychologists respect and protect human and civil rights, and do not knowingly participate or condone unfair discriminatory practice.

The sections of *Ethical Standard 6: Teaching, Training Supervision, Research, and Publication* that deal most directly with human participants in research are

6.06 Planning Research

(a) Psychologists design, conduct, and report research in accordance with recognized standards of scientific competence and ethical research.

(b) Psychologists plan their research so as to minimize the possibility that results will be misleading.

(c) In planning research, psychologists consider its ethical acceptability under the Ethics Code. If an ethical issue is unclear, psychologists seek to resolve the issue through consultation with institutional review boards, animal care and use committees, peer consultation, or other mechanisms.

(d) Psychologists take reasonable steps to implement appropriate protection for the rights and welfare of human participants, other persons affected by the research, and the welfare of animal subjects.

6.07 Responsibility

(a) Psychologists conduct research competently and with due concern for the dignity and welfare of the participants.

(b) Psychologists are responsible for the ethical conduct of research conducted by them or by others under their supervision or control.

(c) Researchers and assistants are permitted to perform only those tasks for which they are appropriately trained and prepared.

(d) As part of the process of development and implementation of research projects, psychologists consult those with expertise concerning any population under investigation or most likely to be affected.

6.08   Compliance with Law and Standards
Psychologists plan and conduct research in a manner consistent with federal and state law and regulations, as well as professional standards governing the conduct of research, and particularly those standards governing research with human participants and animal subjects.

6.09   Institutional Approval
Psychologists obtain from the host institution or origination appropriate approval prior to conducting research, and they provide accurate information about their research proposals. They conduct the research in accordance with the approved research protocol.

6.10   Research Responsibilities
Prior to conducting research (except research involving only anonymous surveys, naturalistic observations, or similar research), psychologists enter into an agreement with participants that clarifies the nature of the research and the responsibilities of each party.

6.11   Informed Consent to Research
(a) Psychologists use language that is reasonable and understandable to the research participants in obtaining their appropriate informed consent (except as provided in Standard 6.12, Dispensing With Informed Consent). Such informed consent is appropriately documented.
(b) Using language that is reasonable to the participants, psychologists inform participants of the nature of the research; they inform participants that they are free to participate or decline to participate or withdraw from the research; they explain the foreseeable consequences of declining or withdrawing; they inform participants of significant factors that may be expected to influence their willingness to participate (such as risks, discomfort, adverse effects, or limitations on confidentiality; except as provided in Standard 6.15, Deception in Research); and they explain other aspects about which the prospective participants inquire.
(c) When psychologists conduct research with individuals such as students or subordinates, psychologists take special care to protect prospective participants from adverse consequences of declining or withdrawing from participation.
(d) When research participation is a course requirement or opportunity for extra credit, the prospective participant is given the choice of equitable alternative activities.
(e) For persons who are legally incapable of giving informed consent, psychologists nevertheless (1) provide an appropriate explanation, (2) obtain the participant's assent, and (3) obtain appropriate permission from a legally authorized person, if such substitution is permitted by law.

6.12  Dispensing with Informed Consent
Before determining that planned research (such as research involving only anonymous questionnaires, naturalistic observations, or certain kinds of archival research) does not require the informed consent of research participants, psychologists consider applicable regulations and institutional review board's requirements, and they consult with colleagues as appropriate.

6.13  Informed Consent in Research Filming or Recording
Psychologists obtain informed consent from research participants prior to filming or recording them in any form, unless the research involves naturalistic observations in public places and it is not anticipated that the recording will be used in a manner that could cause personal identification or harm.

6.14  Offering Inducements for Research Participants
(a) In offering professional services as an inducement to obtain research participants, psychologists make clear the nature of the services, as well as the risks, obligations, and limitations.
(b) Psychologists do not offer excessive or inappropriate financial or other inducements to obtain research participants, particularly when it might tend to coerce participation.

6.15  Deception in Research
(a) Psychologists do not conduct a study involving deception unless they have determined that the use of deceptive techniques is justified by the study's prospective scientific, educational, or applied value and that equally effective alternative procedures that do not use deception are not feasible.
(b) Psychologists never deceive research participants about significant aspects that would affect their willingness to participate, such as physical risks, discomfort, or unpleasant emotional experiences.
(c) Any deception that is an integral feature of the design and conduct of an experiment must be explained to participants as early as is feasible preferably at the conclusion of their participation, but no later than at the conclusion of the research.

6.16  Sharing and Utilizing Data
Psychologists inform research participants of their anticipated sharing or future use of personally identifiable research data and of the possibility of unanticipated future uses.

6.17  Minimizing Invasiveness
In conducting research, psychologists interfere with the participants or milieu from which data are collected in a manner that is warranted by an appropriate research design and that is consistent with psychologists' role as scientific investigators.

6.18    Providing Participants with Information About the Study

(a) Psychologists provide a prompt opportunity for participants to obtain appropriate information about the nature, results, and conclusions of the research, and psychologists attempt to correct any misconceptions that participants may have.

(b) If scientific or humane values justify delaying or withholding this information, psychologists take reasonable measures to reduce the risk of harm.

6.19    Honoring Commitments

Psychologists take reasonable measures to honor all commitments they make to research participants.

It is obvious, considering the above material, that decisions as to what should be considered ethical or unethical are by no means simple; there are no ironclad rules. Each piece in the research puzzle has to be evaluated in terms of its own uniqueness.

## FEDERAL LEGISLATION

On July 12, 1974, the National Research Act (Pub. L. No. 93-348) was signed into law, creating the National Commission for the Protection of Human Subjects of Biomedical and Behavioral Research. The Belmont Report is a summary statement of the basic ethical principles identified by the commission and guidelines that should assist in resolving the ethical problems that surround the conduct of researchers with human subjects. Three focal areas of the report are (a) the boundaries of practice and research, (b) basic ethical principles, and (c) applications.

The first area, boundaries between practice and research, acknowledges the importance of distinguishing between biomedical and behavioral research. The report clearly points out the requirement of distinguishing between what is accepted as therapeutic practice and what is considered research. This is done to more clearly establish what activities ought to undergo review and evaluation for the protection of human subjects. The actual distinction between research and practice, the report points out, is often blurred in part because both often occur together (research designed to evaluate the effect of therapy). Additionally, the report notes that procedures departing from standard practice are often referred to as experimental, though the fact that a procedure is novel does not automatically place it in the category of research. Therefore, when a clinical practitioner deviates in a novel way from what is accepted practice, the use of a new or novel approach does not in itself constitute research. The report defines practice as "interventions that are designed solely to enhance the well-being of an individual patient or client and that have a reasonable expectation of success" (A6-9). Research is defined as "an activity designed to test an hypothesis, permit conclusions to be drawn, and thereby to develop or contribute to general knowledge" (A6-9).

Basic ethical principles refer to general prescriptive judgments relevant to research with human subjects. Three basic principles identified are respect for the person, beneficence, and justice.

Respect for the person involves the ethical principle of autonomy. Respecting the person means acknowledging the individual's self-reliance, independence, and right to participate in decisions, especially as they affect well-being. The ethical principle of autonomy underlies respect for the person and protects the individual's right to self-determination. The report goes on to acknowledge that not all individuals are capable of self-determination. This is a process that increases with maturity and some individuals lose this capacity in part or whole because of illness, accident, or other circumstance. Respect for the incapacity and immaturity of subjects may require others to protect them while they are incapable of being fully autonomous. The report goes on to say that the extent of protection afforded should depend on the risk of harm balanced by the likelihood of benefit.

Ethical treatment of the individual is not defined as solely a matter of respect for autonomy but also includes a duty to secure or help in the establishment of well-being. The term beneficence refers to kindness or acts of charity. In the Belmont Report, beneficence is understood as an obligation, a professional agreement or duty to do no harm and to maximize the possible benefits. This obligation is seen here as applying to both the individual and to the greater society as well. The report acknowledges that the obligation of service to the individual and to the greater society can become complex, with the different claims covered by the principle of beneficence coming into conflict with each other and potentially with other principles.

The third principle addresses the question of who should receive the benefits of research and who should receive the burdens. This question is the question of justice, more succinctly, distributive justice. Recall from a previous chapter that there are several ways to distribute burdens and benefits (e.g., to each an equal share; to each according to individual need). The report notes that during the 19th and early 20th centuries, burdens of serving as research subjects fell largely on the poor while benefits flowed primarily to the more affluent (e.g., Nazi exploitation of unwilling prisoners as research subjects; the Tuskegee syphilis study of rural black men in the 1940s). The concept of justice and its relevance to research with human subjects is plainly exposed (e.g., the selection of subjects made on ease of availability rather than reasons more related to the research; the benefits or advantages provided should not be restricted only to those who can afford them).

The report notes that applying the general principles to the conduct of research requires consideration be given to informed consent, risk/benefit assessment, and the selection of research subjects. These topics were covered at the beginning of the chapter and are consistent with the recommendations made in the report.

Other federal legislation dealing with human subjects research includes the *Code of Federal Regulations,* Title 45, Public Welfare, Part 46-Protection of Human Subjects (45 C.F.R., PART 46). This is the Department of Health and

Human Subjects (DHHS) policy pertaining to human subjects research. These guidelines in subparts A–D specifically address protection of human research subjects, including children and prisoners and the development and related activities involving fetuses, pregnant women, and human in vitro fertilization.

## ANIMAL RESEARCH

Although the focus of this chapter is on ethics of research involving human subjects, it would be incomplete without addressing the ethics of animal research. Animals have been utilized by humans from the beginnings of recorded history for food, clothing, labor, and sport. The obvious difference that exists between animal and human research participants is the almost total control and power researchers hold over animal participants. Allowable risks are considerably greater and include termination of the animal's life. As stewards of all beneath us, the risks to animal participants must still be justified and balanced against potential benefits, just as in research with human participants.

Strict laws and ethical guidelines govern both research with animals and teaching procedures in which animals are used. In addition, institutions in which animal research is conducted must have an Institutional Animal Care and Use Committee (IACUC) composed of at least one research scientist, one veterinarian, and one member of the community. The responsibility of the IACUC is to review animal research procedures and ensure that all regulations are followed.

Section 6.20 of Ethical Standard 6 pertains to animal research and states

(a) Psychologists who conduct research involving animals treat them humanely.

(b) Psychologists acquire, care for, use, and dispose of all animals in compliance with current federal, state, and local laws and regulations, and with professional standards.

(c) Psychologists trained in research methods and experienced in the care of laboratory animals supervise all procedures involving animals and are responsible for ensuring appropriate consideration of their comfort, health, and humane treatment.

(d) Psychologists ensure that all individuals using animals under their supervision have received instruction in research methods and in the care, maintenance, and handling of the species being used, to the extent appropriate to their role.

(e) Responsibilities and activities of individuals assisting in a research project are consistent with their respective competencies.

(f) Psychologists make reasonable efforts to minimize the discomfort, infection, illness, and pain of animal subjects.

(g) A procedure subjecting animals to pain, stress, or privation is used only when an alternative procedure is unavailable and the goal is justified by its prospective scientific, educational, or applied value.

(h) Surgical procedures are performed under appropriate general anesthesia; techniques to avoid infection and minimize pain are followed during and after surgery.

(i) When it is appropriate that the animal's life be terminated, it is done rapidly, with an effort to minimize pain, and in accordance with accepted procedures.

Copyright © 1992 by the American Psychological Association. Reprinted with permission.

Clearly, animal research has been and will continue to be a controversial issue. However, the welfare of the animals utilized in research studies should not be neglected.

## SUMMARY

Beginning formally with the Nuremberg trials, concern has been focused on how research involving human subjects is conducted with concern for the participants' welfare being paramount. Issues involved in ensuring participant well-being, such as informed voluntary consent, assessing benefits and risks, and privacy and confidentiality are multifaceted and complex. The American Psychological Association has taken a leadership role in providing guidance in the formulation of ethical principles. Federal legislation has created commissions and laws for the protection of human subjects involved in research. All of these efforts will reap beneficial harvests if the individual researchers will familiarize themselves with the various policies, procedures, and issues involved in human subject research. The end should never justify the means in research; human subjects should always be seen as the end in themselves.

Our true ability to be ethically accountable is demonstrated not only by how we treat each other, but by the care we take of that which is entrusted to our care. The use of animals in research is controversial; however, the ethical policies that dictate the care of animals used in research are not.

## ADDITIONAL QUESTIONS FOR REFLECTION AND THOUGHT

1. In assessing risk to benefit, on what bases do you make the ultimate determination of how much risk is acceptable and how much benefit is necessary?

2. How do you determine when and under what circumstances deceit is allowable? What is the criteria that must be met?

3. What ethical theories do you find most helpful in addressing the above questions?

4. It has been said that the end never justifies the means used to achieve it. Discuss examples in history where this principle was violated. What do you think went wrong?

5. Relative to the above question, what can you do to ensure that history does not repeat itself?

6. What are our ethical responsibilities to animals? What rights do animals have?

7. Based on the above question, what is your opinion on the necessity of having ethical standards for animal research?

# USING THEORY FOR CONCRETE
# ETHICAL JUDGMENTS

## Ethical Dilemma

You are conducting research in the area of grief and loss at a local bereavement counseling center. Research participants are those who have been bereaved through suicide. As part of your research, participants have been asked to take the MMPI. The answer sheets have been coded to ensure confidentiality of the participants. In scoring the instrument and plotting the profiles, you notice what you consider to be an extreme aberration. This profile has significant elevations on scales 2, 4, 7, and 8. You remember from a class on psychological testing and discussion of the MMPI that there is no "suicidal profile," but that the scales 2, 4, 7, and 8 appear to act in some way as excitors or releasors of suicidal behavior. You are further concerned by the fact that the participant returned the test late and you distinctly remember the individual looking very sad and depressed.

## The Problem

The participant in your research study has been bereaved through the suicide of a family member. As such, he is in a very vulnerable position psychologically. The MMPI suggests the possibility of suicidal thinking and/or potential behavior by the participant. Although you further recall from class that predictions based on the relationships of these scales produce a high false positive rate, you are concerned about the risk for suicide because of the sad and depressed affect. At the beginning of the project, participants were told the information was confidential and their anonymity would be respected. However, your suspicions about the clinical significance of the profile and your observation of the participant have you questioning if you should violate confidentiality and notify the bereavement counseling staff.

## The Decision-Making Process

Utilizing the various ethical approaches you have learned and the information in this chapter on ethics and research with human subjects, determine your course of action and the effective support for it.

# Epilogue

All disciplines within the helping professions have as their common core encounters between human beings; the therapeutic encounter embedded in a moral context. Ethics is both about clinical features that are present in every therapeutic encounter and about the ethical problems that occasionally arise in those encounters. Clinical ethics is a practical discipline that provides a structured approach to assist those in the helping professions in identifying, analyzing, and resolving ethical problems and ethical dilemmas. Good clinical practice, whether in agencies, schools, private practice, or other settings, requires some working knowledge of ethical issues and approaches useful in resolving them. Clinical decisions are made in social, cultural, economic, legal, and educational contexts, each generating certain rights and responsibilities. The primary ethical as well as legal responsibility of the practitioner is to assure the well-being and dignity of those they assist. Concurrently, practitioners have other responsibilities that may, on occasion, conflict with their primary ones. Dilemmas may occur when just claims of other individuals or institutions are taken into account and are incompatible with duties to their clients.

This book has attempted to present a general introduction to the study of moral philosophy as the basis for making concrete moral judgment. The opening chapter was intended to emphasize the need for a process of ethical decision making. The process of ethical decision making is by no means easy, and the ethical dilemmas included in Chapter 1 were designed to underscore this reality. Codes of ethics often provide a good beginning point; however, codes were not designed to provide practitioners with guidance in concrete situations, or a rationale for why a given action is right or wrong in a particular situation. As the dilemmas reflect, many issues cannot be resolved solely by reference to ethical codes.

Part Two of this book attempted to address the need for a more thorough understanding of the process of ethical decision making by returning to the essence of ethics, which is philosophy. Ethics as a branch of philosophy studies moral choices, exploring their implications as well as justifications. Moral philosophy compels mindfulness in that it is the foundation for the process of ethical decision making. As a paradigm, moral philosophy gathers and harvests the thinking and insights of great philosophers. Yet it is a paradigm, a construct that can be justified only by its clinical usefulness. As is the case with all models, there exist some with greater or more inclusive scope than others. The reader will need to decide which method best illuminates the road from theory to concrete ethical judgments.

A characteristic crisis that occurs in the life of any student, especially those who study ethics, takes place when one discovers that there is virtually no conclusion that cannot be defended from plausible premise using plausible methods of reasoning. Clinical ethical decisions, therefore, need solid grounding in moral theory. Which moral theory, stemming from which philosophical position? This book is only an introduction and should be understood as an attempt to begin the discussion of critical issues rather than to resolve them. Ideally, serious readers have begun a never-ending search for the ultimate foundation or bedrock on which to base their ethical judgments. To those who accept the challenge, "Think deep!"

# References

American Association for Marriage and
Family Therapy. (1991). *AAMFT code
of ethics*. Washington, DC: Author.

American Counseling Association (1995).
*Code of ethical standards of practice*.
Alexandria, VA: Author.

American Medical Association. (1991).
*Principles of medical ethics, with
annotation especially applicable to
psychiatry*. Washington, DC: Author.

American Psychological Association.
(1992). *Ethical principles of psychologists*.
Washington, DC: Author.

American School Counselors Association.
(1996). *Ethical standards for school
counselors*. Alexandria, VA: Author.

Anderson, E. (1990). Women and
contracts: No deals. *Michigan Law
Review, 88*, 1792–1793.

Anderson, T. (1979). *The foundation and
structure of Sartrean ethic*. Lawrence, KS:
State Regents Press.

Annas, J. (1981). *An introduction to Plato's
Republic*. Oxford, Clarendon Press.

Aquinas, T. (1952). *The summa theologica
of Saint Thomas Aquinas*. Chicago:
William Benton, Encyclopedia
Britannica.

Aristotle (1987). *The nicomachean ethics*
(J. E. C. Welldon, Trans.). Amherst,
NY: Prometheus Books.

Arras, J. (1986). *Methodology in bioethics:
Applied ethics versus the new casuistry*.
Paper presented at the Institute for the
Medical Humanities of the University
of Texas Forum on Bioethics as an
Intellectual Field, Galveston, Texas.

Arras, J. (1991). Getting down to cases:
The revival of casuistry in bioethics.
*The Journal of Medicine and Philosophy,
16*, 29–51.

Arras, J. (1994). Principles and par-
ticularities: The role of cases in
bioethics. *Indiana Law Journal, 69*,
983–1014.

Ayers, A. (1950). *Language, truth and logic*.
New York: Dover Publications Inc.

Baier, A. (1985). What do women want in
a moral theory? *Nous, 19*, 53–63.

Baier, A. (1985). *Portraits of the mind.* Minneapolis: University of Minnesota Press.

Baier, A. (1986). Trust and antitrust. *Ethics, 96,* 231–260.

Beauchamp, T. & Childress, J. (1979). *Principles of biomedical ethics.* New York: Oxford University Press.

Beauchamp, T. & Childress, J. (1983). *Principles of biomedical ethics.* (2nd ed.) New York: Oxford University Press.

Beauchamp, T., & Childress, J. (1994). *Principles of biomedical ethics.* (3rd ed.). New York: Oxford University Press.

Benedict, R. (1946). *Patterns of culture.* New York: Pelican Books.

Bennett, B., Bryant, B., VandenBos, G., & Greenwood, A. (1990). *Professional liability and risk management.* Washington, DC: American Psychological Association.

Bentham, J. (1988). *The principles of morals and legislation.* Amherst: Prometheus Books (original work published 1781).

Bersoff, D., & Koeppl, P. (1993). The relation between ethical codes and moral principles. *Ethics and Behavior, 3,* 345–357.

Bonhoeffer, D. (1971). After ten years: A reckoning made at New York 1943. In R. Bower & P. de Gasparis (1978). *Ethics in social research.* New York: Praeger.

Braithwaite, V. (1992). Beyond Rokeach's equality-freedom model: Two-dimensional values in a one-dimensional world. *Journal of Social Issues 50,* 67–94.

Braithwaite, V., & Scott, W. (1991). Values. In J. Robinson, P. Shaver, & L. Wrightsman (Eds.), *Measures of Personality and Social Psychological Attitudes, Vol. 1.* San Diego: Academic Press, Inc.

Brandt, R. (1959). *Ethical theory.* Englewood Cliffs, NJ: Prentice-Hall.

Brandt, R. (1967). Some merits of one form of rule utilitarianism. In P. Foot (Ed.), *Theories of Ethics.* London: Oxford University Press.

Brandt, R. (1973). *A theory of the good and the right.* New York: Oxford University Press.

Bray, J., Shepherd, J. & Hays, J. (1985). Legal and ethical issues in informed consent to psychotherapy. *The American Journal of Family Therapy, 13,* 50–60.

Braybrooke, D. (1991). No rules without virtue: No virtues without rules. *Social theory and practice, 17,* 139–156.

Braybrooke, D., & Lindblom, C. (1963). *A strategy of decision: Policy evaluation as a social process.* New York: The Free Press.

Brent, N. (1984). Legal aspects in adult psychiatric nursing. In J. Lancaster (Ed.), *Adult psychiatric nursing.* New Hyde Park, NY: Medical Examination Publishing Co. Inc.

Buber, M. (1970). *I and Thou.* New York: Scribners (original work published 1923).

Buckley Amendment, AKA The Revised Family Education and Privacy Act of 1974, Public Law No. 93-380, 88 Stat. 484, 20 U.S.C. 1232g.

Burnet, J. (1903). *Aristotle on education.* London: Cambridge University Press.

Burt, R. (1979). *Taking care of strangers: The rule of law in doctor-patient relations.* New York: Free Press.

Camblin, L., & Prout, H. (1983). School counselors and the reporting of child abuse. *School Counselor, 30,* 358–367.

Carroll, M., & Rest, J. (1982). Moral Development. In B. Wolman (Ed.), *Handbook of developmental psychology.* Englewood Cliffs: Prentice-Hall.

Chadrow, N. (1978). *The reproduction of mothering.* Berkeley: University of California Press.

Clouser, K., & Bernard, G. (1990). A critique of principlism. *Journal of Medicine and Philosophy, 15,* 219–221.

*Cochran's law lexicon* (5th ed.). (1973). Cincinnati, OH: W. H. Anderson Co.

*Congressional Record* (120-S21487, daily edition, December 3, 1974). Joint statement in explanation of Buckley/ Pell Amendment, Washington, DC: U.S. Government Printing Office.

Corey, G., Corey, M., & Callanan, D. (1984). *Issues and ethics in the helping professions,* (3rd ed.). Belmont, CA: Wadsworth.

Cormier, L., & Bernard, J. (1982). Ethical and legal responsibilities in clinical supervision. *Personnel and Guidance Journal, 60,* 486–490.

Day, C. (1996). *An interdisciplinary approach to the study of values and ethics in resource management in the Australian defense organization.* Paper presented at The Fifth International Conference on Ethics in Public Service, Brisbane, Australia.

Denkowski, K., & Denkowski, G. (1982). Client–counselor confidentiality: An update of rationale, legal status and implications. *Personnel and Guidance Journal, 60,* 371–377.

Dewey, J. (1966). *Democracy and education.* New York: MacMilllan Free Press (original work published 1916).

Diggins, J. (1976). Slavery, race and equality: Jefferson and the pathos of enlightenment. *American Quarterly, 28,* 206–228.

Douglas, M. (1982). *Essays in the sociology of perception.* London: Routledge & Kegan.

Ederhard, B. (Ed.). *Letters and papers from prison.* New York: Macmillan.

Everstine, L., Everstine, D., Heymann, G., True, R., Frey, D., Johnson, H., & Siden, R. (1980). Privacy and confidentiality in psychotherapy. *American Psychologist, 9,* 828–840.

Fabry, J. (1987). *The pursuit of meaning.* Berkeley: Institute of Logotherapy Press.

Feather, N. (1994). Human values and their relation justice. *Journal of Social Issues, 50,* 129–151.

Ferris, P., & Linville, M. (1985). The child's rights. Whose responsibility? *Elementary School Guidance and Counseling, 19,* 172–180.

Fischer, L., & Sorenson, G. (1991). *School law for counselors, psychologists and social workers,* (2nd ed.). New York: Longman.

Fishbein, M., & Ajzen, I. (1975). *Belief, attitude, intention and behavior: An introduction to theory and research.* Reading, MA: Addison-Wesley.

Foot, F. (1978). *Virtues and vices and other essays in moral philosophy.* Berkeley: University of California Press.

Francouer, R. (1983). *Biomedical ethics: A guide to decision making.* New York: John Wiley & Son.

Frankena, W. (1973). The ethics of love conceived as an ethic of virtue. *The Journal of Religious Ethics, 3,* 21–31.

Freeman, S. (1993). To die or not to die: A question of suicide. *Illness, Crisis and Loss, 3,* 81–85.

Freud, S. (1930). *Civilization and its discontents* (Standard Edition 21). 64–145.

Fuchs, J. (1984). *Christian ethics in a secular arena.* Washington, DC: Georgetown University Press.

Gilligan, C. (1979). Woman's place in a man's life cycle. *Harvard Educational Review 49,* 431–446.

Gilligan, C. (1980). *The effects of social institutions on the moral development of children and adolescents. Bulletin of the Menninger Clinic, 44,* 498–523.

Gilligan, C. (1982). *In a different voice.* Cambridge, MA: Harvard University Press.

Gilligan, C., Ward, V., & Taylor, J. (1988). *Mapping the moral domain: A contribution of women's thinking to psychology and education.* Cambridge, MA: Harvard University Press.

Grube, J., Mayton, D., & Ball-Rokeach, S. (1994). Inducing change in values, attitudes and behaviors: Belief system theory and the method of value self-confrontation. *Journal of Social Issues, 50,* 153–173.

Hauerwas, S. (1981). *A community of character.* Notre Dame: University of Notre Dame Press.

Hayek, F. (1952). *Sensory order.* London: Routledge.

Hess, A., & Hess, K. (1983). Psychotherapy supervision: A survey of internship training practices. *Professional Psychology: Research and Practice, 14,* 504–513.

Hess, H. (1980). Enforcement: Procedures, problems and prospects. *Professional Practice of Psychology, 1,* 1–10.

Hobbes, T. (1996). *Leviathan.* (Richard Tuck, Ed.). Cambridge: Cambridge University Press (original work published 1651).

Holmes, R. (1992). *Basic Moral Philosophy.* Belmont, California: Wadsworth.

Hume, D. (1956). *A Treatise of Human Nature.* (E. Rhys, Ed.). New York: E. P. Dutton (original work published 1739).

Ibrahim, F., & Arredondo, P. (1990). Ethical issues in multicultural counseling. In B. Herlihy, & L. Golden (Eds.), *AACD ethical standards case book* (4th ed.). (pp. 137–145). Alexandria, VA: American Association for Counseling and Development.

Janis, I. (1971). Groupthink. *Psychology Today, 5,* 43–76.

Janssins, L. (1977). Norms and priorities in a love ethic. *Louvain Studies, 6,* 207–238.

John Paul II (1995). *The gospel of life: Encyclical letter.* (Vatican translation). Boston: St. Paul Books & Media.

Jonsen, A. (1990a). Case analysis in clinical ethics. *Journal of Clinical Ethics, 1,* 63–65.

Jonsen, A. (1990b). Commentary: Jehovah's Witness and blood. *Journal of Clinical Ethics, 1,* 71–72.

Jonsen, A. (1991). Casuistry as methodology in clinical ethics. *Theoretical Medicine, 12,* 295–307.

Jonsen, A. (1995). Casuistry: An alternative or complement to principles. *Kennedy Institute of Ethics Journal, 5,* 237–251. Used by permission.

Jonsen, A., & Toulmin, S. (1988). *The abuse of casuistry: A history of moral reasoning.* Los Angeles: University of California Press.

Jordan, A., & Meara, N. (1990). Ethics and the professional practice of psychologists: The role of virtues and principles. *Professional Psychology: Research and Practice, 21,* 107–114.

Jordan, A., & Meara, N. (1991). The role of virtues and principles in moral collapse: A response to Miller. *Professional Psychology: Research and Practice, 22,* 228–296.

Kant, E. (1956). *The critique of practical reason.* (L. W. Beck, Trans.) Indianapolis: Liberal Arts Press (original work published 1781).

Kant, E. (1963). *Lectures on ethics.* (L. Infield, Trans.). Indianapolis: Hackett Publishing Co.

Kant, E. (1964). *Groundwork of the metaphysic of morals.* (H. J. Paton, Trans.). New York: Harper Torchbooks (original work published 1785).

Kant, E. (1993). *Grounding for the metaphysics of morals.* (J. W. Ellington, Trans.). Indianapolis: Hackett Publishing Company, Inc. (original work published 1785).

Kass, L. (1992). I will give no deadly drug: Why physicians should not kill. *American College of Surgeons Bulletin, 77,* 6–17.

Katsoff, L. (1947). Observation and interpretation in science. *Philosophy Review, 56,* 682–689.

Katzner, L. (1980). The original position and the veil of ignorance. In G. Blocker & E. Smith (Eds.), *John Rawls' Theory of social justice.* Athens: Ohio University Press.

Keenan, J. (1992). Virtue ethics: Making a case as it comes of age. *Thought, 67,* 115–127.

Keenan, J. (1993). The function of the principle of double effect. *Theological Studies, 54,* 294–315.

Keith-Spiegel, P., & Koocher, G. (1985). *Ethics in psychology.* New York: McGraw Hill. Used by permission.

Kekes, J. (1988). *The examined life.* Lewisberg: Bucknell University.

Kitchener, K. (1984). Institutions, critical evaluations and ethical principles. *The Counseling Psychologist, 12,* 43–55.

Kobasa, S., & Maddi, S. (1977). Existential personality theory. In R. Corsini (Ed.), *Current personality theories.* Itasca, IL: Peacock Publishers, Inc.

Kohlberg, L. (1969). Stage and sequence: The cognitive-developmental approach to socialization. In A. Goslin (Ed.), *Handbook of socialization theory and research.* Chicago: Rand McNally.

Kohlberg, L. (1970). Education for justice. In N. Sizer & T. Sizer (Eds.), *Moral education.* Cambridge, MA: Harvard University Press, 1970.

Kohlberg, L. (1976). Moral stages and moralization. In T. Lickona (Ed.), *Moral Development and Behavior.* New York: Holt, Rinehart & Winston.

Kohlberg, L. (1984). *Essays in moral development: Vol. 2, The psychology of moral development.* New York: Harper & Row.

Kuczewski, M. (1994). Casuistry and its communitarian critics. *Kennedy Institute of Ethics Journal, 4,* 99–116.

Kung, H. (1991). *Global responsibility: In search of a new world ethic.* New York: Crossland.

Ladd, J. (1973). *Ethical relativism.* Belmont, CA: Wadsworth.

Lavine, T. Z. (1984). *From Socrates to Sartre: The philosophy of quest.* New York: Bantam Books.

Levine, S. (1986). *Who dies: An investigation of conscious living and conscious dying.* Garden City, NJ: Anchor Books.

Levy, C. (1974). On the development of a code of ethics. *Social Work, 19,* 207–216.

Lewis, C. (1956). *Mind and the world order.* New York: Dover.

Lewis, C. S. (1962). *The Screwtape letters and Screwtape proposes a toast.* New York: Macmillan.

Linton, R. (1976). An anthropological's approach to ethical principles. In J.

Rachel (Ed.), *Understanding moral philosophy.* Encino, CA: Dickenson Publishing Company, Inc.

Mabe, A., & Rollins, S. (1986). The role of a code of ethical standards in counseling. *Journal of Counseling and Development, 64,* 294–297.

MacIntyre, A. (1981). *After virtue: A study in moral theory.* Notre Dame: University of Notre Dame Press.

MacIntyre, A. (1988). *Whose justice? Which rationality?* Notre Dame: University of Notre Dame Press.

Mackie, J. (1980). *Hume's moral theory.* London: Routledge and Kegan Paul.

Mapples, D., Robb, G., & Engels, D. (1985). Conflicts between ethics and the law in counseling and psychotherapy. *Journal of Counseling and Development, 64,* 246–252.

Meara, N., Schmidt, L., & Day, J. (1996). Principles and virtues: A foundation for ethical decisions, policies and character. *The Counseling Psychologist, 24,* 4–77.

Melton, G. (1981). Children's participation in treatment planning: Psychological and legal issues. *Professional Psychology, 12,* 647–654.

Menninger, C. (1973). *What ever became of sin?* New York: Hawthorn Books, Inc.

Milgram, S. (1974). *Obedience to authority: An experimental view.* New York: Harper & Row.

Mill, J. S. (1969). *Mill's Utilitarianism; text and criticism.* Ed. J. M. Smith & E. Sosa. Belmont, CA: Wadsworth (original work published 1861).

Miller, J. (1977). *Wolf by the ears: Thomas Jefferson and slavery.* New York: Free Press.

Moore, G. (1912). *Ethics.* London: Butterworth.

Moore, G. (1948). *Principia ethica.* New York: Cambridge University Press.

Mower, O. (Ed.). (1967). *Morality and mental health.* Chicago: Rand McNally. National Research Act, Public Law No. 93-348 (1974). Washington, DC: U.S. Government Printing Office.

Neese, L. (1989). Psychological maltreatment in school: Emerging issues for school counselors. *Elementary School Guidance and Counseling, 23,* 194–200.

Noddings, N. (1984). *Caring, a feminine approach to ethics and moral education.* Berkeley, CA: University of California Press. Used by permission.

Oakley, J. (1996). Varieties of virtue ethics. *Ratio, 9,* 128–152.

O'Brien, M. (1972). Protagoras. In R. Sprague (Ed.), *The Older Sophists* (pp. 3–28). Columbus: University of South Carolina Press.

O'Conner v. Donaldson, 422 U.S. 563 (U.S. Supreme Court 1975).

Pederson, P. (1989). Developing multicultural ethical guidelines for psychology. *International Journal of Psychology, 15,* 643–652.

Peirce, C. (1940). How to make your ideas clear. In J. Buchler (Ed.), *The philosophy of Peirce.* London: Routledge.

Peterfreund, S. P., & Denise, T. C. (1992). *Great traditions in ethics* (7th ed.). Belmont, CA: Wadsworth.

Petty, R., & Cacioppo, J. (1981). *Attitudes and persuasion: Classic and contemporary approaches.* Dubuque, IA: W. C. Brown.

Piaget, J. (1932). *The moral judgment of the child.* London: Kegan Paul.

Pincoff, E. (1986). *Quandaries and virtues: Against reductionism in ethics.* Lawrence: University Press of Kansas.

Pope, J., & Vasquez, M. (1991). *Ethics in psychotherapy and counseling: A practical guide for psychologists.* San Francisco: Jossey-Bass.

Punzo, V. (1996). After Kohlberg: Virtue ethics and the recovery of the moral self. *Philosophical Psychology, 9,* 7–23.

Rawls, J. (1971). *A theory of justice.* Cambridge: Harvard University Press.

Remley, T. (1985). The law and ethical practices in elementary and middle schools. *Elementary School Guidance and Counseling 19,* 181–189.

Rest, J. (1980). Understanding the possibilities and conditions of cooperation. *Bulletin of the Menninger Clinic, 44,* 524–561.

Ross, M. (1989). Feminism and the problem of moral character. *Journal of Feminist Studies in Religion, 5,* 57.

Ross, W. (1930). *The right and the good.* New York: Oxford University Press.

Roth, L., Wolford, J., & Meisel, A. (1980) Patients' access to records: Tonic or toxic? *American Journal of Psychiatry, 137,* 592–596.

Rouse v. Cameron, 373 F.2d 451 (D.C. Cir, 1966).

Royce, J. (1974). Cognition and knowledge: Psychological epistemology. In F. C. Carterette & M. P. Freidman (Eds.). *Handbook of perception.* New York: Academic.

Ruskin, J. (1905). *Sesame and lilies.* New York: Ginn & Co.

Schneidman, E. (1984). Aphorisms on suicide and some implications for psychotherapy. *American Journal of Psychotherapy, 3,* 319–328.

Schon, D. (1983). *The reflective practitioner: How professionals think in action.* New York: Basic Books.

Schueller, B. (1980). The debate on the specific character of Christian ethics. *Readings in Moral Theology 2,* 207–233.

Schutte, O. (1984). *Beyond nihilism: Nietzsche without masks.* Chicago: The University of Chicago Press.

Schwartz, S. (1994). Are there universal aspects in the structure and content of human values? *Journal of Social Issues, 50,* 19–45.

Schwitzgebel, R. L., & Schwitzgebel, R. K. (1980). *Law and psychological practice.* New York: Wiley.

Sen, A. (1970) *Collective choice and social welfare.* San Francisco: Holden-Day.

Shah, S. (1969). Privileged communications, confidentiality, and privacy: Privileged communications. *Professional Psychology, 1,* 159–164.

Sheely, V., & Herlihy, B. (1989). Counseling suicidal teens: A duty to warn and protect. *School Counselor, 37,* 89–97.

Sieber, J. (1982). *Ethical dilemmas in social research: Surveys and experiments.* New York: Springer-Verlag.

Siegel, M. (1979). Privacy, ethics, and confidentiality. *Professional Psychology, 10,* 249–258.

Smith, W. (1980) Commentary on Gilligan. In C. Gilligan, The effect of social institutions on the moral development of children and adolescents. *Bulletin of the Menninger Clinic, 44,* 516–522.

Smith, T., McGuire, J., Abbott, D., & Blau, B. (1991). Clinical ethical decision making: An investigation of the rationales used to justify doing less than one believes one should. *Professional Psychology: Research and Practice, 22,* 235–239.

Solomon, R. C. (1993). *Ethics: A short introduction.* Dubuque, IA: Brown & Benchmark.

Spohn, S. (1992). Notes on moral theology. *Theological Studies, 53,* 60–74.

Stevenson, C. (1944). *Ethics and language.* New Haven: Yale University Press.

Strong, C. (1988). Justification in ethics. In B. Brody (Ed.), *Moral theory and moral judgment in medical ethics* (pp. 599–614). Dordrecht: Kluwer Academic Publishers.

Swenson, L. (1997). *Psychology and law.* Pacific Grove: Brooks/Cole Publishing Company.

Swoboda, J., Elwork, A., Sales, B., & Levine, D. (1978). Knowledge and compliance with privileged communication and child abuse reporting laws. *Professional Psychology, 9,* 448–457.

Szasz, T. (1986). The case against suicide prevention. *American Psychologist, 41,* 806–812.

Tarasoff v. Regents of the University of California, 13 Cal. 3d 177, 529 P. 2d 553 (1974), vacated, 17 Cal. 3d 425, 552 p. 2d 334 (1976).

Teehan, J. (1995). Character, integrity and Dewey's virtue ethics. *Translations of the Charles S. Peirce Society, 31,* 841–863.

Tennyson, W., & Strom, S. (1986). Beyond professional standards: Developing responsibleness. *Journal of Counseling and Development, 64,* 298–302.

Thomas, L. (1996). Virtue ethics and the arc of universality: Reflections on Punzo's reading of Kantian and virtue ethics. *Philosophical Psychology, 9,* 25–32.

Thompson, I. (1994). The cost accountability: The social aspects. *Fraud, ethics and accountability.* Sydney: Royal Institute of Public Administration, Australia.

Toulmin, S. (1981). The tyranny of principles. *Hastings Center Report, 11,* 31–39.

Turiel, E. (1968). An experimental test of the sequentiality of developmental stages in the child's moral judgment. *Journal of Personality and Social Psychology, 3,* 618–622.

Turner, M. (1967). *Psychology and the philosophy of science.* New York: Meredith Corporation.

Tymchuk, A. (1981). Ethical decision making and psychological treatment. *Journal of Psychiatric Treatment and Evaluation, 26,* 159–175.

U.S. Department of Health and Human Services, Public Health Service. (1998). *Code of Federal Regulations* (42 C.F.R. Pt2). Washington DC: U.S. Government Printing Office.

U.S. Department of Health and Human Services, (1998). *Code of Federal Regulations* (45 C.F.R. 46). (Regulations governing research with human research participants interpreting the National Research Act of 1974). Washington, DC: U.S. Government Printing Office.

United States v. Holmes, 26 Fed. Cas. 360 (No.15385), (C.C.E.D. Pa., 1842).

Urmsom, J. (1953). The interpretation of the philosophy of J. S. Mill. *Philosophy Quarterly, 3,* 33–39.

VanHoose, W. (1986). Ethical principles in counseling. *Journal of Counseling and Development, 65,* 168–169.

VanHoose, W., & Kottler, J. (1978). *Ethical and legal issues in counseling and psychotherapy.* San Francisco: Jossey-Bass.

VanHoose, W., & Paradise, L. (1979). *Ethics in counseling and psychotherapy.* Cranston, RI: Carroll Press.

Watzlawick, P., Beavin, J., & Jackson, D. (1967). *Pragmatics of human communication: A study of international patterns, pathologies and paradoxes.* New York: Norton.

Wellman, C. (1963) The ethical implications of cultural relativism. *Journal of Philosophy, 60,* 169–84.

Westermack, E. (1932). *Ethical relativity.* London: Routledge & Kegan Paul PLC.

Whitehead, A. (1929). *Process and reality: An essay in cosmology.* New York: MacMillan.

Wilson, J., Thomas, D., & Schuette, L. (1983). Survey of counselors on identifying and reporting cases of child abuse. *School Counselor, 30,* 299–305.

Winter v. Miller, 446 F2d 65 (2nd Cir.), cert. denied., 404 U.S. 985 (U.S. Supreme Court, 1971).

Wyatt v. Strickney, 325 F. Supp.781 (M.D. Ala, 1971), enforcing, 344 F. Supp.373 (M.D. Ala, 1972).

Youniss, J. (1978). Dialectical theory and Piaget on social knowledge. *Human Development, 21,* 324–347.

# Appendixes

A. Ethics and Standards of Practice,
American Counseling Association

B. Ethical Standards for School Counselors,
American School Counselor Association

C. American Mental Health Counselors
Association Code of Ethics

D. American Association for Marriage and Family Therapy
Code of Ethical Principles for Marriage and Family Therapists

E. Ethical Standards of Human Service Professionals

F. Ethical Principles of Psychologists and Code of Conduct

G. National Association of Social Workers Code of Ethics

H. American Medical Association Principles of Medical Ethics
With Annotations Especially Applicable to Psychiatry

Addendum to the 1992 Edition of the Principles of Medical Ethics
With Annotations Especially Applicable to Psychiatry

# A

# Ethics and Standards of Practice

## American Counseling Association Code of Ethics and Standards of Practice

### CODE OF ETHICS PREAMBLE

The American Counseling Association is an educational, scientific, and professional organization whose members are dedicated to the enhancement of human development throughout the lifespan. Association members recognize diversity in our society and embrace a cross-cultural approach in support of the worth, dignity, potential, and uniqueness of each individual.

The specification of a code of ethics enables the association to clarify to current and future members, and to those served by members, the nature of the ethical responsibilities held in common by its members. As the code of ethics of the association, this document establishes principles that define the ethical behavior of association members. All members of the American Counseling Association are required to adhere to the Code of Ethics and the Standards of Practice. The Code of Ethics will serve as the basis for processing ethical complaints initiated against members of the association.

### CODE OF ETHICS

*Section A: The Counseling Relationship*
*Section B: Confidentiality*
*Section C: Professional Responsibility*

*Section D: Relationships with Other Professionals*

*Section E: Evaluation, Assessment, and Interpretation*

*Section F: Teaching, Training, and Supervision*

*Section G: Research and Publication*

*Section H: Resolving Ethical Issues*

## Section A: The Counseling Relationship

1. Client Welfare
   a. Primary Responsibility. The primary responsibility of counselors is to respect the dignity and to promote the welfare of clients.
   b. Positive Growth and Development. Counselors encourage client growth and development in ways that foster the clients' interest and welfare; counselors avoid fostering dependent counseling relationships.
   c. Counseling Plans. Counselors and their clients work jointly in devising integrated, individual counseling plans that offer reasonable promise of success and are consistent with abilities and circumstances of clients. Counselors and clients regularly review counseling plans to ensure their continued viability and effectiveness, respecting clients' freedom of choice. (See A.3.b.)
   d. Family Involvement. Counselors recognize that families are usually important in clients' lives and strive to enlist family understanding and involvement as a positive resource, when appropriate.
   e. Career and Employment Needs. Counselors work with their clients in considering employment in jobs and circumstances that are consistent with the clients' overall abilities, vocational limitations, physical restrictions, general temperament, interest and aptitude patterns, social skills, education, general qualifications, and other relevant characteristics and needs. Counselors neither place nor participate in placing clients in positions that will result in damaging the interest and the welfare of clients, employers, or the public.
2. Respecting Diversity
   a. Nondiscrimination. Counselors do not condone or engage in discrimination based on age, color, culture, disability, ethnic group, gender, race, religion, sexual orientation, marital status, or socioeconomic status. (See C.5.a., C.5.b., and D.1.i.)
   b. Respecting Differences. Counselors will actively attempt to understand the diverse cultural backgrounds of the clients with whom they work. This includes, but is not limited to, learning how the counselor's own cultural/ethnic/racial identity impacts her or his values and beliefs about the counseling process. (See E.8. and F.2.i.)
3. Client Rights
   a. Disclosure to Clients. When counseling is initiated, and throughout the counseling process as necessary, counselors inform clients of the

purposes, goals, techniques, procedures, limitations, potential risks, and benefits of services to be performed, and other pertinent information. Counselors take steps to ensure that clients understand the implications of diagnosis, the intended use of tests and reports, fees, and billing arrangements. Clients have the right to expect confidentiality and to be provided with an explanation of its limitations, including supervision and/or treatment team professionals; to obtain clear information about their case records; to participate in the ongoing counseling plans; and to refuse any recommended services and be advised of the consequences of such refusal. (See E.5.a. and G.2.)

b.  Freedom of Choice. Counselors offer clients the freedom to choose whether to enter into a counseling relationship and to determine which professional(s) will provide counseling. Restrictions that limit choices of clients are fully explained. (See A.1.c.)

c.  Inability to Give Consent. When counseling minors or persons unable to give voluntary informed consent, counselors act in these clients' best interests. (See B.3.)

4.  Clients Served by Others
If a client is receiving services from another mental health professional counselor, with client consent, inform the professional persons already involved and develop clear agreements to avoid confusion and conflict for the client. (See C.6.c.)

5.  Personal Needs and Values
a.  Personal Needs. In the counseling relationship, counselors are aware of the intimacy and responsibilities inherent in the counseling relationship, maintain respect for clients, and avoid actions that seek to meet their personal needs at the expense of clients.

b.  Personal Values. Counselors are aware of their own values, attitudes, beliefs, and behaviors and how these apply in a diverse society, and avoid imposing their values on clients. (See C.5.a.)

6.  Dual Relationships
a.  Avoid When Possible. Counselors are aware of their influential positions with respect to clients, and they avoid exploiting the trust and dependency of clients. Counselors make every effort to avoid dual relationships with clients that could impair professional judgment or increase the risk of harm to clients. (Examples of such relationships include, but are not limited to, familial, social, financial, business, or close personal relationships with clients.) When a dual relationship cannot be avoided, counselors take appropriate professional precautions such as informed consent, consultation, supervision, and documentation to ensure that judgment is not impaired and no exploitation occurs. (See F.1.b.)

b.  Superior/Subordinate Relationships. Counselors do not accept as clients superiors or subordinates with whom they have administrative, supervisory, or evaluative relationships.

7. Sexual Intimacies With Clients
   a. Current Clients. Counselors do not have any type of sexual intimacies with clients and do not counsel persons with whom they have had a sexual relationship.
   b. Former Clients. Counselors do not engage in sexual intimacies with former clients within a minimum of 2 years after terminating the counseling relationship. Counselors who engage in such a relationship after 2 years following termination have the responsibility to examine and document thoroughly that such relations did not have an exploitative nature, based on factors such as duration of counseling, amount of time since counseling, termination circumstances, client's personal history and mental status, adverse impact on the client, and actions by the counselor suggesting a plan to initiate a sexual relationship with the client after termination.

8. Multiple Clients
   When counselors agree to provide counseling services to two or more persons who have a relationship (such as husband and wife, or parents and children), counselors clarify at the outset which person or persons are clients and the nature of the relationships they will have with each involved person. If it becomes apparent that counselors may be called upon to perform potentially conflicting roles, they clarify, adjust, or withdraw from roles appropriately. (See B.2. and B.4.d.)

9. Group Work
   a. Screening. Counselors screen prospective group counseling/therapy participants. To the extent possible, counselors select members whose needs and goals are compatible with goals of the group, who will not impede the group process, and whose well-being will not be jeopardized by the group experience.
   b. Protecting Clients. In a group setting, counselors take reasonable precautions to protect clients from physical or psychological trauma.

10. Fees and Bartering (See D.3.a. and D.3.b.)
    a. Advance Understanding. Counselors clearly explain to clients, prior to entering the counseling relationship, all financial arrangements related to professional services including the use of collection agencies or legal measures for nonpayment. (A.11.c.)
    b. Establishing Fees. In establishing fees for professional counseling services, counselors consider the financial status of clients and locality. In the event that the established fee structure is inappropriate for a client, assistance is provided in attempting to find comparable services of acceptable cost. (See A.10.d., D.3.a., and D.3.b.)
    c. Bartering Discouraged. Counselors ordinarily refrain from accepting goods or services from clients in return for counseling services because such arrangements create inherent potential for conflicts, exploitation, and distortion of the professional relationship. Counselors may participate in bartering only if the relationship is not exploitative,

if the client requests it, if a clear written contract is established, and if such arrangements are an accepted practice among professionals in the community. (See A.6.a.)

    d.  Pro Bono Service. Counselors contribute to society by devoting a portion of their professional activity to services for which there is little or no financial return (pro bono).

11.  Termination and Referral

    a.  Abandonment Prohibited. Counselors do not abandon or neglect clients in counseling. Counselors assist in making appropriate arrangements for the continuation of treatment, when necessary, during interruptions such as vacations, and following termination.

    b.  Inability to Assist Clients. If counselors determine an inability to be of professional assistance to clients, they avoid entering or immediately terminate a counseling relationship. Counselors are knowledgeable about referral resources and suggest appropriate alternatives. If clients decline the suggested referral, counselors should discontinue the relationship.

    c.  Appropriate Termination. Counselors terminate a counseling relationship, securing client agreement when possible, when it is reasonably clear that the client is no longer benefiting, when services are no longer required, when counseling no longer serves the client's needs or interests, when clients do not pay fees charged, or when agency or institution limits do not allow provision of further counseling services. (See A.10.b. and C.2.g.)

12.  Computer Technology

    a.  Use of Computers. When computer applications are used in counseling services, counselors ensure that (1) the client is intellectually, emotionally, and physically capable of using the computer application; (2) the computer application is appropriate for the needs of the client; (3) the client understands the purpose and operation of the computer applications; and (4) a follow-up of client use of a computer application is provided to correct possible misconceptions, discover inappropriate use, and assess subsequent needs.

    b.  Explanation of Limitations. Counselors ensure that clients are provided information as a part of the counseling relationship that adequately explains the limitations of computer technology.

    c.  Access to Computer Applications. Counselors provide for equal access to computer applications in counseling services. (See A.2.a.)

## Section B: Confidentiality

1.  Right to Privacy

    a.  Respect for Privacy. Counselors respect their clients' right to privacy and avoid illegal and unwarranted disclosures of confidential information. (See A.3.a. and B.6.a.)

    b.  Client Waiver. The right to privacy may be waived by the client or his or her legally recognized representative.

    c. Exceptions. The general requirement that counselors keep information confidential does not apply when disclosure is required to prevent clear and imminent danger to the client or others or when legal requirements demand that confidential information be revealed. Counselors consult with other professionals when in doubt as to the validity of an exception.

    d. Contagious, Fatal Diseases. A counselor who receives information confirming that a client has a disease commonly known to be both communicable and fatal is justified in disclosing information to an identifiable third party, who by his or her relationship with the client is at a high risk of contracting the disease. Prior to making a disclosure the counselor should ascertain that the client has not already informed the third party about his or her disease and that the client is not intending to inform the third party in the immediate future. (See B.1.c. and B.1.f.)

    e. Court-Ordered Disclosure. When court ordered to release confidential information without a client's permission, counselors request to the court that the disclosure not be required due to potential harm to the client or counseling relationship. (See B.1.c.)

    f. Minimal Disclosure. When circumstances require the disclosure of confidential information, only essential information is revealed. To the extent possible, clients are informed before confidential information is disclosed.

    g. Explanation of Limitations. When counseling is initiated and throughout the counseling process as necessary, counselors inform clients of the limitations of confidentiality and identify foreseeable situations in which confidentiality must be breached. (See G.2.a.)

    h. Subordinates. Counselors make every effort to ensure that privacy and confidentiality of clients are maintained by subordinates including employees, supervisees, clerical assistants, and volunteers. (See B.1.a.)

    i. Treatment Teams. If client treatment will involve a continued review by a treatment team, the client will be informed of the team's existence and composition.

2. Groups and Families
    a. Group Work. In group work, counselors clearly define confidentiality and the parameters for the specific group being entered, explain its importance, and discuss the difficulties related to confidentiality involved in group work. The fact that confidentiality cannot be guaranteed is clearly communicated to group members.

    b. Family Counseling. In family counseling, information about one family member cannot be disclosed to another member without permission. Counselors protect the privacy rights of each family member. (See A.8., B.3., and B.4.d.)

3. Minor or Incompetent Clients
When counseling clients who are minors or individuals who are unable to give voluntary, informed consent, parents or guardians may be in-

cluded in the counseling process as appropriate. Counselors act in the best interests of clients and take measures to safeguard confidentiality. (See A.3.c.)

4. Records
    a. Requirement of Records. Counselors maintain records necessary for rendering professional services to their clients and as required by laws, regulations, or agency or institution procedures.
    b. Confidentiality of Records. Counselors are responsible for securing the safety and confidentiality of any counseling records they create, maintain, transfer, or destroy whether the records are written, taped, computerized, or stored in any other medium. (See B.1.)
    c. Permission to Record or Observe. Counselors obtain permission from clients prior to electronically recording or observing sessions. (See A.3.a.)
    d. Client Access. Counselors recognize that counseling records are kept for the benefit of clients, and therefore provide access to records and copies of records when requested by competent clients, unless the records contain information that may be misleading and detrimental to the client. In situations involving multiple clients, access to records is limited to those parts of records that do not include confidential information related to another client. (See A.8., B.1. and B.2.b.)
    e. Disclosure or Transfer. Counselors obtain written permission from clients to disclose or transfer records to legitimate third parties unless exceptions to confidentiality exist as listed in Section B.1. Steps are taken to ensure that receivers of counseling records are sensitive to their confidential nature.

5. Research and Training
    a. Data Disguise Required. Use of data derived from counseling relationships for purposes of training, research, or publication is confined to content that is disguised to ensure the anonymity of the individuals involved. (See B.1.g. and G.3.d.)
    b. Agreement for Identification. Identification of a client in a presentation or publication is permissible only when the client has reviewed the material and has agreed to its presentation or publication. (See G.3.d.)

6. Consultation
    a. Respect for Privacy. Information obtained in a consulting relationship is discussed for professional purposes only with persons clearly concerned with the case. Written and oral reports present data germane to the purposes of the consultation, and every effort is made to protect client identity and avoid undue invasion of privacy.
    b. Cooperating Agencies. Before sharing information, counselors make efforts to ensure that there are defined policies in other agencies serving the counselor's clients that effectively protect the confidentiality of information.

## Section C: Professional Responsibility

1. Standards Knowledge

   Counselors have a responsibility to read, understand, and follow the Code of Ethics and the Standards of Practice.

2. Professional Competence

   a. Boundaries of Competence. Counselors practice only within the boundaries of their competence, based on their education, training, supervised experience, state and national professional credentials, and appropriate professional experience. Counselors will demonstrate a commitment to gain knowledge, personal awareness, sensitivity, and skills pertinent to working with a diverse client population.

   b. New Specialty Areas of Practice. Counselors practice in specialty areas new to them only after appropriate education, training, and supervised experience. While developing skills in new specialty areas, counselors take steps to ensure the competence of their work and to protect others from possible harm.

   c. Qualified for Employment. Counselors accept employment only for positions for which they are qualified by education, training, supervised experience, state and national professional credentials, and appropriate professional experience. Counselors hire for professional counseling positions only individuals who are qualified and competent.

   d. Monitor Effectiveness. Counselors continually monitor their effectiveness as professionals and take steps to improve when necessary. Counselors in private practice take reasonable steps to seek out peer supervision to evaluate their efficacy as counselors.

   e. Ethical Issues Consultation. Counselors take reasonable steps to consult with other counselors or related professionals when they have questions regarding their ethical obligations or professional practice. (See H.1.)

   f. Continuing Education. Counselors recognize the need for continuing education to maintain a reasonable level of awareness of current scientific and professional information in their fields of activity. They take steps to maintain competence in the skills they use, are open to new procedures, and keep current with the diverse and/or special populations with whom they work.

   g. Impairment. Counselors refrain from offering or accepting professional services when their physical, mental, or emotional problems are likely to harm a client or others. They are alert to the signs of impairment, seek assistance for problems, and, if necessary, limit, suspend, or terminate their professional responsibilities. (See A.11.c.)

3. Advertising and Soliciting Clients

   a. Accurate advertising. There are no restrictions on advertising by counselors except those that can be specifically justified to protect the public from deceptive practices. Counselors advertise or represent their services to the public by identifying their credentials in an accurate manner that is not false, misleading, deceptive, or fraudulent. Counselors may only advertise the highest degree earned which is in counseling or a closely related field from a college or university that was accredited when the degree was awarded by one of the regional accrediting bodies recognized by the Council on Postsecondary Accreditation.

b. Testimonials. Counselors who use testimonials do not solicit them from clients or other persons who, because of their particular circumstances, may be vulnerable to undue influence.

c. Statements by Others. Counselors make reasonable efforts to ensure that statements made by others about them or the profession of counseling are accurate.

d. Recruiting Through Employment. Counselors do not use their places of employment or institutional affiliation to recruit or gain clients, supervisees, or consultees for their private practices. (See C.5.e.)

e. Products and Training Advertisements. Counselors who develop products related to their profession or conduct workshops or training events ensure that the advertisements concerning these products or events are accurate and disclose adequate information for consumers to make informed choices.

f. Promoting to Those Served. Counselors do not use counseling, teaching, training, or supervisory relationships to promote their products or training events in a manner that is deceptive or would exert undue influence on individuals who may be vulnerable. Counselors may adopt textbooks they have authored for instruction purposes.

g. Professional Association Involvement. Counselors actively participate in local, state, and national associations that foster the development and improvement of counseling.

4. Credentials

a. Credentials Claimed. Counselors claim or imply only professional credentials possessed and are responsible for correcting any known misrepresentations of their credentials by others. Professional credentials include graduate degrees in counseling or closely related mental health fields, accreditation of graduate programs, national voluntary certifications, government-issued certifications or licenses, ACA professional membership, or any other credential that might indicate to the public specialized knowledge or expertise in counseling.

b. ACA Professional Membership. ACA professional members may announce to the public their membership status. Regular members may not announce their ACA membership in a manner that might imply they are credentialed counselors.

c. Credential Guidelines. Counselors follow the guidelines for use of credentials that have been established by the entities that issue the credentials.

   d. Misrepresentation of Credentials. Counselors do not attribute more to their credentials than the credentials represent, and do not imply that other counselors are not qualified because they do not possess certain credentials.
   e. Doctoral Degrees From Other Fields. Counselors who hold a master's degree in counseling or a closely related mental health field, but hold a doctoral degree from other than counseling or a closely related field, do not use the title "Dr." in their practices and do not announce to the public in relation to their practice or status as a counselor that they hold a doctorate.

5. Public Responsibility
   a. Nondiscrimination. Counselors do not discriminate against clients, students, or supervisees in a manner that has a negative impact based on their age, color, culture, disability, ethnic group, gender, race, religion, sexual orientation, or socioeconomic status, or for any other reason. (See A.2.a.)
   b. Sexual Harassment. Counselors do not engage in sexual harassment. Sexual harassment is defined as sexual solicitation, physical advances, or verbal or nonverbal conduct that is sexual in nature, that occurs in connection with professional activities or roles, and that either (1) is unwelcome, is offensive, or creates a hostile workplace environment, and counselors know or are told this; or (2) is sufficiently severe or intense to be perceived as harassment to a reasonable person in the context. Sexual harassment can consist of a single intense or severe act or multiple persistent or pervasive acts.
   c. Reports to Third Parties. Counselors are accurate, honest, and unbiased in reporting their professional activities and judgments to appropriate third parties including courts, health insurance companies, those who are the recipients of evaluation reports, and others. (See B.1.g.)
   d. Media Presentations. When counselors provide advice or comment by means of public lectures, demonstrations, radio or television programs, prerecorded tapes, printed articles, mailed material, or other media, they take reasonable precautions to ensure that (1) the statements are based on appropriate professional counseling literature and practice; (2) the statements are otherwise consistent with the Code of Ethics and the Standards of Practice; and (3) the recipients of the information are not encouraged to infer that a professional counseling relationship has been established. (See C.6.b.)
   e. Unjustified Gains. Counselors do not use their professional positions to seek or receive unjustified personal gains, sexual favors, unfair advantage, or unearned goods or services. (See C.3.d.)

6. Responsibility to Other Professionals
   a. Different Approaches. Counselors are respectful of approaches to professional counseling that differ from their own. Counselors know and

take into account the traditions and practices of other professional groups with which they work.
   b. Personal Public Statements. When making personal statements in a public context, counselors clarify that they are speaking from their personal perspectives and that they are not speaking on behalf of all counselors or the profession. (See C.5.d.)
   c. Clients Served by Others. When counselors learn that their clients are in a professional relationship with another mental health professional, they request release from clients to inform the other professionals and strive to establish positive and collaborative professional relationships. (See A.4.)

## Section D: Relationships with Other Professionals

1. Relationships with Employers and Employees
   a. Role Definition. Counselors define and describe for their employers and employees the parameters and levels of their professional roles.
   b. Agreements. Counselors establish working agreements with supervisors, colleagues, and subordinates regarding counseling or clinical relationships, confidentiality, adherence to professional standards, distinction between public and private material, maintenance and dissemination of recorded information, work load, and accountability. Working agreements in each instance are specified and made known to those concerned.
   c. Negative Conditions. Counselors alert their employers to conditions that may be potentially disruptive or damaging to the counselor's professional responsibilities or that may limit their effectiveness.
   d. Evaluation. Counselors submit regularly to professional review and evaluation by their supervisor or the appropriate representative of the employer.
   e. In-Service. Counselors are responsible for in-service development of self and staff.
   f. Goals. Counselors inform their staff of goals and programs.
   g. Practices. Counselors provide personnel and agency practices that respect and enhance the rights and welfare of each employee and recipient of agency services. Counselors strive to maintain the highest levels of professional services.
   h. Personnel Selection and Assignment. Counselors select competent staff and assign responsibilities compatible with their skills and experiences.
   i. Discrimination. Counselors, as either employers or employees, do not engage in or condone practices that are inhumane, illegal, or unjustifiable (such as considerations based on age, color, culture, disability, ethnic group, gender, race, religion, sexual orientation, or

socioeconomic status) in hiring, promotion, or training. (See A.2.a. and C.5.b.)

j.  Professional Conduct. Counselors have a responsibility both to clients and to the agency or institution within which services are performed to maintain high standards of professional conduct.

k.  Exploitative Relationships. Counselors do not engage in exploitative relationships with individuals over whom they have supervisory, evaluative, or instructional control or authority.

l.  Employer Policies. The acceptance of employment in an agency or institution implies that counselors are in agreement with its general policies and principles. Counselors strive to reach agreement with employers as to acceptable standards of conduct that allow for changes in institutional policy conducive to the growth and development of clients.

2.  Consultation (See B.6.)

a.  Consultation as an Option. Counselors may choose to consult with any other professionally competent persons about their clients. In choosing consultants, counselors avoid placing the consultant in a conflict of interest situation that would preclude the consultant being a proper party to the counselor's efforts to help the client. Should counselors be engaged in a work setting that compromises this consultation standard, they consult with other professionals whenever possible to consider justifiable alternatives.

b.  Consultant Competency. Counselors are reasonably certain that they have or the organization represented has the necessary competencies and resources for giving the kind of consulting services needed and that appropriate referral resources are available.

c.  Understanding With Clients. When providing consultation, counselors attempt to develop with their clients a clear understanding of problem definition, goals for change, and predicted consequences of interventions selected.

d.  Consultant Goals. The consulting relationship is one in which client adaptability and growth toward self-direction are consistently encouraged and cultivated. (See A.1.b.)

3.  Fees for Referral

a.  Accepting Fees From Agency Clients. Counselors refuse a private fee or other remuneration for rendering services to persons who are entitled to such services through the counselor's employing agency or institution. The policies of a particular agency may make explicit provisions for agency clients to receive counseling services from members of its staff in private practice. In such instances, the clients must be informed of other options open to them should they seek private counseling services. (See A.10.a., A.11.b., and C.3.d.)

b.  Referral Fees. Counselors do not accept a referral fee from other professionals.

4. Subcontractor Arrangements

When counselors work as subcontractors for counseling services for a third party, they have a duty to inform clients of the limitations of confidentiality that the organization may place on counselors in providing counseling services to clients. The limits of such confidentiality ordinarily are discussed as part of the intake session. (See B.1.e. and B.1.f.)

## Section E: Evaluation, Assessment, and Interpretation

1. General
   a. Appraisal Techniques. The primary purpose of educational and psychological assessment is to provide measures that are objective and interpretable in either comparative or absolute terms. Counselors recognize the need to interpret the statements in this section as applying to the whole range of appraisal techniques, including test and nontest data.
   b. Client Welfare. Counselors promote the welfare and best interests of the client in the development, publication, and utilization of educational and psychological assessment techniques. They do not misuse assessment results and interpretations and take reasonable steps to prevent others from misusing the information these techniques provide. They respect the client's right to know the results, the interpretations made, and the bases for their conclusions and recommendations.

2. Competence to Use and Interpret Tests
   a. Limits of Competence. Counselors recognize the limits of their competence and perform only those testing and assessment services for which they have been trained. They are familiar with reliability, validity, related standardization, error of measurement, and proper application of any technique utilized. Counselors using computer-based test interpretations are trained in the construct being measured and the specific instrument being used prior to using this type of computer application. Counselors take reasonable measures to ensure the proper use of psychological assessment techniques by persons under their supervision.
   b. Appropriate Use. Counselors are responsible for the appropriate application, scoring, interpretation, and use of assessment instruments, whether they score and interpret such tests themselves or use computerized or other services.
   c. Decisions Based on Results. Counselors responsible for decisions involving individuals or policies that are based on assessment results have a thorough understanding of educational and psychological measurement, including validation criteria, test research, and guidelines for test development and use.
   d. Accurate Information. Counselors provide accurate information and avoid false claims or misconceptions when making statements about assessment instruments or techniques. Special efforts are made to

avoid unwarranted connotations of such terms as IQ and grade equivalent scores. (See C.5.c.)

3. Informed Consent
   a. Explanation to Clients. Prior to assessment, counselors explain the nature and purposes of assessment and the specific use of results in language the client (or other legally authorized person on behalf of the client) can understand, unless an explicit exception to this right has been agreed upon in advance. Regardless of whether scoring and interpretation are completed by counselors, by assistants, or by computer or other outside services, counselors take reasonable steps to ensure that appropriate explanations are given to the client.
   b. Recipients of Results. The examinee's welfare, explicit understanding, and prior agreement determine the recipients of test results. Counselors include accurate and appropriate interpretations with any release of individual or group test results. (See B.1.a. and C.5.c.)

4. Release of Information to Competent Professionals
   a. Misuse of Results. Counselors do not misuse assessment results, including test results, and interpretations, and take reasonable steps to prevent the misuse of such by others. (See C.5.c.)
   b. Release of Raw Data. Counselors ordinarily release data (e.g., protocols, counseling or interview notes, or questionnaires) in which the client is identified only with the consent of the client or the client's legal representative. Such data are usually released only to persons recognized by counselors as competent to interpret the data. (See B.1.a.)

5. Proper Diagnosis of Mental Disorders
   a. Proper Diagnosis. Counselors take special care to provide proper diagnosis of mental disorders. Assessment techniques (including personal interview) used to determine client care (e.g., locus of treatment, type of treatment, or recommended follow-up) are carefully selected and appropriately used. (See A.3.a. and C.5.c.)
   b. Cultural Sensitivity. Counselors recognize that culture affects the manner in which clients' problems are defined. Clients' socioeconomic and cultural experience is considered when diagnosing mental disorders.

6. Test Selection
   a. Appropriateness of Instruments. Counselors carefully consider the validity, reliability, psychometric limitations, and appropriateness of instruments when selecting tests for use in a given situation or with a particular client.
   b. Culturally Diverse Populations. Counselors are cautious when selecting tests for culturally diverse populations to avoid inappropriateness of testing that may be outside of socialized behavioral or cognitive patterns.

7. Conditions of Test Administration
   a. Administration Conditions. Counselors administer tests under the same conditions that were established in their standardization. When

tests are not administered under standard conditions or when unusual behavior or irregularities occur during the testing session, those conditions are noted in interpretation, and the results may be designated as invalid or of questionable validity.

b. Computer Administration. Counselors are responsible for ensuring that administration programs function properly to provide clients with accurate results when a computer or other electronic methods are used for test administration. (See A.12.b.)

c. Unsupervised Test Taking. Counselors do not permit unsupervised or inadequately supervised use of tests or assessments unless the tests or assessments are designed, intended, and validated for self-administration and/or scoring.

d. Disclosure of Favorable Conditions. Prior to test administration, conditions that produce most favorable test results are made known to the examinee.

8. Diversity in Testing
Counselors are cautious in using assessment techniques, making evaluations, and interpreting the performance of populations not represented in the norm group on which an instrument was standardized. They recognize the effects of age, color, culture, disability, ethnic group, gender, race, religion, sexual orientation, and socioeconomic status on test administration and interpretation and place test results in proper perspective with other relevant factors. (See A.2.a.)

9. Test Scoring and Interpretation

a. Reporting Reservations. In reporting assessment results, counselors indicate any reservations that exist regarding validity or reliability because of the circumstances of the assessment or the inappropriateness of the norms for the person tested.

b. Research Instruments. Counselors exercise caution when interpreting the results of research instruments possessing insufficient technical data to support respondent results. The specific purposes for the use of such instruments are stated explicitly to the examinee.

c. Testing Services. Counselors who provide test scoring and test interpretation services to support the assessment process confirm the validity of such interpretations. They accurately describe the purpose, norms, validity, reliability, and applications of the procedures and any special qualifications applicable to their use. The public offering of an automated test interpretation service is considered a professional-to-professional consultation. The formal responsibility of the consultant is to the consultee, but the ultimate and overriding responsibility is to the client.

10. Test Security
Counselors maintain the integrity and security of tests and other assessment techniques consistent with legal and contractual obligations. Counselors do not appropriate, reproduce, or modify published tests or parts thereof without acknowledgment and permission from the publisher.

11. Obsolete Tests and Outdated Test Results
    Counselors do not use data or test results that are obsolete or outdated
    for the current purpose. Counselors make every effort to prevent the
    misuse of obsolete measures and test data by others.

12. Counselors use established scientific procedures, relevant standards, and
    current professional knowledge for test design in the development, publica-
    tion, and utilization of educational and psychological assessment techniques.

## Section F: Teaching, Training, and Supervision

1. Counselor Educators and Trainers
    a. Educators as Teachers and Practitioners. Counselors who are respon-
       sible for developing, implementing, and supervising educational
       programs are skilled as teachers and practitioners. They are knowl-
       edgeable regarding the ethical, legal, and regulatory aspects of the
       profession, are skilled in applying that knowledge, and make students
       and supervisees aware of their responsibilities. Counselors conduct
       counselor education and training programs in an ethical manner and
       serve as role models for professional behavior. Counselor educators
       should make an effort to infuse material related to human diversity
       into all courses and/or workshops that are designed to promote the
       development of professional counselors.
    b. Relationship Boundaries With Students and Supervisees. Counselors
       clearly define and maintain ethical, professional, and social relation-
       ship boundaries with their students and supervisees. They are aware of
       the differential in power that exists and the student's or supervisee's
       possible incomprehension of that power differential. Counselors ex-
       plain to students and supervisees the potential for the relationship to
       become exploitive.
    c. Sexual relationships. Counselors do not engage in sexual relationships
       with students or supervisees and do not subject them to sexual harass-
       ment. (See A.6. and C.5.b.)
    d. Contributions to Research. Counselors give credit to students or su-
       pervisees for their contributions to research and scholarly projects.
       Credit is given through coauthorship, acknowledgment, footnote
       statement, or other appropriate means, in accordance with such con-
       tributions. (See G.4.b. and G.4.c.)
    e. Close Relatives. Counselors do not accept close relatives as students
       or supervisees.
    f. Supervision Preparation. Counselors who offer clinical supervision
       services are adequately prepared in supervision methods and tech-
       niques. Counselors who are doctoral students serving as practicum or
       internship supervisors to master's level students are adequately pre-
       pared and supervised by the training program.
    g. Responsibility for Services to Clients. Counselors who supervise the
       counseling services of others take reasonable measures to ensure that
       counseling services provided to clients are professional.

    h. Endorsement. Counselors do not endorse students or supervisees for certification, licensure, employment, or completion of an academic or training program if they believe students or supervisees are not qualified for the endorsement. Counselors take reasonable steps to assist students or supervisees who are not qualified for endorsement to become qualified.

2. Counselor Education and Training Programs

    a. Orientation. Prior to admission, counselors orient prospective students to the counselor education or training program's expectations, including but not limited to the following: (1) the type and level of skill acquisition required for successful completion of the training, (2) subject matter to be covered, (3) basis for evaluation, (4) training components that encourage self-growth or self-disclosure as part of the training process, (5) the type of supervision settings and requirements of the sites for required clinical field experiences, (6) student and supervisee evaluation and dismissal policies and procedures, and (7) up-to-date employment prospects for graduates.

    b. Integration of Study and Practice. Counselors establish counselor education and training programs that integrate academic study and supervised practice.

    c. Evaluation. Counselors clearly state to students and supervisees, in advance of training, the levels of competency expected, appraisal methods, and timing of evaluations for both didactic and experiential components. Counselors provide students and supervisees with periodic performance appraisal and evaluation feedback throughout the training program.

    d. Teaching Ethics. Counselors make students and supervisees aware of the ethical responsibilities and standards of the profession and the students' and supervisees' ethical responsibilities to the profession. (See C.1. and F.3.e.)

    e. Peer Relationships. When students or supervisees are assigned to lead counseling groups or provide clinical supervision for their peers, counselors take steps to ensure that students and supervisees placed in these roles do not have personal or adverse relationships with peers and that they understand they have the same ethical obligations as counselor educators, trainers, and supervisors. Counselors make every effort to ensure that the rights of peers are not compromised when students or supervisees are assigned to lead counseling groups or provide clinical supervision.

    f. Varied Theoretical Positions. Counselors present varied theoretical positions so that students and supervisees may make comparisons and have opportunities to develop their own positions. Counselors provide information concerning the scientific bases of professional practice. (See C.6.a.)

    g. Field Placements. Counselors develop clear policies within their training program regarding field placement and other clinical experiences. Counselors provide clearly stated roles and responsibilities for the student or supervisee, the site supervisor, and the program supervisor. They confirm that site supervisors are qualified to provide supervision and are informed of their professional and ethical responsibilities in this role.

h. Dual Relationships as Supervisors. Counselors avoid dual relationships such as performing the role of site supervisor and training program supervisor in the student's or supervisee's training program. Counselors do not accept any form of professional services, fees, commissions, reimbursement, or remuneration from a site for student or supervisee placement.

i. Diversity in Programs. Counselors are responsive to their institution's and program's recruitment and retention needs for training program administrators, faculty, and students with diverse backgrounds and special needs. (See A.2.a.)

3. Students and Supervisees
   a. Limitations. Counselors, through ongoing evaluation and appraisal, are aware of the academic and personal limitations of students and supervisees that might impede performance. Counselors assist students and supervisees in securing remedial assistance when needed, and dismiss from the training program supervisees who are unable to provide competent service due to academic or personal limitations. Counselors seek professional consultation and document their decision to dismiss or refer students or supervisees for assistance. Counselors ensure that students and supervisees have recourse to address decisions made to require them to seek assistance or to dismiss them.

   b. Self-Growth Experiences. Counselors use professional judgment when designing training experiences conducted by the counselors themselves that require student and supervisee self-growth or self-disclosure. Safeguards are provided so that students and supervisees are aware of the ramifications their self-disclosure may have on counselors whose primary role as teacher, trainer, or supervisor requires acting on ethical obligations to the profession. Evaluative components of experiential training experiences explicitly delineate predetermined academic standards that are separate and do not depend on the student's level of self-disclosure. (See A.6.)

   c. Counseling for Students and Supervisees. If students or supervisees request counseling, supervisors or counselor educators provide them with acceptable referrals. Supervisors or counselor educators do not serve as counselor to students or supervisees over whom they hold administrative, teaching, or evaluative roles unless this is a brief role associated with a training experience. (See A.6.b.)

   d. Clients of Students and Supervisees. Counselors make every effort to ensure that the clients at field placements are aware of the services rendered and the qualifications of the students and supervisees rendering those services. Clients receive professional disclosure information and are informed of the limits of confidentiality. Client permission is obtained in order for the students and supervisees to use any information concerning the counseling relationship in the training process. (See B.1.e.)

e. Standards for Students and Supervisees. Students and supervisees preparing to become counselors adhere to the Code of Ethics and the Standards of Practice. Students and supervisees have the same obligations to clients as those required of counselors. (See H.1.)

## Section G: Research and Publication

1. Research Responsibilities
   a. Use of Human Subjects. Counselors plan, design, conduct, and report research in a manner consistent with pertinent ethical principles, federal and state laws, host institutional regulations, and scientific standards governing research with human subjects. Counselors design and conduct research that reflects cultural sensitivity appropriateness.
   b. Deviation From Standard Practices. Counselors seek consultation and observe stringent safeguards to protect the rights of research participants when a research problem suggests a deviation from standard acceptable practices. (See B.6.)
   c. Precautions to Avoid Injury. Counselors who conduct research with human subjects are responsible for the subjects' welfare throughout the experiment and take reasonable precautions to avoid causing injurious psychological, physical, or social effects to their subjects.
   d. Principal Research Responsibility. The ultimate responsibility for ethical research practice lies with the principal researcher. All others involved in the research activities share ethical obligations and full responsibility for their own actions.
   e. Minimal Interference. Counselors take reasonable precautions to avoid causing disruptions in subjects' lives due to participation in research.
   f. Diversity. Counselors are sensitive to diversity and research issues with special populations. They seek consultation when appropriate. (See A.2.a. and B.6.)
2. Informed Consent
   a. Topics Disclosed. In obtaining informed consent for research, counselors use language that is understandable to research participants and that (1) accurately explains the purpose and procedures to be followed; (2) identifies any procedures that are experimental or relatively untried; (3) describes the attendant discomforts and risks; (4) describes the benefits or changes in individuals or organizations that might be reasonably expected; (5) discloses appropriate alternative procedures that would be advantageous for subjects; (6) offers to answer any inquiries concerning the procedures; (7) describes any limitations on confidentiality; and (8) instructs that subjects are free to withdraw their consent and to discontinue participation in the project at any time. (See B.1.f.)

b. Deception. Counselors do not conduct research involving deception unless alternative procedures are not feasible and the prospective value of the research justifies the deception. When the methodological requirements of a study necessitate concealment or deception, the investigator is required to explain clearly the reasons for this action as soon as possible.

c. Voluntary Participation. Participation in research is typically voluntary and without any penalty for refusal to participate. Involuntary participation is appropriate only when it can be demonstrated that participation will have no harmful effects on subjects and is essential to the investigation.

d. Confidentiality of Information. Information obtained about research participants during the course of an investigation is confidential. When the possibility exists that others may obtain access to such information, ethical research practice requires that the possibility, together with the plans for protecting confidentiality, be explained to participants as a part of the procedure for obtaining informed consent. (See B.1.e.)

e. Persons Incapable of Giving Informed Consent. When a person is incapable of giving informed consent, counselors provide an appropriate explanation, obtain agreement for participation, and obtain appropriate consent from a legally authorized person.

f. Commitments to Participants. Counselors take reasonable measures to honor all commitments to research participants.

g. Explanations After Data Collection. After data are collected, counselors provide participants with full clarification of the nature of the study to remove any misconceptions. Where scientific or human values justify delaying or withholding information, counselors take reasonable measures to avoid causing harm.

h. Agreements to Cooperate. Counselors who agree to cooperate with another individual in research or publication incur an obligation to cooperate as promised in terms of punctuality of performance and with regard to the completeness and accuracy of the information required.

i. Informed Consent for Sponsors. In the pursuit of research, counselors give sponsors, institutions, and publication channels the same respect and opportunity for giving informed consent that they accord to individual research participants. Counselors are aware of their obligation to future research workers and ensure that host institutions are given feedback information and proper acknowledgment.

3. Reporting Results

a. Information Affecting Outcome. When reporting research results, counselors explicitly mention all variables and conditions known to the investigator that may have affected the outcome of a study or the interpretation of data.

b. Accurate Results. Counselors plan, conduct, and report research accurately and in a manner that minimizes the possibility that results will be misleading. They provide thorough discussions of the limitations of their data and alternative hypotheses. Counselors do not engage in fraudulent research, distort data, misrepresent data, or deliberately bias their results.

   c. Obligation to Report Unfavorable Results. Counselors communicate to other counselors the results of any research judged to be of professional value. Results that reflect unfavorably on institutions, programs, services, prevailing opinions, or vested interests are not withheld.

   d. Identity of Subjects. Counselors who supply data, aid in the research of another person, report research results, or make original data available take due care to disguise the identity of respective subjects in the absence of specific authorization from the subjects to do otherwise. (See B.1.g. and B.5.a.)

   e. Replication Studies. Counselors are obligated to make available sufficient original research data to qualified professionals who may wish to replicate the study.

4. Publication

   a. Recognition of Others. When conducting and reporting research, counselors are familiar with and give recognition to previous work on the topic, observe copyright laws, and give full credit to those to whom credit is due. (See F.1.d. and G.4.c.)

   b. Contributors. Counselors give credit through joint authorship, acknowledgment, footnote statements, or other appropriate means to those who have contributed significantly to research or concept development in accordance with such contributions. The principal contributor is listed first and minor technical or processional contributions are acknowledged in notes or introductory statements.

   c. Student Research. For an article that is substantially based on a student's dissertation or thesis, the student is listed as the principal author. (See F.1.d. and G.4.a.)

   d. Duplicate Submission. Counselors submit manuscripts for consideration to only one journal at a time. Manuscripts that are published in whole or in substantial part in another journal or published work are not submitted for publication without acknowledgment and permission from the previous publication.

   e. Professional Review. Counselors who review material submitted for publication, research, or other scholarly purposes respect the confidentiality and proprietary rights of those who submitted it.

## Section H: Resolving Ethical Issues

1. Knowledge of Standards. Counselors are familiar with the Code of Ethics and the Standards of Practice and other applicable ethics codes from other professional organizations of which they are members, or from certification and licensure bodies. Lack of knowledge or misunderstanding of an ethical responsibility is not a defense against a charge of unethical conduct. (See F.3.e.)

2. Suspected Violations
   a. Ethical Behavior Expected. Counselors expect professional associates to adhere to the Code of Ethics. When counselors possess reasonable cause that raises doubts as to whether a counselor is acting in an ethical manner, they take appropriate action. (See H.2.d. and H.2.e.)
   b. Consultation. When uncertain as to whether a particular situation or course of action may be in violation of the Code of Ethics, counselors consult with other counselors who are knowledgeable about ethics, with colleagues, or with appropriate authorities.
   c. Organization Conflicts. If the demands of an organization with which counselors are affiliated pose a conflict with the Code of Ethics, counselors specify the nature of such conflicts and express to their supervisors or other responsible officials their commitment to the Code of Ethics. When possible, counselors work toward change within the organization to allow full adherence to the Code of Ethics.
   d. Informal Resolution. When counselors have reasonable cause to believe that another counselor is violating an ethical standard, they attempt to first resolve the issue informally with the other counselor if feasible, providing that such action does not violate confidentiality rights that may be involved.
   e. Reporting Suspected Violations. When an informal resolution is not appropriate or feasible, counselors, upon reasonable cause, take action such as reporting the suspected ethical violation to state or national ethics committees, unless this action conflicts with confidentiality rights that cannot be resolved.
   f. Unwarranted Complaints. Counselors do not initiate, participate in, or encourage the filing of ethics complaints that are unwarranted or intend to harm a counselor rather than to protect clients or the public.
3. Cooperation With Ethics Committees. Counselors assist in the process of enforcing the Code of Ethics. Counselors cooperate with investigations, proceedings, and requirements of the ACA Ethics Committee or ethics committees of other duly constituted associations or boards having jurisdiction over those charged with a violation. Counselors are familiar with the ACA Policies and Procedures and use it as a reference in assisting the enforcement of the Code of Ethics.

## STANDARDS OF PRACTICE

All members of the American Counseling Association (ACA) are required to adhere to the Standards of Practice and the Code of Ethics. The Standards of Practice represent minimal behavioral statements of the Code of Ethics. Members should refer to the applicable section of the Code of Ethics for further interpretation and amplification of the applicable Standard of Practice.

*Section A: The Counseling Relationship*
*Section B: Confidentiality*
*Section C: Professional Responsibility*
*Section D: Relationship With Other Professionals*
*Section E: Evaluation, Assessment, and Interpretation*
*Section F: Teaching, Training, and Supervision*
*Section G: Research and Publication*
*Section H: Resolving Ethical Issues*

## Section A: The Counseling Relationship

Standard of Practice One (SP-1): Nondiscrimination. Counselors respect diversity and must not discriminate against clients because of age, color, culture, disability, ethnic group, gender, race, religion, sexual orientation, marital status, or socioeconomic status. (See A.2.a.)

Standard of Practice Two (SP-2): Disclosure to Clients. Counselors must adequately inform clients, preferably in writing, regarding the counseling process and counseling relationship at or before the time it begins and throughout the relationship. (See A.3.a.)

Standard of Practice Three (SP-3): Dual Relationships. Counselors must make every effort to avoid dual relationships with clients that could impair their professional judgment or increase the risk of harm to clients. When a dual relationship cannot be avoided, counselors must take appropriate steps to ensure that judgment is not impaired and that no exploitation occurs. (See A.6.a. and A.6.b.)

Standard of Practice Four (SP-4): Sexual Intimacies With Clients. Counselors must not engage in any type of sexual intimacies with current clients and must not engage in sexual intimacies with former clients within a minimum of two years after terminating the counseling relationship. Counselors who engage in such relationship after two years following termination have the responsibility to examine and document thoroughly that such relations did not have an exploitative nature.

Standard of Practice Five (SP-5): Protecting Clients During Group Work. Counselors must take steps to protect clients from physical or psychological trauma resulting from interactions during group work. (See A.9.b.)

Standard of Practice Six (SP-6): Advance Understanding of Fees. Counselors must explain to clients, prior to their entering the counseling relationship, financial arrangements related to professional services. (See A.10.a.-d. and A.11.c.)

Standard of Practice Seven (SP-7): Termination. Counselors must assist in making appropriate arrangements for the continuation of treatment of clients, when necessary, following termination of counseling relationships. (See A.11.a.)

Standard of Practice Eight (SP-8): Inability to Assist Clients. Counselors must avoid entering or immediately terminate a counseling relationship if it is determined that they are unable to be of professional assistance to a client. The counselor may assist in making an appropriate referral for the client. (See A.11.b.)

## Section B: Confidentiality

Standard of Practice Nine (SP-9): Confidentiality Requirement. Counselors must keep information related to counseling services confidential unless disclosure is in the best interest of clients, is required for the welfare of others, or is required by law. When disclosure is required, only information that is essential is revealed and the client is informed of such disclosure. (See B.1.a.-f.)

Standard of Practice Ten (SP-10): Confidentiality Requirements for Subordinates. Counselors must take measures to ensure that privacy and confidentiality of clients are maintained by subordinates. (See B.1.h.)

Standard of Practice Eleven (SP-11): Confidentiality in Group Work. Counselors must clearly communicate to group members that confidentiality cannot be guaranteed in group work. (See B.2.a.)

Standard of Practice Twelve (SP-12): Confidentiality in Family Counseling. Counselors must not disclose information about one family member in counseling to another family member without prior consent. (See B.2.b.)

Standard of Practice Thirteen (SP-13): Confidentiality of Records. Counselors must maintain appropriate confidentiality in creating, storing, accessing, transferring, and disposing of counseling records. (See B.4.b.)

Standard of Practice Fourteen (SP-14): Permission to Record or Observe. Counselors must obtain prior consent from clients in order to record electronically or observe sessions. (See B.4.c.)

Standard of Practice Fifteen (SP-15): Disclosure or Transfer of Records. Counselors must obtain client consent to disclose or transfer records to third parties, unless exceptions listed in SP-9 exist. (See B.4.e.)

Standard of Practice Sixteen (SP-16): Data Disguise Required. Counselors must disguise the identity of the client when using data for training, research, or publication. (See B.5.a.)

## Section C: Professional Responsibility

Standard of Practice Seventeen (SP-17): Boundaries of Competence. Counselors must practice only within the boundaries of their competence. (See C.2.a.)

Standard of Practice Eighteen (SP-18): Continuing Education. Counselors must engage in continuing education to maintain their professional competence. (See C.2.f.)

Standard of Practice Nineteen (SP-19): Impairment of Professionals. Counselors must refrain from offering professional services when their personal problems or conflicts may cause harm to a client or others. (See C.2.g.)

Standard of Practice Twenty (SP-20): Accurate Advertising. Counselors must accurately represent their credentials and services when advertising. (See C.3.a.)

Standard of Practice Twenty-One (SP-21): Recruiting Through Employment. Counselors must not use their place of employment or institutional affiliation to recruit clients for their private practices. (See C.3.d.)

Standard of Practice Twenty-Two (SP-22): Credentials Claimed. Counselors must claim or imply only professional credentials possessed and must correct any known misrepresentations of their credentials by others. (See C.4.a.)

Standard of Practice Twenty-Three (SP-23): Sexual Harassment. Counselors must not engage in sexual harassment. (See C.5.b.)

Standard of Practice Twenty-Four (SP-24): Unjustified Gains. Counselors must not use their professional positions to seek or receive unjustified personal gains, sexual favors, unfair advantage, or unearned goods or services. (See C.5.e.)

Standard of Practice Twenty-Five (SP-25): Clients Served by Others. With the consent of the client, counselors must inform other mental health professionals serving the same client that a counseling relationship between the counselor and client exists. (See C.6.c.)

Standard of Practice Twenty-Six (SP-26): Negative Employment Conditions. Counselors must alert their employers to institutional policy or conditions that may be potentially disruptive or damaging to the counselor's professional responsibilities, or that may limit their effectiveness or deny clients' rights. (See D.1.c.)

Standard of Practice Twenty-Seven (SP-27): Personnel Selection and Assignment. Counselors must select competent staff and must assign responsibilities compatible with staff skills and experiences. (See D.1.h.)

Standard of Practice Twenty-Eight (SP-28): Exploitative Relationships With Subordinates. Counselors must not engage in exploitative relationships with individuals over whom they have supervisory, evaluative, or instructional control or authority. (See D.1.k.)

## Section D: Relationship With Other Professionals

Standard of Practice Twenty-Nine (SP-29): Accepting Fees from Agency Clients. Counselors must not accept fees or other remuneration for consultation with persons entitled to such services through the counselor's employing agency or institution. (See D.3.a.)

Standard of Practice Thirty (SP-30): Referral Fees. Counselors must not accept referral fees. (See D.3.b.)

## Section E: Evaluation, Assessment, and Interpretation

Standard of Practice Thirty-One (SP-31): Limits of Competence. Counselors must perform only testing and assessment services for which they are competent. Counselors must not allow the use of psychological assessment techniques by unqualified persons under their supervision. (See E.2.a.)

Standard of Practice Thirty-Two (SP-32): Appropriate Use of Assessment Instruments. Counselors must use assessment instruments in the manner for which they were intended. (See E.2.b.)

Standard of Practice Thirty-Three (SP-33): Assessment Explanations to Clients. Counselors must provide explanations to clients prior to assessment about the nature and purposes of assessment and the specific uses of results. (See E.3.a.)

Standard of Practice Thirty-Four (SP-34): Recipients of Tests Results. Counselors must ensure that accurate and appropriate interpretations accompany any release of testing and assessment information. (See E.3.b.)

Standard of Practice Thirty-Five (SP-35): Obsolete Tests and Outdated Test Results. Counselors must not base their assessment or intervention decisions or recommendations on data or test results that are obsolete or outdated for the current purpose. (See E.11.)

## Section F: Teaching, Training, and Supervision

Standard of Practice Thirty-Six (SP-36): Sexual Relationships With Students or Supervisees. Counselors must not engage in sexual relationships with their students and supervisees. (See F.1.c.)

Standard of Practice Thirty-Seven (SP-37): Credit for Contributions to Research. Counselors must give credit to students or supervisees for their contributions to research and scholarly projects. (See F.1.d.)

Standard of Practice Thirty-Eight (SP-38): Supervision Preparation. Counselors who offer clinical supervision services must be trained and prepared in supervision methods and techniques. (See F.1.f.)

Standard of Practice Thirty-Nine (SP-39): Evaluation Information. Counselors must clearly state to students and supervisees in advance of training the levels of competency expected, appraisal methods, and timing of evaluations. Counselors must provide students and supervisees with periodic performance appraisal and evaluation feedback throughout the training program. (See F.2.c.)

Standard of Practice Forty (SP-40): Peer Relationships in Training. Counselors must make every effort to ensure that the rights of peers are not violated when students and supervisees are assigned to lead counseling groups or provide clinical supervision. (See F.2.e.)

Standard of Practice Forty-One (SP-41): Limitations of Students and Supervisees. Counselors must assist students and supervisees in securing remedial assistance, when needed, and must dismiss from the training program students and supervisees who are unable to provide competent service due to academic or personal limitations. (See F.3.a.)

Standard of Practice Forty-Two (SP-42): Self-Growth Experiences. Counselors who conduct experiences for students or supervisees that include self-growth or self-disclosure must inform participants of counselors' ethical obligations to the profession and must not grade participants based on their nonacademic performance. (See F.3.b.)

Standard of Practice Forty-Three (SP-43): Standards for Students and Supervisees. Students and supervisees preparing to become counselors must adhere to the Code of Ethics and the Standards of Practice of Counselors. (See F.3.e.)

### Section G: Research and Publication

Standard of Practice Forty-Four (SP-44): Precautions to Avoid Injury in Research. Counselors must avoid causing physical, social, or psychological harm or injury to subjects in research. (See G.1.c.)

Standard of Practice Forty-Five (SP-45): Confidentiality of Research Information. Counselors must keep confidential information obtained about research participants. (See G.2.d.)

Standard of Practice Forty-Six (SP-46): Information Affecting Research Outcome. Counselors must report all variables and conditions known to the investigator that may have affected research data or outcomes. (See G.3.a.)

Standard of Practice Forty-Seven (SP-47): Accurate Research Results. Counselors must not distort or misrepresent research data, nor fabricate or intentionally bias research results. (See G.3.b.)

Standard of Practice Forty-Eight (SP-48): Publication Contributors. Counselors must give appropriate credit to those who have contributed to research. (See G.4.a. and G.4.b.)

### Section H: Resolving Ethical Issues

Standard of Practice Forty-Nine (SP-49): Ethical Behavior Expected. Counselors must take appropriate action when they possess reasonable cause that raises doubts as to whether counselors or other mental health professionals are acting in an ethical manner. (See H.2.a.)

Standard of Practice Fifty (SP-50): Unwarranted Complaints. Counselors must not initiate, participate in, or encourage the filing of ethics complaints that are unwarranted or intended to harm a mental health professional rather than to protect clients or the public. (See H.2.f.)

Standard of Practice Fifty-One (SP-51): Cooperation With Ethics Committees. Counselors must cooperate with investigations, proceedings, and requirements of the ACA Ethics Committee or ethics committees of other duly constituted associations or boards having jurisdiction over those charged with a violation. (See H.3.)

## REFERENCES

The following documents are available to counselors as resources to guide them in their practices. These resources are not a part of the Code of Ethics and the Standards of Practice.

American Association for Counseling and Development/Association for Measurement and Evaluation in Counseling and Development. (1989). The responsibilities of users of standardized tests (rev.). Washington, DC: Author.

American Counseling Association. (1988). Ethical standards. Alexandria, VA: Author.

American Psychological Association. (1985). Standards for educational and psychological testing (rev.). Washington, DC: Author.

American Rehabilitation Counseling Association, Commission on Rehabilitation Counselor Certification, and National Rehabilitation Counseling Association. (1995). Code of professional ethics for rehabilitation counselors. Chicago, IL: Author.

American School Counselor Association. (1992). Ethical standards for school counselors. Alexandria, VA: Author.

Joint Committee on Testing Practices. (1988). Code of fair testing practices in education. Washington, DC: Author.

National Board for Certified Counselors. (1989). National Board for Certified Counselors Code of Ethics. Alexandria, VA: Author.

Prediger, D.J. (Ed.). (1993, March). Multicultural assessment standards. Alexandria, VA: Association for Assessment in Counseling.

# B

\*

# Ethical Standards for School Counselors

## American School Counselor Association

### PREAMBLE

The American School Counselor Association is a professional organization whose members have a unique and distinctive preparation grounded in the behavioral sciences with training in clinical skills adapted to the school setting. The counselor assists in the growth and development of each individual and uses his/her specialized skills to ensure that the rights of the counselee are properly protected within the structure of the school program. School counselors subscribe to the following basic tenets of the counseling process from which professional responsibilities are derived:

1. Each person has the right to respect and dignity as a human being and to counseling services without prejudice as to person, character, belief or practice.
2. Each person has the right to self-direction and self-development.
3. Each person has the right of choice and the responsibility for decisions reached.
4. Each person has the right to privacy and thereby the right to expect the counselor–client relationship to comply with all laws, policies and ethical standards pertaining to confidentiality.

In this document, the American School Counselor Association has specified the principles of ethical behavior necessary to maintain and regulate the high standards of integrity and leadership among its members. The Association recognizes the basic commitment of its members to the *Ethical Standards* of its parent organization, the American Counseling Association (ACA), and nothing in this document shall be construed to supplant that code. *The Ethical Standards for School Counselors* was developed to complement the ACA standards by clarifying the nature of ethical responsibilities for present and future counselors in the school setting. The purposes of this document are to:

1. Serve as a guide for the ethical practices of all school counselors regardless of level, area, population served, or membership in this Association.

2. Provide benchmarks for both self-appraisal and peer evaluations regarding counselor responsibilities to students, parents, colleagues and professional associates, school and community, self, and the counseling profession.

3. Inform those served by the school counselor of acceptable counselor practices and expected professional deportment.

## A. RESPONSIBILITIES TO PUPILS
The school counselor:

1. Has a primary obligation and loyalty to the pupil, who is to be treated with respect as a unique individual, whether assisted individually or in a group setting.

2. Is concerned with the total needs of the student (educational, vocational, personal, and social) and encourages the maximum growth development of each counselee.

3. Informs the counselee of the purposes, goals, techniques, and rules of procedure under which she/he may receive counseling assistance at or before the time when the counseling relationship is entered. Prior notice includes confidentiality issues such as the possible necessity for consulting with other professionals, privileged communication, and legal or authoritative restraints. The meaning and limits of confidentiality are clearly defined to counselees.

4. Refrains from consciously encouraging the counselee's acceptance of values, lifestyles, plans, decisions, and beliefs that represent only the counselor's personal orientation.

5. Is responsible for keeping abreast of laws relating to students and strives to ensure that the rights of students are adequately provided for and protected.

6. Avoids dual relationships which might impair his/her objectivity and/or increase the risk of harm to the client (e.g., counseling one's family members, close friends or associates). If a dual relationship is unavoidable, the counselor is responsible for taking action to eliminate or reduce the potential for harm. Such safeguards might include informed consent, consultation, supervision, and documentation.

7. Makes appropriate referrals when professional assistance can no longer be adequately provided to the counselee. Appropriate referral necessitates knowledge of available resources.

8. Protects the confidentiality of student records and releases personal data only according to prescribed laws and school policies. Student

information maintained through electronic data storage methods is treated with the same care as traditional student records.

9. Protects the confidentiality of information received in the counseling relationship as specified by law and ethical standards. Such information is only to be revealed to others when informed consent of the counselee and consistent with the obligation of the counselor as a professional person. In a group setting, the counselor sets a norm of confidentiality and stresses its importance, yet clearly states that confidentiality in group counseling cannot be guaranteed.

10. Informs the appropriate authorities when the counselee's condition indicates a clear and imminent danger to the counselee or others. This is to be done after careful deliberation and, where possible, after consultation with other professionals. The counselor informs the counselee of actions to be taken so as to minimize confusion and clarify expectations.

11. Screens prospective group members and maintains an awareness of participants' compatibility throughout the life of the group, especially when the group emphasis is on self-disclosure and self-understanding. The counselor takes reasonable precautions to protect members from physical and/or psychological harm resulting from interaction within the group.

12. Provides explanations of the nature, purposes, and results of tests in language that is understandable to the client(s).

13. Adheres to relevant standards regarding selection, administration, and interpretation of assessment techniques. The counselor recognizes that computer-based testing programs require specific training in administration, scoring, and interpretation which may differ from that required in more traditional assessments.

14. Promotes the benefits of appropriate computer applications and clarifies the limitations of computer technology. The counselor ensures that (1) computer applications are appropriate for the individual needs of the counselee, (2) the counselee understands how to use the application, and (3) follow-up counseling assistance is provided. Members of underrepresented groups are assured of equal access to computer technologies and the absence of discriminatory information and values within computer applications.

15. Has unique ethical responsibilities in working with peer programs. In general, the school counselor is responsible for the welfare of students participating in peer programs under her/his direction. School counselors who function in training and supervisory capacities are referred to the preparation and supervision standards of professional counselor associations.

## B. RESPONSIBILITIES TO PARENTS

The school counselor:

1. Respects the inherent rights and responsibilities of parents for their children and endeavors to establish a cooperative relationship with parents to facilitate the maximum development of the counselee.

2.  Informs parents of the counselor's role, with emphasis on the confidential nature of the counseling relationship between the counselor and counselee.
3.  Provides parents with accurate, comprehensive, and relevant information in an objective and caring manner, as appropriate and consistent with ethical responsibilities to the counselee.
4.  Treats information received from parents in a confidential and appropriate manner.
5.  Shares information about a counselee only with those persons properly authorized to receive such information.
6.  Adheres to laws and local guidelines when assisting parents experiencing family difficulties which interfere with the counselee's effectiveness and welfare.
7.  Is sensitive to changes in the family and recognizes that all parents, custodial and noncustodial, are vested with certain rights and responsibilities for the welfare of their children by virtue of their position and according to law.

## C. RESPONSIBILITIES TO COLLEAGUES AND PROFESSIONAL ASSOCIATES
The school counselor:
1.  Establishes and maintains a cooperative relationship with faculty, staff, and administration to facilitate the provision of optimum guidance and counseling services.
2.  Promotes awareness and adherence to appropriate guidelines regarding confidentiality, the distinction between public and private information, and staff consultation.
3.  Treats colleagues with respect, courtesy, fairness, and good faith. The qualifications, views, and findings of colleagues are represented accurately and fairly to enhance the image of competent professionals.
4.  Provides professional personnel with accurate, objective, concise, and meaningful data necessary to adequately evaluate, counsel, and assist the counselee.
5.  Is aware of and fully utilizes related professions and organizations to whom the counselee may be referred.

## D. RESPONSIBILITIES TO THE SCHOOL AND COMMUNITY
The school counselor:
1.  Supports and protects the educational program against any infringement not in the best interest of students.
2.  Informs appropriate officials of conditions that may be potentially disruptive or damaging to the school's mission, personnel, and property.
3.  Delineates and promotes the counselor's role and function in meeting the needs of those served. The counselor will notify appropriate officials of conditions which may limit or curtail their effectiveness in providing programs and services.
4.  Assist in the development of (1) curricular and environmental conditions appropriate for the school and community, (2) educational pro-

cedures and programs to meet student needs, and (3) a systematic evaluation process for guidance and counseling programs, services, and personnel. The counselor is guided by the findings of the evaluation data in planning programs and services.

5. Actively cooperates and collaborates with agencies, organizations, and individuals in the school and community in the best interest of counselees and without regard to personal reward or remuneration.

## E.  RESPONSIBILITIES TO SELF

The school counselor:

1. Functions within the boundaries of individual professional competence and accepts responsibility for the consequences of his/her actions.
2. Is aware of the potential effects of her/his own personal characteristics on services to clients.
3. Monitors personal functioning and effectiveness and refrains from any activity likely to lead to inadequate professional services or harm to a client.
4. Recognizes that differences in clients relating to age, gender, race, religion, sexual orientation, socioeconomic, and ethnic backgrounds may require specific training to ensure competent services.
5. Strives through personal initiative to maintain professional competence and keep abreast of innovations and trends in the profession. Professional and personal growth is continuous and ongoing throughout the counselor's career.

## F.  RESPONSIBILITIES TO THE PROFESSION

The school counselor:

1. Conducts herself/himself in such a manner as to bring credit to self and the profession.
2. Conducts appropriate research and reports findings in a manner consistent with acceptable educational and psychological research practices. When using client data for research, statistical or program planning purposes, the counselor ensures protection of the identity of the individual client(s).
3. Actively participates in local, state, and national associations which foster the development and improvement of school counseling.
4. Adheres to ethical standards of the profession, other official policy statements pertaining to counseling, and relevant statutes established by federal, state, and local governments.
5. Clearly distinguishes between statements and actions made as a private individual and as a representative of the school counseling profession.
6. Contributes to the development of the profession through the sharing of skills, ideas, and expertise with colleagues.

## G.  MAINTENANCE OF STANDARDS

Ethical behavior among professional school counselors, Association members and nonmembers, is expected at all times. When there exists serious doubt as to the ethical behavior of colleagues, or if counselors are forced to work in situations or abide by policies which do not reflect the standards as outlined in these *Ethical Standards for School Counselors* or the ACA *Ethical Standards*, the counselor is obligated to take appropriate action to rectify the condition. The following procedure may serve as a guide:

1. If feasible, the counselor should consult with a professional colleague to confidentially discuss the nature of the complaint to see if she/he views the situation as an ethical violation.
2. Whenever possible, the counselor should directly approach the colleague whose behavior is in question to discuss the complaint and seek resolution.
3. If resolution is not forthcoming at the personal level, the counselor shall utilize the channels established within the school and/or school district. This may include both informal and formal procedures.
4. If the matter still remains unresolved, referral for review and appropriate action should be made to the Ethics Committees in the following sequence:
   —local counselor association
   —state counselor association
   —national counselor association
5. The ASCA Ethics Committee functions in an educative and consultative capacity and does not adjudicate complaints of ethical misconduct. Therefore at the national level, complaints should be submitted in writing to the ACA Ethics Committee for review and appropriate action. The procedure for submitting complaints may be obtained by writing the ACA Ethics Committee, c/o The Executive Director, American Counseling Association, 5999 Stevenson Avenue, Alexandria, VA 22304.

## H. RESOURCES

School counselors are responsible for being aware of, and acting in accord with, the standards and positions of the counseling profession as represented in official documents such as those listed below.

*Code of Ethics* (1989). National Board for Certified Counselors. Alexandria, VA.

*Code of Ethics for Peer Helping Professionals* (1989). National Peer Helpers Association. Glendale, CA.

*Ethical Guidelines for Group Counselors* (1989). Association for Specialists in Group Work. Alexandria, VA

*Ethical Standards* (1988). American Association for Counseling and Development. Alexandria, VA

*Position Statement: The School Counselor and Confidentiality* (1986). American School Counselor Association. Alexandria, VA

*Position Statement: The School Counselor and Peer Facilitation* (1984). American School Counselor Association. Alexandria, VA.

*Position Statement: The School Counselor and Student Rights* (1992). American School Counselor Association. Alexandria, VA.

*Ethical Standards for School Counselors* was adopted by the ASCA Delegate Assembly, March 19, 1984. This revision was approved by the ASCA Delegate Assembly, March 27, 1992.

As of July 1, 1992 the American Association for Counseling and Development (AACD) becomes the American Counseling Association (ACA).

Reprinted by permission of the American Counseling Association.

# C

✳

# American Mental Health Counselors Association Code of Ethics

## PREAMBLE

Mental health counselors believe in the dignity and worth of the individual. They are committed to increasing knowledge of human behavior and understanding of themselves and others. While pursuing these endeavors, they make every reasonable effort to protect the welfare of those who seek their services or of any subject that may be the object of study. They use their skills only for purposes consistent with these values and do not knowingly permit their misuse by others. While demanding for themselves freedom of inquiry and community, mental health counselors accept the responsibility this freedom confers: competence, objectivity in the application of skills and concern for the best interests of clients, colleagues, and society in general. In the pursuit of these ideals, mental health counselors subscribe to the following principles:

**Principle 1. Responsibility**
In their commitment to the understanding of human behavior, mental health counselors value objectivity and integrity, and in providing services they maintain the highest standards. They accept responsibility for the consequences of their work and make every effort to insure that their services are used appropriately.

a. Mental health counselors accept ultimate responsibility for selecting appropriate areas for investigation and the methods relevant to minimize the possibility that their finding will be misleading. They provide thorough discussion of the limitations of their data and alternative hypotheses, especially where their work touches on social policy or might be misconstrued to the detriment of specific age, sex, ethnic, socio-economic, or other social categories. In publishing reports of their work, they never discard observations that may modify the interpretation of results. Mental health counselors take credit only for the work they have actually done. In pursuing research, mental health counselors ascertain that their efforts will not lead to changes in individuals or organizations unless such changes are part of the agreement at the time of obtaining informal consent. Mental health counselors clarify in advance the expectations for sharing and utilizing research data. They avoid dual relationships which may limit objectivity, whether theoretical, political, or monetary, so that interference with data, subjects, and milieu is kept to a minimum.

b. As employees of an institution or agency, mental health counselors have the responsibility of remaining alert to institutional pressures which may distort reports of counseling findings or use them in ways counter to the promotion of human welfare.

c. When serving as members of governmental or other organizational bodies, mental health counselors remain accountable as individuals to the Code of Ethics of the American Mental Health Counselors Association (AMHCA).

d. As teachers, mental health counselors recognize their primary obligation to help others acquire knowledge and skill. They maintain high standards of scholarship and objectivity by presenting counseling information fully and accurately, and by giving appropriate recognition to alternative viewpoints.

e. As practitioners, mental health counselors know that they bear a heavy social responsibility because their recommendations and professional actions may alter the lives of others. They, therefore, remain fully cognizant of their impact and alert to personal, social, organizational, financial or political situations or pressures which might lead to misuse of their influence.

f. Mental health counselors provide reasonable and timely feedback to employees, trainees, supervisors, students, clients, and others whose work they may evaluate.

## Principle 2. Competence

The maintenance of high standards of professional competence is a responsibility shared by all mental health counselors in the interest of the public and the profession as a whole. Mental health counselors recognize the boundaries of their competence and the limitations of their techniques and only provide services, use techniques, or offer opinions as professionals that meet recognized standards. Throughout their careers, mental health counselors maintain knowledge of professional information related to the services they render.

a. Mental health counselors accurately represent their competence, education, training, and experience.

b. As teachers, mental health counselors perform their duties based on careful preparation so that their instruction is accurate, up-to-date and scholarly.

c. Mental health counselors recognize the need for continuing training to update themselves to serve persons of all ages and cultural backgrounds. They are open to procedures and sensitive to differences between groups of people and changes in expectations and values over time.

d. Mental health counselors with the responsibility for decisions involving individuals or policies based on test results should know and understand literature relevant to the tests used and testing problems with which they deal.

e. Mental health counselors and practitioners recognize that their effectiveness depends in part upon their ability to maintain sound interpersonal relations, that temporary or more enduring aberrations on their part may interfere with their abilities or distort their appraisal of others. Therefore, they refrain from undertaking any activity in which their personal problems are likely to lead to inadequate professional services or harm to a client, or, if they are already engaged in such activity when they become aware of their personal problems, they would seek competent professional assistance to determine whether they should suspend or terminate service to one or all of their clients.

f. The mental health counselor has a responsibility both to the individual who is served and to the institution with which the service is performed to maintain high standards of professional conduct. The mental health counselor strives to maintain the highest level of professional services offered to the individuals to be served. The mental health counselor also strives to assist the agency, organization or institution in providing the highest caliber of professional services. The acceptance of employment in an institution implies that the mental health counselor is in substantial agreement with the general policies and principles of the institution. If despite concerted efforts, the member cannot reach agreement with the employer as to acceptable standards of conduct that allow for changes in the institutional policy conducive to the positive growth and development of counselees, then terminating the affiliation should be seriously considered.

g. Ethical behavior among professional associates, mental health counselors and nonmental health counselors, is expected at all times. When information is possessed which raises serious doubt as to the ethical behavior of professional colleagues, whether Association members or not, the mental health counselor is obligated to take action to attempt to rectify such a condition. Such action shall utilize the institution's channels first and then utilize procedures established by the state, division, or Association.

h. The mental health counselor is aware of the intimacy of the counseling relationship and maintains a healthy respect for the personhood of the client and avoids engaging in activities that seek to meet the mental health counselor's personal needs at the expense of the client. Through awareness of the negative impact of both racial and sexual stereotyping and discrimination, the member strives to ensure the individual rights and personal dignity of the client in the counseling relationship.

### Principle 3. Moral and Legal Standards

Mental health counselors' moral, ethical, and legal standards of behavior are a personal matter to the same degree as they are for any other citizen, except as these may compromise the fulfillment of their professional responsibilities, or reduce the trust in counseling or counselors held by the general public. Regarding their own behavior, mental health counselors should be aware of the prevailing community standards and of the possible impact upon the quality of professional services provided by their conformance to or deviation from these standards. Mental health counselors should also be aware of the possible impact of their public behavior upon the ability of colleagues to perform their professional duties.

a. To protect public confidence in the profession of counseling, mental health counselors will avoid public behavior that is clearly in violation of accepted moral and legal standards.

b. To protect students, mental health counselors/teachers will be aware of the diverse backgrounds of students and, when dealing with topics that may give offense, will see that the material is treated objectively, that it is clearly relevant to the course, and that it is treated in a manner for which the student is prepared.

c. Providers of counseling services conform to the statutes relating to such services as established by their state and its regulating professional board(s).

d. As employees, mental health counselors refuse to participate in employer's practices which are inconsistent with the moral and legal standards established by federal or state legislation regarding the treatment of employees or of the public. In particular and for example, mental health counselors will not condone practices which result in illegal or otherwise unjustifiable discrimination on the basis of race, sex, religion or national origin in hiring, promotion or training.

e. In providing counseling services to clients mental health counselors avoid any action that will violate or diminish the legal and civil rights of clients or of others who may be affected by the action.

f. Sexual conduct, not limited to sexual intercourse, between mental health counselors and clients is specifically in violation of this code of ethics. This does not, however, prohibit the use of explicit instructional aids including films and videotapes. Such use is within accepted practices of trained and competent sex therapists.

### Principle 4. Public Statements

Mental health counselors in their professional roles may be expected or required to make public statements providing counseling information, professional opinions, or supply information about the availability of counseling products and services. In making such statement, mental health counselors take full account of the limits and uncertainties of present counseling knowledge and techniques. They represent, as objectively as possible, their professional qualifications, affiliations, and functions, as well as those of the institutions or organizations with which the statements may be associated. All public statements, announcements of services, and promotional activities should serve the purpose of providing sufficient information to aid the consumer public in making informed judgments and choices on matters that concern it.

a.  When announcing professional counseling services, mental health counselors limit the information to: name, highest relevant degree conferred, certification or licensure, address, telephone number, office hours, cost of services, and a brief explanation of the other types of services offered but not evaluative as to their quality or uniqueness. They will not contain testimonials by implication. They will not claim uniqueness of skill or methods beyond those acceptable and public scientific evidence.

b.  In announcing the availability of counseling services or products, mental health counselors will not display their affiliations with organizations or agencies in a manner that implies the sponsorship or certification of the organization or agency. They will not name their employer or professional associations unless the services are in fact to be provided by or under the responsible, direct supervision and continuing control of such organizations or agencies.

c.  Mental health counselors associated with the development of promotion of counseling device, books or other products offered for commercial sale will make every effort to insure that announcements and advertisements are presented in a professional and factually informative manner without unsupported claims of superiority and must be supported by scientifically acceptable evidence or by willingness to aid and encourage independent professional scrutiny or scientific test.

d.  Mental health counselors engaged in radio, television or other public media activities will not participate in commercial announcements recommending to the general public the purchase or use of any proprietary or single-source product or service.

e.  Mental health counselors who describe counseling or the services of professional counselors to the general public accept the obligation to present the material fairly and accurately, avoiding misrepresentation through sensationalism, exaggeration or superficiality. Mental health counselors will be guided by the primary obligation to aid the public in forming their own informed judgments, opinions, and choices.

f.  As teachers, mental health counselors ensure their statements in catalogs and course outlines are accurate, particularly in terms of subject matter to be covered, bases for grading, and nature of classroom experiences.

g.  Mental health counselors accept the obligation to correct others who may represent their professional qualifications or associations with products or services in a manner incompatible with these guidelines.

h.  Mental health counselors providing consultation, workshops, training, and other technical services may refer to previous satisfied clients in their advertising, provided there is no implication that such advertising refers to counseling services.

## Principle 5. Confidentiality

Mental health counselors have a primary obligation to safeguard information about individuals obtained in the course of teaching, practice, or research. Personal information is communicated to others only with the person's written consent or in those circumstances where there is clear and imminent danger to the client, to others or to society. Disclosures of counseling information are restricted to what is necessary, relevant, and verifiable.

a.  All materials in the official record shall be shared with the client who shall have the right to decide what information may be shared with anyone beyond the immediate provider of service and to be informed of the implications of the materials to be shared.

b.  The anonymity of clients served in public and other agencies is preserved, if at all possible, by withholding names and personal identifying data. If external conditions require reporting such information, the client shall be so informed.

c.  Information received in confidence by one agency or person shall not be forwarded to another person or agency without the client's written permission.

d.  Service providers have a responsibility to insure the accuracy and to indicate the validity of data shared with their parties.

e.  Case reports presented in classes, professional meetings, or in publications shall be so disguised that no identification is possible unless the client or responsible authority has read the report and agreed in writing to its presentation or publication.

f.  Counseling reports and records are maintained under conditions of security and provisions are made for their destruction when they have outlived their usefulness. Mental health counselors insure that privacy and confidentiality are maintained by all persons in their employ or volunteers, and community aides.

g.  Mental health counselors who ask that an individual reveal personal information in the course of interviewing, testing or evaluation, or who allow such information to be divulged, do so only after making certain that the person or authorized representative is fully aware of the purposes of the interview, testing or evaluation and of the ways in which the information will be used.

h.  Sessions with clients are taped or otherwise recorded only with their written permission or the written permission of a responsible guardian. Even with guardian written consent one should not record a session against the expressed wishes of a client.

i.  Where a child or adolescent is the primary client, the interests of the minor shall be paramount.

j. In work with families, the rights of each family member should be safeguarded. The provider of service also has the responsibility to discuss the contents of the record with the parent and/or child, as appropriate, and to keep separate those parts which should remain the property of each family member.

## Principle 6. Welfare of the Consumer

Mental health counselors respect the integrity and protect the welfare of the people and groups with whom they work. When there is a conflict of interest between the client and the mental health counselor employing institution, the mental health counselors clarify the nature and direction of their loyalties and responsibilities and keep all parties informed of their commitments. Mental health counselors fully inform consumers as to the purpose and nature of any evaluative, treatment, educational or training procedure, and they freely acknowledge that clients, students, or subjects have freedom of choice with regard to participation.

a. Mental health counselors are continually cognizant both of their own needs and of their inherently powerful position "vis-a-vis" clients, in order to avoid exploiting the client's trust and dependency. Mental health counselors make every effort to avoid dual relationships with clients and/or relationships which might impair their professional judgment or increase the risk of client exploitation. Examples of such dual relationships include treating an employee or supervisor, treating a close friend or family relative and sexual relationships with clients.

b. Where mental health counselors' work with members of an organization goes beyond reasonable conditions of employment, mental health counselors recognize possible conflicts of interest that may arise. When such conflicts occur, mental health counselors clarify the nature of the conflict and inform all parties of the nature and directions of the loyalties and responsibilities involved.

c. When acting as supervisors, trainers, or employers, mental health counselors accord recipients informed choice, confidentiality, and protection from physical and mental harm.

d. Financial arrangements in professional practice are in accord with professional standards that safeguard the best interests of the client and that are clearly understood by the client in advance of billing. This may best be done by the use of a contract. Mental health counselors are responsible for assisting clients in finding needed services in those instances where the payment of the usual fee would be a hardship. No commission or rebate or other form of remuneration may be given or received for referral of clients for professional services, whether by an individual or by an agency.

e. Mental health counselors are responsible for making their services readily accessible to clients in a manner that facilitates the client's ability to make an informed choice when selecting a service provider.

This responsibility includes a clear description of what the client may expect in the way of tests, reports, billing, therapeutic regime, and schedules and the use of the mental health counselor's Statement of Professional Disclosure.

f.  Mental health counselors who find that their services are not beneficial to the client have the responsibility to make this known to the responsible persons.

g.  Mental health counselors are accountable to the parties who refer and support counseling services and to the general public and are cognizant of the indirect or long-range effects of their intervention.

h.  The mental health counselor attempts to terminate a private service or consulting relationship when it is reasonably clear to the mental health counselor that the consumer is not benefiting from it. If a consumer is receiving services from another mental health professional, mental health counselors do not offer their services directly to the consumer without informing the professional persons already involved in order to avoid confusion and conflict for the consumer.

i.  The mental health counselor has the responsibility to screen prospective group participants, especially when the emphasis is on self-understanding and growth through self-disclosure. The member should maintain an awareness of the group participants' compatibility throughout the life of the group.

j.  The mental health counselor may choose to consult with any other professionally competent person about a client. In choosing a consultant, the mental health counselor should avoid placing the consultant in a conflict of interest situation that would preclude the consultant's being a proper party to the mental health counselors' efforts to help the clients.

k.  If the mental health counselor is unable to be of professional assistance to the client, the mental health counselor should avoid initiating the counseling relationship or the mental health counselor terminates the relationship. In either event, the member is obligated to suggest appropriate alternatives. (It is incumbent upon the mental health counselors to be knowledgeable about referral resources so that a satisfactory referral can be initiated.) In the event the client declines the suggested referral, the mental health counselor is not obligated to continue the relationship.

l.  When the mental health counselor has other relationships, particularly of an administrative, supervisory, and/or evaluative nature, with an individual seeking counseling services, the mental health counselor should not serve as the counselor but should refer the individual to another professional. Only in instances where such an alternative is unavailable and where the individual's situation definitely warrants counseling intervention should the mental health counselor enter into and/or maintain a counseling relationship. Dual relationships with clients which might impair the member's objectivity and professional judgment (such as with close friends or relatives, sexual intimacies with any client, etc.) must be avoided and/or the counseling relationship terminated through referral to another competent professional.

m. All experimental methods of treatment must be clearly indicated to prospective recipients, and safety precautions are to be adhered to by the mental health counselor instituting treatment.

n. When the member is engaged in short-term group treatment/training programs e.g., marathons and other encounter-type or growth groups, the member ensures that there is professional assistance available during and following the group experience.

**Principle 7. Professional Relationships**

Mental health counselors act with due regard to the needs and feelings of their colleagues in counseling and other professions. Mental health counselors respect the prerogatives and obligations of the institutions or organizations with which they are associated.

a. Mental health counselors understand the areas of competence of related professions and make full use of other professional, technical, and administrative resources which best serve the interests of consumers. The absence of formal relationships with other professional workers does not relieve mental health counselors from the responsibility of securing for their clients the best possible professional service; indeed, this circumstance presents a challenge to the professional competence of mental health counselors, requiring special sensitivity to problems outside their areas of training, and foresight, diligence, and tact in obtaining the professional assistance needed by clients.

b. Mental health counselors know and take into account the traditions and practices of other professional groups with which they work and cooperate fully with members of such groups when research, services, and other functions are shared or in working for the benefit of public welfare.

c. Mental health counselors strive to provide positive conditions for those they employ and they spell out clearly the conditions of such employment. They encourage their employees to engage in activities that facilitate their further professional development.

d. Mental health counselors respect the viability, reputation, and the proprietary right of organizations which they serve. Mental health counselors show due regard for the interest of their present or prospective employers. In those instances where they are critical of policies, they attempt to effect change by constructive action within the organization.

e. In the pursuit of research, mental health counselors give sponsoring agencies, host institutions, and publication channels the same respect and opportunity for giving informed consent that they accord to individual research participants. They are aware of their obligation to future research workers and insure that host institutions are given feedback information and proper acknowledgment.

f. Credit is assigned to those who have contributed to a publication, in proportion to their contribution.

g. When a mental health counselor violates ethical standards, mental health counselors who know firsthand of such activities should, if possible, attempt to rectify the situation. Failing an informal solution, mental health counselors should bring such unethical activities to the attention of the appropriate state, and/or national committee on ethics and professional conduct. Only after all professional alternatives have been utilized will a mental health counselor begin legal action for resolution.

## Principle 8. Utilization of Assessment Techniques

In the development, publication, and utilization of counseling assessment techniques, mental health counselors follow relevant standards. Individuals examined, or their legal guardians, have the right to know the results, the interpretations made, and where appropriate, the particulars on which final judgment was based. These users should take precautions to protect test security but not at the expense of an individual's right to understand the basis for decisions that adversely affect that individual or that individual's dependents.

a. The client has the right to have and the provider has the responsibility to give explanations of test results in language the client can understand.

b. When a test is published or otherwise made available for operational use, it should be accompanied by a manual (or other published or readily available information) that makes every reasonable effort to describe fully the development of the test, the rationale, specifications followed in writing items analysis or other research. The test, the manual, the record forms, and other accompanying material should help users make correct interpretations of the test results and should warn against common misuses. The test manual should state explicitly the purposes and applications for which the test is recommended and identify any special qualifications required to administer the test and to interpret it properly. Evidence of validity and reliability, along with other relevant research data, should be presented in support of any claims made.

c. Norms presented in test manuals should refer to defined and clearly described populations. These populations should be the groups with whom users of the test will ordinarily wish to compare the persons tested. Test users should consider the possibility of bias in tests or in test items. When indicated, there should be an investigation of possible differences in validity for ethnic, sex, or other subsamples that can be identified when the test is given.

d. Mental health counselors who have the responsibility for decisions about individuals or policies that are based on test results should have a thorough understanding of counseling or educational measurement and of validation and other test research.

e.  Mental health counselors should develop procedures for systematically eliminating from data files test score information that has, because of the lapse of time, become obsolete.

f.  Any individual or organization offering test scoring and interpretation services must be able to demonstrate that their programs are based on appropriate research to establish the validity of the programs and procedures used in arriving at interpretations. The public offering of an automated test interpretation service will be considered as a professional-to-professional consultation. In this the formal responsibility of the consultant is to the consultee but his/her ultimate and overriding responsibility is to the client.

g.  Counseling services for the purpose of diagnosis, treatment, or personalized advice are provided only in the context of a professional relationship, and are not given by means of public lectures or demonstrations, newspapers or magazine articles, radio or television programs, mail, or similar media. The preparation of personnel reports and recommendations based on test data secured solely by mail is unethical unless such appraisals are an integral part of a continuing client relationship with a company, as a result of which the consulting clinical mental health counselor has intimate knowledge of the client's personal situation and can be assured thereby that his written appraisals will be adequate to the purpose and will be properly interpreted by the client. These reports must not be embellished with such detailed analyses of the subject's personality traits as would be appropriate only for intensive interviews with the subjects.

**Principle 9. Pursuit of Research Activities**
The decision to undertake research should rest upon a considered judgment by the individual mental health counselor about how best to contribute to counseling and to human welfare. Mental health counselors carry out their investigations with respect for the people who participate and with concern for their dignity and welfare.

a.  In planning a study the investigator has the personal responsibility to make a careful evaluation of its ethical acceptability, taking into account the following principles for research with human beings. To the extent that this appraisal, weighing scientific and human values, suggests a deviation from any principle, the investigator incurs an increasingly serious obligation to seek ethical advice and to observe more stringent safeguards to protect the rights of the human research participants.

b.  Mental health counselors know and take into account the traditions and practices of other professional groups with members of such groups when research, services, and other functions are shared or in working for the benefit of public welfare.

c.  Ethical practice requires the investigator to inform the participant of all features of the research that reasonably might be expected to influence willingness to participate, and to explain all other aspects of the research about which the participant inquires. Failure to make full disclosure gives added emphasis to the investigator's abiding responsibility to protect the welfare and dignity of the research participant.

d. Openness and honesty are essential characteristics of the relationship between investigator and research participant. When the methodological requirements of a study necessitate concealment or deception, the investigator is required to insure as soon as possible the participant's understanding of the reasons for this action and to restore the quality of the relationship with the investigator.

e. In the pursuit of research, mental health counselors give sponsoring agencies, host institutions, and publication channels the same respect and opportunity for giving informed consent that they accord to individual research participants. They are aware of their obligation to future research workers and insure that host institutions are given feedback information and proper acknowledgment.

f. Credit is assigned to those who have contributed to a publication, in proportion to their contribution.

g. The ethical investigator protects participants from physical and mental discomfort, harm and danger. If the risk of such consequences exists, the investigator is required to inform the participant of that fact, secure consent before proceeding, and take all possible measures to minimize distress. A research procedure may not be used if it is likely to cause serious and lasting harm to participants.

h. After the data are collected, ethical practice requires the investigator to provide the participant with a full clarification of the nature of the study and to remove any misconceptions that may have arisen. Where scientific or humane values justify delaying or withholding information the investigator acquires a special responsibility to assure that there are no damaging consequences for the participants.

i. Where research procedure may result in undesirable consequences for the participant, the investigator has the responsibility to detect and remove or correct these consequences, including, where relevant, long-term after effects.

j. Information obtained about the research participants during the course of an investigation is confidential. When the possibility exists that others may obtain access to such information, ethical research practice requires that the possibility, together with the plans for protecting confidentiality, be explained to the participants as a part of the procedure for obtaining informed consent.

## Principle 10. Private Practice

a. A mental health counselor should assist where permitted by legislation or judicial decision the profession in fulfilling its duty to make counseling services available in private settings.

b. In advertising services as a private practitioner the mental health counselor should advertise the services in such a manner so as to accurately inform the public as to services, expertise, profession, techniques of counseling in a professional manner. A mental health counselor who assumes an executive leadership role in the organization shall not permit his/her name to be used in professional notices during periods when not actively engaged in the private practice of counseling.

The mental health counselor may list the following: Highest relevant degree, type and level of certification or license, type and/or description of services and other relevant information. Such information should not contain false, inaccurate, misleading, partial, out-of-context or deceptive material or statements.

c. The mental health counselors may join in partnership/corporation with other mental health counselors and/or other professionals provided that each mental health counselor of the partnership or corporation makes clear the separate specialties by name in compliance with the regulations of the locality.

d. A mental health counselor has an obligation to withdraw from a counseling relationship if it is believed that employment will result in violation of the code of ethics, if their mental capacity or physical condition renders it difficult to carry out an effective professional relationship, or if the mental health counselor is discharged by the client because the counseling relationship is no longer productive for the client.

e. A mental health counselor should adhere to and support the regulations for private practice of the locality where the services are offered.

f. Mental health counselors are discouraged from deliberate attempts to utilize one's institutional affiliation to recruit clients for one's private practice. Mental health counselors are to refrain from offering their services in the private sector, when they are employed by an institution in which this is prohibited by stated policies reflecting conditions for employment.

## Principle 11. Consulting

a. The mental health counselor acting as consultant must have a high degree of self-awareness of his/her own values, knowledge, skills and needs in entering a helping relationship which involves human and/or organizational change and that the focus of the relationship be on the issues to be resolved and not on the person(s) presenting the problem.

b. There should be understanding and agreement between the mental health counselor and client for the problem definition, change goals and predicted consequences of interventions selected.

c. The mental health counselor must be reasonably certain that she/he or the organization represented has the necessary compentencies and resources for giving the kind of help which is needed now or may develop later and that appropriate referral resources are available to the consultant, if needed later.

d. The mental health counselor relationship must be one in which client adaptability and growth toward self-direction are encouraged and cultivated. The mental health counselor must maintain this role consistently and not become a decision maker or substitute for the client.

e.   When announcing consultant availability for services, the mental health counselor conscientiously adheres to professional standards.

f.   The mental health counselor is expected to refuse a private fee or other remuneration for consultation with persons who are entitled to these services through the member's employing institution or agency. The policies of a particular agency may make explicit provisions for private practice with agency counselees by members of its staff. In such instances, the counselees must be apprised of other options open to them should they seek private counseling services.

## Principle 12. Clients' Rights

The following apply to all consumers of mental health services, including both in- and outpatients in all state, county, local, and private care mental health facilities, as well as clients of mental health practitioners in private practice.

*The client has the right:*

a.   to be treated with consideration and respect;

b.   to expect quality service provided by concerned, competent staff;

c.   to a clear statement of the purposes, goals, techniques, rules of procedure, and limitations as well as potential dangers of the services to be performed and all other information related to or likely to affect the ongoing counseling relationship;

d.   to obtain information about their case record and to have this information explained clearly and directly;

e.   to full, knowledgeable, and responsible participation in the ongoing treatment plan, to the maximum feasible extent;

f.   to expect complete confidentiality and that no information will be released without written consent;

g.   to see and discuss their charges and payment records; and

h.   to refuse any recommended services and be advised of the consequences of this action.

Reprinted by permission of the American Counseling Association.

# D

＊

# American Association for Marriage and Family Therapy Code of Ethical Principles for Marriage and Family Therapists

The Board of Directors of the American Association for Marriage and Family Therapy (AAMFT) hereby promulgates, pursuant to Article II, Section (1)(C) of the Association's Bylaws, the Revised AAMFT Code of Ethical Principles for Marriage and Family Therapists, effective August 1, 1988.

The AAMFT Code of Ethical Principles for Marriage and Family Therapists is binding on all Members of AAMFT (Clinical, Student, and Associate) and on all AAMFT Approved Supervisors.

If an AAMFT Member or an AAMFT Approved Supervisor resigns in anticipation of or during the course of an ethics investigation, the Ethics Committee will complete its investigation. Any publication of action taken by the Association will include the fact that the Member attempted to resign during the investigation.

Marriage and family therapists are encouraged to report alleged unethical behavior of colleagues to appropriate professional associations and state regulatory bodies.

1. Responsibility to Clients
   Marriage and family therapists are dedicated to advancing the welfare of families and individuals, including respecting the rights of those persons seeking their assistance, and making reasonable efforts to ensure that their services are used appropriately.

1.1 Marriage and family therapists do not discriminate against or refuse professional service to anyone on the basis of race, sex, religion, or national origin.

1.2 Marriage and family therapists are cognizant of their potentially influential position with respect to clients, and they avoid exploiting the trust and dependency of such persons. Marriage and family therapists therefore make every effort to avoid dual relationships with clients that could impair their professional judgment or increase the risk of exploitation. Examples of such dual relationships include, but are not limited to, business or close personal relationships with clients. Sexual intimacy with clients is prohibited. Sexual intimacy with former clients for two years following the termination of therapy is prohibited.

1.3 Marriage and family therapists do not use their professional relationship with clients to further their own interests.

1.4 Marriage and family therapists respect the right of clients to make decisions and help them to understand the consequences of those decisions. Marriage and family therapists clearly advise a client that a decision on marital status is the responsibility of the client.

1.5 Marriage and family therapists continue therapeutic relationships only so long as it is reasonably clear that clients are benefiting from the relationship.

1.6 Marriage and family therapists assist persons in obtaining other therapeutic services if a marriage and family therapist is unable or unwilling, for appropriate reasons, to see a person who has requested professional help.

1.7 Marriage and family therapists do not abandon or neglect clients in treatment without making reasonable arrangements for the continuation of such treatment.

1.8 Marriage and family therapists obtain informed consent of clients before taping, recording, or permitting third party observation of their activities.

2. Confidentiality
   Marriage and family therapists have unique confidentiality problems because the "client" in a therapeutic relationship may be more than one person. The overriding principle is that marriage and family therapists respect the confidences of their client(s).

   2.1 Marriage and family therapists cannot disclose client confidences to anyone, except: (1) as mandated by law; (2) to prevent a clear and immediate danger to a person or persons; (3) where the marriage and family therapist is a defendant in a civil, criminal or disciplinary action arising from the therapy (in which case client confidences may only be disclosed in the course of that action); or (4) if there is a waiver previously obtained in writing, and then such information may only be revealed in accordance with the terms of the waiver. In circumstances where more than one person in a family is receiving therapy, each such family member who is legally competent to execute a waiver must agree to the waiver required by subparagraph (4). Absent such a waiver from each family member legally competent to execute a waiver, a marriage and family therapist cannot disclose information received from any family member.

2.2 Marriage and family therapists use client and/or clinical materials in teaching, writing, and public presentations only if a written waiver has been received in accordance with subprinciple 2.1 (4), or when appropriate steps have been taken to protect client identity.

2.3 Marriage and family therapists store or dispose of client records in ways that maintain confidentiality.

3. Professional Competence and Integrity
   Marriage and family therapists are dedicated to maintaining high standards of professional competence and integrity.

   3.1 Marriage and family therapists who (a) are convicted of felonies, (b) are convicted of misdemeanors (related to their qualifications or functions), (c) engage in conduct which could lead to conviction of felonies, or misdemeanors related to their qualifications or functions, (d) are expelled from other professional organizations, (e) have their licenses or certificates suspended or revoked, (f) are no longer competent to practice marriage and family therapy because they are impaired due to physical or mental causes or the abuse of alcohol or other substances, or (g) fail to cooperate with the Association at any stage of an investigation of an ethical complaint of his/her conduct by the AAMFT Ethics Committee or Judicial Council, are subject to termination of membership or other appropriate action.

   3.2 Marriage and family therapists seek appropriate professional assistance for their own personal problems or conflicts that are likely to impair their work performance and their clinical judgment.

   3.3 Marriage and family therapists, as teachers, are dedicated to maintaining high standards of scholarship and presenting information that is accurate.

   3.4 Marriage and family therapists seek to remain abreast of new developments in family therapy knowledge and practice through both educational activities and clinical experiences.

   3.5 Marriage and family therapists do not engage in sexual or other harassment or exploitation of clients, students, trainees, employees, colleagues, research subjects, or actual or potential witnesses or complainants in ethical proceedings.

   3.6 Marriage and family therapists do not attempt to diagnose, treat, or advise on problems outside the recognized boundaries of their competence.

   3.7 Marriage and family therapists attempt to prevent the distortion or misuse of their clinical and research findings.

3.8 Marriage and family therapists are aware that, because of their ability to influence and alter the lives of others, they must exercise special care when making public their professional recommendations and opinions through testimony or other public statements.

4. Responsibility to Students, Employees, and Supervisees
Marriage and family therapists do not exploit the trust and dependency of students, employees, and supervisees.

4.1 Marriage and family therapists are cognizant of their potentially influential position with respect to students, employees, and supervisees, and they avoid exploiting the trust and dependency of such persons. Marriage and family therapists, therefore, make every effort to avoid dual relationships that could impair their professional judgment or increase the risk of exploitation. Examples of such dual relationships include, but are not limited to, provision of therapy to students, employees, or supervisees, and business or close personal relationships with students, employees, or supervisees. Sexual intimacy with students or supervisees is prohibited.

4.2 Marriage and family therapists do not permit students, employees, or supervisees to perform or to hold themselves out as competent to perform professional services beyond their training, level of experience, and competence.

5. Responsibility to the Profession
Marriage and family therapists respect the rights and responsibilities of professional colleagues; carry out research in an ethical manner; and participate in activities which advance the goals of the profession.

5.1 Marriage and family therapists remain accountable to the standards of the profession when acting as members or employees of organizations.

5.2 Marriage and family therapists assign publication credit to those who have contributed to a publication in proportion to their contributions and in accordance with customary professional publication practices.

5.3 Marriage and family therapists who are the authors of books or other materials that are published or distributed should cite appropriately persons to whom credit for original ideas is due.

5.4 Marriage and family therapists who are the authors of books or other materials published or distributed by an organization take reasonable precautions to ensure that the organization promotes and advertises the materials accurately and factually.

5.5 Marriage and family therapists, as researchers, must be adequately informed of and abide by relevant laws and regulations regarding the conduct of research with human participants.

5.6 Marriage and family therapists recognize a responsibility to participate in activities that contribute to a better community and society, including devoting a portion of their professional activity to services for which there is little or no financial return.

5.7 Marriage and family therapists are concerned with developing laws and regulations pertaining to marriage and family therapy that serve the public interest, and with altering such laws and regulations that are not in the public interest.

5.8 Marriage and family therapists encourage public participation in the designing and delivery of services and in the regulation of practitioners.

6. Financial Arrangements

Marriage and family therapists make financial arrangements with clients and third party payers that conform to accepted professional practices and that are reasonably understandable.

6.1 Marriage and family therapists do not offer or accept payment for referrals.

6.2 Marriage and family therapists do not charge excessive fees for services.

6.3 Marriage and family therapists disclose their fee structure to clients at the onset of treatment.

6.4 Marriage and family therapists are careful to represent facts truthfully to clients and third party payers regarding services rendered.

7. Advertising

Marriage and family therapists engage in appropriate informational activities, including those that enable laypersons to choose marriage and family services on an informed basis.

7.1 Marriage and family therapists accurately represent their competence, education, training, and experience relevant to their practice of marriage and family therapy.

7.2 Marriage and family therapists claim as evidence of educational qualifications in conjunction with their AAMFT membership only those degrees (a) from regionally accredited institutions or (b) from institutions recognized by states which license or certify marriage and family therapists, but only if such regulation is accepted by AAMFT.

7.3 Marriage and family therapists assure that advertisements and publications, whether in directories, announcement cards, newspapers, or on radio or television, are formulated to convey information that is necessary for the public to make an appropriate selection. Information could include: (1) office information, such as name, address, telephone number, credit card acceptability, fee structure, languages spoken, and office hours; (2) appropriate degrees, state licensure and/or certification, and AAMFT Clinical Member status; and (3) description of practice.

7.4 Marriage and family therapists do not use a name which could mislead the public concerning the identity, responsibility, source, and status of those practicing under that name and do not hold themselves out as being partners or associates of a firm if they are not.

7.5 Marriage and family therapists do not use any professional identification (such as a professional card, office sign, letterhead, or telephone or association directory listing) if it includes a statement or claim that is false, fraudulent, misleading, or deceptive. A statement is false, fraudulent, misleading, or deceptive if it (a) contains a material misrepresentation of fact: (b) fails to state any material fact necessary to make the statement, in light of all circumstances, not misleading; or (c) is intended to or is likely to create an unjustified expectation.

7.6 Marriage and family therapists correct, wherever possible, false, misleading, or inaccurate information and representations made by others concerning the marriage and family therapist's qualifications, services, or products.

7.7 Marriage and family therapists make certain that the qualifications of persons in their employ are represented in a manner that is not false, misleading, or deceptive.

7.8 Marriage and family therapists may represent themselves as specializing within a limited area of marriage and family therapy, but may not hold themselves out as specialists without being able to provide evidence of training, education, and supervised experience in settings which meet recognized professional standards.

7.9 Only marriage and family therapist Clinical Members, Approved Supervisors, and Fellows—**not** Associate Members, Student Members, or organizations—may identify these AAMFT designations in public information or advertising materials.

7.10 Marriage and family therapists may not use the initials AAMFT following their name in the manner of an academic degree.

7.11 Marriage and family therapists may not use the AAMFT name, logo, and the abbreviated initials AAMFT. The Association (which is the sole owner of its name, logo, and the abbreviated initials AAMFT) and its committees and regional divisions, operating as such, may use the name, logo, and the abbreviated initials AAMFT. A regional division of AAMFT may use the AAMFT insignia to list its individual Clinical Members as a group (e.g., in the Yellow Pages); when all Clinical Members practicing within a directory district have been invited to list themselves in the directory, any one or more members may do so.

7.12 Marriage and family therapists use their membership in AAMFT only in connection with their clinical and professional activities.

Violations of this Code should be brought in writing to the attention of the AAMFT Ethics Committee at the central office of AAMFT, 1100 17th Street, NW, Tenth Floor, Washington, DC 20036.

Reprinted from the AAMFT Code of Ethics.

# E

＊

# Ethical Standards of Human Service Professionals

## National Organization for Human Service Education Council for Standards in Human Service Education

### PREAMBLE

Human services is a profession developing in response to and in anticipation of the direction of human needs and human problems in the late twentieth century. Characterized particularly by an appreciation of human beings in all of their diversity, human services offers assistance to its clients within the context of their community and environment. Human service professionals, regardless of whether they are students, faculty or practitioners, promote and encourage the unique values and characteristics of human services. In so doing human service professionals uphold the integrity and ethics of the profession, partake in constructive criticism of the profession, promote client and community well-being, and enhance their own professional growth.

The ethical guidelines presented are a set of standards of conduct which the human service professional considers in ethical and professional decision making. It is hoped that these guidelines will be of assistance when the human service professional is challenged by difficult ethical dilemmas. Although ethical codes are not legal documents, they may be used to assist in the adjudication of issues related to ethical human service behavior.

Human service professionals function in many ways and carry out many roles. They enter into professional–client relationships with individuals, families, groups, and communities who are all referred to as "clients" in these standards. Among their roles are caregiver, case manager, broker, teacher/educator, behavior changer, consultant, outreach professional, mobilizer, advocate, community planner, community change organizer, evaluator, and administrator. The following standards are written with these multifaceted roles in mind.

## THE HUMAN SERVICE PROFESSIONAL'S RESPONSIBILITY TO CLIENTS

**Statement 1** Human service professionals negotiate with clients the purpose, goals, and nature of the helping relationship prior to its onset as well as inform clients of the limitations of the proposed relationship.

**Statement 2** Human service professionals respect the integrity and welfare of the client at all times. Each client is treated with respect, acceptance, and dignity.

**Statement 3** Human service professionals protect the client's right to privacy and confidentiality except when such confidentiality would cause harm to the client or others, when agency guidelines state otherwise, or under other stated conditions (e.g., local, state, or federal laws). Professionals inform clients of the limits of confidentiality prior to the onset of the helping relationship.

**Statement 4** If it is suspected that danger or harm may occur to the client or to others as a result of a client's behavior, the human service professional acts in an appropriate and professional manner to protect the safety of those individuals. This may involve seeking consultation, supervision, and/or breaking the confidentiality of the relationship.

**Statement 5** Human service professionals protect the integrity, safety, and security of client records. All written client information that is shared with other professionals, except in the course of professional supervision, must have the client's prior written consent.

**Statement 6** Human service professionals are aware that in their relationships with clients power and status are unequal. Therefore they recognize that dual or multiple relationships may increase the risk of harm to, or exploitation of, clients, and may impair their professional judgment. However, in some communities and situations it may not be feasible to avoid social or other nonprofessional contact with clients. Human service professionals support the trust implicit in the helping relationship by avoiding dual relationships that may impair professional judgment, increase the risk of harm to clients or lead to exploitation.

**Statement 7** Sexual relationships with current clients are not considered to be in the best interest of the client and are prohibited. Sexual relationships with previous clients are considered dual relationships and are addressed in Statement 6 (above).

**Statement 8** The client's right to self-determination is protected by human service professionals. They recognize the client's right to receive or refuse services.

**Statement 9** Human service professionals recognize and build on client strengths.

## THE HUMAN SERVICE PROFESSIONAL'S RESPONSIBILITY TO THE COMMUNITY AND SOCIETY

**Statement 10** Human service professionals are aware of local, state, and federal laws. They advocate for change in regulations and statutes when such legislation conflicts with ethical guidelines and/or client rights. Where laws are harmful to individuals, groups or communities, human service professionals consider the conflict between the values of obeying the law and the values of serving people and may decide to initiate social action.

**Statement 11** Human service professionals keep informed about current social issues as they affect the client and the community. They share that information with clients, groups, and community as part of their work.

**Statement 12** Human service professionals understand the complex interaction between individuals, their families, the communities in which they live, and society.

**Statement 13** Human service professionals act as advocates in addressing unmet client and community needs. Human service professionals provide a mechanism for identifying unmet client needs, calling attention to these needs, and assisting in planning and mobilizing to advocate for those needs at the local community level.

**Statement 14** Human service professionals represent their qualifications to the public accurately.

**Statement 15** Human service professionals describe the effectiveness of programs, treatments, and/or techniques accurately.

**Statement 16** Human service professionals advocate for the rights of all members of society, particularly those who are members of minorities and groups at which discriminatory practices have historically been directed.

**Statement 17**  Human service professionals provide services without discrimination or preference based on age, ethnicity, culture, race, disability, gender, religion, sexual orientation or socioeconomic status.

**Statement 18**  Human service professionals are knowledgeable about the cultures and communities within which they practice. They are aware of multiculturalism in society and its impact on the community as well as individuals within the community. They respect individuals and groups, their cultures and beliefs.

**Statement 19**  Human service professionals are aware of their own cultural backgrounds, beliefs, and values, recognizing the potential for impact on their relationships with others.

**Statement 20**  Human service professionals are aware of sociopolitical issues that differentially affect clients from diverse backgrounds.

**Statement 21**  Human service professionals seek the training, experience, education, and supervision necessary to ensure their effectiveness in working with culturally diverse client populations.

## THE HUMAN SERVICE PROFESSIONAL'S RESPONSIBILITY TO COLLEAGUES

**Statement 22**  Human service professionals avoid duplicating another professional's helping relationship with a client. They consult with other professionals who are assisting the client in a different type of relationship when it is in the best interest of the client to do so.

**Statement 23**  When a human service professional has a conflict with a colleague, he or she first seeks out the colleague in an attempt to manage the problem. If necessary, the professional then seeks the assistance of supervisors, consultants or other professionals in efforts to manage the problem.

**Statement 24**  Human service professionals respond appropriately to unethical behavior of colleagues. Usually this means initially talking directly with the colleague and, if no resolution is forthcoming, reporting the colleague's behavior to supervisory or administrative staff and/or to the professional organization(s) to which the colleague belongs.

**Statement 25**  All consultations between human service professionals are kept confidential unless to do so would result in harm to clients or communities.

## THE HUMAN SERVICE PROFESSIONAL'S RESPONSIBILITY TO THE PROFESSION

**Statement 26** Human service professionals know the limit and scope of their professional knowledge and offer services only within their knowledge and skill base.

**Statement 27** Human service professionals seek appropriate consultation and supervision to assist in decision making when there are legal, ethical or other dilemmas.

**Statement 28** Human service professionals act with integrity, honesty, genuineness, and objectivity.

**Statement 29** Human service professionals promote cooperation among related disciplines (e.g., psychology, counseling, social work, nursing, family and consumer sciences, medicine, education) to foster professional growth and interests within the various fields.

**Statement 30** Human service professionals promote the continuing development of their profession. They encourage membership in professional associations, support research endeavors, foster educational advancement, advocate for appropriate legislative actions, and participate in other related professional activities.

**Statement 31** Human service professionals continually seek out new and effective approaches to enhance their professional abilities.

## THE HUMAN SERVICE PROFESSIONAL'S RESPONSIBILITY TO EMPLOYERS

**Statement 32** Human service professionals adhere to commitments made to their employers.

**Statement 33** Human service professionals participate in efforts to establish and maintain employment conditions which are conducive to high-quality client services. They assist in evaluating the effectiveness of the agency through reliable and valid assessment measures.

**Statement 34** When a conflict arises between fulfilling the responsibility to the employer and the responsibility to the client, human service professionals advise both of the conflict and work conjointly with all involved to manage the conflict.

# THE HUMAN SERVICE PROFESSIONAL'S RESPONSIBILITY TO SELF

**Statement 35** Human service professionals strive to personify those characteristics typically associated with the profession (eg., accountability, respect for others, genuineness, empathy, pragmatism).

**Statement 36** Human service professionals foster self-awareness and personal growth in themselves. They recognize that when professionals are aware of their own values, attitudes, cultural background, and personal needs, the process of helping others is less likely to be negatively impacted by those factors.

**Statement 37** Human service professionals recognize a commitment to life-long learning and continually upgrade knowledge and skills to serve the populations better.

October 1994

[1.] Southern Regional Education Board (1967). Roles and Functions Mental Health Workers: A Report of a Symposium. Atlanta, GA: Community Mental Health Worker Project.

Reprinted by permission of William L. McKinney, University of Rhode Island.

# F

# Ethical Principles
of Psychologists
and Code of Conduct

## INTRODUCTION

The American Psychological Association's (APA's) Ethical Principles of Psychologists and Code of Conduct (hereinafter referred to as the Ethics Code) consists of an Introduction, a Preamble, six General Principles (A–F), and specific Ethical Standards. The Introduction discusses the intent, organization, procedural considerations, and scope of application of the Ethics Code. The Preamble and General Principles are *aspirational* goals to guide psychologists toward the highest ideals of psychology. Although the Preamble and General Principles are not themselves enforceable rules, they should be considered by psychologists in arriving at an ethical course of action and may be considered by ethics bodies in interpreting the Ethical Standards. The Ethical Standards set forth *enforceable* rules for conduct as psychologists. Most of the Ethical Standards are written broadly, in order to apply to psychologists in varied roles, although the application of an Ethical Standard may vary depending on the context. The Ethical Standards are not exhaustive. The fact that a given conduct is not specifically addressed by the Ethics Code does not mean that it is necessarily either ethical or unethical.

Membership in the APA commits members to adhere to the APA Ethics Code and to the rules and procedures used to implement it. Psychologists and students, whether or not they are APA members, should be aware that the Ethics Code may be applied to them by state psychology boards, courts, or other public bodies.

This Ethics Code applies only to psychologists' work-related activities, that is, activities that are part of the psychologists' scientific and professional functions or that are psychological in nature. It includes the clinical or counseling practice of psychology, research, teaching, supervision of trainees, development of assessment instruments, conducting assessments, educational counseling, organizational consulting, social intervention, administration, and other activities as well. These work-related activities can be distinguished from the purely private conduct of a psychologist, which ordinarily is not within the purview of the Ethics Code.

The Ethics Code is intended to provide standards of professional conduct that can be applied by the APA and by other bodies that choose to adopt them. Whether or not a psychologist has violated the Ethics Code does not by itself determine whether he or she is legally liable in a court action, whether a contract is enforceable, or whether other legal consequences occur. These results are based on legal rather than ethical rules. However, compliance with or violation of the Ethics Code may be admissible as evidence in some legal proceedings, depending on the circumstances.

In the process of making decisions regarding their professional behavior, psychologists must consider this Ethics Code, in addition to applicable laws and psychology board regulations. If the Ethics Code establishes a higher standard of conduct than is required by law, psychologists must meet the higher ethical standard. If the Ethics Code standard appears to conflict with the requirements of law, then psychologists make known their commitment to the Ethics Code and take steps to resolve the conflict in a responsible manner. If neither law nor the Ethics Code resolves an issue, psychologists should consider other professional materials and the dictates of their own conscience, as well as seek consultation with others within the field when this is practical.

The procedures for filing, investigating, and resolving complaints of unethical conduct are described in the current Rules and Procedures of the APA Ethics Committee. The actions that APA may take for violations of the Ethics Code include actions such as reprimand, censure, termination of APA membership, and referral of the matter to other bodies. Complainants who seek remedies such as monetary damages in alleging ethical violations by a psychologist must resort to private negotiation, administrative bodies, or the courts. Actions that violate the Ethics Code may lead to the imposition of sanctions on a psychologist by bodies other than APA, including state psychological associations, other professional groups, psychology boards, other state or federal agencies, and payors for health services. In addition to actions for violation of the Ethics Code, the APA Bylaws provide that APA may take action against a member after his or her conviction of a felony, expulsion or suspension from an affiliated state psychological association, or suspension or loss of licensure.

## PREAMBLE

Psychologists work to develop a valid and reliable body of scientific knowledge based on research. They may apply that knowledge to human behavior in a variety of contexts. In doing so, they perform many roles, such as researcher, educator, diagnostician, therapist, supervisor, consultant, administrator, social interventionist, and expert witness. Their goal is to broaden knowledge of behavior and, where appropriate, to apply it pragmatically to improve the condition of both the individual and society. Psychologists respect the central importance of freedom of inquiry and expression in research, teaching, and publication. They also strive to help the public in developing informed judgments and choices concerning human behavior. This Ethics Code provides a common set of values upon which psychologists build their professional and scientific work.

This Code is intended to provide both the general principles and the decision rules to cover most situations encountered by psychologists. It has as its primary goal the welfare and protection of the individuals and groups with whom psychologists work. It is the individual responsibility of each psychologist to aspire to the highest possible standards of conduct. Psychologists respect and protect human and civil rights, and do not knowingly participate in or condone unfair discriminatory practices.

The development of a dynamic set of ethical standards for a psychologist's work-related conduct requires a personal commitment to a lifelong effort to act ethically; to encourage ethical behavior by students, supervisees, employees, and colleagues, as appropriate; and to consult with others, as needed, concerning ethical problems. Each psychologist supplements, but does not violate, the Ethics Code's values and rules on the basis of guidance drawn from personal values, culture, and experience.

## GENERAL PRINCIPLES

### Principle A: Competence

Psychologists strive to maintain high standards of competence in their work. They recognize the boundaries of their particular competencies and the limitations of their expertise. They provide only those services and use only those techniques for which they are qualified by education, training, or experience. Psychologists are cognizant of the fact that the competencies required in serving, teaching, and/or studying groups of people vary with the distinctive characteristics of those groups. In those areas in which recognized professional standards do not yet exist, psychologists exercise careful judgment and take appropriate precautions to protect the welfare of those with whom they work. They maintain knowledge of relevant scientific and professional information related to the services they render, and they recognize the need for ongoing education. Psychologists make appropriate use of scientific, professional, technical, and administrative resources.

### Principle B: Integrity

Psychologists strive to promote integrity in the science, teaching, and practice of psychology. In these activities psychologists are honest, fair, and respectful of others. In describing or reporting their qualifications, services, products, fees, research, or teaching, they do not make statements that are false, misleading, or deceptive. Psychologists strive to be aware of their own belief systems, values, needs, and limitations and the effect of these on their work. To the extent feasible, they attempt to clarify for relevant parties the roles they are performing and to function appropriately in accordance with those roles. Psychologists avoid improper and potentially harmful dual relationships.

### Principle C: Professional and Scientific Responsibility

Psychologists uphold professional standards of conduct, clarify their professional roles and obligations, accept appropriate responsibility for their behavior, and adapt their methods to the needs of different populations. Psychologists consult with, refer to, or cooperate with other professionals and institutions to the extent needed to serve the best interests of their patients, clients, or other recipients of their services. Psychologists' moral standards and conduct are personal matters to the same degree as is true for any other person, except as psychologists' conduct may compromise their professional responsibilities or reduce the public's trust in psychology and psychologists. Psychologists are concerned about the ethical compliance of their colleagues' scientific and professional conduct. When appropriate, they consult with colleagues in order to prevent or avoid unethical conduct.

### Principle D: Respect for People's Rights and Dignity

Psychologists accord appropriate respect to the fundamental rights, dignity, and worth of all people. They respect the rights of individuals to privacy, confidentiality, self-determination, and autonomy, mindful that legal and other obligations may lead to inconsistency and conflict with the exercise of these rights. Psychologists are aware of cultural, individual, and role differences, including those due to age, gender, race, ethnicity, national origin, religion, sexual orientation, disability, language, and socioeconomic status. Psychologists try to eliminate the effect on their work of biases based on those factors, and they do not knowingly participate in or condone unfair discriminatory practices.

### Principle E: Concern for Others' Welfare

Psychologists are aware of their professional and scientific responsibilities to the community and the society in which they work and live. They apply and make public their knowledge of psychology in order to contribute to human welfare. Psychologists are concerned about and work to mitigate the causes of human suffering. When undertaking research, they strive to advance human welfare and the science of psychology. Psychologists try to avoid misuse of their work. Psychologists comply with the law and encourage the development of law and social policy that serve the interests of their patients and clients and the public. They are encouraged to contribute a portion of their professional time for little or no personal advantage.

# ETHICAL STANDARDS

## 1. GENERAL STANDARDS

These General Standards are potentially applicable to the professional and scientific activities of all psychologists.

1.01 Applicability of the Ethics Code.

The activity of a psychologist subject to the Ethics Code may be reviewed under these Ethical Standards only if the activity is part of his or her work-related functions or the activity is psychological in nature. Personal activities having no connection to or effect on psychological roles are not subject to the Ethics Code.

1.02 Relationship of Ethics and Law.

If psychologists' ethical responsibilities conflict with law, psychologists make known their commitment to the Ethics Code and take steps to resolve the conflict in a responsible manner.

1.03 Professional and Scientific Relationship.

Psychologists provide diagnostic, therapeutic, teaching, research, supervisory, consultative, or other psychological services only in the context of a defined professional or scientific relationship or role. (See also Standards 2.01, Evaluation, Diagnosis and Interventions in Professional Context, and 7.02, Forensic Assessments.)

1.04 Boundaries of Competence.

(a) Psychologists provide services, teach, or conduct research only within the boundaries of their competence, based on their education, training, supervised experience, or appropriate professional experience.

(b) Psychologists provide services, teach, or conduct research in new areas or involving new techniques only after first undertaking appropriate study, training, supervision, and/or consultation from persons who are competent in those areas or techniques.

(c) In those emerging areas in which generally recognized standards for preparatory training do not yet exist, psychologists nevertheless take reasonable steps to ensure the competence of their work and to protect patients, clients, students, research participants, and others from harm.

1.05 Maintaining Expertise.

Psychologists who engage in assessment, therapy, teaching, research, organizational consulting, or other professional activities maintain a reasonable level of awareness of current scientific and professional information in their fields of activity, and undertake ongoing efforts to maintain competence in the skills they use.

1.06 Basis for Scientific and Professional Judgments.

Psychologists rely on scientifically and professionally derived knowledge when making scientific or professional judgments or when engaging in scholarly or professional endeavors.

1.07 Describing the Nature and Results of Psychological Services.
  (a) When psychologists provide assessment, evaluation, treatment, counseling, supervision, teaching, consultation, research, or other psychological services to an individual, a group, or an organization, they provide, using language that is reasonably understandable to the recipient of those services, appropriate information beforehand about the nature of such services and appropriate information later about results and conclusions. (See also Standard 2.09, Explaining Assessment Results.)
  (b) If psychologists will be precluded by law or by organizational roles from providing such information to particular individuals or groups, they so inform those individuals or groups at the outset of the service.
1.08 Human Differences.
  Where differences of age, gender, race, ethnicity, national origin, religion, sexual orientation, disability, language, or socioeconomic status significantly affect psychologists' work concerning particular individuals or groups, psychologists obtain the training experience, consultation, or supervision necessary to ensure the competence of their services, or they make appropriate referrals.
1.09 Respecting Others.
  In their work-related activities, psychologists respect the rights of others to hold values, attitudes, and opinions that differ from their own.
1.10 Nondiscrimination.
  In their work-related activities, psychologists do not engage in unfair discrimination based on age, gender, race, ethnicity, national origin, religion, sexual orientation, disability, socioeconomic status, or any basis proscribed by law.
1.11 Sexual Harassment.
  (a) Psychologists do not engage in sexual harassment. Sexual harassment is sexual solicitation, physical advances, or verbal or nonverbal conduct that is sexual in nature, that occurs in connection with the psychologist's activities or roles as a psychologist, and that either: (1) is unwelcome, is offensive, or creates a hostile workplace environment, and the psychologist knows or is told this; or (2) is sufficiently severe or intense to be abusive to a reasonable person in the context. Sexual harassment can consist of a single intense or severe act or of multiple persistent or pervasive acts.
  (b) Psychologists accord sexual-harassment complainants and respondents dignity and respect. Psychologists do not participate in denying a person academic admittance or advancement, employment, tenure, or promotion, based solely upon their having made, or their being the subject of, sexual harassment charges.

This does not preclude taking action based upon the outcome of such proceedings or consideration of other appropriate information.

1.12 Other Harassment.

Psychologists do not knowingly engage in behavior that is harassing or demeaning to persons with whom they interact in their work based on factors such as those persons' age, gender, race, ethnicity, national origin, religion, sexual orientation, disability, language, or socioeconomic status.

1.13 Personal Problems and Conflicts.

(a) Psychologists recognize that their personal problems and conflicts may interfere with their effectiveness. Accordingly, they refrain from undertaking an activity when they know or should know that their personal problems are likely to lead to harm to a patient, client, colleague, student, research participant, or other person to whom they may owe a professional or scientific obligation.

(b) In addition, psychologists have an obligation to be alert to signs of, and to obtain assistance for, their personal problems at an early stage, in order to prevent significantly impaired performance.

(c) When psychologists become aware of personal problems that may interfere with their performing work-related duties adequately, they take appropriate measures, such as obtaining professional consultation or assistance, and determine whether they should limit, suspend, or terminate their work-related duties.

1.14 Avoiding Harm.

Psychologists take reasonable steps to avoid harming their patients or clients, research participants, students, and others with whom they work, and to minimize harm where it is foreseeable and unavoidable.

1.15 Misuse of Psychologists' Influence.

Because psychologists' scientific and professional judgments and actions may affect the lives of others, they are alert to and guard against personal, financial, social, organizational, or political factors that might lead to misuse of their influence.

1.16 Misuse of Psychologists' Work.

(a) Psychologists do not participate in activities in which it appears likely that their skills or data will be misused by others, unless corrective mechanisms are available. (See also Standard 7.04, Truthfulness and Candor.)

(b) If psychologists learn of misuse or misrepresentation of their work, they take reasonable steps to correct or minimize the misuse or misrepresentation.

1.17 Multiple Relationships.

(a) In many communities and situations, it may not be feasible or reasonable for psychologists to avoid social or other nonprofessional contacts with persons such as patients, clients, students, supervisees, or research participants. Psychologists must always be sensitive to the potential harmful effects of other contacts on their work and on those persons with whom they deal. A psychologist refrains from entering into or promising another personal, scientific, professional, financial, or other relationship with such persons if it appears likely that such a relationship reasonably might impair the psychologist's objectivity or otherwise interfere with the psychologist's effectively performing his or her functions as a psychologist, or might harm or exploit the other party.

(b) Likewise, whenever feasible, a psychologist refrains from taking on professional or scientific obligations when preexisting relationships would create a risk of such harm.

(c) If a psychologist finds that, due to unforeseen factors, a potentially harmful multiple relationship has arisen, the psychologist attempts to resolve it with due regard for the best interests of the affected person and maximal compliance with the Ethics Code.

1.18 Barter (With Patients or Clients).

Psychologists ordinarily refrain from accepting goods, services, or other nonmonetary remuneration from patients or clients in return for psychological services because such arrangements create inherent potential for conflicts, exploitation, and distortion of the professional relationship. A psychologist may participate in bartering only if (1) it is not clinically contraindicated, and (2) the relationship is not exploitative. (See also Standards 1.17, Multiple Relationships, and 1.25, Fees and Financial Arrangements.)

1.19 Exploitative Relationships

(a) Psychologists do not exploit persons over whom they have supervisory, evaluative, or other authority such as students, supervisees, employees, research participants, and clients or patients. (See also Standards 4.05–4.07 regarding sexual involvement with clients or patients.)

(b) Psychologists do not engage in sexual relationships with students or supervisees in training over whom the psychologist has evaluative or direct authority, because such relationships are so likely to impair judgment or be exploitative.

1.20 Consultation and Referrals.

(a) Psychologists arrange for appropriate consultations and referrals based principally on the best interests of their patients or clients, with appropriate consent, and subject to other relevant considerations, including applicable law and contractual obligations. (See also Standards 5.01, Discussing the Limits of Confidentiality, and 5.06, Consultations.)

(b) When indicated and professionally appropriate, psychologists cooperate with other professionals in order to serve their patients or clients effectively and appropriately.

(c) Psychologists' referral practices are consistent with law.

1.21 Third-Party Requests for Services.

(a) When a psychologist agrees to provide services to a person or entity at the request of a third party, the psychologist clarifies to the extent feasible, at the outset of the service, the nature of the relationship with each party. This clarification includes the role of the psychologist (such as therapist, organizational consultant, diagnostician, or expert witness), the probable uses of the services provided or the information obtained, and the fact that there may be limits to confidentiality.

(b) If there is a foreseeable risk of the psychologist's being called upon to perform conflicting roles because of the involvement of a third party, the psychologist clarifies the nature and direction of his or her responsibilities, keeps all parties appropriately informed as matters develop, and resolves the situation in accordance with this Ethics Code.

1.22 Delegation to and Supervision of Subordinates.

(a) Psychologists delegate to their employees, supervisees, and research assistants only those responsibilities that such persons can reasonably be expected to perform competently, on the basis of their education, training, or experience, either independently or with the level of supervision being provided.

(b) Psychologists provide proper training and supervision to their employees or supervisees and take reasonable steps to see that such persons perform services responsibly, competently, and ethically.

(c) If institutional policies, procedures, or practices prevent fulfillment of this obligation, psychologists attempt to modify their role or to correct the situation to the extent feasible.

1.23 Documentation of Professional and Scientific Work.

(a) Psychologists appropriately document their professional and scientific work in order to facilitate provision of services later by them or by other professionals, to ensure accountability, and to meet other requirements of institutions or the law.

(b) When psychologists have reason to believe that records of their professional services will be used in legal proceedings involving recipients of or participants in their work, they have a responsibility to create and maintain documentation in the kind of detail and quality that would be consistent with reasonable scrutiny in an adjudicative forum. (See also Standards 7.01, Professionalism, under Forensic activities.)

1.24 Records and Data.

Psychologists create, maintain, disseminate, store, retain, and dispose of records and data relating to their research, practice, and other work in accordance with law and in a manner that permits compliance with the requirements of this Ethics Code. (See also Standard 5.04, Maintenance of Records.)

1.25 Fees and Financial Arrangements.
    (a) As early as is feasible in a professional or scientific relationship, the psychologist and the patient, client, or other appropriate recipient of psychological services reach an agreement specifying the compensation and the billing arrangements.
    (b) Psychologists do not exploit recipients of services or payers with respect to fees.
    (c) Psychologists' fee practices are consistent with law.
    (d) Psychologists do not misrepresent their fees.
    (e) If limitations to services can be anticipated because of limitations in financing, this is discussed with the patient, client, or other appropriate recipient of services as early as is feasible. (See also Standard 4.08, Interruption of Services.)
    (f) If the patient, client, or other recipient of services does not pay for services as agreed, and if the psychologist wishes to use collection agencies or legal measures to collect the fees, the psychologist first informs the person that such measures will be taken and provides that person an opportunity to make prompt payment. (See also Standard 5.11, Withholding Records for Nonpayment.)

1.26 Accuracy in Reports to Payers and Funding Sources.
In their reports to payers for services or sources of research funding, psychologists accurately state the nature of the research or service provided, the fees or charges, and where applicable, the identity of the provider, the findings, and the diagnosis. (See also Standard 5.05, Disclosure.)

1.27 Referrals and Fees.
When a psychologist pays, receives payment from, or divides fees with another professional other than in an employer–employee relationship, the payment to each is based on the services (clinical, consultative, administrative, or other) provided and is not based on the referral itself.

## 2. EVALUATION, ASSESSMENT, OR INTERVENTION

2.01 Evaluation, Diagnosis, and Interventions in Professional Context.
    (a) Psychologists perform evaluations, diagnostic services, or interventions only within the context of a defined professional relationship. (See also Standards 1.03, Professional and Scientific Relationship.)
    (b) Psychologists' assessments, recommendations, reports, and psychological diagnostic or evaluative statements are based on information and techniques (including personal interviews of the individual when appropriate) sufficient to provide appropriate substantiation for their findings. (See also Standard 7.02, Forensic Assessments.)

2.02 Competence and Appropriate Use of Assessments and Interventions.

(a) Psychologists who develop, administer, score, interpret, or use psychological assessment techniques, interviews, tests, or instruments do so in a manner and for purposes that are appropriate in light of the research on or evidence of the usefulness and proper application of the techniques.

(b) Psychologists refrain from misuse of assessment techniques, interventions, results, and interpretations and take reasonable steps to prevent others from misusing the information these techniques provide. This includes refraining from releasing raw test results or raw data to persons, other than to patients or clients as appropriate, who are not qualified to use such information. (See also Standards 1.02, Relationship of Ethics and Law, and 1.04, Boundaries of Competence.)

2.03 Test Construction.

Psychologists who develop and conduct research with tests and other assessment techniques use scientific procedures and current professional knowledge for test design, standardization, validation, reduction or elimination of bias, and recommendations for use.

2.04 Use of Assessment in General and With Special Populations.

(a) Psychologists who perform interventions or administer, score, interpret, or use assessment techniques are familiar with the reliability, validation, and related standardization or outcome studies of, and proper applications and uses of, the techniques they use.

(b) Psychologists recognize limits to the certainty with which diagnoses, judgments, or predictions can be made about individuals.

(c) Psychologists attempt to identify situations in which particular interventions or assessment techniques or norms may not be applicable or may require adjustment in administration or interpretation because of factors such as individuals' gender, age, race, ethnicity, national origin, religion, sexual orientation, disability, language, or socioeconomic status.

2.05 Interpreting Assessment Results.

When interpreting assessment results, including automated interpretations, psychologists take into account the various test factors and characteristics of the person being assessed that might affect psychologists' judgments or reduce the accuracy of their interpretations. They indicate any significant reservations they have about the accuracy or limitations of their interpretations.

2.06 Unqualified Persons.

Psychologists do not promote the use of psychological assessment techniques by unqualified persons. (See also Standard 1.22, Delegation to and Supervision of Subordinates.)

2.07 Obsolete Tests and Outdated Test Results.

(a) Psychologists do not base their assessment or intervention decisions or recommendations on data or test results that are outdated for the current purpose.

(b) Similarly, psychologists do not base such decisions or recommendations on tests and measures that are obsolete and not useful for the current purpose.

2.08 Test Scoring and Interpretation Services.

(a) Psychologists who offer assessment or scoring procedures to other professionals accurately describe the purpose, norms, validity, reliability, and applications of the procedures and any special qualifications applicable to their use.

(b) Psychologists select scoring and interpretation services (including automated services) on the basis of evidence of the validity of the program and procedures as well as on other appropriate considerations.

(c) Psychologists retain appropriate responsibility for the appropriate application, interpretation, and use of assessment instruments, whether they score and interpret such tests themselves or use automated or other services.

2.09 Explaining Assessment Results.

Unless the nature of the relationship is clearly explained to the person being assessed in advance and precludes provision of an explanation of results (such as in some organizational consulting, preemployment or security screenings, and forensic evaluations), psychologists ensure that an explanation of the results is provided using language that is reasonably understandable to the person assessed or to another legally authorized person on behalf of the client. Regardless of whether the scoring and interpretation are done by the psychologist, by assistants, or by automated or other outside services, psychologists take reasonable steps to ensure that appropriate explanations of results are given.

2.10 Maintaining Test Security.

Psychologists make reasonable efforts to maintain the integrity and security of tests and other assessment techniques consistent with law, contractual obligations, and in a manner that permits compliance with the requirements of this Ethics Code. (See also Standard 1.02, Relationship of Ethics and Law.)

# 3. ADVERTISING AND OTHER PUBLIC STATEMENTS

3.01 Definition of Public Statements.

Psychologists comply with this Ethics Code in public statements relating to their professional services, products, or publications or to the field of psychology. Public statements include but are not limited to paid or unpaid advertising, brochures, printed matter, directory listings, personal resumes or curriculum vitae, interviews or comments for use in media, statements in legal proceedings, lectures and public oral presentations, and published materials.

3.02 Statements by Others.

(a) Psychologists who engage others to create or place public statements that promote their professional practice, products, or activities retain professional responsibility for such statements.

(b) In addition, psychologists make reasonable efforts to prevent others whom they do not control (such as employers, publishers, sponsors, organizational clients, and representatives of the print or broadcast media) from making deceptive statements concerning psychologists' practice or professional or scientific activities.

(c) If psychologists learn of deceptive statements about their work made by others, psychologists make reasonable efforts to correct such statements.

(d) Psychologists do not compensate employees of press, radio, television, or other communications media in return for publicity in a news item.

(e) A paid advertisement relating to the psychologist's activities must be identified as such, unless it is already apparent from the context.

3.03 Avoidance of False or Deceptive Statements.

(a) Psychologists do not make public statements that are false, deceptive, misleading, or fraudulent, either because of what they state, convey, or suggest or because of what they omit, concerning their research, practice, or other work activities or those of persons or organizations with which they are affiliated. As examples (and not in limitation) of this standard, psychologists do not make false or deceptive statements concerning (1) their training, experience, or competence; (2) their academic degrees; (3) their credentials; (4) their institutional or association affiliations; (5) their services; (6) the scientific or clinical basis for, or results or degree of success of, their services; (7) their fees; or (8) their publications or research findings. (See also Standards 6.15, Deception in Research, and 6.18, Providing Participants With Information About the Study.)

(b) Psychologists claim as credentials for their psychological work, only degrees that (1) were earned from a regionally accredited educational institution or (2) were the basis for psychology licensure by the state in which they practice.

3.04 Media Presentations.

When psychologists provide advice or comment by means of public lectures, demonstrations, radio or television programs, prerecorded tapes, printed articles, mailed material, or other media, they take reasonable precautions to ensure that (1) the statements are based on appropriate psychological literature and practice, (2) the statements are otherwise consistent with this Ethics Code, and (3) the recipients of the information are not encouraged to infer that a relationship has been established with them personally.

3.05 Testimonials.

Psychologists do not solicit testimonials from current psychotherapy clients or patients or other persons who because of their particular circumstances are vulnerable to undue influence.

3.06 In-Person Solicitation.

Psychologists do not engage, directly or through agents, in uninvited in-person solicitation of business from actual or potential psychotherapy patients or clients or other persons who because of their particular circumstances are vulnerable to undue influence. However, this does not preclude attempting to implement appropriate collateral contacts with significant others for the purpose of benefiting an already engaged therapy patient.

## 4.  THERAPY

4.01 Structuring the Relationship.

(a) Psychologists discuss with clients or patients as early as is feasible in the therapeutic relationship appropriate issues, such as the nature and anticipated course of therapy, fees, and confidentiality. (See also Standards 1.25, Fees and Financial Arrangements, and 5.01, Discussing the Limits of Confidentiality.)

(b) When the psychologist's work with clients or patients will be supervised, the above discussion includes that fact, and the name of the supervisor, when the supervisor has legal responsibility for the case.

(c) When the therapist is a student intern, the client or patient is informed of that fact.

(d) Psychologists make reasonable efforts to answer patients' questions and to avoid apparent misunderstandings about therapy. Whenever possible, psychologists provide oral and/or written information, using language that is reasonably understandable to the patient or client.

4.02 Informed Consent to Therapy.

(a) Psychologists obtain appropriate informed consent to therapy or related procedures, using language that is reasonably understandable to participants. The content of informed consent will vary depending on many circumstances; however, informed consent generally implies that the person (1) has the capacity to consent, (2) has been informed of significant information concerning the procedure, (3) has freely and without undue influence expressed consent, and (4) consent has been appropriately documented.

(b) When persons are legally incapable of giving informed consent, psychologists obtain informed permission from a legally authorized person, if such substitute consent is permitted by law.

(c) In addition, psychologists (1) inform those persons who are legally incapable of giving informed consent about the proposed interventions in a manner commensurate with the persons' psychological capacities, (2) seek their assent to those interventions, and (3) consider such persons' preferences and best interests.

4.03 Couple and Family Relationships.

(a) When a psychologist agrees to provide services to several persons who have a relationship (such as husband and wife or parents and children), the psychologist attempts to clarify at the outset (1) which of the individuals are patients or clients and (2) the relationship the psychologist will have with each person. This clarification includes the role of psychologist and the probable uses of the services provided or the information obtained. (See also Standard 5.01, Discussing the Limits of Confidentiality.)

(b) As soon as it becomes apparent that the psychologist may be called on to perform potentially conflicting roles (such as marital counselor to husband and wife, and then witness for one party in a divorce proceeding), the psychologist attempts to clarify and adjust, or withdraw from, roles appropriately. (See also Standard 7.03, Clarification of Role, under Forensic Activities.)

4.04 Providing Mental Health Services to Those Serviced by Others.
In deciding whether to offer or provide services to those already receiving mental health services elsewhere, psychologists carefully consider the treatment issues and the potential patient's or client's welfare. The psychologist discusses these issues with the patient or client, or another legally authorized person on behalf of the client, in order to minimize the risk of confusion and conflict, consults with the other service providers when appropriate, and proceeds with caution and sensitivity to the therapeutic issues.

4.05 Sexual Intimacies With Current Patients or Clients.
Psychologists do not engage in sexual intimacies with current patients or clients.

4.06 Therapy With Former Sexual Partners.
Psychologists do not accept as therapy patients or clients persons with whom they have engaged in sexual intimacies.

4.07 Sexual Intimacies With Former Therapy Patients.

(a) Psychologists do not engage in sexual intimacies with a former therapy patient or client for at least two years after cessation or termination of professional services.

(b) Because sexual intimacies with a former therapy patient or client are so frequently harmful to the patient or client, and because such intimacies undermine public confidence in the psychology profession and thereby deter the public's use of needed services, psychologists do not engage in sexual intimacies with former therapy patients and clients even after a two-year interval except in the most unusual circumstances. The psychologist who engages in such activity after the two years following cessation or termination of treatment bears the burden of demonstrating that there has been no exploitation, in light of all relevant factors, including (1) the amount of time that has passed since therapy terminated, (2) the nature and duration of the therapy, (3) the circumstances of termination, (4) the patient's or client's personal history, (5) the patient's or client's current mental status, (6) the likelihood of adverse impact on the patient or client and others, and (7) any statements or actions made by the therapist during the course of therapy suggesting or inviting the possibility of a post-termination sexual or romantic relationship with the patient or client. (See also Standard 1.17, Multiple Relationships.)

4.08 Interruption of Services.

(a) Psychologists make reasonable efforts to plan for facilitating care in the event that psychological services are interrupted by factors such as the psychologist's illness, death, unavailability, or relocation or by the client's relocation or financial limitations. (See also Standard 5.09, Preserving Records and Data.)

(b) When entering into employment or contractual relationships, psychologists provide for orderly and appropriate resolution of responsibility for patient or client care in the event that the employment or contractual relationship ends, with paramount consideration given to the welfare of the patient or client.

4.09 Terminating the Professional Relationship.

(a) Psychologists do not abandon patients or clients. (See also Standard 1.25e, under Fees and Financial Arrangements.)

(b) Psychologists terminate a professional relationship when it becomes reasonably clear that the patient or client no longer needs the service, is not benefiting or is being harmed by continued service.

(c) Prior to termination for whatever reason, except where precluded by the patient's or client's conduct, the psychologist discusses the patient's or client's views and needs, provides appropriate predetermination counseling, suggests alternative service providers as appropriate, and takes other reasonable steps to facilitate transfer of responsibility to another provider if the patient or client needs one immediately.

5. **PRIVACY AND CONFIDENTIALITY**

These Standards are potentially applicable to the professional and scientific activities of all psychologists.

5.01 Discussing the Limits of Confidentiality.

(a) Psychologists discuss with persons and organizations with whom they establish a scientific or professional relationship (including, to the extent feasible, minors and their legal representatives) (1) the relevant limitations on confidentiality, including limitations where applicable in group, marital, and family therapy or in organizational consulting, and (2) the foreseeable uses of the information generated through their services.

(b) Unless it is not feasible or is contraindicated, the discussion of confidentiality occurs at the outset of the relationship and thereafter as new circumstances may warrant.

(c) Permission for electronic recording of interviews is secured from clients and patients.

5.02 Maintaining Confidentiality.

Psychologists have a primary obligation and take reasonable precautions to respect the confidentiality rights of those with whom they work or consult, recognizing that confidentiality may be established by law, institutional rules, or professional or scientific relationships. (See also Standard 6.26, Professional Reviewers.)

5.03 Minimizing Intrusions on Privacy.

  (a) In order to minimize intrusions on privacy, psychologists include in written and oral reports, consultations, and the like, only information germane to the purpose for which the communication is made.

  (b) Psychologists discuss confidential information obtained in clinical or consulting relationships, or evaluative data concerning patients, individual or organizational clients, students, research participants, supervisees, and employees only for appropriate scientific or professional purposes and only with persons clearly concerned with such matters.

5.04 Maintenance of Records.

Psychologists maintain appropriate confidentiality in creating, storing, accessing, transferring, and disposing of records under their control whether these are written, automated, or in any other medium. Psychologists maintain and dispose of records in accordance with law and in a manner that permits compliance with the requirements of this Ethics Code.

5.05 Disclosures.

  (a) Psychologists disclose confidential information without the consent of the individual only as mandated by law, or where permitted by law for a valid purpose, such as (1) to provide needed professional services to the patient or the individual or organizational client, (2) to obtain appropriate professional consultations, (3) to protect the patient or client or others from harm, or (4) to obtain payment for services, in which instance disclosure is limited to the minimum that is necessary to achieve the purpose.

  (b) Psychologists also may disclose confidential information with the appropriate consent of the patient or the individual or organizational client (or of another legally authorized person on behalf of the patient or client), unless prohibited by law.

5.06 Consultations.

When consulting with colleagues, (1) psychologists do not share confidential information that reasonably could lead to the identification of a patient, client, research participant, or other person or organization with whom they have a confidential relation unless they have obtained the prior consent of the person or organization or the disclosure cannot be avoided, and (2) they share information only to the extent necessary to achieve the purposes of the consultation. (See also Standard 5.02, Maintaining Confidentiality.)

5.07 Confidential Information in Databases.

(a) If confidential information concerning recipients of psychological services is to be entered into databases or systems of records available to persons whose access has not been consented to by the recipient, the psychologists use coding or other techniques to avoid the inclusion of personal identifiers.

(b) If a research protocol approved by an institutional review board or similar body requires the inclusion of personal identifiers, such identifiers are deleted before the information is made accessible to persons other than those of whom the subject was advised.

(c) If such deletion is not feasible, then before psychologists transfer such data to others or review such data collected by others, they take reasonable steps to determine that appropriate consent of personally identifiable individuals has been obtained.

5.08 Use of Confidential Information for Didactic or Other Purposes.

(a) Psychologists do not disclose in their writings, lectures, or other public media, confidential, personally identifiable information concerning their patients, individual or organizational clients, students, research participants, or other recipients of their services that they obtained during the course of their work, unless the person or organization has consented in writing or unless there is other ethical or legal authorization for doing so.

(b) Ordinarily, in such scientific and professional presentations, psychologists disguise confidential information concerning such persons or organizations so that they are not individually identifiable to others and so that discussions do not cause harm to subjects who might identify themselves.

5.09 Preserving Records and Data.

A psychologist makes plans in advance so that confidentiality of records and data is protected in the event of the psychologist's death, incapacity, or withdrawal from the position or practice.

5.10 Ownership of Records and Data.

Recognizing that ownership of records and data is governed by legal principles, psychologists take reasonable and lawful steps so that records and data remain available to the extent needed to serve the best interests of patients, individual or organizational clients, research participants, or appropriate others.

5.11 Withholding Records for Nonpayment.

Psychologists may not withhold records under their control that are requested and imminently needed for a patient's or client's treatment solely because payment has not been received, except as otherwise provided by law.

6. **TEACHING, TRAINING SUPERVISION, RESEARCH, AND PUBLISHING**

6.01 Design of Education and Training Programs.

Psychologists who are responsible for education and training programs seek to ensure that the programs are competently designed, provide the proper experiences, and meet the requirements for licensure, certification, or other goals for which claims are made by the program.

6.02 Descriptions of Education and Training Programs.

    (a) Psychologists responsible for education and training programs seek to ensure that there is a current and accurate description of the program content, training goals and objectives, and requirements that must be met for satisfactory completion of the program. This information must be made readily available to all interested parties.

    (b) Psychologists seek to ensure that statements concerning their course outlines are accurate and not misleading, particularly regarding the subject matter to be covered, bases for evaluating progress, and the nature of course experiences. (See also Standard 3.03, Avoidance of False or Deceptive Statements.)

    (c) To the degree to which they exercise control, psychologists responsible for announcements, catalogs, brochures, or advertisements describing workshops, seminars, or other nondegree-granting educational programs ensure that they accurately describe the audience for which the program is intended, the educational objectives, the presenters and the fees involved.

6.03 Accuracy and Objectivity in Teaching.

    (a) When engaged in teaching or training, psychologists present psychological information accurately and with a reasonable degree of objectivity.

    (b) When engaged in teaching or training, psychologists recognize the power they hold over students or supervisees and therefore make reasonable efforts to avoid engaging in conduct that is personally demeaning to students or supervisees. (See also Standards 1.09, Respecting Others, and 1.12, Other Harassment.)

6.04 Limitation on Teaching.

Psychologists do not teach the use of techniques or procedures that require specialized training, licensure, or expertise, including but not limited to hypnosis, biofeedback, and projective techniques, to individuals who lack the prerequisite training, legal scope of practice, or expertise.

6.05 Assessing Student and Supervisee Performance.

    (a) In academic and supervisory relationships, psychologists establish an appropriate process for providing feedback to students and supervisees.

    (b) Psychologists evaluate students and supervisees on the basis of their actual performance on relevant and established program requirements.

6.06 Planning Research.

    (a) Psychologists design, conduct, and report research in accordance with recognized standards of scientific competence and ethical research.

(b) Psychologists plan their research so as to minimize the possibility that results will be misleading.

(c) In planning research, psychologists consider its ethical acceptability under the Ethics Code. If an ethical issue is unclear, psychologists seek to resolve the issue through consultation with institutional review boards, animal care and use committees, peer consultations, or other proper mechanisms.

(d) Psychologists take reasonable steps to implement appropriate protections for the rights and welfare of human participants, other persons affected by the research, and the welfare of animal subjects.

6.07 Responsibility.

(a) Psychologists conduct research competently and with due concern for the dignity and welfare of the participants.

(b) Psychologists are responsible for the ethical conduct of research conducted by them or by others under their supervision or control.

(c) Researchers and assistants are permitted to perform only those tasks for which they are appropriately trained and prepared.

(d) As part of the process of development and implementation of research projects, psychologists consult those with expertise concerning any special population under investigation or most likely to be affected.

6.08 Compliance With Law and Standards.

Psychologists plan and conduct research in a manner consistent with federal and state law and regulations, as well as professional standards governing the conduct of research, and particularly those standards governing research with human participants and animal subjects.

6.09 Institutional Approval.

Psychologists obtain from host institutions or organizations appropriate approval prior to conducting research, and they provide accurate information about their research proposals. They conduct the research in accordance with the approved research protocol.

6.10 Research Responsibilities.

Prior to conducting research (except research involving only anonymous surveys, naturalistic observations, or similar research), psychologists enter into an agreement with participants that clarifies the nature of the research and the responsibilities of each party.

6.11 Informed Consent to Research.

(a) Psychologists use language that is reasonably understandable to research participants in obtaining their appropriate informed consent (except as provided in Standard 6.12, Dispensing with Informed Consent). Such informed consent is appropriately documented.

(b) Using language that is reasonably understandable to participants, psychologists inform participants of the nature of the research;

they inform participants that they are free to participate or to decline to participate or to withdraw from the research; they explain the foreseeable consequences of declining or withdrawing; they inform participants of significant factors that may be expected to influence their willingness to participate (such as risks, discomfort adverse effects, or limitations on confidentiality, except as provided in Standard 6.15, Deception in Research); and they explain other aspects about which the prospective participants inquire.

(c) When psychologists conduct research with individuals such as students or subordinates, psychologists take special care to protect the prospective participants from adverse consequences of declining or withdrawing from participations.

(d) When research participation is a course requirement or opportunity for extra credit, the prospective participant is given the choice of equitable alternative activities.

(e) For persons who are legally incapable of giving informed consent, psychologists nevertheless (1) provide an appropriate explanation, (2) obtain the participant's assent, and (3) obtain appropriate permission from a legally authorized person, if such substitute consent is permitted by law.

6.12 Dispensing With Informed Consent.

Before determining that planned research (such as research involving only anonymous questionnaires, naturalistic observations, or certain kinds of archival research) does not require the informed consent of research participants, psychologists consider applicable regulations and institutional review board requirements, and they consult with colleagues as appropriate.

6.13 Informed Consent in Research Filming or Recording.

Psychologists obtain informed consent from research participants prior to filming or recording them in any form, unless the research involves simply naturalistic observations in public places and it is not anticipated that the recording will be used in a manner that could cause personal identification or harm.

6.14 Offering Inducements for Research Participants.

(a) In offering professional services as an inducement to obtain research participants, psychologists make clear the nature of the services, as well as the risks, obligations, and limitations. (See also Standard 1.18, Barter [With Patients or Clients].)

(b) Psychologists do not offer excessive or inappropriate financial or other inducements to obtain research participants, particularly when it might tend to coerce participation.

6.15 Deception in Research.

(a) Psychologists do not conduct a study involving deception unless they have determined that the use of deceptive techniques is justified by the study's prospective scientific, educational, or applied value and that equally effective alternative procedures that do not use deception are not feasible.

(b) Psychologists never deceive research participants about significant aspects that would affect their willingness to participate, such as physical risks, discomfort, or unpleasant emotional experiences.

(c) Any other deception that is an integral feature of the design and conduct of an experiment must be explained to participants as early as is feasible, preferably at the conclusion of their participation, but no later than at the conclusion of the research. (See also Standard 6.18, Providing Participants With Information About the Study.)

6.16 Sharing and Utilizing Data.

Psychologists inform research participants of their anticipated sharing or further use of personally identifiable research data and of the possibility of unanticipated future uses.

6.17 Minimizing Invasiveness.

In conducting research, psychologists interfere with the participants or milieu from which data are collected only in a manner that is warranted by an appropriate research design and that is consistent with psychologists' roles as scientific investigators.

6.18 Providing Participants With Information About the Study.

(a) Psychologists provide a prompt opportunity for participants to obtain appropriate information about the nature, results, and conclusions of the research, and psychologists attempt to correct any misconceptions that participants may have.

(b) If scientific or humane values justify delaying or withholding this information, psychologists take reasonable measures to reduce the risk of harm.

6.19 Honoring Commitments.

Psychologists take reasonable measures to honor all commitments they have made to research participants.

6.20 Care and Use of Animals in Research.

(a) Psychologists who conduct research involving animals treat them humanely.

(b) Psychologists acquire, care for, use, and dispose of animals in compliance with current federal, state, and local laws and regulations, and with professional standards.

(c) Psychologists trained in research methods and experienced in the care of laboratory animals supervise all procedures involving animals and are responsible for ensuring appropriate consideration of their comfort, health, and humane treatment.

(d) Psychologists ensure that all individuals using animals under their supervision have received instruction in research methods and in the care, maintenance, and handling of the species being used, to the extent appropriate to their role.

(e) Responsibilities and activities of individuals assisting in a research project are consistent with their respective competencies.

(f) Psychologists make reasonable efforts to minimize the discomfort, infection, illness, and pain of animal subjects.

(g) A procedure subjecting animals to pain, stress, or privation is used only when an alternative procedure is unavailable and the goal is justified by its prospective scientific, educational, or applied value.

(h) Surgical procedures are performed under appropriate anesthesia; techniques to avoid infection and minimize pain are followed during and after surgery.

(i) When it is appropriate that the animal's life be terminated, it is done rapidly, with an effort to minimize pain, and in accordance with accepted procedures.

6.21 Reporting of Results.

(a) Psychologists do not fabricate data or falsify results in their publications.

(b) If psychologists discover significant errors in their published data, they take reasonable steps to correct such errors in a correction, retraction, erratum, or other appropriate publication means.

6.22 Plagiarism.

Psychologists do not present substantial portions or elements of another's work or data as their own, even if the other work or data source is cited occasionally.

6.23 Publication Credit.

(a) Psychologists take responsibility and credit, including authorship credit, only for work they have actually performed or to which they have contributed.

(b) Principal authorship and other publication credits accurately reflect the relative scientific or professional contributions of the individuals involved, regardless of their relative status. Mere possession of an institutional position, such as Department Chair, does not justify authorship credit. Minor contributions to the research or to the writing for publications are appropriately acknowledged, such as in footnotes or in an introductory statement.

(c) A student is usually listed as principal author on any multiple-authored article that is substantially based on the student's dissertation or thesis.

6.24 Duplicate Publication of Data.

Psychologists do not publish, as original data, data that have been previously published This does not preclude republishing data when they are accompanied by proper acknowledgment.

6.25 Sharing Data.

After research results are published, psychologists do not withhold the data on which their conclusions are based from other competent professionals who seek to verify the substantive claims through reanalysis and who intend to use such data only for that purpose, provided that the confidentiality of the participants can be protected and unless legal rights concerning proprietary data preclude their release.

6.26 Professional Reviewers. Psychologists who review material submitted for publication, grant, or other research proposal review respect the confidentiality of and the proprietary rights in such information of those who submitted.

# 7. FORENSIC ACTIVITIES

7.01 Professionalism.

Psychologists who perform forensic functions, such as assessments, interviews, consultations, reports, or expert testimony, must comply with all other provisions of this Ethics Code to the extent that they apply to such activities. In addition, psychologists base their forensic work on appropriate knowledge of and competence in the areas underlying such work, including specialized knowledge concerning special populations. (See also Standards 1.06, Basis for Scientific and Professional Judgments; 1.08, Human Differences; 1.15, Misuse of Psychologists' Influence; and 1.23, Documentation of Professional and Scientific Work.)

7.02 Forensic Assessments.

(a) Psychologists' forensic assessments, recommendations, and reports are based on information and techniques (including personal interviews of the individual, when appropriate) sufficient to provide appropriate substantiation for their findings. (See also Standards 1.03, Professional and Scientific Relationship; 1.23, Documentation of Professional and Scientific Work; 2.01, Evaluation, Diagnosis, and Interventions in Professional Context; and 2.05, Interpreting Assessment Results.)

(b) Except as noted in (c), below, psychologists provide written or oral forensic reports or testimony of the psychological characteristics of an individual only after they have conducted an examination of the individual adequate to support their statements or conclusions.

(c) When, despite reasonable efforts, such an examination is not feasible, psychologists clarify the impact of their limited information on the reliability and validity of their reports and testimony, and they appropriately limit the nature and extent of their conclusions or recommendations.

7.03 Clarification of Role.

In most circumstances, psychologists avoid performing multiple and potentially conflicting roles in forensic matters. When psychologists may be called on to serve in more than one role in a legal proceeding—for example, as consultant or expert for one party or for the court and as a fact witness—they clarify role expectations and the extent of confidentiality in advance to the extent feasible, and thereafter as changes occur, in order to avoid compromising their

professional judgment and objectivity and in order to avoid misleading others regarding their role.

7.04 Truthfulness and Candor.

(a) In forensic testimony and reports, psychologists testify truthfully,
honestly, and candidly and, consistent with applicable legal procedures, describe fairly the bases for their testimony and
conclusions.

(b) Whenever necessary to avoid misleading, psychologists acknowledge the limits of their data or conclusions.

7.05 Prior Relationships.

A prior professional relationship with a party does not preclude psychologists from testifying as fact witnesses or from testifying to their
services to the extent permitted by applicable law. Psychologists appropriately take into account ways in which the prior relationship
might affect their professional objectivity or opinions and disclose the
potential conflict to the relevant parties.

7.06 Compliance With Law and Rules.

In performing forensic roles, psychologists are reasonably familiar
with the rules governing their roles. Psychologists are aware of the
occasionally competing demands placed upon them by these principles and the requirements of the court system, and attempt to resolve
these conflicts by making known their commitment to this Ethics
Code and taking steps to resolve the conflict in a responsible manner.
(See also Standard 1.02, Relationship of Ethics and Law.)

## 8. RESOLVING ETHICAL ISSUES

8.01 Familiarity With Ethics Code.

Psychologists have an obligation to be familiar with this Ethics Code,
other applicable ethics codes, and their application to psychologists'
work. Lack of awareness or misunderstanding of an ethical standard is
not itself a defense to a charge of unethical conduct.

8.02 Confronting Ethical Issues.

When a psychologist is uncertain whether a particular situation or
course of action would violate this Ethics Code, the psychologist ordinarily consults with other psychologists knowledgeable about ethical issues, with state or national psychology ethics committees, or
with other appropriate authorities in order to choose a proper
response.

8.03 Conflicts Between Ethics and Organizational Demands.

If the demands of an organization with which psychologists are affiliated conflict with this Ethics Code, psychologists clarify the nature of
the conflict, make known their commitment to the Ethics Code, and
to the extent feasible, seek to resolve the conflict in a way that permits the fullest adherence to the Ethics Code.

8.04 Informal Resolution of Ethical Violations.

When psychologists believe that there may have been an ethical violation by another psychologist, they attempt to resolve the issue by

bringing it to the attention of that individual if an informal resolution appears appropriate and the intervention does not violate any confidentiality rights that may be involved.

8.05 Reporting Ethical Violations.

If an apparent ethical violation is not appropriate for informal resolution under Standard 8.04 or is not resolved properly in that fashion, psychologists take further action appropriate to the situation, unless such action conflicts with confidentiality rights in ways that cannot be resolved. Such action might include referral to state or national committees on professional ethics or to state licensing boards.

8.06 Cooperating With Ethics Committees.

Psychologists cooperate in ethics investigations, proceedings, and resulting requirements of the APA or any affiliated state psychological association to which they belong. In doing so, they make reasonable efforts to resolve any issues as to confidentiality. Failure to cooperate is itself an ethics violation.

8.07 Improper Complaints.

Psychologists do not file or encourage the filing of ethics complaints that are frivolous and are intended to harm the respondent rather than to protect the public.

# G

*

# National Association
# of Social Workers
# Code of Ethics

## PREAMBLE

The primary mission of the social work profession is to enhance human well-being and help meet the basic human needs of all people, with particular attention to the needs and empowerment of people who are vulnerable, oppressed, and living in poverty. A historic and defining feature of social work is the profession's focus on individual well-being in a social context and the well-being of society. Fundamental to social work is attention to the environmental forces that create, contribute to, and address problems in living.

Social workers promote social justice and social change with and on behalf of clients. "Clients" is used inclusively to refer to individuals, families, groups, organizations, and communities. Social workers are sensitive to cultural and ethnic diversity and strive to end discrimination, oppression, poverty, and other forms of social injustice. These activities may be in the form of direct practice, community organizing, supervision, consultation, administration, advocacy, social and political action, policy development and implementation, education, and research and evaluation. Social workers seek to enhance the capacity of people to address their own needs. Social workers also seek to promote the responsiveness of organizations, communities, and other social institutions to individuals' needs and social problems.

The mission of the social work profession is rooted in a set of core values. These core values, embraced by social workers throughout the profession's history, are the foundation of social work's unique purpose and perspective:

service

social service

dignity and worth of the person

importance of human relationships

integrity

competence.

This constellation of core values reflects what is unique to the social work profession. Core values, and the principles that flow from them, must be balanced within the context and complexity of the human experience.

## PURPOSE OF THE NASW CODE OF ETHICS

Professional ethics are at the core of social work. The profession has an obligation to articulate its basic values, ethical principles, and ethical standards. The *NASW Code of Ethics* sets forth these values, principles, and standards to guide social workers' conduct.

The *Code* is relevant to all social workers and social work students, regardless of their professional functions, the settings in which they work, or the populations they serve.

The *NASW Code of Ethics* serves six purposes:

1. The *Code* identifies core values on which social work's mission is based.

2. The *Code* summarizes broad ethical principles that reflect the profession's core values and establishes a set of specific ethical standards that should be used to guide social work practice

3. The *Code* is designed to help social workers identify relevant considerations when professional obligations conflict or ethical uncertainties arise.

4. The *Code* provides ethical standards to which the general public can hold the social work profession accountable.

5. The *Code* socializes practitioners new to the field to social work's mission, values, ethical principles, and ethical standards.

6. The *Code* articulates standards that the social work profession itself can use to assess whether social workers have engaged in unethical conduct. NASW has formal procedures to adjudicate ethics complaints filed against its members. (For information on NASW adjudication procedures, see *NASW Procedures for the Adjudication of Grievances.*) In subscribing to the *Code*, social workers are required to cooperate in its implementation, participate in NASW adjudication proceedings, and abide by any NASW disciplinary rulings or sanctions based on it.

The *Code* offers a set of values, principles, and standards to guide decision making and conduct when ethical issues arise. It does not provide a set of rules that prescribe how social workers should act in all situations. Specific applications of the *Code* must take into account the context in which it is being considered and the possibility of conflicts among the *Code's* values, principles, and standards. Ethical responsibilities flow from all human relationships, from the personal and familial to the social and professional.

Further, the *NASW Code of Ethics* does not specify which values, principles, and standards are most important and ought to outweigh others in instances when they conflict. Reasonable differences of opinion can and do exist among social workers with respect to the ways in which values, ethical principles, and ethical standards should be rank ordered when they conflict. Ethical decision making in a given situation must apply the informed judgment of the individual social worker and should also consider how the issues would be judged in a peer review process where the ethical standards of the profession would be applied.

Ethical decision making is a process. There are many instances in social work where simple answers are not available to resolve complex ethical issues. Social workers should take into consideration all the values, principles, and standards in this *Code* that are relevant to any situation in which ethical judgment is warranted. Social workers' decisions and actions should be consistent with the spirit as well as the letter of this *Code*.

In addition to the *Code*, there are many other sources of information about ethical thinking that may be useful. Social workers should consider ethical theory and principles generally, social work theory and research, laws, regulations, agency policies, and other relevant codes of ethics, recognizing that among codes of ethics social workers should consider the *NASW Code of Ethics* as their primary source. Social workers also should be aware of the impact on ethical decision making of their clients' and their own personal values and cultural and religious beliefs and practices. They should be aware of any conflicts between personal and professional values and deal with them responsibly. For additional guidance social workers should consult the relevant literature on professional ethics and ethical decision making and seek appropriate consultation when faced with ethical dilemmas. This may involve consultation with an agency-based or social work organization's ethics committee, a regulatory body, knowledgeable colleagues, supervisors, or legal counsel.

Instances may arise when social workers' ethical obligations conflict with agency policies or relevant laws or regulations. When such conflicts occur, social workers must make a responsible effort to resolve the conflict in a manner that is consistent with the values, principles, and standards expressed in this *Code*. If a reasonable resolution of the conflict does not appear possible social workers should seek proper consultation before making a decision.

The *NASW Code of Ethics* is to be used by NASW and by individuals, agencies, organizations, and bodies (such as licensing and regulatory boards, professional liability insurance providers, courts of law, agency boards of directors, government agencies, and other professional groups) that choose to adopt it or use it as a frame of reference. Violation of standards in this Code does not automatically imply legal liability or violation of the law. Such determination can only be made in the context of legal and judicial proceedings. Alleged violations of the *Code* would be subject to a peer review process. Such processes are generally separate from legal or administrative procedures and insulated from legal review or proceedings to allow the profession to counsel and discipline its own members.

A code of ethics cannot guarantee ethical behavior. Moreover, a code of ethics cannot resolve all ethical issues or disputes or capture the richness and complexity involved in striving to make responsible choices within a moral community. Rather, a code of ethics sets forth values, ethical principles, and ethical standards to which professionals aspire and by which their actions can be judged. Social workers' ethical behavior should result from their personal commitment to engage in ethical practice. The *NASW Code of Ethics* reflects the commitment of all social workers to uphold the profession's values and to act ethically. Principles and standards must be applied by individuals of good character who discern moral questions and, in good faith, seek to make reliable ethical judgments.

## ETHICAL STANDARDS

The following ethical standards are relevant to the professional activities of all social workers. These standards concern (1) social workers' ethical responsibilities to clients, (2) social workers' ethical responsibilities to colleagues, (3) social workers' ethical responsibilities in practice settings, (4) social workers' ethical responsibilities as professionals, (5) social workers' ethical responsibilities to the social work profession, and (6) social workers' ethical responsibilities to the broader society.

Some of the standards that follow are enforceable guidelines for professional conduct, and some are aspirational. The extent to which each standard is enforceable is a matter of professional judgment to be exercised by those responsible for reviewing alleged violations of ethical standards.

## ETHICAL PRINCIPLES

The following broad ethical principles are based on social work's core values of service, social justice, dignity and worth of the person, importance of human relationships, integrity, and competence. These principles set forth ideals to which all social workers should aspire.

**Value** *Service*

**Ethical Principle** *Social workers' primary goal is to help people in need and to address social problems.*

Social workers elevate service to others above self-interest. Social workers draw on their knowledge, values, and skills to help people in need and to address social problems. Social workers are encouraged to volunteer some portion of their professional skills with no expectation of significant financial return (pro bono service).

**Value** *Social Justice*

**Ethical Principle** *Social workers challenge social injustice.*
Social workers pursue social change, particularly with and on behalf of vulnerable and oppressed individuals and groups of people. Social workers' social change efforts are focused primarily on issues of poverty, unemployment, discrimination, and other forms of social injustice. These activities seek to promote sensitivity to and knowledge about oppression and cultural and ethnic diversity. Social workers strive to ensure access to needed information, services, and resources; equality of opportunity; and meaningful participation in decision making for all people.

**Value** *Dignity and Worth of the Person*

**Ethical Principle** *Social workers respect the inherent dignity and worth of the person.*
Social workers treat each person in a caring and respectful fashion, mindful of individual differences and cultural and ethnic diversity. Social workers promote clients' socially responsible self-determination. Social workers seek to enhance clients' capacity and opportunity to change and to address their own needs. Social workers are cognizant of their dual responsibility to clients and to the broader society. They seek to resolve conflicts between clients' interests and the broader society's interests in a socially responsible manner consistent with the values, ethical principles, and ethical standards of the profession.

**Value** *Importance of Human Relationships*

**Ethical Principle** *Social workers recognize the central importance of human relationships.*
Social workers understand that relationships between and among people are an important vehicle for change. Social workers engage people as partners in the helping process. Social workers seek to strengthen relationships among people in a purposeful effort to promote, restore, maintain, and enhance the well-being of individuals, families, social groups, organizations, and communities.

**Value** *Integrity*

**Ethical Principle** *Social workers behave in a trustworthy manner.*
Social workers are continually aware of the profession's mission, values, ethical principles, and ethical standards and practice in a manner consistent with them. Social workers act honestly and responsibly and promote ethical practices on the part of the organizations with which they are affiliated.

**Value** *Competence*

**Ethical Principle** *Social workers practice within their areas of competence and develop and enhance their professional expertise.*

Social workers continually strive to increase their professional knowledge and skills and to apply them in practice. Social workers should aspire to contribute to the knowledge base of the profession.

## ETHICAL STANDARDS

### 1. Social Workers' Ethical Responsibilities to Clients

#### 1.01 Commitment to Clients

Social workers' primary responsibility is to promote the well-being of clients. In general, clients' interests are primary. However, social workers' responsibility to the larger society or specific legal obligations may on limited occasions supersede the loyalty owed clients, and clients should be so advised. (Examples include when a social worker is required by law to report that a client has abused a child or has threatened to harm self or others.)

#### 1.02 Self-Determination

Social workers respect and promote the right of clients to self-determination and assist clients in their efforts to identify and clarify their goals. Social workers may limit clients' right to self-determination when, in the social workers' professional judgment, clients' actions or potential actions pose a serious, foreseeable, and imminent risk to themselves or others.

#### 1.03 Informed Consent

(a) Social workers should provide services to clients only in the context of a professional relationship based, when appropriate, on valid informed consent. Social workers should use clear and understandable language to inform clients of the purpose of the services, risks related to the services, limits to services because of the requirements of a third-party payer, relevant costs, reasonable alternatives, clients' right to refuse or withdraw consent, and the timeframe covered by the consent. Social workers should provide clients with an opportunity to ask questions.

(b) In instances when clients are not literate or have difficulty understanding the primary language used in the practice setting, social workers should take steps to ensure clients' comprehension. This may include providing clients with a detailed verbal explanation or arranging for a qualified interpreter or translator whenever possible.

(c) In instances when clients lack the capacity to provide informed consent, social workers should protect clients' interests by seeking permission from an appropriate third party, informing clients consistent with the clients' level of understanding. In such instances social workers should seek to ensure that the third party acts in a manner consistent with clients' wishes and interests. Social workers should take reasonable steps to enhance such clients' ability to give informed consent.

(d) In instances when clients are receiving services involuntarily, social workers should provide information about the nature and extent of services and about the extent of clients' right to refuse service.

(e) Social workers who provide services via electronic media (such as computer, telephone, radio, and television) should inform recipients of the limitations and risks associated with such services.

(f) Social workers should obtain clients' informed consent before audiotaping or videotaping clients or permitting observation of services to clients by a third party.

### 1.04 Competence

(a) Social workers should provide services and represent themselves as competent only within the boundaries of their education, training, license, certification, consultation received, supervised experience, or other relevant professional experience.

(b) Social workers should provide services in substantive areas or use intervention techniques or approaches that are new to them only after engaging in appropriate study, training, consultation, and supervision from people who are competent in those interventions or techniques.

(c) When generally recognized standards do not exist with respect to an emerging area of practice, social workers should exercise careful judgment and take responsible steps (including appropriate education, research, training, consultation, and supervision) to ensure the competence of their work and to protect clients from harm.

### 1.05 Cultural Competence and Social Diversity

(a) Social workers should understand culture and its function in human behavior and society, recognizing the strengths that exist in all cultures.

(b) Social workers should have a knowledge base of their clients' cultures and be able to demonstrate competence in the provision of services that are sensitive to clients' cultures and to differences among people and cultural groups.

(c) Social workers should obtain education about and seek to understand the nature of social diversity and oppression with respect to race, ethnicity, national origin, color, sex, sexual orientation, age, marital status, political belief, religion, and mental or physical disability.

### 1.06  Conflicts of Interests

(a) Social workers should be alert to and avoid conflicts of interest that interfere with the exercise of professional discretion and impartial judgment. Social workers should inform clients when a real or potential conflict of interest arises and take reasonable steps to resolve the issue in a manner that makes the clients' interests primary and protects clients' interests to the greatest extent possible. In some cases, protecting clients' interests may require termination of the professional relationship with proper referral of the client.

(b) Social workers should not take unfair advantage of any professional relationship or exploit others to further their personal, religious, political, or business interests.

(c) Social workers should not engage in dual or multiple relationships with clients or former clients in which there is a risk of exploitation or potential harm to the client. In instances when dual or multiple relationships are unavoidable, social workers should take steps to protect clients and are responsible for setting clear, appropriate, and culturally sensitive boundaries. (Dual or multiple relationships occur when social workers relate to clients in more than one relationship, whether professional, social, or business. Dual or multiple relationships can occur simultaneously or consecutively.)

(d) When social workers provide services to two or more people who have a relationship with each other (for example, couples, family members), social workers should clarify with all parties which individuals will be considered clients and the nature of social workers' professional obligations to the various individuals who are receiving services. Social workers who anticipate a conflict of interest among the individuals receiving services or who anticipate having to perform in potentially conflicting roles (for example, when a social worker is asked to testify in a child custody dispute or divorce proceedings involving clients) should clarify their role with the parties involved and take appropriate action to minimize any conflict of interest.

### 1.07  Privacy and Confidentiality

(a) Social workers should respect clients' right to privacy. Social workers should not solicit private information from clients unless it is essential to providing services or conducting social work evaluation or research. Once private information is shared, standards of confidentiality apply.

(b) Social workers may disclose confidential information when appropriate with valid consent from a client or a person legally authorized to consent on behalf of a client.

(c) Social workers should protect the confidentiality of all information obtained in the course of professional service, except for compelling professional reasons. The general expectation that social workers will keep information confidential does not apply when disclosure is necessary to prevent serious, foreseeable, and imminent harm to a client or other identifiable person or when laws or regulations require disclosure without a client's consent. In all instances, social workers should disclose the least amount of confidential information necessary to achieve the desired purpose; only information that is directly relevant to the purpose for which the disclosure is made should be revealed.

(d) Social workers should inform clients, to the extent possible, about the disclosure of confidential information and the potential consequences, when feasible before the disclosure is made. This applies whether social workers disclose confidential information on the basis of a legal requirement or client consent.

(e) Social workers should discuss with clients and other interested parties the nature of confidentiality and limitations of clients' right to confidentiality. Social workers should review with clients circumstances where confidential information may be requested and where disclosure of confidential information may be legally required. This discussion should occur as soon as possible in the social worker–client relationship and as needed throughout the course of the relationship.

(f) When social workers provide counseling services to families, couples, or groups, social workers should seek agreement among the parties involved concerning each individual's right to confidentiality and obligation to preserve the confidentiality of information shared by others. Social workers should inform participants in family, couples, or group counseling that social workers cannot guarantee that all participants will honor such agreements.

(g) Social workers should inform clients involved in family, couples, marital, or group counseling of the social worker's, employer's, and agency's policy concerning the social worker's disclosure of confidential information among the parties involved in the counseling.

(h) Social workers should not disclose confidential information to third-party payers unless clients have authorized such.

(i) Social workers should not discuss confidential information in any setting unless privacy can be ensured. Social workers should not discuss confidential information in public or semipublic areas such as hallways, waiting rooms, elevators, and restaurants.

(j) Social workers should protect the confidentiality of clients during legal proceedings to the extent permitted by law. When a court of law or other legally authorized body orders social workers to disclose confidential or privileged information without a client's consent and such disclosure could cause harm to the client, social workers should request that the court withdraw the order or limit the order as narrowly as possible or maintain the records under seal, unavailable for public inspection.

(k) Social workers should protect the confidentiality of clients when responding to requests from members of the media.

(l) Social workers should protect the confidentiality of clients' written and electronic records and other sensitive information. Social workers should take reasonable steps to ensure that clients' records are stored in a secure location and that clients' records are not available to others who are not authorized to have access.

(m) Social workers should take precautions to ensure and maintain the confidentiality of information transmitted to other parties through the use of computers, electronic mail, facsimile machines, telephones and telephone answering machines, and other electronic or computer technology. Disclosure of identifying information should be avoided whenever possible.

(n) Social workers should transfer or dispose of clients' records in a manner that protects clients' confidentiality and is consistent with state statutes governing records and social worker licensure.

(o) Social workers should take reasonable precautions to protect client confidentiality in the event of the social worker's termination of practice, incapacitation, or death.

(p) Social workers should not disclose identifying information when discussing clients for teaching or training purposes unless the client has consented to disclosure of confidential information.

(q) Social workers should not disclose identifying information when discussing clients with consultants unless the client has consented to disclosure of confidential information or there is a compelling need for such disclosure.

(r) Social workers should protect the confidentiality of deceased clients consistent with the preceding standards.

**1.08  Access to Records**

(a) Social workers should provide clients with reasonable access to records concerning the clients. Social workers who are concerned that clients' access to their records could cause serious misunderstanding or harm to the client should provide assistance in interpreting the records and consultation with the client regarding the records. Social workers should limit clients' access to their records, or portions of their records, only in exceptional circumstances when there is compelling evidence that such access would cause serious harm to the client. Both clients' requests and the rationale for withholding some or all of the record should be documented in clients' files.

(b) When providing clients with access to their records, social workers should take steps to protect the confidentiality of other individuals identified or discussed in such records.

### 1.09 Sexual Relationships
(a) Social workers should under no circumstances engage in sexual activities or sexual contact with current clients, whether such contact is consensual or forced.

(b) Social workers should not engage in sexual activities or sexual contact with clients' relatives or other individuals with whom clients maintain a close personal relationship when there is a risk of exploitation or potential harm to the client. Sexual activity or sexual contact with clients' relatives or other individuals with whom clients maintain a personal relationship has the potential to be harmful to the client and may make it difficult for the social worker and client to maintain appropriate professional boundaries. Social workers—not their clients, their clients' relatives, or other individuals with whom the client maintains a personal relationship—assume the full burden for setting clear, appropriate, and culturally sensitive boundaries.

(c) Social workers should not engage in sexual activities or sexual contact with former clients because of the potential for harm to the client. If social workers engage in conduct contrary to this prohibition or claim that an exception to this prohibition is warranted because of extraordinary circumstances, it is social workers—not their clients—who assume the full burden of demonstrating that the former client has not been exploited, coerced, or manipulated, intentionally or unintentionally.

(d) Social workers should not provide clinical services to individuals with whom they have had a prior sexual relationship. Providing clinical services to a former sexual partner has the potential to be harmful to the individual and is likely to make it difficult for the social worker and individual to maintain appropriate professional boundaries.

### 1.10 Physical Contact
Social workers should not engage in physical contact with clients when there is a possibility of psychological harm to the client as a result of the contact (such as cradling or caressing clients). Social workers who engage in appropriate physical contact with clients are responsible for setting clear, appropriate, and culturally sensitive boundaries that govern such physical contact.

### 1.11 Sexual Harassment
Social workers should not sexually harass clients. Sexual harassment includes sexual advances, sexual solicitation, requests for sexual favors, and other verbal or physical conduct of a sexual nature.

### 1.12 Derogatory Language
Social workers should not use derogatory language in their written or verbal communications to or about clients. Social workers should use accurate and respectful language in all communications to and about clients.

### 1.13  Payment for Services

(a) When setting fees, social workers should ensure that the fees are fair, reasonable, and commensurate with the services performed. Consideration should be given to clients' ability to pay.

(b) Social workers should avoid accepting goods or services from clients as payment for professional services. Bartering arrangements, particularly involving services, create the potential for conflicts of interest, exploitation, and inappropriate boundaries in social workers' relationships with clients. Social workers should explore and may participate in bartering only in very limited circumstances when it can be demonstrated that such arrangements are an accepted practice among professionals in the local community, considered to be essential for the provision of services, negotiated without coercion, and entered into at the client's initiative and with the client's informed consent. Social workers who accept goods or services from clients as payment for professional services assume the full burden of demonstrating that this arrangement will not be detrimental to the client or the professional relationship.

(c) Social workers should not solicit a private fee or other remuneration for providing services to clients who are entitled to such available services through the social workers' employer or agency.

### 1.14  Clients Who Lack Decision-Making Capacity

When social workers act on behalf of clients who lack the capacity to make informed decisions, social workers should take reasonable steps to safeguard the interests and rights of those clients.

### 1.15  Interruption of Services

Social workers should make reasonable efforts to ensure continuity of services in the event that services are interrupted by factors such as unavailability, relocation, illness, disability, or death.

### 1.16  Termination of Services

(a) Social workers should terminate services to clients and professional relationships with them when such services and relationships are no longer required or no longer serve the clients' needs or interests.

(b) Social workers should take reasonable steps to avoid abandoning clients who are still in need of services. Social workers should withdraw services precipitously only under unusual circumstances, giving careful consideration to all factors in the situation and taking care to minimize possible adverse effects. Social workers should assist in making appropriate arrangements for continuation of services when necessary.

(c) Social workers in fee-for-service settings may terminate services to clients who are not paying an overdue balance if the financial contractual arrangements have been made clear to the client, if the client does not pose an imminent danger to self or others, and if the clinical and other consequences of the current nonpayment have been addressed and discussed with the client.

(d) Social workers should not terminate services to pursue a social, financial, or sexual relationship with a client.

(e) Social workers who anticipate the termination or interruption of services to clients should notify clients promptly and seek the transfer, referral, or continuation of services in relation to the clients' needs and preferences.

(f) Social workers who are leaving an employment setting should inform clients of appropriate options for the continuation of services and of the benefits and risks of the options.

# H

✳

# The Principles of Medical Ethics

## With Annotations Especially Applicable to Psychiatry

In 1973, the American Psychiatric Association published the first edition of THE PRINCIPLES OF MEDICAL ETHICS WITH ANNOTATIONS ESPECIALLY APPLICABLE TO PSYCHIATRY. Subsequently, revisions were published as the Board of Trustees and the Assembly approved additional annotations. In July of 1980, the American Medical Association approved a new version of the Principles of Medical Ethics (the first revision since 1957) and the APA Ethics Committee[1] incorporated many of its annotations into the new Principles, which resulted in the 1981 edition and subsequent revisions.

### FOREWORD

All physicians should practice in accordance with the medical code of ethics set forth in the Principles of Medical Ethics of the American Medical Association. An up-to-date expression and elaboration of these statements is found in the Opinions and Reports of the Council on Ethical and Judicial Affairs of the

---

[1]The committee included Herbert Klemmer, M.D., Chairperson, Miltiades Zaphiropoulos, M.D., Ewald Busse, M.D., John R. Saunders, M.D., and Robert McDevitt, M.D. J. Brand Brickman, M.D., William P. Camp, M.D., and Robert A. Moore, M.D. served as consultants to the APA Ethics Committee.

American Medical Association.[2] Psychiatrists are strongly advised to be familiar with these documents.[3]

# PRINCIPLES OF MEDICAL ETHICS
# AMERICAN MEDICAL ASSOCIATION

## Preamble

The medical profession has long subscribed to a body of ethical statements developed primarily for the benefit of the patient. As a member of this profession, a physician must recognize responsibility not only to patients but also to society, to other health professionals, and to self. The following principles, adopted by the American Medical Association, are not laws but standards of conduct, which define the essentials of honorable behavior for the physician.

## Section 1

A physician shall be dedicated to providing competent medical service with compassion and respect for human dignity.

## Section 2

A physician shall deal honestly with patients and colleagues, and strive to expose those physicians deficient in character or competence, or who engage in fraud or deception.

## Section 3

A physician shall respect the law and also recognize a responsibility to seek changes in those requirements which are contrary to the best interests of the patient.

## Section 4

A physician shall respect the rights of patients, of colleagues, and of other health professionals, and shall safeguard patient confidences within the constraints of the law.

---

[2]Current Opinions of the Council on Ethical and Judicial Affairs, Chicago, American Medical Association, 1992.

[3]Chapter 8, Section 1 of the Bylaws of the American Psychiatric Association states, "All members of the American Psychiatric Association shall be bound by the ethical code of the medical profession, specifically defined in the Principles of Medical Ethics of the American Medical Association." In interpreting the APA Constitution and Bylaws, it is the opinion of the Board of Trustees that inactive status in no way removes a physician member from responsibility to abide by the Principles of Medical Ethics.

## Section 5

A physician shall continue to study, apply, and advance scientific knowledge, make relevant information available to patients, colleagues, and the public, obtain consultation, and use the talents of other health professionals when indicated.

## Section 6

A physician shall, in the provision of appropriate patient care, except in emergencies, be free to choose whom to serve, with whom to associate, and the environment in which to provide medical services.

## Section 7

A physician shall recognize a responsibility to participate in activities contributing to an improved community.

# PRINCIPLES WITH ANNOTATIONS

Following are each of the AMA Principles of Medical Ethics printed separately along with annotations especially applicable to psychiatry.

## Preamble

*The medical profession has long subscribed to a body of ethical statements developed primarily for the benefit of the patient. As a member of this profession, a physician must recognize responsibility not only to patients but also to society, to other health professionals, and to self. The following Principles, adopted by the American Medical Association, are not laws but standards of conduct, which define the essentials of honorable behavior for the physician.*[4]

## Section 1

*A physician shall be dedicated to providing competent medical service with compassion and respect for human dignity.*

1.  The patient may place his/her trust in his/her psychiatrist knowing that the psychiatrist's ethics and professional responsibilities preclude him/her gratifying his/her own needs by exploiting the patient. The psychiatrist shall be ever vigilant about the impact that his/her conduct has upon the boundaries of the doctor/patient relationship, and thus upon the well-being of the patient. These requirements become particularly important because of the essentially private, highly personal, and sometimes intensely emotional nature of the relationship established with the psychiatrist.

---

[4]Statements in italics are taken directly from the American Medical Association's Principles of Medical Ethics.

2. A psychiatrist should not be a party to any type of policy that excludes, segregates, or demeans the dignity of any patient because of ethnic origin, race, sex, creed, age, socioeconomic status, or sexual orientation.

3. In accord with the requirements of law and accepted medical practice, it is ethical for a physician to submit his/her work to peer review and to the ultimate authority of the medical staff executive body and the hospital administration and its governing body. In case of dispute, the ethical psychiatrist has the following steps available.

   a. Seek appeal from the medical staff decision to a joint conference committee, including members of the medical staff executive committee and the executive committee of the governing board. At this appeal, the ethical psychiatrist could request that outside opinions be considered.

   b. Appeal to the governing body itself.

   c. Appeal to state agencies regulating licensure of hospitals if, in the particular state, they concern themselves with matters of professional competency and quality of care.

   d. Attempt to educate colleagues through development of research projects and data and presentations at professional meetings and in professional journals.

   e. Seek redress in local courts, perhaps through an enjoining injunction against the governing body.

   f. Public education as carried out by an ethical psychiatrist would not utilize appeals based solely upon emotion, but would be presented in a professional way and without any potential exploitation of patients through testimonials.

4. A psychiatrist should not be a participant in a legally authorized execution.

## Section 2

*A physician shall deal honestly with patients and colleagues, and strive to expose those physicians deficient in character or competence, or who engage in fraud or deception.*

1. The requirement that the physician conduct himself/herself with propriety in his/her profession and in all the actions of his/her life is especially important in the case of the psychiatrist because the patient tends to model his/her behavior after that of his/her psychiatrist by identification. Further, the necessary intensity of the treatment relationship may tend to activate sexual and other needs and fantasies on the part of both patient and psychiatrist, while weakening the objectivity necessary for control. Additionally, the inherent inequality in the doctor–patient relationship may lead to exploitation of the patient. Sexual activity with a current or former patient is unethical.

2. The psychiatrist should diligently guard against exploiting information furnished by the patient and should not use the unique position of power af-

forded him/her by the psychotherapeutic situation to influence the patient in any way not directly relevant to the treatment goals.

3. A psychiatrist who regularly practices outside his/her area of professional competence should be considered unethical. Determination of professional competence should be made by peer review boards or other appropriate bodies.

4. Special consideration should be given to those psychiatrists who, because of mental illness, jeopardize the welfare of their patients and their own reputations and practices. It is ethical, even encouraged, for another psychiatrist to intercede in such situations.

5. Psychiatric services, like all medical services, are dispensed in the context of a contractual arrangement between the patient and the treating physician. The provisions of the contractual arrangement, which are binding on the physician as well as on the patient, should be explicitly established.

6. It is ethical for the psychiatrist to make a charge for a missed appointment when this falls within the terms of the specific contractual agreement with the patient. Charging for a missed appointment or for one not canceled 24 hours in advance need not, in itself, be considered unethical if a patient is fully advised that the physician will make such a charge. The practice, however, should be resorted to infrequently and always with the utmost consideration for the patient and his/her circumstances.

7. An arrangement in which a psychiatrist provides supervision or administration to other physicians or nonmedical persons for a percentage of their fees or gross income is not acceptable; this would constitute fee-splitting. In a team of practitioners, or a multidisciplinary team, it is ethical for the psychiatrist to receive income for administration, research, education, or consultation. This should be based upon a mutually agreed upon and set fee or salary, open to renegotiation when a change in the time demand occurs. (See also Section 5, Annotations, 2, 3, and 4.)

## Section 3

*A physician shall respect the law and also recognize a responsibility to seek changes in those requirements which are contrary to the best interests of the patient.*

1. It would seem self-evident that a psychiatrist who is a lawbreaker might be ethically unsuited to practice his/her profession. When such illegal activities bear directly upon his/her practice, this would obviously be the case. However, in other instances, illegal activities such as those concerning the right to protest social injustices might not bear on either the image of the psychiatrist or the ability of the specific psychiatrist to treat his/her patient ethically and well. While no committee or board could offer prior assurance that any illegal activity would not be considered unethical, it is conceivable that an individual could violate a law without being guilty of professionally unethical behavior. Physicians lose no right of citizenship on entry into the profession of medicine.

2. Where not specifically prohibited by local laws governing medical practice, the practice of acupuncture by a psychiatrist is not unethical per se. The psychiatrist should have professional competence in the use of acupuncture. Or, if he/she is supervising the use of acupuncture by non-medical individuals, he/she should provide proper medical supervision. (See also Section 5, Annotations 3 and 4.)

## Section 4

*A physician shall respect the rights of patients, of colleagues, and of other health professionals, and shall safeguard patient confidences within the constraints of the law.*

1. Psychiatric records, including even the identification of a person as a patient, must be protected with extreme care. Confidentiality is essential to psychiatric treatment. This is based in part on the special nature of psychiatric therapy as well as on the traditional ethical relationship between physician and patient. Growing concern regarding the civil rights of patients and the possible adverse effects of computerization, duplication equipment, and data banks makes the dissemination of confidential information an increasing hazard. Because of the sensitive and private nature of the information with which the psychiatrist deals, he/she must be circumspect in the information that he/she chooses to disclose to others about a patient. The welfare of the patient must be a continuing consideration.

2. A psychiatrist may release confidential information only with the authorization of the patient or under proper legal compulsion. The continuing duty of the psychiatrist to protect the patient includes fully apprising him/her of the connotations of waiving the privilege of privacy. This may become an issue when the patient is being investigated by a government agency, is applying for a position, or is involved in legal action. The same principles apply to the release of information concerning treatment to medical departments of government agencies, business organizations, labor unions, and insurance companies. Information gained in confidence about patients seen in student health services should not be released without the students' explicit permission.

3. Clinical and other materials used in teaching and writing must be adequately disguised in order to preserve the anonymity of the individuals involved.

4. The ethical responsibility of maintaining confidentiality holds equally for the consultations in which the patient may not have been present and in which the consultee was not a physician. In such instances, the physician consultant should alert the consultee to his/her duty of confidentiality.

5. Ethically the psychiatrist may disclose only that information which is relevant to a given situation. He/she should avoid offering speculation as fact. Sensitive information such as an individual's sexual orientation or fantasy material is usually unnecessary.

6. Psychiatrists are often asked to examine individuals for security purposes, to determine suitability for various jobs, and to determine legal competence. The psychiatrist must fully describe the nature and purpose and lack of confidentiality of the examination to the examinee at the beginning of the examination.

7. Careful judgment must be exercised by the psychiatrist in order to include, when appropriate, the parents or guardian in the treatment of a minor. At the same time, the psychiatrist must assure the minor proper confidentiality.

8. Psychiatrists at times may find it necessary, in order to protect the patient or the community from imminent danger, to reveal confidential information disclosed by the patient.

9. When the psychiatrist is ordered by the court to reveal the confidences entrusted to him/her by patients, he/she may comply or he/she may ethically hold the right to dissent within the framework of the law. When the psychiatrist is in doubt, the right of the patient to confidentiality and, by extension, to unimpaired treatment, should be given priority. The psychiatrist should reserve the right to raise the question of adequate need for disclosure. In the event that the necessity for legal disclosure is demonstrated by the court, the psychiatrist may request the right to disclosure of only that information which is relevant to the legal question at hand.

10. With regard for the person's dignity and privacy and with truly informed consent, it is ethical to present a patient to a scientific gathering, if the confidentiality of the presentation is understood and accepted by the audience.

11. It is ethical to present a patient or former patient to a public gathering or to the news media only if the patient is fully informed of enduring loss of confidentiality, is competent, and consents in writing without coercion.

12. When involved in funded research, the ethical psychiatrist will advise human subjects of the funding source, retain his/her freedom to reveal data and results, and follow all appropriate and current guidelines relative to human subject protection.

13. Ethical considerations in medical practice preclude the psychiatric evaluation of any person charged with criminal acts prior to access to, or availability of, legal counsel. The only exception is the rendering of care to the person for the sole purpose of medical treatment.

14. Sexual involvement between a faculty member or supervisor and a trainee or student, in those situations in which an abuse of power can occur, often takes advantage of inequalities in the working relationship and may be unethical because: (a) any treatment of a patient being supervised may be deleteriously affected; (b) it may damage the trust relationship between teacher and student; and (c) teachers are important professional role models for their trainees and affect their trainees' future professional behavior.

## Section 5

*A physician shall continue to study, apply, and advance scientific knowledge, make relevant information available to patients, colleagues, and the public, obtain consultation, and use the talents of other health professionals when indicated.*

1. Psychiatrists are responsible for their own continuing education and should be mindful of the fact that theirs must be a lifetime of learning.

2. In the practice of his/her specialty, the psychiatrist consults, associates, collaborates, or integrates his/her work with that of many professionals, including psychologists, psychometricians, social workers, alcoholism counselors, marriage counselors, public health nurses, etc. Furthermore, the nature of modern psychiatric practice extends his/her contacts to such people as teachers, juvenile and adult probation officers, attorneys, welfare workers, agency volunteers, and neighborhood aides. In referring patients for treatment, counseling, or rehabilitation to any of these practitioners, the psychiatrist should ensure that the allied professional or paraprofessional with whom he/she is dealing is a recognized member of his/her own discipline and is competent to carry out the therapeutic task required. The psychiatrist should have the same attitude toward members of the medical profession to whom he/she refers patients. Whenever he/she has reason to doubt the training, skill, or ethical qualifications of the allied professional, the psychiatrist should not refer cases to him/her.

3. When the psychiatrist assumes a collaborative or supervisory role with another mental health worker, he/she must expend sufficient time to assure that proper care is given. It is contrary to the interests of the patient and to patient care if he/she allows himself/herself to be used as a figurehead.

4. In relationships between psychiatrists and practicing licensed psychologists, the physician should not delegate to the psychologist or, in fact, to any nonmedical person any matter requiring the exercise of professional medical judgment.

5. The psychiatrist should agree to the request of a patient for consultation or to such a request from the family of an incompetent or minor patient. The psychiatrist may suggest possible consultants, but the patient or family should be given free choice of the consultant. If the psychiatrist disapproves of the professional qualifications of the consultant or if there is a difference of opinion that the primary therapist cannot resolve, he/she may, after suitable notice, withdraw from the case. If this disagreement occurs within an institution or agency framework, the differences should be resolved by the mediation or arbitration of higher professional authority within the institution or agency.

## Section 6

*A physician shall, in the provision of appropriate patient care, except in emergencies be free to choose whom to serve, with whom to associate, and the environment in which to provide medical services.*

1. Physicians generally agree that the doctor–patient relationship is such a vital factor in effective treatment of the patient that preservation of optimal conditions for development of a sound working relationship between a doctor and his/her patient should take precedence over all other considerations. Professional courtesy may lead to poor psychiatric care for physicians and their families because of embarrassment over the lack of a complete give-and-take contract.

2. An ethical psychiatrist may refuse to provide psychiatric treatment to a person who, in the psychiatrist's opinion, cannot be diagnosed as having a mental illness amenable to psychiatric treatment.

## Section 7

*A physician shall recognize a responsibility to participate in activities contributing to an improved community.*

1. Psychiatrists should foster the cooperation of those legitimately concerned with the medical, psychological, social, and legal aspects of mental health and illness. Psychiatrists are encouraged to serve society by advising and consulting with the executive, legislative, and judiciary branches of the government. A psychiatrist should clarify whether he/she speaks as an individual or as a representative of an organization. Furthermore, psychiatrists should avoid cloaking their public statements with the authority of the profession (e.g., "Psychiatrists know that . . .").

2. Psychiatrists may interpret and share with the public their expertise in the various psychosocial issues that may affect mental health and illness. Psychiatrists should always be mindful of their separate roles as dedicated citizens and as experts in psychological medicine.

3. On occasion psychiatrists are asked for an opinion about an individual who is in the light of public attention, or who has disclosed information about himself/herself through public media. It is unethical for a psychiatrist to offer a professional opinion unless he/she has conducted an examination and has been granted proper authorization for such a statement.

4. The psychiatrist may permit his/her certification to be used for the involuntary treatment of any person only following his/her personal examination of that person. To do so, he/she must find that the person, because of mental illness, cannot form a judgment as to what is in his/her own best interests and that, without such treatment, substantial impairment is likely to occur to the person or others.

## PROCEDURES FOR HANDLING COMPLAINTS OF UNETHICAL CONDUCT

The medical profession has long subscribed to a body of ethical statements developed primarily for the benefit of the patient. As a member of this profession, a physician must recognize responsibility not only to patients but also to society, to other health professionals, and to self. The prior Principles, adopted by the American Medical Association, are not laws but standards of conduct, which define the essentials of honorable behavior for the physician.

Complaints charging members of the Association with unethical behavior or practices shall be investigated, processed, and resolved in accordance with procedures approved by the Assembly and the Board.

If a complaint of unethical conduct against a member is sustained, the member shall receive a sanction ranging from admonishment to expulsion. Any decision to expel a member must be approved by a two-thirds affirmative vote of all members of the Board present and voting.[5]

## Procedures

1. All formal complaints charging a member of the American Psychiatric Association (APA) with unethical behavior shall be made in writing, signed by the complainant, and addressed to the accused member's district branch or, if addressed to the APA, shall be referred by the APA to the accused member's district branch for investigation[6] and decision in accordance with the procedures set out in paragraphs 4 through 9 below.[7] If the accused member is a member-at-large of the APA, the complaint shall be referred to an ad hoc investigating committee, as provided for in paragraph 2 below.

2. If, after receiving a written complaint, the district branch determines that there are compelling reasons why it would not be the appropriate body to consider the complaint, the district branch shall write to the Chair of the APA Ethics Committee, requesting that it be excused, providing a detailed explanation of the reasons for its request. If the Chair of the APA Ethics Committee determines that the district branch should not be excused, the district branch shall proceed with the complaint. If the Chair of the APA Ethics Committee agrees that the district branch should be excused from considering the complaint, the Chair shall then appoint three Fellows of the APA to serve as an ad hoc investigating committee to conduct the investigation and to render a decision.[8] When possible, these Fellows shall reside in the same area as the accused member and in no event shall any such Fellow be a mem-

---

[5]Chapter 10, Sections 1 and 2, Bylaws, American Psychiatric Association, 1993 edition.

[6]As used in these procedures, the term "investigation" is meant to include both an information-gathering or investigatory phase of a case and a hearing phase. This term does not apply to the process by which a district branch initially determines whether or not a complaint merits investigation.

[7]Paragraphs 4 through 9, below, set out minimum requirements. Each district branch should comply with any additional or more stringent requirements of state law.

[8]Unless otherwise indicated, whenever these procedures refer to activities of a district branch, the same requirements shall apply to the ad hoc investigating committee when it performs an investigation.

ber of the APA Ethics Committee, the APA Ethics Appeals Board, or the APA Board of Trustees.

3. If the district branch finds it cannot determine that the complaint merits investigation under the ethical standards established by *The Principles of Medical Ethics with Annotations Especially Applicable to Psychiatry*, the district branch shall so notify the complainant, requesting additional information when appropriate. If the district branch determines that the charges do not merit investigation it shall notify the complainant, stating the basis for the conclusion and informing the complainant that he/she may address a request for a review of this decision to the Secretary of the APA. If the Secretary determines that the complaint merits investigation, the complaint shall be referred to the Chair of the APA Ethics Committee, who will appoint an ad hoc investigating committee as provided for in paragraph 2 above. When an ad hoc investigating committee is appointed, the district branch shall be so notified by the Chair of the APA Ethics Committee.

4. If the district branch determines that a complaint merits investigation under the ethical standards established by *The Principles of Medical Ethics with Annotations Especially Applicable to Psychiatry*, the district branch shall advise the Secretary of the APA as well as the complainant and the accused member that it will be conducting the investigation, and that it will notify the complainant and the accused member in accordance with the provisions of paragraphs 16–24 below. The district branch shall also send a copy of the complaint to the accused member, along with copies of *The Principles of Medical Ethics with Annotations Especially Applicable to Psychiatry* and of these procedures. The accused member shall further be informed that he/she has the right to be represented by counsel; that he/she has the right to a hearing; and, that, at the hearing he/she will have the rights set out in paragraph 8 below. The member will also be informed of his/her right to appeal an adverse decision to the APA Ethics Appeals Board in accordance with the provisions of paragraphs 18–23 below.

5. The district branch investigation shall be comprehensive and fair and conducted as provided herein. A hearing conducted in accordance with the provisions of paragraph 8 below shall be held unless the accused member has voluntarily waived his/her right to a hearing or the district branch, prior to the hearing, has determined that there has been no ethical violation. The accused member's waiver of a hearing shall not prevent the district branch from meeting with, and hearing the evidence of, the complainant and other witnesses and reaching a decision in the case.

6. The accused member will be notified of the hearing by certified mail, at least 30 days in advance of the hearing. The notice will include the following:
   a. The date, time, and place of the hearing;
   b. A list of witnesses expected to testify;

c. Notification of the member's right to representation by legal counsel or another individual of the member's choice;

d. Notification of the accused member's right to appeal any adverse decision to the APA Ethics Appeals Board.

7. The initial, information-gathering stages of the investigation, which may include preliminary interviews of the complainant and the accused member, may be conducted by any single member or a subcommittee of the ethics committee. In all cases in which there may be a decision adverse to the accused member, unless the accused member has waived his/her right to a hearing, there must be a hearing before the district branch ethics committee or a specially constituted panel of at least three (3) members, at least one (1) of whom must be a member of the district branch ethics committee.

8. The hearing shall provide fairness and respect for both the accused member and the complainant. The following procedures shall apply:

a. The accused member may be represented by counsel or other person. The counsel or other person may answer questions addressed to him/her, advise his/her client, introduce evidence, examine and cross-examine witnesses, and make opening and closing statements. Counsel's participation is subject to the continuing direction and control of the Chair. The Chair shall exercise its discretion so as to prevent the intimidation or harassment of the complainant and/or other witnesses and with regard to the peer review nature of the proceedings. Questions addressed by members of the committee or panel to the accused member shall be answered by the member.

b. Except when the district branch concludes that it is prepared to proceed solely on the basis of extrinsic evidence,[9] the complainant must be present at the hearing unless excused by the committee or panel Chair. The complainant will be excused only when he/she has so requested and, in the judgment of the Chair, participation would be harmful to him/her.

c. Except when the district branch concludes that it is prepared to proceed solely on the basis of extrinsic evidence or the complainant is excused pursuant to paragraph 8(b) above, the complainant shall testify regarding his/her charges.

d. The accused member or his/her attorney may challenge material presented by the complainant or the complainant's witnesses: (i) by appropriate direct challenge through cross-examination; or (ii) if the

---

[9]For these purposes, "extrinsic evidence" shall mean documents whose validity and accuracy appear to be clear on their face and which do not rely on the assertions or opinions of the complainant and/or his/her witnesses. Examples of such evidence include admissions by the accused member, formal judicial or administrative reports, sworn deposition or trial testimony that was subject to cross-examination, photographs, medical or hospital records, hotel or credit card receipts, etc. When the district branch decides to rely solely on such extrinsic evidence, it should take appropriate steps to ensure that members of the hearing panel do not take into account any information from the complainant or other witnesses and base their decision solely on the available extrinsic evidence.

complainant asked to be excused from such direct challenge and the Chair determined that such direct challenge will be harmful to the complainant, by written questions submitted by the accused member and posed to the complainant by the Chair, with answers to be provided orally or in writing as the Chair in his/her discretion determines is appropriate.

e. The accused member may choose not to be present at the hearing and to present his/her defense through other witnesses and counsel.

f. The accused member may testify on his/her own behalf, call and examine supporting witnesses, and introduce relevant evidence in support of his/her case. Evidence may not be excluded solely on the grounds that it would be inadmissible in a court of law.

g. Members of the hearing panel may ask pertinent questions during the hearing.

h. A stenographic or tape record shall be made of the proceedings and a copy shall subsequently be made available to the accused member at a reasonable charge.

i. The accused member may make an oral statement and/or submit a written statement at the close of the hearing.

9. All ethics committee or panel recommendations shall be in writing and shall include a statement of the basis for recommendation. If the investigation has been conducted by a panel, the panel shall make a recommendation only as to whether there has been an ethics violation and the district branch ethics committee shall review this recommendation and add its recommendation as to sanction, if any.

10. Upon completion of the investigation and any internal review procedures required by the district branch's governing documents, the district branch shall render a decision as to whether an ethics violation has occurred and, if so, what sanction is appropriate. If the investigation has been conducted by an ad hoc investigating committee, the ad hoc investigating committee shall make the decision as to both violation and sanction. The district branch decision shall be in writing and shall include a statement of the basis of the decision. In all cases, the district branch shall seek to reach a decision as expeditiously as possible. This should usually be within nine (9) months from the time that the complaint was received.

11. The four possible sanctions are as follows:
    a. admonishment—an informal warning;
    b. reprimand—a formal censure;
    c. suspension (for a period not to exceed five years);[10]
    d. expulsion.

---

[10]A suspended member will be required to pay dues and will be eligible for APA benefits, except that such a member will lose his/her rights to hold office, vote, nominate candidates, propose referenda or amendments to the Constitution or Bylaws, and serve on any APA committee or component, including the Board of Trustees and the Assembly. If the suspended member is a Fellow or Life Fellow, the Fellowship will be suspended for the same period of time. Each district branch shall decide which, if any, district branch privileges and benefits shall be denied during the period of suspension.

12. In addition to the above sanctions, a district branch may, but is not required to, impose certain conditions, such as educational or supervisory requirements, on a suspended member.[11] When such conditions are imposed, the following procedures shall apply:
    a. if the district branch imposes conditions, it shall monitor compliance;
    b. if the ad hoc investigating committee imposes conditions, the Chair of the APA Ethics Committee shall establish a means for monitoring compliance;
    c. if a member fails to satisfy the conditions, the district branch or the APA monitoring body established by the Chair of the APA Ethics Committee may decide to expel the member;
    d. if it is determined that a member should be expelled for noncompliance with conditions, the member may appeal pursuant to the provisions set forth in paragraphs 18–23 below;
    e. if a member expelled for noncompliance with conditions does not appeal, the APA Board of Trustees shall review the expulsion in accordance with the provisions of paragraph 17 below.

13. After the district branch completes its investigation and arrives at its decision, the decision and any pertinent information concerning the procedures followed or relating to the action taken shall be forwarded to the APA Ethics Committee for review in accordance with the provisions of paragraphs 14–16 below. If the Chair of the APA Ethics Committee determines that these review functions are best carried out by a subcommittee, he/she shall designate such a subcommittee (or subcommittees) which shall include at least three (3) voting members of the APA Ethics Committee, and which shall be authorized to undertake these review functions on behalf of the full APA Ethics Committee. The review proceedings shall be undertaken expeditiously, in no instance exceeding ninety (90) days from the receipt of the district branch's report before the district branch is informed of the APA Ethics Committee's opinion, conclusion, or need for clarification of the material received. If the APA Ethics Committee fails to act within ninety (90) days, the district branch may inform the accused member in accordance with paragraph 16 below.

14. In all cases where the district branch renders a decision, including those where the district branch finds that an ethics violation has not occurred, the APA Ethics Committee shall review the information submitted by the district branch to assure that the complaint received an investigation that was comprehensive and fair and in accordance with these procedures, shall consider the appropriateness of the sanction imposed. If the APA Ethics Committee or subcommittee concludes that the sanction is appro-

---

[11]Personal treatment may be recommended, but not required, and any such recommendation shall be carried out in accordance with the ethical requirements governing confidentiality as set forth in *The Principles of Medical Ethics with Annotations Especially Applicable to Psychiatry*. In appropriate cases, the district branch may in addition refer the psychiatrist in question to a component responsible for considering impaired or physically ill physicians.

priate, it shall so notify the district branch. If the APA Ethics Committee or subcommittee concludes that the sanction should be reconsidered by the district branch, it shall provide a statement of reasons explaining the basis for its opinion, and the district branch shall reconsider the sanction. After reconsideration, the decision of the district branch shall stand, even if the district branch decides to adhere to the original sanction, except that the sanction may be modified as provided for in paragraphs 17, 21, or 23 below.

15. In cases where the district branch has found that an ethics violation has occurred, the APA Ethics Committee or subcommittee, after ascertaining that the investigation was comprehensive and fair and in accordance with these procedures, shall consider the appropriateness of the sanction imposed. If the APA Ethics Committee or subcommittee concludes that the sanction is appropriate, it shall so notify the district branch. If the APA Ethics Committee or subcommittee concludes that the sanction should be reconsidered by the district branch, it shall provide a statement of reasons explaining the basis for its opinion, and the district branch shall reconsider the sanction. After reconsideration, the decision of the district branch shall stand, even if the district branch decides to adhere to the original sanction, except that the sanction may be modified as provided for in paragraphs 17, 21, or 23 below.

16. After the APA Ethics Committee or subcommittee completes the review process, the district branch shall notify the accused member of the decision and sanction, if any, by certified mail. The accused member shall be provided copies of the district branch ethics committee and/or panel recommendation(s) and of the district branch decision. If the decision is that no ethics violation has occurred, the case shall be terminated, and the district branch shall also notify the complainant of this decision by certified mail. If the decision is that an ethics violation has occurred, the accused member shall be advised that he/she has thirty (30) days to file a written letter of appeal with the Secretary of the APA. In such circumstances, unless the complainant is requested to appear before the Ethics Appeals Board as provided for in paragraph 19 below, the complainant shall not be advised of any action until after the appeal has been completed or until the Secretary of the APA notifies the district branch that no appeal has been taken or that the procedures provided for in paragraph 17 below have been completed.

17. If, after review by the APA Ethics Committee or upon a finding of noncompliance with conditions as provided for in paragraph 12(c), above, the decision is to expel a member, and the member fails to appeal the decision, the APA Board of Trustees at its next meeting shall review the expulsion on the basis of a presentation by the Chair of the APA Ethics Committee and the documentary record in the case. A decision to affirm an expulsion must be by a vote of two-thirds (2/3) of those Trustees present and voting. A decision to impose a lesser sanction shall be by a

majority vote. If necessary, the APA Board of Trustees may request further information from the district branch before voting on the decision to expel.

18. All appeals shall be heard by the APA Ethics Appeals Board, which shall be chaired by the Secretary of the APA, and shall include two past presidents of the APA, a past Speaker of the APA Assembly, the Chair of the APA Ethics Committee, and a current Chair of a district branch ethics committee. The Secretary and Chair of the APA Ethics Committee shall serve during their respective terms of office. All other members of the Appeals Board shall be appointed by the President for a three-year term. All members of the Ethics Appeals Board, including the Chair, shall be entitled to one vote on all matters. If any of the above cannot serve, the President is authorized to appoint a replacement.

19. The appeal shall be based on one or more of the following grounds:
    a. that there have been significant procedural irregularities or deficiencies in the case;
    b. that *The Principles of Medical Ethics with Annotations Especially Applicable to Psychiatry* have been improperly applied;
    c. that the findings of or sanction imposed by the district branch are not supported by substantial evidence;
    d. that substantial new evidence has called into question the findings and conclusions of the district branch.

20. The accused member shall be entitled to file a written statement with the Ethics Appeals Board and must appear before the Board alone, or accompanied by counsel. The Ethics Appeals Board shall request a representative of the district branch, accompanied by counsel if the district branch so requests, to attend the appeal. In addition, the Ethics Appeals Board may request any information from the district branch and may also request the complainant, accompanied by counsel if he/she so requests, to attend the appeal. The APA counsel and other necessary APA staff may also attend if the Ethics Appeals Board so requests. Time limits and other procedural requirements concerning the appeal shall be established by the Ethics Appeal Board.

21. After hearing the appeal and reviewing the record, the Ethics Appeals Board may take any of the following actions:
    a. affirm the decision, including the sanction imposed by the district branch;
    b. affirm the decision, but alter the sanction imposed by the district branch;
    c. reverse the decision of the district branch and terminate the case;
    d. remand these to the district branch with specific instructions as to what further information or action is necessary.[12] After the district

---

[12]Remands will be employed only in rare cases, such as when new information has been presented on appeal or when there is an indication that important information is available and has not been considered.

branch or panel has completed remand proceedings, the case shall be handled in accordance with procedures in paragraphs 13 through 21.

22. After the Ethics Appeals Board reaches a decision as set forth in paragraph 21(a), (b), or (c), if the decision is anything other than to expel a member, the APA Secretary shall notify the district branch of the decision and that it is final.

23. If the decision of the Ethics Appeals Board is to expel a member, the APA Board of Trustees at its next meeting shall review the action solely on the basis of the presentation of the Secretary of the APA (or his/her designee) and the documentary record in the case. The Board of Trustees may affirm the sanction, impose a lesser sanction, or remand to the Ethics Appeals Board for further action or consideration. A decision to affirm an expulsion must be by a vote of two-thirds (2/3) of those Trustees present and voting. All other actions shall be by majority vote. Members of the Board of Trustees who participated as members of the APA Ethics Appeals Board shall not vote when the Board of Trustees considers the case. Once the Board of Trustees has acted or, in a case of a remand, has approved the action taken on remand, the APA Secretary shall notify the district branch of the decision and that it is final.

24. Once a final decision is reached, the district branch shall notify the complainant and the accused member by certified mail.

25. Except as described in paragraph 26 below, disclosure by members of the APA of the name of the accused member, the fact that a complaint has been lodged, the substance of the complaint, or the identity of any witnesses, shall be limited to persons who need this information to assure the orderly and effective administration of these procedures.

26. To assure proper protection of the public, there are times when disclosure of the identity of an accused member may be essential. Such disclosure is authorized in the following instances:[13]

    a.  The name of any member who is expelled from the APA for an ethics violation, along with an explanation of the nature of the violation, shall be reported in PSYCHIATRIC NEWS and in the district branch newsletter or other usual means of communication with its membership. The name of any member who is expelled from the APA for an ethics violation, along with an explanation of the nature of the violation, shall also be reported to the medical licensing authority in all states in which the member is licensed. In addition, the name of any member who is also a member of a foreign psychiatric society or association and who is expelled shall be reported to the international society or association to which the member belongs.[14]

---

[13]State and/or federal law may impose additional reporting requirements with which district branches or the APA must comply.

[14]Reporting shall include a press release to the media in the area in which the expelled member lives.

b.  The name of any member who is suspended from the APA for an ethics violation, along with an explanation of the nature of the violation, shall be reported in PSYCHIATRIC NEWS and in the district branch newsletter or other usual means of communication with its membership. The name of any member who is suspended from the APA for an ethics violation, along with an explanation of the nature of the violation, shall also be reported to the medical licensing authority in all states in which the member is licensed.

c.  The name of any member who resigns from the APA after an ethics complaint against him/her is received shall be reported in PSYCHI-ATRIC NEWS and in the district branch newsletter or other usual means of communication with its membership. The name of a member against whom an ethics complaint is filed within 90 days after the member submits a resignation may be reported to the membership and to the National Practitioner Data Bank by the APA.

d.  The Board of Trustees or, after approval by the APA Ethics Committee, any district branch's governing council may report an ethics charge or a decision finding that a member has engaged in unethical conduct to any medical licensing authority, medical society, hospital, clinic, or other institutions or persons where such disclosure is deemed appropriate to protect the public.[15]

Code of Medical Ethics, Current Opinion, American Medical Association, Copyright 1992. Used with permission.

---

[15]Chapter 10, Sections 1 and 2, Bylaws, American Psychiatric Association, 1993 edition.

# Addendum to the 1992 Edition of the Principles of Medical Ethics

## With Annotations Especially Applicable to Psychiatry

The APA Ethics Committee receives frequent requests for opinions on the "Procedures for Handling Complaints of Unethical Conduct" (see pages 10–18 of the PRINCIPLES). The questions and answers that follow have been received and developed since 1973.

1. **Question** Ethics proceedings sometimes involve serious unethical conduct. Under what circumstances should information about ethics cases be disclosed to the membership, government authorities, or other interested organizations and persons?

   **Answer** APA ethics cases are conducted in secrecy. As a general matter, the complainant's charges, the identity of the accused member and other information are made available only to persons participating directly in the proceedings. Even within the APA and the district branches, information should not be passed on to peer review, membership, and other components. (October 1976; November 1977)

   In some circumstances, however, disclosure of information about an ethics case is necessary to assure proper protection of the public. For example, many states now require reporting to government agencies concerning members who have been found to have engaged in unethical conduct. The timing of such required reports, the amount and specificity of information to be disclosed and other matters will vary from state to state. District branches should consult applicable state statutes to assure that these requirements are adhered to. The National Practitioner Data

Bank requires that the APA report suspensions and expulsions. (March 1985; November 1989)

The APA's Bylaws, as amended in 1985, also require the reporting to the membership of any member who is expelled from the APA because of an ethics violation. Such reports will identify the expelled member and specify the ethics violation for which he was expelled. (March 1985)

If a member charged with an ethics violation resigns from the APA before completion of the ethics proceeding, this fact will be noted in the APA's records and the member will not be permitted to rejoin the APA until the ethics case is resolved. In addition, a member who resigns under these circumstances may be reported to the membership, following approval by the APA Ethics Committee. (March 1985)

Apart from these specific guidelines, public safety considerations may justify reporting before completion of formal proceedings. If a complainant, deemed highly credible, alleges unethical conduct on the part of a member that would pose a serious danger to the safety of patients, the district branch could report the allegations to an appropriate state agency, following consultation with legal counsel. (October 1977; March 1985)

2. **Question** Does an Inactive Member have the responsibility to abide by *The Principles of Medical Ethics?*

**Answer** These principles apply equally to all members except Corresponding Fellows and Corresponding Members (see Question 16). (October 1973)

3. **Question** For the sake of educating our members and showing our diligence to the public, should the results of ethical hearings be made public? Such results could be printed in the district branch newsletter or in *Psychiatric News.*

**Answer** Undoubtedly, such publication would accomplish the above goals; but, it might also discourage complainants and district branch ethics committees from proceeding. However, if the penalty is expulsion, the name is to be published with the offense specified. If a member resigns during an ethics investigation, the name may be published with the approval of the APA Ethics Committee. (March 1974; March 1985)

For educational purposes, we also encourage district branch ethics committees to extract the lessons from ethical hearings to illustrate the tensions between ethical principles and member behavior and their resolution by the hearing. The purpose is to alert our members to possible vulnerability to allegations of unethical conduct. (September 1979)

In addition, the APA may publish disguised ethics cases in *Psychiatric News* in order to educate members and the public as to what matters are being reported and how they are being handled. (Board of Trustees, December 1981)

**4. Question** Aren't our members who participate in ethics hearings or who bring complaints taking a risk of being sued?

**Answer** Local laws vary and one should check with local attorneys. In general, if procedures are followed properly and all involved act without malice, there should be no serious risk. In many states, specific immunity has been granted by laws. In fact, the public expects professional organizations to police themselves and courts have held that professional peers are best qualified to judge the actions of each other. The most a disgruntled member could sue for would be a rehearing, not damages, unless he can prove malice on the part of those who judged him. It should be understood that anyone can file a suit at any time. To date, there has never been a successful suit. (April 1976; March 1985)

**5. Question** What does a complainant have to gain except potential embarrassment and harassment?

**Answer** Patient complainants may be seeking vindication or revenge. Occasionally they see an ethics procedure as a route to financial reward. There have been complaints who demonstrate a sincere desire to obtain help for the defendant psychiatrist. Colleague complainants are usually seeking to protect the reputation of the profession. As a general statement, the only gain a complainant can expect is the realization that he has brought to our profession's attention a possible break in our ethical standards. From then on, it is up to us. Local laws vary, but in most jurisdictions complainants who bring ethics charges without malice receive legal protection. (June 1976; March 1985)

**6. Question** In an ethics hearing, should the complainant and defendant be heard together?

**Answer** The Procedures now require that the complainant and the accused member be heard together under most circumstances. Exceptions include cases in which the member has waived his right to a hearing, cases in which the committee or panel chair has determined that requiring the complainant and the accused member to appear together would be harmful to the accused member, and cases in which the accused member decides not to appear, but to present his cases through counsel and other witnesses. (November 1989)

**7. Question** Can various specialty groups within psychiatry develop their own code of ethics?

**Answer** Since we are members of the medical profession first, we are responsible to *The Principles of Medical Ethics*, formulated by the American Medical Association. The APA added "With Annotations Especially Applicable to Psychiatry." These annotations were additive, and in no case did they subtract from or change any elements of *The Principles of Medical Ethics*. Nothing precludes another psychiatric society from developing a code that addresses the special needs of that group as long as it is additive to *The Principles of Medical Ethics with Annotations Especially Applicable to Psychiatry* and does not subtract or change any elements of the above. To allow anything else would be to create much confusion for our membership and the public and lead to legal challenges. (July 1976)

8. **Question** To whom at the district branch should formal complaints be directed?

   **Answer** That is to be determined by each district branch. We recommend they be directed to the president of the district branch. We prefer the president to be the initial recipient because of his elected status and because there is frequent turnover in the office. Occasionally a chair of an ethics committee remains in that position for several years and it would be unwise for him to be not only the initial recipient of complaints but also the recipient of charges of member harassment or complaint suppression. (October 1976)

9. **Question** Should a district branch provide an appeal mechanism?

   **Answer** There are ample appeal mechanisms available under the procedures. Nothing prevents a district branch from setting up an appeal to its local membership as long as it follows its own procedures as well as those of the APA. We do not recommend it. (January 1977; March 1977)

10. **Question** Can an ex-member dropped for ethical reasons be readmitted to membership?

    **Answer** Yes, if he demonstrates a return to ethical conduct. We should strongly encourage and reward efforts toward rehabilitation. (March 1977)

11. **Question** If a member is undergoing legal investigation for an alleged crime or is involved in a malpractice suit and a formal complaint has been received by the district branch, should its ethics committee proceed?

    **Answer** If the ethics committee decides to proceed, the member may object because he might fear that information produced at the ethics hearing could be subpoenaed for the trial, although the district branch would be advised to use all legal means to resist the subpoena. For this reason, or others, the district branch might determine it was more prudent to defer the charge for the time being. However, it is incumbent upon the ethics committee to monitor the investigation and trial so that an ethics hearing can be conducted as soon after their completion as possible. (April 1977; August 1977; November 1977; January 1978; September 1979)

12. **Question** If a district branch covers a large area, can one of its chapters act on an ethical complaint?

    **Answer** "The Procedures for Handling Complaints of Unethical Conduct" would allow the council of the district branch to appoint a special hearing body composed of chapter members that would investigate the complaint and make recommendations to the council as long as at least one member of the hearing panel is a member of the district branch ethics committee. However, only the council can make an official decision on the merits of the complaint. (April 1977; October 1989)

**13. Question** What are the "rights" of a complainant in an ethics hearing?

**Answer** The complainant has the right to be heard and the complaint to be taken seriously even though it may eventually be found to be without merit. While the complainant can be accompanied by an attorney to the hearing and can ask the attorney for advice, the attorney should not be allowed to argue his client's complaint or cross-examine the defendant-member or his witnesses. The complainant can gain nothing from the procedure of a tangible nature. He can gain only appreciation for assisting us in maintaining the integrity of our profession. (June 1977)

**14. Question** What are the "rights" of a member against whom a formal complaint has been filed?

**Answer** A member complained against has the right to be informed of the complaint, to be notified in advance of any hearing or investigation, to have legal counsel, to bring witnesses in his defense, to be allowed to present his defense in detail, to expect the hearing panel and the decision-making body to make a decision that is fair and without malice, and to be notified of the decision and of his avenue of appeal. The defendant-member and/or his attorney have a right, in most cases, to confront his accusers and to cross-examine those accusers and other witnesses against him. There is a significant issue here—the member's right of confrontation v. the concern as to the harm this might do to a complainant—so each hearing chairperson will decide the form the challenge will take, whether by direct challenge or by written response. (June 1977; October 1989)

**15. Question** If a component committee, council, or task force of the American Psychiatric Association comes across evidence of unethical behavior of a member, should it make a formal ethical complaint as a matter of routine?

**Answer** Yes, with one exception. If the component was gathering confidential information for another purpose and had advised the member of this confidentiality, it should not make a formal complaint unless the unethical behavior is of such magnitude as to constitute a severe and immediate risk to the public or other members. (September 1977)

**16. Question** Does a Corresponding Fellow or Member living in another country have to follow all ethical proscriptions of the American Psychiatric Association?

**Answer** Our Constitution and Bylaws make no exceptions for a Corresponding Fellow or Member in the requirement to live by *The Principles of Medical Ethics*. However, this code was developed for members practicing in the United States, and a Corresponding Fellow or Member is expected to follow codes of ethics of the country where he lives or practices. A formal complaint can be sent to the Ethics Committee of the World Psychiatric Association. (October 1977)

**17. Question** Does a patient-complainant have to give permission to a defendant-psychiatrist to reveal information about the treatment relationship?

**Answer** No. To bring a complaint is to consent to an investigation. In such a circumstance, the psychiatrist may ethically reveal only that information relevant to the hearing of the complaint. (November 1977)

18. **Question** If the public press reports the conviction of a member-psychiatrist of a crime or the loss of a malpractice suit that raises a very serious question about moral competency to practice, what is the responsibility of the district branch?

    **Answer** If no other member of the district branch nor anyone else makes a formal complaint, it would be appropriate for an officer of the district branch to do so. (January 1978; January 1979)

19. **Question** Can the district branch send to the APA Secretary a code number rather than the name of the defendant? If the member has been found innocent, can we expunge our records of the complaint?

    **Answer** Most district branches send the name; a few send initials or a code number. We prefer the former but accept the latter. The APA believes, however, that the use of code numbers and initials presents serious administrative problems. If code numbers are used, be sure to use the same number if a second complaint is received. If suspension or expulsion is the recommended action, the name must be submitted. This information is kept in a secure place at APA headquarters so fear of loss of confidentiality is unwarranted. A card file is maintained after the original material is destroyed so that we can maintain a history of ethical questions involving our profession. The district branch can expunge its record if it chooses, but might also wish to maintain such history. (April 1978; June 1978)

20. **Question** When a member transfers from one district branch to another, can information about a finding of unethical conduct be sent to the second district branch?

    **Answer** With the written permission of the transferring member, the transferring district branch can send information about an ethical charge and the results of the investigation to the new district branch council as confidential correspondence. Unless the member is suspended or expelled, he remains an APA member and does not lose his right to transfer. However, the receiving district branch has a right to challenge his transfer. (May 1978)

21. **Question** Our district branch ethics committee is investigating an ethical complaint against one of our members. The member is moving to another district branch area. Do we drop the investigation or pass the information on to the new district branch?

    **Answer** This question presents problems. The member might use moving and transferring as a way of avoiding the investigation and possible censure by peers. To pass the information on to the new district branch for continued investigation would create a very difficult problem for them, the complainant, and witnesses. Further, at this time, the information the first district branch received is to be considered confidential. (April 1978) Therefore, the Board of Trustees has made the following addition to the *Operations Manual:*

A transfer from one district branch to another will be delayed until resolution of any charge of unethical conduct. (May 1978)

22. **Question** Should a member who is mentally ill and, as a result, behaved unethically be suspended or expelled?

**Answer** We would recommend he be placed on Inactive Status and encouraged to seek treatment under the "impaired physician" act adopted in many states. Since he may also have had his medical license suspended or revoked, his return to active membership would require that the local licensing body had returned his medical license. The district branch would want to assure itself he had recovered and was again capable of ethical practice. The ultimate goal of such proceedings is rehabilitation of our colleague. The Board of Trustees has made the following addition to the *Operations Manual:*

Members who lose their license as a result of illness should not be removed from APA membership rolls but placed on Inactive Status until their recovery is such that they can return to practice and full membership. (May 1978)

23. **Question** What should the composition of a district branch ethics committee be?

**Answer** That is up to the district branch to decide. The committee should consist of members whose judgment is respected, obviously, but there are no specific requirements. Some district branches use their executive council, but it is more common to establish a standing committee. Only the APA Ethics Committee has a constitutional definition of its membership: six members, appointed for three years, with one to be a Past-President of the APA. (August 1978)

24. **Question** If a complainant refuses to participate in a formal hearing, should the complaint be dropped?

**Answer** Not necessarily. While not willing to participate in a formal hearing, the complainant might present written information sufficient to proceed or point the way to other evidence that would be relevant. The role of the complainant is not that of a prosecutor but that of a person bringing a potential problem to our attention (see Questions 5, 6, 13, and 14). (February 1979)

25. **Question** When a member is suspended from membership in the district branch and in the APA, what privileges does he lose?

**Answer** A suspended member will now lose privileges cited in Chapter 8, Sections 2, 3, and 5 of the APA Bylaws. A suspended member will lose the right to vote, to nominate candidates for office, to propose referenda and amendments to the Constitution and Bylaws, and to serve on components. He may not hold elected office and may not initiate referenda to change actions of the Board of Trustees. The suspended member will be expected to pay dues and assessments and will remain eligible for other benefits of membership such as participation in the insurance programs. Suspension may also result in the loss of other district branch privileges. (September 1981; March 1985)

26. **Question (Part A)** On occasion, a member charged with unethical behavior may settle out of court with the complainant in a parallel civil suit. Part of the settlement requires the complainant not to pursue the ethical charge. Should we not establish a rule that it is unethical in itself for a member to be a party to such an agreement?

    **Answer** This "back door exit" from ethical complaints concerns us, and if used to stifle a bona fide complaint, is unethical.

    **Question (Part B)** Even though the complainant drops the charge, can the process be continued?

    **Answer** If the alleged behavior is known to others, such as district branch officers, and from sources other than that provided by the original complainant, another complaint may be brought by whomever has that information. Obviously, the original complainant would not be available to provide information nor to appear at a hearing. (March 1988)

27. **Question** For an ethics charge, is there a time limit between the alleged behavior and complaint beyond which the complaint cannot be accepted? Can ethics information be shared with other appropriate committees of the district branch?

    **Answer** There is no "statute of limitations" for an ethical complaint; frequently, allegedly harmed patients take years to develop the courage, often with additional treatment, to come forward. To the second question, ethical material is confidential. The president of the district branch needs to be informed if he plans to appoint a suspended member to a committee. At the APA, the chair of the Membership Committee will be advised by staff if a disciplined member is proposed for Fellowship and the President will be informed about a suspended member being considered for a committee or component appointment. (December 1986)

28. **Question** What is the effect of an accused member's refusal to participate in the investigation or hearing? Is that, in itself, unethical?

    **Answer** The investigation and hearing can proceed with the evidence at hand and reach its conclusion in the absence of the accused member's participation, though the right of appeal is not lost. A charge of unethical conduct upon this action itself would not be sufficient to constitute a sustainable complaint. (October 1977)

29. **Question** We have learned that a member has been found guilty of sexual misconduct with a patient by the Board of Medical Examiners. They revoked his license, stayed the revocation, suspended his license for 6 months, and gave him 7 years of probation. Can we suspend him without going through all the repetitive procedures?

**Answer** APA policy does not allow automatic suspension at the time of license suspension but requires an investigation. Thus, while a fair procedure must be followed, it is likely this will not have to be exhaustive under the circumstances. (January 1988)

30. **Question** A serious ethical allegation about a member was received shortly after he resigned from our district branch and the APA, presumably because he was aware of the impending complaint. Should we publish that he resigned while under investigation?

    **Answer** No, because he wasn't under investigation when he resigned. He "beat the system," by his view at least, but will have to face the complaint if he wishes to rejoin the Association at some later time. (July 1988)

31. **Question** It is alleged that a member engaged in sexual activities with a patient during his residency, which ended in December 1973. He joined the APA in 1976 and now comes the complaint. Can we proceed?

    **Answer** Yes. The dates do not constitute an obstacle. The APA annotation prohibiting sexual activity was published in 1973 but medical ethics has prohibited such activity since the origin of the Hippocratic Oath. If the complaint had surfaced prior to his approval for membership, he would have had to face it since the APA Constitution and Bylaws require, and did then, that a prospective member abide by the *Principles of Medical Ethics*. As to the delay in making the complaint, see Question 27. (September 1988)

32. **Question** Our district branch is quite large and has a heavy volume of complaints. Thus, we have divided the ethics committee into several hearing panels all of whose members belong to the ethics committee. Paragraph 9 of the "Procedures" gives to a panel only the responsibility to determine if there has been a violation, and the recommendation of the ethics committee is required for the penalty. This would overburden us.

    **Answer** This requirement for a panel to recommend only the finding of unethical conduct but not the penalty was meant for panels not entirely comprised of ethics committee members. If all of the panel members are on the ethics committee, they may recommend the sanction, too. (April 1990)

33. **Question** Although we found a member not to have behaved unethically, we feel he is impaired. Can the ethics committee refer him to the Impaired Physician Committee?

    **Answer** While the rules protecting confidentiality in the processing of ethical complaints do not address this, we believe a discreet referral to the Impaired Physician Committee is permissible. (June 1990)

34. **Question** Should our district branch executive council discuss matters from the ethics committee in executive session? Should minutes be kept and, if so, how complete?

**Answer** Discussion should be in executive session and complete minutes kept, including the reasoning leading to the decision and the vote to reach a decision. (January 1991)

35. **Question** Are there circumstances in which a reprimand can be published?

   **Answer** No. Publication is limited to suspension or expulsion (see paragraph 26 of "Procedures for Handling Complaints of Unethical Conduct"). If you feel publication is indicated, you may wish to review your sanction. (February 1991)

# Name Index

**A**

Abbott, 18, 195
Ajzen, 105, 191
Anderson, E., 118, 189
Anderson, T., 47, 189
Annas, 40, 189
Aquinas, 76–87, 94, 95
Aristotle, 88, 92, 95, 109, 118, 132, 134–135, 189
Arras, 109, 135, 136, 189
Arredendo, 18, 192
Ayers, 47, 189

**B**

Baier, 96, 114, 116, 118–120, 189
Ball-Rokeach, 105, 191
Beauchamp, 94, 124, 127, 133, 135, 167, 190
Bennett, 20, 190
Bentham, 50–51, 190
Bernard, 160, 190
Bersoff, 94, 190
Blau, 18, 194
Bonhoeffer, 36, 190

Braithwaite, x, 105, 190
Brandt, 32, 190
Bray, 145, 190
Braybrooke, 89, 94,–96, 190
Brent, 155, 158–159, 190
Bryant, 20, 190
Buber, 121, 190
Burnet, 107, 190
Burt, 24, 190

**C**

Cacioppo, 105, 194
Callanan, 149, 191
Camblin, 168, 190
Carroll, 100, 190
Chadrow, 123, 191
Childress, 94, 124, 127, 133–135, 167, 190
Clouser, 135, 190
Corey, G., 149, 190
Corey, M., 149, 190
Cormier, 169, 191

**D**

Day, 25, 94, 191

# Subject Index